DISASTER MOVIES

A Loud, Long, Explosive, Star-Studded Guide to Avalanches, Earthquakes, Floods, Meteors, Sinking Ships, Twisters, Viruses, Killer Bees, Nuclear Fallout, and Alien Attacks in the Cinema!!!!

Glenn Kay and Michael Rose

CHICAGO
REVIEW
PRESS

D1198703

A Capella Book

Library of Congress Cataloging-in-Publication Data

Kay, Glenn.

Disaster movies : a loud, long, explosive, star-studded guide to avalanches, earthquakes, floods, meteors, sinking ships, twisters, viruses, killer bees, nuclear fallout, and alien attacks in the cinema!!!! / Glenn Kay and Michael Rose.— 1st ed.

p. cm.

An A Cappella book.

ISBN-13: 978-1-55652-612-1

ISBN-10: 1-55652-612-1

1. Disaster films—History and criticism. I. Rose, Michael, 1973– II. Title.

PN1995.9.D55K39 2006

791.43'6556—dc22

2005030182

Cover and interior design: Emily Brackett/Visible Logic
Cover photos: (meteor) ImageBank; (flames) Getty Images/Photodisc
Interior illustrations: Greg Hyland
Questions and comments may be directed to disasterthebook@hotmail.com

Published in the United States by Chicago Review Press, Incorporated
814 North Franklin Street
Chicago, Illinois 60610

Published worldwide by Mosaic Press
1251 Speers Road
Oakville ON L6L 5N9 Canada
www.mosaic-press.com

ISBN-13: 978-1-55652-612-1
ISBN-10: 1-55652-612-1
Printed in the United States of America
5 4 3 2 1

CONTENTS

Foreword by Mike Nelson, host of *Mystery Science Theater 3000* ... v
Acknowledgments ... vii
Introduction by Glenn Kay ... ix
Introduction by Michael Rose ... xii

A Brief History of Disaster Movies ... 1
I'll Never Fly with This Airline Again! ... 7
Shake, Rattle, and Roll ... 51
Disaster Movies' Greatest Stars ... 79
Fun with Snow ... 86
Hot Molten Lava ... 104
The Best Disaster Movies Never Made ... 124
Sinking Ships ... 127
Don't Be a Hero: The Disaster Movie's Hardest Lesson ... 170
Big Space Rocks ... 172
Now That's a Fire ... 194
The Most Ridiculous Disaster Movie Concepts Ever ... 224
Really Bad Storms ... 228
Just a Little Radiation ... 259
What's with All the Love Themes? ... 306
Mad Bombers, Killer Bees, and Wild Animals ... 308
The Highest-Grossing Disaster Movies of All Time ... 347
Those Darn Aliens! ... 349
Movies That Sound Like They're Disaster Films, But Aren't ... 369
Disaster Movie Parodies ... 371
Our Ultimate Disaster Movie Lists ... 382

Index ... 384

FOREWORD

by Mike Nelson, host of *Mystery Science Theater 3000*

Do this simple experiment: grab a boy under the age of 15, any boy that's handy, give him crayons, paper, and half an hour's time, and tell him to create the image of his choosing. (OK, I assume you're back now, having done that.) What did he create? A lush image of a fragrant copse filled with daisies, buttercups, and prancing fairies? A crude but poignantly beautiful spring wedding, the misty-eyed bride gazing lovingly at her future husband while pastel-clad guests weep with joy into lacy handkerchiefs? Still life of fruit? No, huh?

Let me guess—he drew a picture of missiles crashing into a densely populated city. Or perhaps Godzilla rampaging through the financial district, gouts of fire spouting from his hideous maw. Or, if he's a little more talented, perhaps he rendered the effects of a massive and devastating earthquake, complete with details of the earth's crust opening and swallowing train cars like ladyfingers, or skyscrapers crumbling as though made of pasteboard.

Now give a grown man a camera, a crew, and eight weeks of filming, and what will he create? *Pillow Talk? That Touch of Mink? When Harry Met Sally?* No, not bloody likely. He'll make *Earthquake*, of course, and if he's even half a man he'll make the damn thing in Sensurround just to make sure you don't miss the point.

Let's face it, it's deep in our subconscious to want to see Charlton Heston try to survive a massive geological upheaval while simultaneously being forced to choose between his wife and a beautiful mistress. Written right in our genetic code is a desire to witness Paul Newman, Steve McQueen, William Holden, Faye Dunaway, and Robert Wagner battle a building fire caused by faulty wiring. We wouldn't be human if we didn't wake every day with a hunger for it.

Thank heavens for disaster films, or our needs would go unmet. We would have to settle for *The Wedding Planner*, and I for one would not be prepared to go on living in a world like that.

Earthquake was my first disaster film, and yes, I saw it in Sensurround. I was 10 years old and I'll never forget the drama, the devastation, the terrifyingly creepy performance of Marjoe Gortner as Jody (perhaps the only time a character named Jody has ever had the power to frighten anyone in the slightest).

Playing right to my 10-year-old sensibilities, the movie saw fit to include an homage to Evel Knievel, only instead of being a suicidal, drug-addled numskull from Montana, he was all groovy and Richard Roundtree-ish (which was easy, as he was played by Richard Roundtree). You did not want to be caught flat-footed at school when Brian Fisher asked, "Did you guys see *Earthquake* in Sensurround when that one guy was going to take his motorcycle into the loop-de-loop thing?" You wanted—no, *had*—to be able to come back with, "Yeah, that was so cool when he was about to do the stunt and the earthquake knocked his track down." Not to do so brought only scorn, derision, and the possibility of a very serious and painful stint at the bottom of an Indian pile.

But it is the image of Victoria Principal that made the biggest impression. Victoria played Rosa Amici and had the good sense to do so wearing a fright wig and a tight leather jumpsuit. She looked like Sexxo the Clown. Which was fine with me—and still is.

Who knows why we love to watch misery, tragedy, and disaster onscreen? (If you're really interested, you could probably read Aeschylus or Euripides or something, though I don't know why you would want to when *Twister* is due up on cable at any moment.) But love it we do, especially when George Kennedy is involved.

Disaster Movies is a loving, exhaustive, and funny look at all of the best of these films. (All of the worst, too, though sometimes it is hard to tell them apart.) You will find yourself consulting this book often, marveling as you do that they just don't make 'em like they used to, not even knowing for sure whether or not that is a good thing.

ACKNOWLEDGMENTS

The authors would like to thank the following for their
contributions, support, and encouragement:

Sean Armstrong

The Arts & Letters Club of Toronto

Malina Bakowski

Al Bigongiari

John Brooks

Steven Chiodo

Joe Dante

Brad Darch

Carlos Diaz

Alex Gershon

Gunter, Andrea, Alec, Zach, and Evan Hinz

Hollywood Renaissance Movie Memorabilia

Bob Hoo

Greg Hyland

Igo Kantor

Iain and Sharon Kay

Don McKellar

John and Angela Migliore

Mike Nelson

O Entertainment

Chris Owen

Barbara, Alan, and Kathryn Rose

Joe Sudak

Nola Weaver

And all of the writers, artists, performers, and technicians
who made these movies possible

All of Glenn Kay's profits earned as coauthor of *Disaster Movies*
will be donated to charity.

INTRODUCTION
by Glenn Kay

Why would anybody want to watch a disaster film? What makes them so popular? Why would anyone want to write a book on the subject? Why would anyone read it? These are all questions that have plagued me. Well, OK, maybe they haven't *plagued* me. I haven't lost any sleep over them. But I've put some thought into it. To find an answer, I had to think back to my childhood and try to remember what I originally found so appealing about these films.

I suppose that, at first, it was a morbid fascination with what the end of the world might look like. The special effects that depicted the destruction of buildings, streets, cities—even the planet—always struck me as cool. I watched these films, jaw agape, captivated with fear. When I walked past the local cinema, I marveled at the disaster movie posters, their graphic images luridly foretelling the calamitous events that occurred in the films. Who wouldn't become hooked?

As I got older, I found that I was watching them for a different reason: they're cheesy and hilarious. Many of the special effects in the older films don't look quite so special anymore, and most of the films involve cornball subplots, a surprising amount of flag waving, and, at times, some really bad acting.

And, strangely enough, I watch disaster movies to see famous celebrities die horribly violent deaths. That's what I like best about them—I'll happily admit it. It's all about seeing A-list actors get blown up, or fall 50 stories and crash to their deaths on the city streets below. You'd never see an event this tragic or disturbing in a typical Hollywood film. But in this genre, any star is as likely to buy the farm as any other.

This is the guide to all movies disastrous in the 20th and early 21st centuries. We divided movie reviews and listings into three types. Long Reviews offer in-depth plot analyses and discussions of major releases new and old, with particular attention paid to the elaborate and often hilarious ends of its characters. Brief Reviews are reserved for movies that we felt we didn't have quite as much to comment on or that aren't quite as important. Rare, Obscure, and Less Important

Titles are simply listings of, well, rare, obscure, and less important titles, with the thinking that people don't want to read a lot about movies they'll have a hard time finding.

Films in the first two categories are rated as one of the following:

HIGHLY RECOMMENDED

RECOMMENDED

AT YOUR OWN RISK

AVOID AT ALL COSTS

SO BAD IT'S GOOD

So what defines a "disaster movie"? Michael and I agreed upon a set of criteria, which includes all or a significant combination of the following:

- A cavalcade of recognizable faces and big stars playing characters of various social backgrounds

- A powerful force of nature beyond the control of humankind, and a protagonist who is constantly warning the community of the impending danger, to no avail

- Scenes of self-sacrifice, mass destruction, and citizens in peril

- Spectacular special effects and panicked crowds running toward the camera always help

- There's often a love theme in these films, and, as I mentioned previously, horribly gruesome and elaborate death scenes

If there's a title that hasn't been included that you think should be in here, we're sorry. We probably thought it was close but didn't quite meet our definition of what a disaster film is.

A note about some of the original movie posters featured in this book. Unfortunately, these posters were shipped to theaters folded—not rolled—until the late '80s (and, believe it or not, theater owners were supposed to destroy promotional materials after the run of the movie. Thank goodness a lot of people held on to the stuff!). For some of the major hits, like *The Towering Inferno*, reprints were shipped rolled in tubes. But for the majority of these early films, all that exists are posters that are deeply creased after some 30 years of storage in folded form. We've reproduced them here as well as we can.

But enough of my endless rambling. Now read Michael's rambling for a bit, and then on with the show. Enjoy, thanks for reading, and, of course, happy viewing.

Hamilton, Ontario, September 2005

INTRODUCTION
by Michael Rose

I love movies, and I love to write. Ask me to write about movies, and I'm all over it like white on rice, or something. Of course, there are some kinds of movies that suit my tastes and my writing style more closely than others; you might not find me frothing at the mouth to write a book chronicling the films of Merchant Ivory, but a book about disaster movies is just my thing. I knew that it was important to make this book both entertaining and informative, but I always felt that my central obligation to the reader was to write about these movies with the same enthusiasm that drew me to the project, and that inspired Glenn to come up with the idea in the first place.

Over the last few decades disaster films have come to rely more on high-tech visual effects and contrived moralizing than on the classic combination of old-school opticals and miniature effects, old-fashioned storytelling, and unapologetic violence. But there are a few things that didn't change, because you can't completely alter the nature of the beast no matter how hard you try. This is a genre in which a lack of subtlety and an exploitive nature are almost required elements. Today's disaster movies are just as silly and make as little sense as the old ones, and though the effects are a lot better, they're still just spiffed-up versions of the classic disaster highlights we've come to recognize with fondness. There are only so many ways to show a terrified crowd running away from a huge explosion, or tidal wave, or alien attack, or whatever. Still, there's a certain simple charm to the 1970s disaster movie—a kind of inevitable, straightforward quality that's missing in today's explosive, overstuffed disaster fare.

Yet, the genre had to evolve, and in doing so it created a whole new set of rules and subgenres. It amazes me how much the genre has always been and continues to be relevant to our times. It is an ever-changing showcase for the terrors we face, certain political realities (and unrealities), the nature of celebrity over the decades, and how technology can be used to bring all of this to the screen. As silly as these films may be, they have the potential to capture the essence of an era as well as any other genre. Plus, they offer more bang for the buck than your everyday movie.

Note that Glenn and I made the decision not to always favor theatrically released films over made-for-TV disaster movies. There are a lot of these small-screen flicks out there, and it seemed improper to give short shrift to movies seen by potentially millions of people through a medium as direct and immediate as television.

Finally, a warning: many of these reviews and essays reveal not only important plot points of these movies, but in most cases, the endings as well. Most of these films have been around for a while though, and I'm not gonna lose sleep over revealing the ending of, say, *The Towering Inferno*, which was made over 30 years ago. This is just a disclaimer, so that you'll know this is gonna happen and won't get all pissy about it.

So let's not waste any more time. I know you're eager to delve into the strange and disturbing world of the disaster movie. Let the feature presentation begin!

Toronto, Ontario, September 2005

A BRIEF HISTORY OF DISASTER MOVIES

The disaster movie genre is as old as film itself. Ever since some of the first silent films were produced, catastrophe and spectacle have been important parts of the movies. Just think about it: one of the first images ever shot was that of a locomotive speeding down the rails toward a camera. Audiences at the time were terrified, thinking that the locomotive itself would crash through the screen and strike them. Was it then that filmmakers considered the possibility that filming a train crash itself and the reactions of those on board would be even more worth capturing? Or perhaps the early pioneers of cinema wondered to themselves, why not plunge that impressive piece of machinery off of a cliff for good measure? Could this have been how it all began?

So that may not be a completely accurate representation of the beginnings of the genre, but consider this: before film, there were books, like *The Last Days of Pompeii* (1833) by Sir Edward George Bulwer-Lytton, that whet people's appetites for mass destruction. Clearly, we've all been obsessed with disasters for a very long time. Horrible tragedy and conflict are the stuff of great drama, things that all good works of dramatic fiction and nonfiction possess.

The turn of the 20th century produced some major, real disasters. This included the Great 1906 San Francisco Earthquake and the sinking of the *Titanic* in 1911. These events actually jumpstarted the disaster movie genre. Dozens of short silent films depicted these tragedies, many serving as news footage. (Sadly, although you may have seen every *Titanic* film reviewed in this book, you will more than likely never have a chance to view the many more *Titanic*-related films of the silent era that were also produced.) Then, as now, audiences were fascinated with these images.

The little-seen Italian silent film *The Last Days of Pompeii* (1913), an adaptation of Lytton's book, may be the first attempt at a narrative film of a disaster story. About 15 years later, British International Pictures produced *Atlantic* (1929), a weak, highly fictionalized reworking of the *Titanic* sinking that can be found in North America under the title *Titanic: Disaster in the Atlantic*.

The 1930s saw the first real wave of narrative disaster films from major Hollywood studios. As film technology progressed, sound became commonly used, and special effects improved. Producers, understanding the appeal of catastrophes, created palatable, fictionalized works based on real events, altering the facts of each to include a romantic subplot or a greater degree of melodrama (maybe even a musical number!). Voilà, they had themselves a disaster film! The earthquake film *Deluge* (1933) may be the earliest big-studio disaster title. It is not difficult to assume that the filmmakers must have been influenced by the San Francisco earthquake. Although this title is currently hidden away in some film vault and is unavailable, it was an extremely successful film in its day. Another early film was yet another version of *The Last Days of Pompeii* (1935), a dramatization of the volcanic eruption in ancient Rome. John Ford's classic *The Hurricane* (1937) followed. The films *San Francisco* (1936) and *In Old Chicago* (1937) met with even greater financial success. Another earthquake/flood picture called *The Rains Came* (1939) sprouted during this period. But for the next 10 or so years, few disaster movies followed this intense decade of releases. With the exception of *Titanic* (1943), a German Nazi propaganda film that went unseen by most of the world, the genre lay dormant until after World War II, when it reemerged slightly morphed from its previous incarnations.

The newfound popularity of science fiction in the 1950s influenced producer George Pal to produce *When Worlds Collide* (1951), which depicted the end of the world when a star and planet from another solar system approach Earth. The sometimes outrageous concepts of fantasy-minded follow-ups like *The War of the Worlds* (1953) allowed filmmakers to attempt new and spectacular visual effects, including the destruction of buildings and cities on a large scale. In fact, these two movies were awarded with Oscars for their elaborate effects.

But what about all of those disaster movie fans out there in the '50s and '60s who preferred their films more reality based? Interestingly enough, the options all included ships in peril. Perhaps it was a result of the money required, but it wasn't until 1953 that any major Hollywood studio would attempt another lavish, big-screen re-creation of the *Titanic*'s tragic maiden voyage. While then-unavailable elaborate special effects would have been required to convincingly sink the world's largest luxury liner on celluloid, I assume if audiences of the day could buy low-tech films about aliens attempting to destroy the world, then maybe it was possible to adequately depict the White Star Line ship sinking into the Atlantic. *Titanic* was a huge success, but those wanting to see a more realistic presentation of events would have to wait.

In the meantime, there were many *When Worlds Collide* copycats, like 1957's *The Night the World Exploded* and 1958's *The Day the Sky Exploded* (which would make for a perfectly confusing double bill at the drive-in . . . "So, honey, what's exploding in this movie?"). These films combined elements of popular science fiction magazines with end-of-the-world scenarios.

In 1958 came *A Night to Remember*, an enormous successful and darn good movie about the *Titanic* based on a book by Walter Lord. This was followed by *The Last Voyage* (1960), an entertaining "fire in the hull" feature that was obviously inspired by both *Titanic* and *A Night to Remember*, but one that would hint stylistically (with its big-scale sets) of things to come in the 1970s. By the mid '60s, however, with the exception of a few titles like *The Flight of the Phoenix* (1965) things were drying up once again. During this period, the quality of the sci-fi disaster features took a turn for the worse, as is evidenced by titles like *Planet on the Prowl* (1966) and the mostly snore-inducing *Crack in the World* (1965). It seemed that both science fiction films and disaster movies were becoming stale and falling out of favor.

But the disaster film evolved with the times, and writers discovered a new, untapped source for terror—commercial airlines. *Airport* (1970) was a hugely popular novel that read more like a soap opera. Universal Pictures spent an enormous amount of money making the film version and wisely cast big stars to portray the many characters—all of which resulted in a phenomenal box-office hit and a complete rebirth of the genre as the '70s began.

Of course, everyone knows that the 1970s were the golden age of disaster movie cinema. This is thanks to one man, Irwin Allen, a TV producer in love with the idea of making his own *Titanic*-style disaster movie, perhaps on an even larger scale than other disaster films that had been made. Perhaps he wished to top *Airport* by creating the biggest spectacle on film that he could possibly imagine. *The Poseidon Adventure* (1972) was truly that. Allen kept the soap opera elements of *Airport* and threw in even more stars, incredible sets, better effects work, and—most welcome of all (for me at least)—a mean streak that involved killing off many of the major characters unexpectedly. Audiences went berserk. Both *Airport* and *The Poseidon Adventure* broke records, and every studio began producing disaster sequels. The '70s saw three *Airport* sequels and even an unlikely *Poseidon Adventure* follow-up, *Beyond the Poseidon Adventure* (1979).

Many '70s disaster movies followed the same successful formula that had been employed in *Airport* and *The Poseidon Adventure*, using every possible scenario Hollywood could think up. All of these films also seemed to feature Charlton Heston, George Kennedy, Ava Gardner, Ernest Borgnine, or Red Buttons. There were earthquakes, avalanches, floods, and meteors. Volcanoes, raging fires, and hurricanes burst across the screen, all vying for the public's entertainment dollars. The popularity of these films was so great that Allen even produced numerous made-for-TV disaster movies, presumably for those who couldn't make it out to the theater.

As the '70s came to a close, so did the ideas, and audiences were left with the dregs of the studios' preposterous concepts, like killer bees, which were depicted in several movies. Even Allen couldn't resist the allure of killer bees stinging A-list stars to death; he gave us the big-budget turkey *The Swarm* (1978). The box-office failure of this movie, coupled with *Beyond the Poseidon Adventure* and Allen's ultimate turkey, *When Time Ran Out...* (1980), led to hard times for the genre. Even Universal's *Airport* franchise had dried up. The good news was that audiences were treated to a couple of incredibly funny parodies of the genre in the form of *Airplane!* (1980) and *Airplane II: The Sequel* (1982).

But even still, the genre would not die. In fact, it was once again morphing into something new. The dawn of the "nuclear" disaster picture had arrived. Personally, I'm not particularly fond of this period. While an earlier film, *On the Beach* (1959), addresses the issue in a subtle and playful way, the nuclear disaster films of the 1980s are too serious and real downers to watch. Topical and current (and soon to become very outdated) made-for-TV movies like *The Day After* (1983) and *Threads* (1984) played across our television screens. The intention was to show the horrors of what could happen to all of us if nuclear war broke out. These movies certainly did that, but it seems to me that most of the people who tuned into these flicks were kids around my age who watched them simply because their parents had gone out for the evening and told them not to. The meltdown of Chernobyl in the USSR further encouraged these fears. Thankfully, this style of disaster film began dying out as relations between the USSR and the United States improved and the Cold War came to an end. The release of laughable stinkers like *Control* (1987) marked the beginning of the end of the period, which at least managed to end with a strong film, *Miracle Mile* (1988).

In the 1990s, with the rise of mass media, CNN, and immediate access to news from around the planet, stories in the headlines became fodder for dramatic TV disaster films. The early '90s saw movies based on Chernobyl, the Korean airline tragedy, another earthquake in Southern California, and even the *Exxon Valdez* oil spill. At movie theaters, right-wing, big-budget action films had been all the rage. Buddy-cop films and spectacular Sylvester Stallone and Arnold Schwarzenegger special-effects extravaganzas took center stage. But there was only so much witty banter amid car chases and buildings being blown up that audiences could take before the '80s action film found itself merging with the disaster movie formula.

Die Hard 2 (1991), about a group of airplanes in peril above Washington Dulles International Airport on Christmas Eve, was one of the most successful films of the year and used elements from the *Airport* series. Not only that, but it also featured shoot-outs and big-scale explosions that were staples of the '80s action film. Perhaps this is what gave producers the idea to return to disaster films in the '90s. Filmmakers like Roland Emmerich openly admitted his love for '70s disaster movies, and he formatted his huge box-office hit *Independence Day* (1996) after them (he also pays obvious homage to the sci-fi disaster films of the 1950s, particularly *The War of The Worlds*). Tim Burton's great science fiction flick/disaster movie/comedy *Mars Attacks!* (1996) would follow the same year.

Moviemakers in the '90s realized that they could milk every concept from the past. Back were airlines in peril, and audiences were treated to the fact-based *Alive* (1993), as well as to the very non-fact-based *Executive Decision* (1996) and *Turbulence* (1997). Once again, the *Titanic* films made a comeback, with James Cameron's *Titanic* (1997) becoming the highest-grossing film of all time to date. *Dante's Peak* (1997) and *Volcano* (1997), a pair of volcano movies, were followed the next year by a pair of meteor movies, *Armageddon* (1998), which ended up being the highest-grossing film of the year, and *Deep Impact* (1998). In fact, it seemed that there was always a pair of disaster flicks competing in the marketplace, vying for our attention. The only disappointing thing about these modern-day disaster films was that many avoided showing the violent carnage that their '70s counterparts had (with the notable exception of *Mars Attacks!*). Perhaps this can be attributed to the escalating costs of these films and the need to attract as wide a market as possible.

As the new century dawns, the films just keep on coming. In the past few years we've gotten a real mix of scenarios dredged up from disaster films of the past, including a submarine disaster movie based on a true story, *K-19: The Widowmaker* (2002), and a '50s sci-fi-inspired disaster flick, *The Core* (2003). The summer of 2004 brought us *The Day After Tomorrow*, a picture depicting another ice age. A new *War of the Worlds* was released in 2005, directed by none other than Steven Spielberg. As of this writing, a *When Worlds Collide* remake is in development. And *The Poseidon Adventure* is also making a return voyage thanks to Wolfgang Petersen, director of *The Perfect Storm* (2000). It may be upsetting to many, but producers have also already developed film and TV adaptations of the 9/11 tragedy.

In the end, it's difficult to say exactly what the attraction is to these pictures, and psychologists could have a field day with our love of the genre. Perhaps their appeal is similar to what some have claimed of horror films: they're a way for audiences to deal with real-life terrors and to leave the theater feeling moved, uplifted, or simply alive. The movies may even provide a perverse thrill, not unlike the thrill motorists experience as they slow to a crawl to catch a glimpse of an accident scene. Although it may be impossible to predict exactly where the genre will head next, we can rest assured that it will continue to thrive and give audiences around the world the disturbing thrills that it has always delivered since the birth of narrative film. **(GK)**

I'll Never Fly with This Airline Again!

The fear of flying is an easy subject to exploit. Putting your life in the hands of an overworked pilot and airport crew whom you don't know anything about can be quite stressful. If something goes wrong, it's all over. It can happen to anyone, and since most of us have been on planes, we can relate to the frightening prospect of a catastrophe in the air. Not too many people can identify with facing the end of humanity as a giant meteor hurls toward Earth. That's probably why some, but thankfully not all, airplane disaster films tend to be a little more serious than your average apocalyptic asteroid flick. Many even strive to be more realistic (which, in some instances, really works against them). But at least I can understand why.

I recall having a window seat over a wing of a major airline's plane once and being told that the flight would be delayed while technicians checked into a warning light that was appearing on the control panel. I witnessed them walking out to the wing and watched them study the wing flaps. What did they do? Looked at each other, shrugged, squirted a water bottle of red fluid on the gears, and walked away. That was a little disconcerting. (However, in their defense, I did get to where I was going.). When the turbulence hits onscreen, we can all identify with the characters' dread that something really, really bad is about to happen.

While there hasn't been a major airplane disaster movie in theaters in some time, no doubts about the popularity of such films are evident in the direct-to-video market. Whether you like them or find them utterly tasteless, you can bet that airplane disaster films will eventually return to the big screen and garner success like they always have (or at least, like some of them have).

Here are some reviews of the biggest and baddest disaster films set at airports and in airplanes. I apologize if there are some halfway serious reviews in this section. It won't happen again. **(GK)**

Airport (1970)
Universal Pictures   137 minutes

AT YOUR OWN RISK

☢

DIRECTOR: George Seaton

WRITER: George Seaton (based on the novel by Arthur Hailey)

CAST: Burt Lancaster, Dean Martin, Jean Seberg, Jacqueline Bisset, George Kennedy, Helen Hayes, Van Heflin, Maureen Stapleton, Barry Nelson, Dana Wynter, Lloyd Nolan, Barbara Hale, Gary Collins, John Findlater, Jesse Royce Landis

Imagine this: You're about to leave on a flight to Rome. You sit back in your seat, relaxing. The captain's voice becomes audible over the intercom. It sounds familiar, almost slurred. The jet takes off before you realize it. Oh, no! Your pilot is . . . Dean Martin!!!

Of course, with Dino in the cockpit, disaster is inevitable. Martin stars as the heroic, martini-sipping, chain-smoking, womanizing, and frequently (who are we kidding? perpetually) blitzed pilot in this all-star extravaganza. Budgeted at an astronomical $10 million (it was practically the *Titanic* of its day), this monstrous success ended up taking in roughly $45.22 million at the box office and spawned a slew of sequels and imitations. *Airport*, which may be the most famous disaster film of all time, has the distinction of being Universal Pictures' highest-grossing film up until that time. Its success is also partially responsible for the saturation of disaster films that the '70s have become famous for.

How does it hold up over 30 years later? The answer is not very well. This is a plot-heavy movie, where the soap-opera dramatics of the characters' love lives are more important than the so-called disaster during the flight. Should Burt Lancaster's character divorce his hag of a wife and shack up with beautiful coworker Jean Seberg? Should Dino dump his wife for pregnant stewardess Jacqueline Bisset? Can George Kennedy (who gets all of the best lines) dig the plane out of the snow in time to get back home for a little "action" with his woman? And, most important, how are such old, out-of-shape guys managing to sleep with women at least half their age?!

Yes, there is a mad bomber. And yes, the plane is put into peril. Unfortunately, this doesn't occur until over 100 minutes into the film. Don't expect any spectacular special effects when the bomb does go off, either. The explosion itself is kept offscreen. Basically, a very fake-looking hole is blown open in the bathroom of a fake-looking set. End of story. It left me scratching my head and disappointed. I'd expected a lot more than I got.

Strangely enough, *Airport* was well received by critics. Helen Hayes won Best Supporting Actress at the 1971 Academy Awards for her groan-inducing comic-relief work (she drops some real clunkers on the audience—you can almost hear the rim shot) as a kindly, elderly stowaway. *Airport* was nominated for an additional nine Oscars, including Best Picture, and Maureen Stapleton won a Golden Globe for her performance as the mad bomber's harried wife. Go figure.

Most Spectacular Moment of Carnage

Unfortunately, in *Airport* (unlike in *The Towering Inferno* or *Earthquake*), the celebrities are saved. There is only one casualty, that of the mad bomber, who is presumably blown up (again, it occurs offscreen) and sucked out of the airplane by the explosion. The Most Spectacular Moment of Carnage award, therefore, goes to stewardess Bisset's eye being punctured by a splinter during the chaos. **(GK)**

Airport 1975 (1974)
Universal Pictures   107 minutes

RECOMMENDED

⚠

"Something hit us... the crew is dead... help us, please, please help us!"

An all **NEW** movie inspired by the film "AIRPORT" based on the novel by Arthur Hailey.

© Universal Pictures

DIRECTOR: Jack Smight

WRITER: Don Ingalls

CAST: Charlton Heston, Karen Black, George Kennedy, Gloria Swanson, Efrem Zimbalist, Jr., Susan Clark, Helen Reddy, Linda Blair, Dana Andrews, Roy Thinnes, Sid Caesar, Myrna Loy, Ed Nelson, Nancy Olson, Larry Storch, Martha Scott, Jerry Stiller, Norman Fell, Erik Estrada, Sharon Gless

Airport 1975 is a significant improvement over the original *Airport* for many reasons. The film has a campy, "everything but the kitchen sink" feel. It claims to feature "22 of the World's Greatest Stars," although I'm not sure if Norman Fell and Erik Estrada really qualify as some of the "World's Greatest Stars."

It's highly entertaining to witness the movie's producers attempts to throw in every '70s celebrity imaginable, and it's even more entertaining to see those celebrities cast in such bizarre roles. Feminist musician Helen Reddy essays the role of a guitar-playing, singing nun! She spends the entire movie caring for a saccharine-sweet child in need of a kidney transplant, played by *The Exorcist*'s Linda Blair. Sadly, Blair does not vomit on Helen Reddy, but this bizarre combo is still worth seeing.

Another plus is that the filmmakers decided to use footage of a real 747 and perform a live, spectacular aerial stunt. Phony-looking projection gimmicks, while present, are thankfully kept to a minimum. A marked improvement in both realism and special effects (well, they're not like *Star Wars* or anything, but they are an improvement) really helps the film. This sequel may have been made for just $4 million, less than half of what was spent on the original, but it looks much costlier.

The only returning character is George Kennedy's (the series staple) Joe Patroni. This time, his wife (played by *Webster*'s mom, Susan Clark!) and child are on the plane and in peril. After a midair collision with a small plane, the safety of the 747 is jeopardized. One copilot is blown out of the cockpit, the other blinded before falling unconscious. The shrapnel also presumably kills "Poncho," leaving only Karen Black (playing a plucky stewardess) to fly the plane.

On the ground, Kennedy, along with Black's boyfriend, played by Charlton Heston, coaches her to the ground with helpful flying tips like "Climb, baby! Climb!" and, "Go do your thing, baby." Kennedy and Heston do most of the yelling in the film, shouting things like "Oh, daahhmmm!!!" at regular intervals and generally acting more panicked than the passengers on the plane. To be fair, though, the performances are entertaining and, overall, they seem much less stiff and dated in this sequel. The climax features a spectacular midair transfer in which a fed-up Heston shimmies across a strengthened wire from a helicopter to the 747.

Airport 1975 grossed a very profitable $25 million. Even more surprising, Helen Reddy was nominated for a Golden Globe in 1975 for Most Promising Newcomer with her gripping portrayal of the singing nun.

Most Spectacular Moment of Carnage

Again, disaster is averted, and very few people are killed. The copilot's expulsion from the aircraft during the midair collision probably qualifies as the winner, but it's a close call with the air force pilot who gets sucked away as he tries to enter the 747's cockpit during a midair transfer. **(GK)**

Airport '77 (1977)
Universal Pictures   114 minutes

RECOMMENDED

DIRECTOR: Jerry Jameson

WRITERS: Michael Scheff, David Spector

CAST: Jack Lemmon, Lee Grant, Brenda Vaccaro, Joseph Cotten, Olivia de Havilland, James Stewart, George Kennedy, Darren McGavin, Christopher Lee, Robert Foxworth, Robert Hooks, Monte Markham, Kathleen Quinlan, Gil Gerard, James Booth, Monica Lewis, Maidie Norman, M. Emmet Walsh

Obviously influenced by the success of *The Poseidon Adventure*, this second sequel takes the action out of the airport and sets it in the underwater depths of the Bermuda

Triangle. Jack Lemmon takes over the role of hapless pilot, whose superluxurious 747 (you can even play video games like Pong on it!) carrying valuable cargo to Jimmy Stewart's Bermuda mansion is suddenly taken hostage by thieves. Gassed asleep along with the rest of the passengers, Lemmon is helpless as the robbers crash the plane, leaving it perched precariously on a cliff ledge underwater.

Surprisingly, this is the most entertaining film of the series. There's a lot more tension in this sequel, too. Finally, audiences get to see a spectacular crash. The leaking plane and threat of drowning further amplify tensions between the passengers, crew, and thieves. In the end it's up to Jimmy Stewart to save the day. He goes berserk, decks the bad guys, escapes, and swims for help. Just kidding! Actually, Stewart spends the movie in his mansion, guffawing. Jack Lemmon makes an unusual hero for this type of film, but he pulls it off well. And the underwater photography is quite striking.

Still, there are a lot of unnecessary characters and subplots. Watch for Kathleen Quinlan's brief and bizarre romantic subplot involving the 747's blind piano player. What's the deal there? And I suppose it wouldn't be a disaster film without a bickering husband and wife (played by the great Christopher Lee and Lee Grant). And Mr. Gil Gerard—Buck Rogers himself—has a small role as Grant's boyfriend. But when disaster strikes, he isn't particularly heroic. I suppose he could've used some help from Twiki. As for Kennedy's Joe Patroni, he makes a brief appearance, offering insight on how to rescue the plane (like he's suddenly become an expert on navy underwater retrieval missions?!). In reality, his part is just a glorified cameo.

Once again, the Academy saw fit to nominate *Airport '77*, although this time it was for Best Art Direction and Best Costume Design. Domestically, the film grossed a profitable but disappointing $16.2 million at the box office. Still, *Airport '77* did end up being one of the 10 highest moneymakers of the year in the United Kingdom, which meant that Universal would decide that yet another (but ill-fated) follow-up was in order.

Most Spectacular Moment of Carnage

There are more casualties in this sequel, most occurring from drowning or exposure. Most notable is Christopher Lee's death as he attempts a dangerous swim to the surface with Lemmon. The kicker occurs when his body floats by the passenger window, right where his wife is sitting, for all to see. **(GK)**

The Concorde: Airport '79 (1979)

Universal Pictures   113 minutes

SO BAD IT'S GOOD

At twice the speed of sound, can the Concorde evade attack?

© Universal City Studios, Inc.

DIRECTOR: David Lowell Rich

WRITER: Eric Roth

CAST: Alain Delon, Susan Blakely, Robert Wagner, Sylvia Kristel, George Kennedy, Eddie Albert, Bibi Andersson, Charo, John Davidson, Andrea Marcovicci, Martha Raye, Cicely Tyson, Jimmie Walker, David Warner, Mercedes McCambridge, Sybil Danning, Ed Begley, Jr.

A note for bad movie fans out there: this series killer has the dubious distinction of qualifying as one of the worst (or best, depending on your taste in film) disaster films ever made. Besides being a blatant and obvious advertisement for the Concorde company, it is ridiculous beyond words, guaranteed to leave you rolling on the floor in laughter.

George Kennedy, sick of his second-fiddle role in the series, takes the pilot's seat for a cross-continental flight to wackiness. And with a passenger roster including B-list celebrities Eddie Albert, Charo, John Davidson (and his hair), Martha Raye, and a saxophone-playing Jimmy Walker, you know you're in for trouble. Thankfully, Kennedy's Joe Patroni is a driven, take-no-bull kind of guy with a Concorde to fly and save. He's *the man*. And he proves it early on in the film as he preps for takeoff by barking to a stewardess, "They don't call it the cockpit for nothing, honey!"

The ever-so-suave Robert Wagner plays the heavy, an industrialist involved in illegal arms sales. When his newscaster girlfriend, Susan Blakely, witnesses a killing in her own home and later receives documents proving the shocking truth, Wagner tells her that he can explain everything. He convinces her he'll meet her and clear it up in Paris during a layover on the Concorde pre-Olympic goodwill flight bound for Moscow. What to do now? Wagner decides to subtly blow the Concorde up using any means necessary. As such, the Concorde must skillfully avoid heat-seeking missiles and survive a dogfight with fighter planes.

Kennedy has an interesting way of handling the aircraft during the crisis. It involves thrashing the steering wheel around and grimacing as hard as he can. He flies the Concorde as if it's the Millennium Falcon, taking it for a series of 360-degree loops in the sky. At one point, Kennedy even rolls down the cockpit window and fires a flare out of it to destroy one of the aforementioned missiles. The pathetic special effects of the plane's loop-de-loops, superimposed missiles, and so on only heighten the comedy.

But the action's not only in the skies. After a hard day's work avoiding terrorist attacks, what does Kennedy do to relax? How about sleeping with a French prostitute? Yes, midway through

the film, during a brief stop in Paris to assess the plane's condition, Kennedy goes for drinks with his French copilot in a local bar. A horrifying fireside love scene ensues (although it is kept mercifully short) between Kennedy and a local woman. After learning that she's a hooker hired by his copilot, Kennedy shouts jubilantly, "She was great!"

to which the copilot responds, laughing, "What are friends for?" It brings a tear to your eye, doesn't it?

Shockingly, intended target Blakely doesn't realize that the attack was because of her, and she gets *back* on the Concorde *again* to finish the flight (whereupon, she tells Wagner, she'll announce her findings to the media. Talk about painting a bull's-eye on your forehead! I suppose she couldn't just talk to the reporters in Paris that morning. That would make too much sense!), pointlessly endangering the lives of the crew and passengers. This time, there's a device set to open the lower cargo door during flight. The "explosive decompression" tears a hole in the aircraft, almost sucking Eddie Albert into oblivion. But his airplane seat jams in the hole and, after being rescued from certain death, he jovially responds, "I had the best seat in the house!" Huh? Kennedy lands the Concorde safely on a ski hill (although it still manages to explode), and Wagner puts a gun to his head (we know how he feels) before the movie ends.

It goes without saying that this film bombed both critically and commercially upon release. Charo was not nominated for Best Supporting Actress at the Oscars that year. Sadly, it looks like *The Concorde: Airport '79* finally managed to shut the *Airport* series down. But don't let that stop you from checking it out. If bad taste is your thing, this is the *Airport* movie to see!

Most Spectacular Moment of Carnage

The entire film. But the Concorde mechanic who plants the bomb does manage to get himself run down by the Concorde itself during liftoff. That's pretty impressive, and it deserves a special mention. **(GK)**

Airspeed (1998)
Lions Gate Films   88 minutes

AVOID AT ALL COSTS

DIRECTOR: Robert Tinnel

WRITERS: Richard Goudreau, Roc LaFortune (based on the novel by Andrew Sands)

CAST: Elisha Cuthbert, Bronwen Booth, Joe Mantegna, Lynne Adams, Charles Powell, Yvan Ponton, Roc LaFortune, and lots of other French-Canadian actors

As a Canadian, I am often subjected to low-budget Canadian knockoffs of big-budget American films. I just want everyone out there to know that, yes, they're terrible, and I apologize to everyone around the world who has been hoodwinked into watching any of them.

The box cover of this direct-to-video stink bomb depicts a jumbo jet flying through a city street with skyscrapers on either side, a visual that is nowhere to be seen in the actual film. This is a no-money knockoff disaster film made to profit on the incredible nonsuccess of *Turbulence*, and it features some seriously bad acting. Many of the performers are trying unsuccessfully to hide their French-Canadian accents. You're expecting someone in the control tower to bring in poutine (in case you're interested, poutine is a French-Canadian french fry treat) and start digging in. There's terrible model and effects work, the score is rotten, and worst of all, the script is just plain bad.

If you're still reading this review at this point, you might be interested to learn that the thin plot involves a luxury Teknacom 727, which is transporting the daughter of a famous Bill Gates-type owner of a computer firm. He's played by Joe Mantegna, who, we hope, picked up a fat check for two or three days' work. This kid, a young, pre-*24* Elisha Cuthbert, is one of the brattiest characters ever to be filmed. Why anyone would watch the first 10 minutes and not want her to come to a grisly end is beyond me.

Through a series of ridiculous incidents, Cuthbert is alone, piloting the plane. Enter a hipster/doofus air traffic controller, played by Charles Powell, who manages to make contact with her. Mantegna arrives at the control booth to join in the exposition. Before long, Powell, our hero, is delivering lines like "I'm gonna be your Charlton Heston," with a straight face. Honestly, Powell is no Charlton Heston, mostly because he never grinds his teeth or barks lines like "Climb, baby, climb!"

Trying to break the monotony of shooting mostly in two locations, the director employs a bizarre editing technique I've never seen before. When the characters briefly lose radio contact with Cuthbert, the dialogue scene that follows is edited using nothing but a series of dissolves, for no reason whatsoever.

Come on, guys. Just because you throw in one significant American actor doesn't mean you can fool everyone into thinking you've made a big American film. Will we Canadians ever learn?

Most Spectacular Moment of Carnage
The pilot's electrocution, displayed via dime-store special effects, is by far the cheesiest, most unintentionally hilarious moment in the film.

Note: To make poutine, fry up some french fries and dump as many cheese curds on top of them as you can. In the meantime, heat a pan of brown gravy. Pour the gravy over the fries and cheese curds, kiss your arteries goodbye, and enjoy. (GK)

Alive (1993)

Touchstone Pictures   126 minutes

HIGHLY RECOMMENDED

⚠

Director: Frank Marshall

Writer: John Patrick Shanley (based on the book by Piers Paul Read)

Cast: Ethan Hawke, Vincent Spano, Josh Hamilton, Bruce Ramsay, John Newton, David Kriegel, Kevin Breznahan, Sam Behrens, Illeana Douglas, Jack Noseworthy, Christian J. Meoli, Jake Carpenter, John Malkovich

After sitting through films like *Survive!* and *Cyclone* that have exploited the cannibalistic aspects of this true story about a horrifying plane crash, I approached yet another telling of the story with a great deal of trepidation. Surprisingly, *Alive* is an excellent film that was made with the full cooperation of the survivors. Based on the bestselling book by Piers Paul Read and scripted by Oscar winner John Patrick Shanley, the film takes the time to fully develop its characters.

Following a brief introduction (from an uncredited John Malkovich), we are introduced to the passengers just minutes before they crash. Writer Shanley and director Marshall manage to introduce the many characters efficiently without slowing down the film. These people are really likable, and a relatively big budget allows the filmmakers to realistically depict such frightening moments as the plane crash (some people are sucked out of the plane as it breaks in two; some are crushed as their section hits the mountain) and, later, a claustrophobic avalanche sequence in which the characters, portrayed in abject terror, are submerged under many feet of snow. There are also great moments of intensity (one of the characters slips and dangles from a mountain ledge) during expeditions to find food and help.

It was a wise move to avoid cutting back to civilization (family members and those looking for the group) like previous versions had. This way, the audience experiences what the characters did, without a break. I could really sense the hopelessness that the characters must have been experiencing after enduring hardship after hardship for 72 straight days. Yet the film also has a surprising sense of humor, as the characters are quick to make light of their situation. Watch for a makeshift snowball birthday cake with a cigarette candle.

The cannibalistic aspects of the story are well handled and work as a minor element of the story, rather than the only reason for the story. What could have been simply exploitative (not that there's anything wrong with that) instead turns out to be a downright inspirational film. The movie grossed $36 million domestically, but it didn't garner the award nominations you might expect. Still, this film is highly recommended; it's one of the best of the genre you're likely to see. If you want to learn more about the real-life events that took place afterward, check out *Alive: 20 Years Later*, a short documentary that was released on video in conjunction with the film's release.

Most Spectacular Moment of Carnage

Naturally, the plane crash, where a big special-effects budget captures the horrifying reality of what it's like to go down. Passengers are sucked out of the plane, thrown around, and crushed. **(GK)**

Die Hard 2 (1990)

Twentieth Century Fox   124 minutes

HIGHLY RECOMMENDED

© Twentieth Century Fox

DIRECTOR: Renny Harlin

WRITERS: Steven E. de Souza, Doug Richardson (based on the novel *58 Minutes* by Walter Wager)

CAST: Bruce Willis, Bonnie Bedelia, William Atherton, William Sadler, Reginald VelJohnson, Franco Nero, John Amos, Dennis Franz, Art Evans, Fred Dalton Thompson, Tom Bower, Sheila McCarthy, Don Harvey, Robert Patrick, John Leguizamo, Colm Meaney

So how does this Bruce Willis action blockbuster qualify as a disaster movie? At first glance, it may not seem like one (probably because it's so well made), but in fact it has all the trappings of what you'd expect from an *Airport*-style disaster flick.

It has an extremely varied cast of characters, including a New York cop, an obnoxious captain of security, a deposed South American cocaine-smuggling general (!), an arrogant news reporter, a crazy janitor, and even a foul-mouthed, Taser-wielding old lady.

All of these characters are trapped either on the ground in the vicinity of Washington Dulles International Airport on Christmas Eve during a snowstorm or in one of the numerous 747s circling above during said snowstorm. Terrorists have shut down the airport's power, leaving no landing lights for the planes or ability to communicate with the watchtower. There are even shots of a panicked crowd crashing through glass doors, trying to escape the doomed airport in terror. Hell, this movie *is* *Airport*, only much better.

Perhaps most preoccupied with getting planes down safely is Willis's character John McClane, whose wife is a passenger on one of the circling 747s. It seems that a team of right-wing military extremists, led by William Sadler, is pretty keen on rescuing its evil extradited general from authorities, to the point of seizing control of the airport. The guys are threatening to crash the fuel-challenged planes above. Willis discovers this almost immediately, and the action begins 10 minutes in with a great fight scene in the airport baggage handling area. Unfortunately, brutally killing one of the terrorists puts Willis at odds with the security captain, played by Dennis Franz, which leads to various barbs and insults, including my favorite from Willis: "What sets off the metal detectors first? The lead in your ass or the shit in your brains?" I'm not sure how "shit" is supposed to set off a metal detector, but who cares?

Baffling comments like those leave Willis on his own for most of the film as he runs around underneath the airport and tries to predict what the terrorists will do. Director Renny Harlin is highly skilled at shooting and cutting action scenes, and this film features some of his best, including a skywalk shoot-out and a snowmobile chase.

Particularly enjoyable about this film (and others like it) is that even when our "hero" does all the right things, terrible events still manage to happen. When Sadler decides to intentionally down a plane, Willis does everything humanly possible to stop it from happening. Yet it still crashes spectacularly, killing hundreds.

Die Hard 2 was one of the biggest hits of 1990, grossing $117 million domestically and finishing somewhere around $237 million worldwide.

Most Spectacular Moment of Carnage

Do planes explode? Yes, three explode, and in a big way. In addition, you'll see heavily blood-squibbed shootings, a beating with a golf club, a head crushing (or flattening—you be the judge) and many shootings through glass. But that's not all, folks! There's a fatal crushing under scaffolding (my second favorite death in the film), a strangulation, a bullet to the head, an icicle driven through the eye (the hands-down winner), a throat slashing, and finally, the sucking of a man into a jumbo jet's propeller. To make your viewing experience of this flick even more enjoyable, gather some friends together to watch it and drink a shot every time a violent act is committed. **(GK)**

Executive Decision (1996)

Warner Bros.   133 minutes

AT YOUR OWN RISK

DIRECTOR: Stuart Baird

WRITERS: Jim Thomas, John Thomas

CAST: Kurt Russell, Steven Seagal, Halle Berry, John Leguizamo, Oliver Platt, Joe Morton, David Suchet, B. D. Wong, Len Cariou, Whip Hubley, Andreas Katsulas, Mary Ellen Trainor, Marla Maples Trump, J. T. Walsh

After the huge success of *Die Hard 2*, producer Joel Silver decided to try his luck again, this time with less impressive results. Directed by Stuart Baird (who coedited *Die Hard 2*), who clearly showed he can cut and shoot action, the film does have some exciting moments toward the end. But this is a patchwork taken from better films, and the good stuff comes too little, too late.

In a confusing series of shots and scenes that almost look as though they were cut from another movie, an Islamic terrorist leader is abducted and taken into U.S. custody. The sequence is impossible to follow. We see a church, priests shooting bazookas and machine guns, and people being shot, and none of it makes any sense. The film is sepia toned in this montage for no apparent reason. We cut to Greece, where a 747 is taking off for Dulles airport (Silver really has a thing for Dulles airport) in Washington. Then, in London, an Islamic terrorist blows up a restaurant. We watch all of this in bewilderment, until finally the 747 is taken hostage by Islamic terrorists. It seems they have a stolen Soviet nerve toxin called DZ-5 onboard. Their plan is to force the release of their leader, then set the plane down in Washington and blow up the city with the toxin.

The passengers onboard include flight attendants Halle Berry, Marla Maples Trump (ex of "The Donald," she has few lines, but her "worried" performance is worth focusing on), and a senator played by J. T. Walsh. There's also an overweight cop traveling back home, packing heat and waiting for his chance to save the day. On the ground below, government officials try to figure out how to handle the situation, unsure if the DZ-5 really is aboard.

Kurt Russell stars as Dr. Phil David Grant, a brain with no military experience who is working for "Intelligence." Steven Seagal plays Austin Travis, a lieutenant colonel who is immediately at odds with Russell and who displays it with his one facial expression (which garnered him a Razzie, or Golden Raspberry Award, nomination). Seagal suggests a spectacular midair transfer of his anti-terrorist team onto the plane by means of an adapted "130" F-14 (at least, I think that's what it is). An aerospace engineer (Oliver Platt) and Russell are forced to accompany the anti-terrorist squad as witnesses and technical advisors.

Platt, Russell, and squad sneak up on the plane and begin boarding (how does no one onboard the 747 notice this?). The squad drills holes above and below the passenger cabin (no one hears this?) and sets up cameras. All the while there's a lot of goofy and laughable dialogue. Additionally, Russell recruits the help of flight attendant Berry in identifying the terrorists and figuring out which one has the detonator. Later, she misidentifies the bomber, who turns out to be a diamond thief!

As the implausibility builds, they locate the bomb, and the "expert" must coach the device's nervous inventor, Platt, as he disarms it. All the while, fighter planes circle around the 747, and eventually they are ordered to go ahead and shoot it down. As expected, chaos results. Russell and Berry have an incredibly difficult time landing the plane, at one point causing a runway full of miniatures to explode.

To be honest, the last 20 minutes of this film are actually fun and exciting. But we've seen it all before, and we've seen it done better. It's acceptable entertainment, if there's *really* nothing better out there. The film garnered Blockbuster Entertainment Awards for Russell and Berry as Favorite Actor and Actress, respectively, in an Adventure/Drama and grossed a healthy $133 million worldwide (it was budgeted at $55 million).

Most Spectacular Moment of Carnage
The winner is Steven Seagal's spectacular death by suction during the midair transfer. It comes as a welcome surprise. I only wish that his demise had been a little more violent. In a perfect world, his body would have decompressed and exploded instead of just being sucked (offscreen) at 30,000 feet, but I'll take what I can get. **(GK)**

Fearless (1993)

Warner Bros.   122 minutes

RECOMMENDED

© Warner Bros.

DIRECTOR: Peter Weir

WRITER: Rafael Yglesias

CAST: Jeff Bridges, Isabella Rossellini, Rosie Perez, Tom Hulce, John Turturro, Benicio Del Toro, Deirdre O'Connell, John De Lancie

Fearless opens with an image of businessman Max Klein, played by Jeff Bridges. Baby in one arm, child in his other hand, he is walking through a cornfield. In a wide shot, we see smoke, the wreckage of an airliner, fire trucks, screaming passengers, and a scrambling emergency crew. Amid all this, Bridges remains perfectly calm, almost distant. After giving the children to the crew, he walks away, and thus begins *Fearless*, one of the most unusual disaster films ever made. Unfortunately, carnage fans, we never do see the crash itself, but instead focus on the character and the effect these events have on him.

Bridges's wife, family, and psychologist are at a loss as how to treat his mental state. Having faced death and survived it, he no longer seems to care about anything, and, as the title suggests, becomes "fearless." He begins behaving as though he is invincible, slapping his lawyer, Tom Hulce, and walking into traffic and along the ledges of tall buildings. This attitude does not impress his family, including his wife, played by Isabella Rossellini. Yet Bridges refuses to modify his behavior or talk about the accident because he believes they can't relate to what he has experienced. He just wants to stare blankly into space and eat strawberries. Yes, eat strawberries.

Through flashbacks we begin to see what transpired during the flight. The chaotic shaking, the realization of the passengers and crew that they are about to crash and die. We see Bridges, accepting his oncoming death, rise from his seat. Almost euphoric, he calmly helps the other passengers, comforting them and eventually leading them to safety.

After the crash, Bridges will only open up to fellow survivor Rosie Perez, who is struggling to get over the loss of her baby. She blames herself for losing grip of her only child during the flight. Bridges eventually proves to her that it wasn't her fault by strapping her into a car, making her hold onto a toolbox, and driving the vehicle into a brick wall. Amazingly, this works miracles, and despite almost killing them both, it cures her!

Unfortunately for Bridges, his family relations crumble further, and Perez must try to help him return to planet Earth and restore his relations with his wife and kids. This process involves more strawberries (what's with all the strawberries in this movie?).

The film is beautifully shot, the story is unique and interesting, and the performances are great (Rosie Perez was nominated for an Oscar and won both the Chicago and Los Angeles Film Critics Awards). The result is a quite thoughtful and moving film—the last thing a bunch of guys sitting around the TV, eating corn chips, drinking beer, and waiting for celebrities to bite the big one would want to see. I'm glad I was in the right mood for it at the time.

Most Spectacular Moment of Carnage

It would be tasteless to take such a serious, meaningful film and reduce it to a few moments of carnage. Ha! Who am I kidding? Unfortunately, since the crash itself is kept offscreen, I can't come up with anything. The closest thing would probably involve Jeff Bridges's character choking on a strawberry. That's it. Sorry. (**GK**)

The Flight of the Phoenix (1965)

Twentieth Century Fox   142 minutes

HIGHLY RECOMMENDED

⚠

DIRECTOR: Robert Aldrich

WRITER: Lukas Heller (based on the novel by Elleston Trevor)

CAST: James Stewart, Richard Attenborough, Peter Finch, Hardy Krüger, Ernest Borgnine, Ian Bannen, Ronald Fraser, Christian Marquand, Dan Duryea, George Kennedy, Gabriele Tinti, Alex Montoya, Peter Bravos, William Aldrich, Barrie Chase

The Flight of the Phoenix is a highly entertaining adventure film that draws upon classic disaster movie themes to tell a compelling story about a group of disparate characters trapped in a seemingly hopeless situation. The first half of the film effectively lays out the story's logistics, and the second half of the film depicts the superhuman struggles involved in assembling this new aircraft under very adverse conditions. Central to the plot is the unbridled hatred that exists between Jimmy Stewart, a guilt-ridden, emasculated pilot, and Hardy Krüger, a German airplane designer and erstwhile asshole of the universe. Stewart feels responsible for the crash and the resulting deaths, yet he still attempts to maintain control over the situation. Krüger thinks Stewart is a moron, and he resents having to answer to him. If only these two men could learn to respect each other, damn it! Krüger, in an amazing slow-burn performance, angrily blasts out dialogue like "You behave as if stupidity were a virtue!" and "That is precisely the re-action I would have expected from a man of your obvious limitations!" Among a very fine cast, his performance is perhaps the most compelling.

We meet our merry band on the plane that Stewart is piloting from the Arabco Oil Company site to a nearby vacation spot. He's a veteran pilot who doesn't seem to worry about this older plane's mechanical problems, such as the radio fritzing out and something called a voltage regulator being out of service. Ten minutes into the film, a freak sandstorm engulfs the plane, causing the engines to give out and causing Stewart to crash land in the desert. Two secondary characters are killed; another is mortally wounded and spends the rest of the film dying slowly on a cot inside the wrecked plane. The rest of the men are uninjured, and the first hour of the film covers the next few days as they set up shop, tend to their dying comrade, and begin to ration the water and the only food they've got, a veritable shitload of pressed dates. Among the central characters are Richard Attenborough as Stewart's longtime friend and copilot; Peter Finch and Ronald Fraser as a British army captain and sergeant, respectively; Ian Bannen, masterfully acerbic and condescending, with a sharp word for every occasion; Christian Marquand as a soft-spoken and ruggedly handsome doctor; George Kennedy, who doesn't have all that much to do, really; and Ernest Borgnine, who doesn't waste any time establishing his character as a bug-eyed madman. Borgnine revels in the chance to pitch screaming and crying fits, probably because his character only survives to the film's halfway mark; he obviously wanted to chew as much scenery as he could before his character runs into the desert with no water or supplies and drops dead.

A little more than a half hour into the movie, Krüger suggests to Stewart his idea to tear apart the wreck and build a new plane. Stewart doesn't listen, however, and the film progresses with every passing day bringing more sandstorms and sunburns, and less hope that they'll be rescued. Eventually, Krüger reveals that he's actually an airplane designer, which for some reason he didn't mention earlier, and he manages to convince everyone that his plan might be feasible. However, this is still an urgent and desperate situation, in that they need to finish construction before their water runs out. Plus, there is no guarantee that the engine will start or that the plane will actually fly. This, and the continuing power struggle between Krüger and Stewart, constantly threatens to derail the entire plan.

And then a band of 12 Arabs on camels sets up camp below a nearby sand dune. Everyone decides that they're obviously dangerous marauders, but until the boys know for sure, they have to stop construction so as not to be detected. Finch and Marquand make the mistake of going out and asking them for help, and they end up with their throats slit. Then the Arabs vanish, leaving behind an injured camel that no one thinks might make a tasty meal. Perhaps they just really loved their pressed dates, but I for one would have been all over that delicious camel with a knife and fork.

Construction resumes and the end of the project is in sight, but all of the men are fighting exhaustion, lack of food and water, and the relentless sun. Then, after one final blowout between our two protagonists, during which Krüger hurls a large wrench directly at Stewart's head, there is a reconciliation that allows for the project to reach completion. Oh, and Krüger also chooses this moment to reveal that he's actually a *model* airplane designer and that he has never actually designed a full-size aircraft. He doesn't think this is a very big deal, and he actually makes a good case for his skills being easily transferable to the real thing. As the film draws to a close, Stewart manages to start the engine and keep it running long enough for the plane to be dragged to a clearing, after which he gets it into the air and all the way back to Arabco. It's a very exciting conclusion made all the more meaningful by the way in which the hard-earned trust that Krüger and Stewart begrudgingly place in one another pays off.

There are other interesting subplots involving the two British army officers, Borgnine and the dying young man and a transistor radio, exhaustion-induced visions of a belly dancer, and the care and feeding of a little monkey, but I'll leave it to you to discover those pleasures for yourself. By doing so, you'll see how a film such as this could have a "love theme" performed by Connie Francis. This is a well-made adventure film that plays faster than its actual length and features performances that are surprisingly contemporary in tone.

Most Spectacular Moment of Carnage
This movie does not offer the kind of large-scale violence often seen in the disaster genre. Therefore, one must look for the small pleasures, such as the untimely death of Robert Aldrich's son William about 10 minutes in. He's the poor bastard who, after paging through a copy of *Playboy*, gets crushed by some large pieces of what looks like drilling equipment as the plane goes down, but not before looking behind him and letting out a high-pitched shriek of terror. William Aldrich later went on to produce such classy cinematic fare as *Who Is Killing the Great Chefs of Europe?* **(MR)**

Flight of the Phoenix (2004)

Twentieth Century Fox   113 minutes

AT YOUR OWN RISK

DIRECTOR: John Moore

WRITERS: Scott Frank, Edward Burns (from the 1965 screenplay by Lukas Heller and based on the novel by Elleston Trevor)

CAST: Dennis Quaid, Tyrese Gibson, Giovanni Ribisi, Miranda Otto, Tony Curran, Sticky Fingaz, Jacob Vargas, Hugh Laurie

I knew there was going to be trouble about five seconds in. Is that Johnny Cash, I thought, singing "I've Been Everywhere"? I like Johnny as much as the next guy, but you need to be making a hell of a movie to justify using one of his classic tunes over the opening credits. Sadly, this pointless remake of Robert Aldrich's 1965 adventure epic is tedious and silly, though this does result in a few unintentional laughs.

In this version, an oil rig in Mongolia is being shut down, and Dennis Quaid is the pilot sent to take the entire crew back to Beijing. This may seem like an arbitrary change from the original movie, but it's actually intended to provide a thematic back-story for the people on the plane and the hopelessness of their situation. It doesn't work. But I'll get to that.

Most of the characters from the original movie are not represented in this film. Quaid has taken on the Jimmy Stewart role, and he does have a copilot just like Stewart did, but the similarities end there. Some of the other characters do or say things reminiscent of other original characters, but that's pretty much it. The only exception is Giovanni Ribisi, in the role originally played by Hardy Krüger. Though he has a different name and isn't German, he's still a model airplane designer, and he still sports bleach-blond hair, wire rim glasses, and the same prim superiority. However, the filmmakers so clearly intended to establish him as mysterious and enigmatic that they never really explain why he's on the plane. According to rig foreperson Miranda Otto, he's not a member of the crew; he just showed up one day and never left. What's the chief designer of a successful model airplane company doing wandering around Mongolia? I don't know either.

After a maddening setup in which pretty much everyone comes off as obnoxious pricks, the plane gets caught in a huge, fake-looking sandstorm, and soon one of the engines explodes and the plane crashes spectacularly in the Gobi Desert. Aside from the crappy sandstorm effects, the plane crash is very exciting and much longer and more violent than the one shown in the original film. I did enjoy how one of the propellers spins right off of the engine and slams into the plane, slicing through the forward cabin. But is one great plane crash enough to justify watching an entire movie?

Once everyone emerges from the wreck, they find that they have about 30 days' worth of water and plenty of canned food. Oh, and they discover that a couple of people were killed in the crash, by the way. Then one of the other characters, a superstitious young fellow, decides to go outside at night in a sandstorm to take a piss, and he can't find his way back to the plane, so he ends up dead as well.

It's at this point that the thematic underpinning of the film is fully established. See, the crew Quaid was transporting has been all but tossed away by the company they work for, so they no longer matter. Hugh Laurie, as the accountant, admits that a search to find them would be considered too expensive an undertaking. The movie heavy-handedly continues to remind us of this fact as various characters comment from time to time about how the world has tossed them away. Even Quaid and his copilot describe their jobs, at the beginning of the film, as "taking out the trash." OK, we get it! Funny how in the original film, it was enough for the radio to be broken and the plane to have crashed a couple hundred miles off course for us to believe no one would find them. Here, though, we apparently need some sort of treatise on the value of human life for the story to work. And that's ironic, as I found these people stupid and annoying, no matter how hard the film tries to endear us to them.

About a half hour in, Ribisi tells everyone he's got a plan to rebuild the wreck into a brand new plane. Quaid will have none of this, though, and he is soon forced to go find and bring back one of the men, who has walked off into the desert alone. When Quaid catches up with him among his plane's scattered wreckage, he finds not only evidence of murderous scavengers, but also an armchair philosopher in the wandering oil-rig worker, a towheaded young man wont to say things like "I think a man only needs one thing in life—someone to love," and "I find it hard to believe that a man who learned to fly never had a dream." In an obvious attempt to shut him up, Quaid agrees to build the plane.

More boring stuff, then a huge explosion, then a very strange montage sequence cut to Outkast's "Hey Ya." Camaraderie ensues. An electrical storm begins. Will the fuel-filled plane explode? Nope. Will Quaid and Miranda Otto, formerly at odds, warm up to one another? Sure. Will the murderous scavengers show up? You bet. Will an impromptu meeting with these lowlifes go well? Not so much, due to all those machine guns. Quaid ends up killing most of them, allowing one to escape. Think that'll cause some problems later? Still paying attention?

Next thing you know, Ribisi flips his lid, in a fantastic freak-out that I thoroughly enjoyed. After he makes everyone beg him to continue building the plane (the titular "*Phoenix*"), we see that the group is being watched by a couple of the same folks who tried to kill them earlier. Uh-oh! Shit, there's more bad news: Ribisi is a *model* plane engineer! For some reason, even though the plane's already finished when everyone finds out, they're all furious! But then a big gust of wind picks up the plane and everyone calms down when they see it is capable of becoming airborne. Of course, many objects—even those of a large size, like cars and houses—can become airborne during high winds. Sadly, the film prolongs its foregone conclusion by having a sandstorm bury the *Phoenix*, causing Quaid to once again remind us of the film's "point" by declaring, "We're not garbage!" in an attempt to motivate everyone to dig out the plane. This is one easily discouraged bunch of oilmen, but the situation is nothing a very short, ridiculous speech can't fix.

So they get the plane moving, but they are soon being shot at by an army of marauders on horseback. Other problem: the plane's heading toward the edge of a cliff. Think they'll get off the ground? You know, it really is never too late to visit the concession stand or the refrigerator. You don't need to see the end of this movie, as it holds few surprises.

As I watched the credits roll with Steve Winwood's "Gimme Some Lovin'" blasting on the soundtrack, I pondered what went wrong with this movie. In spite of some striking locales, interesting photography, a couple of intriguing scenes, and Ribisi's fascinating performance, the movie falls apart. It makes the fatal mistake of altering the original material so that the characters of the pilot and the airplane designer are no longer the two key figures in this story. That structural approach was central to the original film's success, and it created a real sense of urgency that is never present in this remake. Unlike with the original, I never identified with this film's characters or situation, never emotionally connected to their struggle for survival. I'm not interested in a bunch of asswipes cracking bad jokes and getting all up in each other's grills. This movie telegraphs every aspect of the story with dutiful regularity while paying little attention to character development. It is so intent on being "current" in its approach to the material that, like many contemporary films, it substitutes glib irony for intelligent dialogue. The film simply wants to speedily move from one hackneyed scene to another, offering up simpleminded interpretations of human behavior wrapped in a condescending moral package that is far too laughable to be taken seriously.

Still, that was a cool explosion.

Most Spectacular Moment of Carnage

As the plane goes down, the tail rips off and sucks one poor bastard out. He falls to the desert sand below and lands with a comical thud, as if in a Wile E. Coyote cartoon. I do declare, in reality the human body would probably explode gruesomely under such circumstances. I guess, then, that this is actually the "Most Spectacular *Imagined* Moment of Carnage." Damn stupid movie. **(MR)**

The Hindenburg (1975)

Universal Studios   125 minutes

AT YOUR OWN RISK

⚠

DIRECTOR: Robert Wise

WRITER: Nelson Gidding (based on the novel by Michael M. Mooney)

CAST: George C. Scott, Anne Bancroft, William Atherton, Roy Thinnes, Gig Young, Burgess Meredith, Charles Durning, Richard A. Dysart, Robert Clary, Rene Auberjonois, Katherine Helmond

Famed director Robert Wise (*The Sound of Music, The Day the Earth Stood Still, The Haunting*) jumps into the disaster movie realm, and while the results are a little disappointing, there are some interesting moments. George C. Scott stars as a Nazi security officer (General Patton himself playing a Nazi?) posted on the *Hindenburg*'s historic flight to America. He is told that there is a saboteur onboard, plotting to blow up the ship. Scott's character, who is also doubtful about the Nazi party and its beliefs, must discover the plot. This leads to minor tension and melodrama as the passengers are searched and questioned by the officers. It's an interesting way to play up conflict between German civilians and the evil Nazi party.

This mystery would be intriguing, if not for the fact that it isn't much of a mystery. I could guess who the assassin was almost immediately, thanks to an unnecessary shot of one the characters as the blimp takes off. The minute I saw the expression on his face (he may as well grin and laugh maniacally), there were no doubts. Not only does that dilute the tension, but I also knew that Scott has to fail in his quest to save the ship. So I had to endure the competently acted and presented, but typical, disaster melodrama between characters. It's only in the last third of the movie, where Scott must find the bomb and disarm it, that the film actually kicks into high gear.

One nice touch is the use of actual black-and-white newsreel footage in the film. The opening, showing a history of blimps and aircraft, is effective and gives a lot of background information. The climax incorporates actual footage of the *Hindenburg* disaster with newly shot footage. In the film, the disaster is shown in black and white to match the newsreel. Surprisingly, it works much better than expected, and it is quite eerie to watch. Besides being nominated for Oscars in the categories of sound, cinematography, and art direction, the film won a statue for its Special Achievement in Sound and Visual Effects (easily some of the best things in the film). But I was most amazed and impressed that the filmmakers managed to work a musical number into a period drama about the *Hindenburg*. This proves my theory that every '70s disaster flick was required by law to have some sort of love theme or musical number in it. At least this particular number works reasonably well within the context of the film.

Most Spectacular Moment of Carnage

Hero George C. Scott discovers the bomb only in time to watch it explode, whereupon he is vaporized at ground zero. It's a good shock and, of course, a spectacular death. **(GK)**

Starflight: The Plane That Couldn't Land (1983)

Orion Pictures   116 minutes

AT YOUR OWN RISK

DIRECTOR: Jerry Jameson

WRITER: Robert M. Young

CAST: Lee Majors, Hal Linden, Lauren Hutton, Ray Milland, Gail Strickland, George DiCenzo, Tess Harper

Starflight is the farfetched yet languidly paced story of what happens when the world's first hypersonic jet airliner becomes trapped in space after a series of, er, unfortunate events. No stranger to the disaster genre, director Jerry Jameson (*Raise the Titanic,* *Airport '77, Terror on the 40th Floor, Hurricane*) attempts to drag the genre into the space age with the help of visual effects supervisor John Dykstra, of *Star Wars* and *Battlestar Galactica* fame. Though this is one of the better films of Jameson's oeuvre, that's not saying much. Still, the optical effects are generally quite good for their time, and the made-for-TV movie is sufficiently ridiculous to hold the interest of the disaster movie fan.

The first sign of trouble comes when scientist Hal Linden voices his concerns, to deaf ears, about the safety of the plane's rocket boosters. More than this, though, he just has a bad feeling about the launch, which is scheduled to take place in a mere 24 hours. And he should: to achieve the required velocity and altitude for hypersonic travel, the plane has to ascend vertically before leveling out at a terrifying cruising altitude of 100,000 feet and a speed of 2,500 miles per hour. Plus, many a man has been befallen by a terrible fate by ignoring the concerns of Hal Linden. But I suppose the numerous risks are worth it to be able to fly from California to Sydney, Australia, in a couple of hours, even if those risks include being hurled into space if the rocket boosters can't be shut off.

Note to travelers: if Lee Majors is your captain, chances are he's not only banging one of the flight attendants, but that he's also going to make aviation history in the worst possible way. It's not really his fault, though, that a wayward, malfunctioning rocket is on a collision course with his plane. And it's also not his fault that when the rocket is manually destroyed, a sky full of debris comes hurtling toward his plane at hypersonic speeds. And it's definitely not his fault that when he fires the rockets to climb above the debris, a chunk hits the rockets, causing an electrical short that prevents him from shutting them down, causing the *Starflight* to be shot into a decaying Earth orbit. I'm still not sure whose fault it is that his marriage is crumbling, but I don't blame him for falling into Lauren Hutton's arms. I do blame her, though, for letting him get away with being a really bad kisser. When she plants one on him during the film's climax, he just stands there and lets her mash her lips into his expressionless face. I don't know, maybe I've been doing it wrong.

Out of fuel and without a heat shield, they're pretty much screwed. And weightless! This movie ambitiously tries to depict a zero-gravity environment, but it doesn't really succeed. Some objects float while others don't, and most of the floating objects look like either someone just out of frame is slowly moving them around or that they are hanging from invisible filament. And why have the actors been told to simulate weightlessness by moving around really slowly? It just makes the movie longer.

So the space shuttle is sent up to refuel the plane, even though without a heat shield it wouldn't survive reentry. While the shuttle crew is at it, they decide to rescue Hal Linden so that he can supervise additional rescue attempts from the safety of Earth. They want to use a floating airlock, but that doesn't work very well, as is evidenced when the poor bastard who volunteers to test it is unable to close the hatch and gets sucked out into space. Then they decide to move Linden to the shuttle by putting him inside a coffin! I don't know much about coffins, but when you close one, is it really "hermetically sealed"? Can a coffin also insulate a living person from the coldness of space? It seems to make sense to the people in the movie, and the shuttle returns to Earth with Linden onboard.

Within a couple of hours, the shuttle is launched again. I would have thought it takes a little longer than that to refuel, check the computer systems, repair broken or missing heat tiles, restock the cigarette machine, and the like, but what do I know? This time the shuttle crew brings along a "universal docking device," which is a long tunnel that's connected to both vehicles for the passengers to crawl through. They manage to rescue five people before the tunnel is destroyed when it makes contact with sparks from the rocket's exposed wires. With nothing left to do, the shuttle returns to Earth.

Then Linden decides to use a huge, empty rocket-booster tank to collect as many passengers as possible and bring them back to Earth in the shuttle's cargo bay. So they launch the shuttle again! How did they get the tank on site and into the shuttle, and then get the shuttle back on the launch pad and into the air, in two hours? Seems unlikely, doesn't it? Anyway, as it appears that no matter when they launch the shuttle, it is always on a direct course for the orbiting *Starflight*, they make it back there in no time, load up the tank with most of the passengers, and return the tank to the shuttle. Meanwhile, the damage to the rockets is repaired from space, allowing them full rocket control, if only there were some safe way to return to Earth . . .

Well, they could just follow the other shuttle already in space that no one mentioned until now, allowing them to stay in the shuttle's "shadow" during reentry. And since it seems to be no problem for that shuttle to find them, that's the plan they choose. Even more conveniently, after reentry Majors manages to pilot the plane to a perfect landing on the very same runway he took off from, even though they weren't anywhere near North America when they reentered the atmosphere.

There are a lot of other things about this movie that don't make sense. I was bemused by every shot of the space shuttle taking off and landing, as it's always shown in broad daylight even if it's supposed to be happening in the middle of the night. Also, it's never clear where the shuttle is landing, though that would have to be the same place it's being launched from, which is Texas, I think. But near the end of the movie, just a few minutes after the shuttle lands for the last time, some of the passengers appear in the *Starflight* control room, which is in California. And what were all those gold bars doing in the cargo hold? And why didn't the space shuttle supply the *Starflight* with more oxygen? That would have been much more helpful than the case of crap-ass astronaut food that nobody ate anyway.

Most Spectacular Moment of Carnage

When the docking tunnel explodes, there are five people inside, including an old woman and the guy who played Bernie in *Weekend at Bernie's*. It's a big explosion, and it kills all five people at the same time. Who knew that crawling through a flimsy tunnel between two space vessels could be so dangerous? **(MR)**

Survive! (1976)
Paramount Pictures   85 minutes

AVOID AT ALL COSTS

DIRECTOR: René Cardona

WRITER: René Cardona, Jr. (based on the book by Charles Blair, Jr.)

CAST: Hugo Stiglitz, Norma Lazareno, Luz María Auguilar, Fernando Larrañaga, Pablo Ferrel

This hard-to-find, very-low-budget Mexican take on a real life incident (also depicted in the American film *Alive*) that occurred in 1972 involves a group of Uruguayan rugby players who crash in the Andes and are forced to fend for themselves, eventually eating the dead to survive. *Survive!* is led by the star powers of Pablo Ferrel and Hugo Stiglitz (I don't know, maybe they're famous in Mexico).

To its credit, the movie seems accurate in its portrayal of the facts and, despite the producers' limited resources (as is evidenced by a model airplane crash and lots of confetti snow), the filmmakers seem, at first, to have attempted to be earnest and do a decent job. But the film is so preoccupied with reporting the "facts" that the characters are never really fleshed out. I couldn't tell anyone apart. The American version of the film is also awkwardly dubbed in English, and a lot of the characters sound ridiculous. And frankly, zooming the camera in on the passengers' injuries for cheap gore shots doesn't help to establish credibility, either. There is also a startling voiceover that crops up almost every 10 minutes to explain what is happening, in case people can't figure it out for themselves. The jet flies too low into the mountain range and a voiceover explains, "The plane was flying too low."

Unlike *Alive*, this movie features a series of scenes involving the government and the families of the crash victims, who are unsuccessfully trying to locate the plane. As helicopters fly around, finding nothing, the omnipresent voiceover relays yet more important information to the presumably slow audience, like, "Their calculations had been incorrect . . . the wreckage was actually many miles away."

This is a gory film, with a heavier emphasis on the cannibalistic aspects of the story than other versions. Scenes of the survivors cutting up the crash victims and eating them are quite graphic. Interestingly enough, the bits of human flesh look just like bacon! Mmmm! It goes without saying that this would have been more fun to watch if I didn't know that it had really happened. Most of the movie consists of seemingly endless scenes of cannibalism and characters sitting outside the plane and freezing. Finally, three of the men journey over the mountains and find someone who looks like Juan Valdez (on a field, presumably growing coffee beans with his donkey). They are rescued while the inevitable voiceover explains this. Frankly, I think you'd be better off just frying some bacon instead of renting this flick.

Most Spectacular Moment of Carnage
The aftermath of the plane crash. There are wonderful close-ups of bleeding faces and carnage. One passenger helps another, who has been sliced along the stomach, by pushing an exposed piece of his small intestine back into his stomach. Thanks, guys. (**GK**)

The Survivor (1981)

GUO   98 minutes

AT YOUR OWN RISK

⚠

DIRECTOR: David Hemmings

WRITER: David Ambrose (based on the novel by James Herbert)

CAST: Robert Powell, Jenny Agutter, Joseph Cotten, Angela Punch-McGregor, Peter Sumner

This pre-*X-Files* disaster/sci-fi/horror/art-house flick wants to creep viewers out, but there's nothing in it more terrifying than the whacked out late-'70s hairstyles and fashions. The film gets off to a decidedly weird start, as children frolic in a park with an aircraft flying overhead. A lot of this widescreen film is shot in close-ups, which means that if you happen to be watching this at home on VHS, you're seeing half of a face, or, in some cases, you don't even know what you're looking at. Before you can say, "What the f*ck is going on here?" the film cuts to that evening, as pilot Robert Powell veers a 747 into the park, crashing through trees and lampposts. These shots are effective (if only they were clearly visible), depicting panicked crowds as they grasp trees or run for cover.

A photographer and his wife who live in a cabin that is grazed by the plane chase after the aircraft for photos. The 747 explodes into a fireball amid screams, and naturally, the insensitive photographer snaps pictures of the charred corpses, children's dolls, and wreckage. The pilot suddenly wanders out from the flames, the sole survivor, completely unharmed except for a case of amnesia. From this moment on the film gets even stranger, as the pilot (along with a stuffy crash investigator) tries to figure out what happened and why. Powell gives us lots of long, intense stares, and he delivers little dialogue. He hangs out around the wreckage site because he "has to know why." Meanwhile, a medium named Hobbs (played by Jenny Agutter), who is living in a cabin the park, hears the screams of the dead whistling in the wind through the trees. I'm not sure how she managed to find a cabin in a public park to live in, but oh well.

The ghosts of the dead get decidedly nastier, and the film suddenly switches gears. The corpses in the photographs stare back at the actors, and there are some eerie images of the ghost of a charred dead girl stalking various characters.

Powell decides to reenact the events with Agutter to try to determine exactly what happened. They seek out a priest, played by Joseph Cotten. He gives a long diatribe on God and, after refusing to help, follows them to the crash site anyway. He then vanishes from the film completely. Hope he was well paid by the producers.

Powell discovers that there was a bomb onboard and he travels to a nearby hangar, where the wreckage sits. To make a long story short (you know you're not going to go out and rent this one), Powell finds out who set the bomb. This would be exciting except for the fact that Powell and the newly discovered villain merely engage in a long conversation about why it was done. "Trophies for the hunter . . . they hang on my wall," the villain babbles. The character informs Powell that "they [the dead] want you" and goes on about the sound of "death rattles" and other nonsense before the wreckage bursts into flames.

Was Powell brought back to solve the mystery and avenge the passengers? Is he a ghost? What is the reason for his hairdo? Unfortunately, these questions go unanswered. All that is shown before the credits is Agutter walking away into the park with some children, and all of them freezing in a bizarre tableau.

Strictly a curiosity piece, this movie should not be viewed in the irritating pan-and-scan format, which subverts and destroys the artsy-fartsy potential the film might have possessed. In Australia (where it was filmed), *The Survivor* was nominated for four Australian Film Institute awards (the "Australian Oscars"), including Best Achievement in Cinematography, Best Achievement in Production Design, Best Achievement in Sound, and Best Actress in a Lead Role.

Most Spectacular Moment of Carnage

As the photographer's wife develops a snapshot of a charred body, we see that its eyes are wide open and staring right at her. She screams and, as if possessed, inexplicably places her wrist under the blade of a paper cutter. The slicing noises and what must be a bucket of blood seeping under the crack in the door suggest the rest. **(GK)**

Turbulence (1997)

Rysher Entertainment   102 minutes

AT YOUR OWN RISK

© Rysher Entertainment

DIRECTOR: Robert Butler

WRITER: Jonathan Brett

CAST: Ray Liotta, Lauren Holly, Brendan Gleeson, Hector Elizondo, Rachel Ticotin, Jeffrey DeMunn, John Finn, Ben Cross, Catherine Hicks

Here's a slick, good-looking disaster movie that nonetheless fails to engage. Its ridiculous plot makes even the usual suspension of disbelief required for disaster films impossible. Ray Liotta stars as Ryan Weaver, the "Lonely Hearts Strangler," a serial killer who likes to give his girlfriends teddy bears before raping and strangling them. Lauren Holly plays flight attendant Teri Halloran, who's just been dumped by her fiancé. In FBI custody, Liotta and a bank robber, played by Brendan Gleeson, are put on a commercial flight traveling from New York to L.A.

I have found that your typical major airport is one of the worst places to be during the holidays. *Turbulence* is set on Christmas Eve, and we are led to believe that no one travels anywhere on this day. The jumbo 747 is almost completely empty, with only five other passengers introduced, including such disaster movie staples as a grumpy old couple and a skateboarding kid. Despite the fact that these are the only passengers, the flight is not canceled, and the crew is ridiculously large; there are at least four flight attendants (one for each passenger, almost). This would all be perfectly acceptable if something entertaining were done with—or, more to the point—*to* the characters. But they are locked away in a storage room by Liotta, who has gotten loose, and they aren't seen again until the end of the film.

With Liotta running amuck, it doesn't take long for things to go haywire. On the ground, air traffic controllers, FBI agents, and detectives argue endlessly. Liotta is quick to point out that his goal is to crash the plane, and he maniacally threatens a corrupt detective, played by Hector Elizondo, that he will be the "first fucking cop to die with a plane up his ass." Sadly, while seeing an airplane ram itself up Hector Elizondo's ass and kill him on the runway is a visual that I think would have punched the movie up considerably, it doesn't happen. In fact, Liotta's and the detective's relationship is never properly resolved.

Throughout this wackiness, the pilot is killed and Lauren Holly attempts to fly the plane under the coaching of another pilot/unnecessary love interest (Ben Cross). Still unsure if Liotta is a madman (even though his screaming and tendency to run around belting out Christmas carols should be a dead giveaway), Holly is convinced by Liotta to unlock the cockpit door and let him in, so she can check on the crew members locked away in storage.

By now, a "class six" storm has found its way into the plane's path. As a deluge of rain pours onto the streets of Los Angeles below, Liotta (a fine actor, doing everything that he can to keep things interesting) continues to laugh hysterically (which, frankly, is getting a bit grating at this point).

The visual effects are average, the score weak. The filmmakers try very hard to make this situation believable, but it isn't for a nanosecond. All of the subplots and bells and whistles are distracting enough, but with a heroine who isn't clever enough to realize immediately that the villain is crazed, or that she might be wise to kill him, and a plane filled (such as it is) with forgettable characters, who cares if the damn thing goes down or not?

Turbulence tanked, grossing a lean $11.46 million domestically. It was nominated for two major awards—unfortunately, both were Razzies—for Worst Actress and Worst Reckless Disregard for Human Life and Public Property. From the director of *The Computer Wore Tennis Shoes*.

Most Spectacular Moment of Carnage
There is a shootout early on that leaves many characters dead, but frankly, it's not anything you wouldn't see in your average cop film. While the most unnecessary damage occurs when the plane crashes through a hotel karaoke bar, my favorite bit is Liotta's death scene, where he takes a bullet in the forehead. There's some blood spray and a brief shot of the back of his head being blown off. **(GK)**

The Doomsday Flight (1966)
Universal TV   100 minutes

RECOMMENDED

Passengers and crew on a routine flight learn that there is a bomb aboard that will explode once they descend to 4,000 feet. What to do? Well, land the plane in Denver. This made-for-TV movie features Edward Asner, Richard Carlson, Katherine Crawford, Van Johnson, Jack Lord, Greg Morris, Edmond O'Brien, Michael Sarrazin, John Saxon, and Don Stewart, and it was directed by William A. Graham. *Hawaii Five-O*'s Lord plays the FBI agent assigned to the case, and his wife just happens to be onboard the plane. He's good, but Edmond O'Brien steals the movie with his over-the-top performance as a mad, bespectacled bomber. He spends much of the film giggling maniacally, his wandering eyes appearing huge through his thick glasses. How this guy could walk around an airport unnoticed is beyond me, but you won't care because he's so entertaining. One of the best TV disaster movies I've seen. The plot-twist-laden screenplay was written by Rod Serling, of *Twilight Zone* fame. **(GK)**

Fire and Rain (1989)
Wilshire Court Productions   89 minutes

AT YOUR OWN RISK

A made-for-TV reenactment of the tragic 1985 Delta Airlines crash at the Dallas-Ft. Worth International Airport. With Charles Haid, John Beck, Tom Bosley, Penny Fuller, Robert Guillaume, David Hasselhoff, Dean Jones, Patti LaBelle, Lawrence Pressman, Susan Ruttan, and Angie Dickinson. Directed by Jerry Jameson, who also gave us the decent *Airport '77*. **(GK)**

Murder on Flight 502 (1975)

ABC   97 minutes

SO BAD IT'S GOOD

A fun, cheeseball made-for-TV flick with Robert Stack, Farrah Fawcett, Sonny Bono, Ralph Bellamy, and a stack of other stars. The preposterous murder plot involves a psychopath and a raging fire. Passengers include a cop, a priest, a practical joker, and an assortment of other absurd caricatures, each of whom could be responsible for the murder. Robert Stack's deadpan delivery of some pretty amusing dialogue might make you believe you're watching *Airplane!*, only the laughs aren't intentional this time. This one is an enjoyable, good-for-a-laugh piece of '70s camp. **(GK)**

Zero Hour! (1957)

Warner Bros.   81 minutes

SO BAD IT'S GOOD

Written by Arthur Hailey (author of the novel *Airport*), *Zero Hour!* tells the story of a plane in peril after the pilots fall prey to food poisoning. Sound familiar? That's because this flick is the inspiration for *Airplane!*, the classic comedy. With Dana Andrews, Linda Darnell, Sterling Hayden, Elroy "Crazylegs" Hirsch, and some other actors I've never heard of. This isn't currently available on DVD or video, but it's a must-see if you ever do get an opportunity to catch it on TV. Directed by Hall Bartlett. **(GK)**

RARE, OBSCURE, AND LESS IMPORTANT TITLES

Air Rage (2001) Straight-to-video

And I Alone Survived (1978) Made-for-TV

Back from Eternity (1956)

Challenger (1990) Made-for-TV

Concorde Affair '79 (1979)

Crash (1978) Made-for-TV

Crash: The Mystery of Flight 1501 (1990) Made-for-TV

Crash Landing: The Rescue of Flight 232 (1992) Made-for-TV

The Crowded Sky (1961)

Falling from the Sky: Flight 174 (1995) Made-for-TV

Fate Is the Hunter (1964)

Final Descent (1997) Made-for-TV

Flight into Danger (1956)

The Ghost of Flight 401 (1978) Made-for-TV

The High and the Mighty (1954)

Miracle Landing (1990) Made-for-TV

Seven in Darkness (1969) Made-for-TV

Skyjacked (1972)

Sonic Impact (1999) Straight-to-video

SST: Death Flight (1977) Made-for-TV

Submerged (2000) Straight-to-video

Tailspin: Behind the Korean Airliner Tragedy (1989) Made-for-TV

Terror in the Sky (1971) Made-for-TV

The Tragedy of Flight 103: The Inside Story (1990) Made-for-TV

Turbulence 2: Fear of Flying (2000) Made-for-TV

Turbulence 3: Heavy Metal (2001) Straight-to-video

Shake, Rattle, and Roll

It seems like most places on Earth fall into one earthquake zone or another, and most people have felt at least a tremor or two in their lives, so it's strange that earthquakes haven't been exploited in film as much as one would expect. There were two major films in the '30s (one of which could almost have fallen into the Really Bad Storms section), but no period since has devoted much attention to quakes. The 1994 Los Angeles earthquake inspired several television movies, but no theatrical features. Perhaps no one thinks that they can top *Earthquake*, the granddaddy of all earthquake films. And I can't blame them. Whatever the reason may be, we've included all that we could find in this chapter. Enjoy! **(GK)**

10.5 (2004)

NBC   164 minutes

AVOID AT ALL COSTS

DIRECTOR: John Lafia

WRITERS: Christopher Canaan, John Lafia, Ronnie Christensen

CAST: Beau Bridges, Kim Delaney, Fred Ward, Ivan Sergei, John Schneider, Kaley Cuoco, David Cubitt, Rebecca Jenkins, Dulé Hill

This TV miniseries is supposed to be a comedy, right? If the filmmakers had wanted us to take this movie seriously for even a second, they wouldn't have given us one of the most preposterous opening sequences in the genre's history. This miniseries starts off with an "extreme" mountain biker doing flips through the streets of Seattle to an obnoxious soundtrack. It's all meant to play like some kind of Gatorade commercial, as if we'd be more intrigued by a knockoff soda ad than the miniseries we've tuned in for.

Things get off to a rollicking start when the first earthquake immediately hits, and our extreme biker performs some bitchin' stunts to escape falling debris, exploding glass, and even the Seattle Space Needle crashing down behind him via terrible digital effects. I still can't stop laughing at the overreaction of the biker to the Space Needle coming down, or at the fact that he pedals furiously to try to get away instead of banking left or right and avoiding it altogether.

Thus the stage is set for an over-the-top cheesefest, and for the first hour or so this miniseries delivers. The characters repeatedly yell lines at each other like "We need to talk!" or "The public needs to know!" Kim Delaney, as Dr. Samantha Hill, is a heroic seismologist and a loose cannon. Hill is the type of arrogant character who poses outrageous theories, like detonating nuclear warheads to stop an earthquake, that in the real world would get you fired and perhaps committed, but who in the world of *10.5* is always right. Beau Bridges, as the president, is so earnest, so concerned about the health and welfare of the nation, so noble, and so unflappable, that, sadly enough, he seems almost inhuman.

The camera technique is unbearable. Apparently director John Lafia believes himself to be Lars Von Trier. The entire program is shot with the camera constantly roaming and randomly zooming in and out—perhaps in an attempt to convey tension, give the show a chaotic, realistic tone, and emulate what the human eye would see. Maybe my eye *would* see that, if I were having a seizure, had a zoom lens in my eyeball, or were experiencing severe trouble with my equilibrium.

But back to the story. There's a superfault that threatens to sink a large portion of the entire West Coast into the Pacific Ocean. The loss of Starbucks being too much to bear, Delaney and the team decide that the best course of action is to detonate a series of nuclear warheads underground to stop the chain reaction of earthquakes. The theory is that detonating, say, seven nuclear warheads doesn't really cause any damage to the environment as long as it's underground. (Yeah, tell that to the cast and crew of *The Conqueror*, a 1956 film that was shot in the desert at St. George, Utah, within 100 miles of a U.S. military site where nuclear bomb tests had been conducted a few years earlier. Over the next two decades over 90 of the approximately 200 cast and crew members contracted terminal cancer, including stars John Wayne, Susan Hayward, Agnes Moorehead, and the film's director, Dick Powell.)

There's nothing more exciting than drilling action and the sight of characters sitting around waiting for the work to be completed. Sadly, this comprises most of the second part of *10.5*, and any camp value the miniseries might have displayed up to this point dries up.

10.5's effects range from passable to hilariously bad. The movie also features a terrible score that sounds like it was performed on a Casio keyboard, circa 1983 (with an operatic choir chiming in during the climax). Oftentimes a disaster film can be silly and over-the-top and still work. *10.5* isn't one such example.

Most Spectacular Moment of Carnage

There is little onscreen gore, although a minor character is crushed by a falling wall and several people are washed away in the film's climax. Only Fred Ward dies in spectacular disaster movie fashion. Taking a page from Bruce Willis in *Armageddon*, Ward decides to detonate a nuclear warhead manually and save the West Coast. In the process, he falls into a drill site and lands on his back on the rocky bottom. Naturally, the warhead he's attempting to detonate shakes free and falls on top of him, crushing his chest. Luckily, Ward is able to continue speaking with a number of the main characters for minutes on end, during which time he makes amends, shares his feelings, and gives out delicious recipes (just kidding!) before being vaporized in a nuclear blast. **(GK)**

Aftershock: Earthquake in New York
(1999)
Hallmark Entertainment/Artisan   139 minutes

AT YOUR OWN RISK

☢

DIRECTOR: Mikael Salomon

WRITERS: Paul Eric Myers, David Stevens, Loren Boothby (based on the novel by Chuck Scarborough)

CAST: Tom Skerritt, Sharon Lawrence, Charles S. Dutton, Lisa Nicole Carson, Jennifer Garner, Rachel Ticotin, Fred Weller, Erika Eleniak-Goglia, Mitch Ryan, Cicely Tyson

Aftershock is a fairly run-of-the-mill TV movie, made watchable by the decent production values of the quake itself and the destruction it leaves behind. You already know you're not in for a masterpiece by the opening credits, which features a totally inappropriate title theme. I'm not sure what the music is meant to suggest—perhaps only that New York loves its jazz.

Tom Skerritt stars as a fire chief who's about to resign, due partly to his dislike for Mayor Charles S. Dutton. During the first half hour we meet both of them and members of their families and see how their lives intersect with other characters. None of this is very interesting. We also meet an apartment-dwelling family who has no connection whatsoever to the other intersecting plot lines. The husband and wife are having marital problems, and the wife is wracked with guilt over the permanent limp that she feels responsible for giving to her young son in a car accident. This kid is a huge soccer fan, and there are a couple of scenes that deal with his desire to pick up the new Pelé videotape (does any nine-year-old kid living in Manhattan know who Pelé is, or care about soccer?). At no point in the film is this soccer obsession relevant. I was waiting for the kid to do some kind of elaborate backward somersault kick off of a falling ledge during the earthquake, but it never happened.

At least the earthquake scene is well handled—eight full minutes of total chaos. Signs fall, streets break up, panicked crowds litter the streets, cars crash through windows, and even famous New York landmarks like the Museum of Modern Art and the

Statue of Liberty crumble. This director has a good eye for shooting and for cutting action scenes together, and the art department deserves some credit for its impressive sets. The Emmy-winning digital effects are very good, and, thankfully, Solomon doesn't rely on them as heavily as other recent TV disaster movies have.

There aren't a lot of deaths in this film, and the people that do die tend to pontificate greatly before doing so. While lying in extreme pain under the stairs of the building, one character manages to inspire a young man by telling him an allegorical story about the importance of life. (I'm pretty if I were caught under hundreds of pounds of concrete, I wouldn't have the energy to tell stories or mutter anything other than the occasional "aarrghhhh!") In fact, by the end of the movie, you get the impression that many of the characters feel that the earthquake was the best thing that ever happened to them, in spite of the tragedy of all the people who were maimed and killed in it, of course.

The climax involves the Pelé-loving boy getting trapped in the fourth-floor washroom of his elementary school. His mother, an experienced mountain climber, orders the police to lend her their climbing gear. They do, and then they watch, dumbfounded, as she uses it to rescue her son and re-earn his trust in the process (she also has the time to have a meaningful talk with her son about trust in the midst of the rescue).

Aftershock is passable entertainment, although it's certainly not spectacular. The big earthquake comes early in the film, and what's left are scenes of most of the characters crawling around in the dust.

Most Spectacular Moment of Carnage

During the earthquake a character is hit by a car, which then crashes through a storefront window. A psychopathic character trapped in the subway with a lawyer also dies impressively, climbing a ladder to the surface and then falling off it to his death. The impact isn't seen, but his clenched hand is shown sticking out from beneath a pile of bricks. How that many bricks got on top of him is beyond me. **(GK)**

Crack in the World (1965)

Paramount Pictures   96 minutes

AT YOUR OWN RISK

© Paramount Pictures and Security Pictures Inc.

DIRECTOR: Andrew Marton

WRITERS: John Manchip White, Julian Zimet

CAST: Dana Andrews, Janette Scott, Kieron Moore, Alexander Knox

Dana Andrews stars in this sci-fi disaster flick as Stephen Sorenson, head of an international team attempting to harness power from the earth's core. It all starts in Africa at an elaborate, high-security, underground lab and headquarters for the project, which is clearly labeled to passersby as "Project Innerspace." Andrews explains to visitors at the base exactly what the team is attempting. Apparently, it's much like eating a Cadbury Cream Egg, where under the chocolate crust lies tasty, sweet fluid, a limitless source of energy. He goes on to explain that by setting off a nuclear device at the core of the earth, the final layer of crust can be broken and magma will be freed to rise to the surface. No one seems to think that setting off a nuclear weapon at the center of the earth is a bad idea, except for Dr. Ted Rampion (Kieron Moore),who is rightfully concerned that this may trigger some negative events around the globe.

Of course, Andrews doesn't take any heed of Moore's theory, possibly because he's already nearing the project deadline, and perhaps also because he resents being called wrong in front of his young wife Maggie, played by Janette Scott. As is the case in all of these types of movies, Scott and Moore were once involved themselves, which leads to further tension. But worst of all, Andrews is dying of some kind of mystery illness that he refuses to tell anyone about. This disease causes periods of impotency (accompanied by a loud music cue to accentuate his embarrassment with his wife) and a great deal of pain in his body. Before long he is stumbling around the underground lab wearing sunglasses, his hands wrapped up in gauze, looking like Michael Jackson. Despite this, Scott is shocked (toward the end of the movie) to learn that her husband is ill at all.

Before he can be stopped, Andrews and the others fire the nuclear missile into the earth's core, causing the launchpad (OK, a model of the launchpad) to explode spectacularly. Red fluid bursts up from the earth and fills the sky to cheers of "magma!" from the scientists below. Unfortunately, the "Crack in the World" emerges, moving east, causing earthquakes and rampant destruction. We know this because we see stock footage of lava flowing through a forest and a squirrel's subsequent daring escape.

Our hero Moore takes over. His plan is to stop the progression of the crack by detonating another nuclear device in its path, with the intention of causing a pressure drop. This doesn't seem like a great idea either, but the team suits up and heads to a volcano on a remote island in the Indian Ocean. Moore and two other men volunteer to enter the volcano and plant the bomb, leaving them "20 minutes to evacuate everyone from Fortune Island." A little optimistic, I would say, unless we're not planning on helping the natives of the island get out.

This explosion doesn't have the desired effect either, as it is learned that the crack has changed directions and is heading right back for the lab in Africa. Instead of heading as far away from there as humanly possible, everyone's immediate reaction is to rush back to the lab and certain death. It is also determined that the crack will intersect with its original point and be shot into outer space, taking 20,000 miles of the surface of the earth with it.

Moore and Scott attempt to save the locals and those around the lab before they are swept up with the chunk of earth. Unfortunately, what could have been a great effect is depicted with only an explosion and a glowing white orblike light flying into the sky.

It goes without saying that none of this makes any sense and is very slow going. You have to wait an awfully long time for your five minutes of destruction. This film is not yet available on video or DVD, but you'll see it on late-night television now and again.

Most Spectacular Moment of Carnage

Sending someone flying off the planet on a chunk of the earth's surface could have been an image for the ages, but the filmmakers don't take advantage of the opportunity. The winner, therefore, goes to a team member who attempts to plant a nuclear device in a volcano. After the bomb gets stuck, he helps to free it, only to fall into the bubbling lava of the active volcano below. **(GK)**

Daylight (1997)
Universal Pictures   115 minutes

© Universal Pictures

DIRECTOR: Rob Cohen

WRITER: Leslie Bohem

CAST: Sylvester Stallone, Amy Brenneman, Viggo Mortensen, Dan Hedaya, Jay O. Sanders, Karen Young, Claire Bloom, Colin Fox, Sage Stallone, Barry Newman

Sylvester Stallone plays the improbably named Kit Latura in this sometimes clumsy but very entertaining thriller, which is chock-full of all the things that make a disaster film great, plus Dan Hedaya. It's very difficult to tell that Stallone's character's name is Kit, because it sounds like people are calling him "kid" all the way through the movie. Nonetheless, if you can make it through the boring patches, you will find a surprisingly well-made movie with lavish production values and a solid performance from Sly. But is it goofy? Oh, my, yes!

Stallone, a former paramedic, now a New York City cab driver, is compelled to offer his superhuman assistance when a carload of young punks loses control and careens into a convoy of trucks carrying toxic waste, causing a devastating explosion in a commuter tunnel linking New York to New Jersey. At the same time, a number of other people are converging on the scene for various unrelated reasons, offering up a veritable chef's salad of disaster movie clichés. There's an older couple (Claire Bloom and Colin Fox) out with their dog; another, squabbling couple (Jay O. Sanders and Karen Young) and their precocious teenage daughter; type-A sporting goods entrepreneur Viggo Mortensen; a police bus carrying several teenage felons (including Stallone's son, Sage); young struggling playwright Amy Brenneman, whose life is totally collapsing because she's basically an idiot; a security guard who works in the tunnel; and, of course, Sly himself (or Kit Latura, or "Kid").

Anyway, what we're really waiting for is the big disaster scene—and, for once, none-too-subtle director Rob Cohen's taste for excess is put to good use; the explosion sets off an incredible chain reaction of destruction. It's a fantastic sequence, extremely well photographed and edited, in which huge toxic fireballs race through the tunnel, engulfing cars and crisping their occupants. As well, huge chunks of concrete are brought down onto people and vehicles, crushing hapless motorists flat as pancakes. The explosions seal the tunnel at both ends, trapping all but Stallone inside with the middle of the underwater tunnel hanging precariously and about to collapse.

Inside the tunnel, the survivors emerge in a daze, except for Viggo Mortensen, who happens to have mountain climbing gear with him and who decides to try to climb his way out through the rubble. It's terrifying to hear this very fine actor have to say lines like "I was born six weeks premature. My own mother couldn't keep me in!"

Meanwhile, outside in the tunnel's control center, Stallone is desperately trying to convince acting EMS chief Dan Hedaya and, um, generally-the-guy-in-charge-of-everything Barry Newman that he should somehow go in there to rescue these people. Everyone agrees; they're obviously not prepared for a situation like this and are willing to accept Stallone's ludicrous plan. He decides to enter the tunnel through the ventilation fans, and there are four of these enormous structures, but he can't shut them down or else he'll risk cutting the oxygen supply to the tunnel. It's an incredibly dangerous task, and this is the one other unquestionably great scene in the film, perfectly executed to generate actual suspense.

Stallone manages to navigate through the fans and survives the crushing force of their combined blowing power. Even though he's risked his life to try to help these people, and they have no other option but to let him try, they're the most ungrateful bunch of assholes imaginable. I kept thinking to myself, we're supposed to want him to save them, but now, I really don't. On the other hand, maybe they were still angry at him for having made *Lock Up*.

Soon the ceiling starts to collapse, and more water floods in. I thought it was funny how Stallone just stands there watching it like he can't believe it's happening. *Yeah, maybe if I don't move and do nothing, everything will be fine.* Eventually he uses explosives to seal the breach, and there's a really cool goopy mud effect when the explosion creates a wall of slime that dams up the tunnel. Later, the security guard or cop or transit officer or whatever the hell he is gets trapped underneath a car when the pavement he's standing on suddenly erupts, and as the water level rises, everyone desperately tries to save him. (Disaster movie fans will recognize this as one of the genre's many sadistic flourishes; often, when someone is injured and a great effort is made to save him, he will survive with serious injuries, only to die a horrible death later.) After this, Stallone explains to Brenneman about his sordid past and why he was fired from the EMS, and it's supposed to give us insight into his psychology and why he would undertake the nearly impossible task of trying to save these people, and it does, but I thought it was funny when he admits to her that he never had a plan to get them out.

As the water level continues to rise, Stallone takes a swim and finds an old bunkroom from when the tunnel was originally built, which allows a pensive Claire Bloom to describe the death of her son. In a moment that I find riotously funny in its unnecessarily complicated silliness, she reveals that her son was killed while "trekking in Nepal," where he contracted a deadly fever.

They soon come across a flight of stairs leading up to possible freedom, but at that moment a tremor rocks the place and the stairs begin to collapse. They quickly run to the top, but once there, Stallone looks back to see a character's damn dog swimming toward them! And since dogs aren't allowed to die in disaster movies, he risks his life to go back and save the mutt. In return for his kindness, Stallone is knocked into the water when a huge beam smashes into the stairs, destroying them. He begs the others not to try to save him, but for some reason they still try, obviously not realizing what happens to people when they try to be heroes in disaster movies. So the only thing left to do is to set some explosives to create a climactic "blowout." A vacuum is created, and it sucks them up rapidly to the surface through murky visual effects. Eventually they explode from the water, with the New York skyline cheaply composited into the background.

Daylight is well worth seeing for its two great action scenes and its many interesting moments scattered throughout, as well as for Stallone's gentle perfor-mance—which may have been an attempt to play Latura as an idiot savant. Check out his facial expressions and his general indecision, as well as his incredibly agree-able nature. No matter what anyone says to him, he agrees with them, even if they're insulting him. While this appears to be meant as an indication of Latura's expertise at dealing with hot tempers and dangerous emotions in a time of crisis, I thought it made him come off like a sweet, lumbering simpleton. Not your average movie hero!

Daylight was nominated for an Oscar (Best Sound Effects Editing) as well, sadly, as two Razzies (Worst Actor and Worst Original Song).

Most Spectacular Moment of Carnage
Lots of people die in the first explosion sequence, which is great because it means that later we see loads of charred bodies all over the place. How can you go wrong with toxic fire incinerating people and huge chunks of concrete flattening cars? Answer: you can't. **(MR)**

Earthquake (1974)
Universal Pictures   123 minutes

HIGHLY RECOMMENDED

⚠️

© Universal Pictures

DIRECTOR: Mark Robson

WRITERS: George Fox, Mario Puzo

CAST: Charlton Heston, Ava Gardner, George Kennedy, Lorne Greene, Geneviève Bujold, Richard Roundtree, Marjoe Gortner, Barry Sullivan, Lloyd Nolan, Victoria Principal, Walter Matthau

A prime example of large-scale '70s disaster filmmaking, *Earthquake* is a connoisseur's delight, loaded with mass destruction, death, and carnage, and the decidedly outsized acting style of the legendary Charlton Heston. It's a tribute to excess, lacking the subtlety of other films in its genre but oozing with exploitative, bloodthirsty excitement.

This one actually lives up to the violent and spectacular illustration on its poster. *Earthquake* was the third highest grossing film of 1974, raking in over $79 million.

Heston plays a construction engineer working for Lorne Greene. He is mired in a loveless marriage to Greene's daughter, played by Ava Gardner (veteran of disaster flicks *The Cassandra Crossing* and *City on Fire*). This casting of the father and daughter is problematic, because Gardner looks to be about as old as Greene, and in reality the actors were born only seven years apart. Heston is screwing around with the tiny, boyish Geneviève Bujold, whose husband, an old friend of Heston's, has died. Heston's head seems to be three or four times bigger than hers, and he could probably break her in half if he rolled over on top of her during the night. Thankfully, we never actually see their sex scene, but we do see them "afterward," and that's quite enough.

Disaster movie hero George Kennedy appears as a disillusioned cop who also happens to be friends with daredevil Richard Roundtree, who wears a ridiculous leather daredevil outfit for the entire movie. Victoria Principal, sporting a smokin' Afro, is the sister of Roundtree's mechanic, and is also the object of supermarket checkout guy Marjoe Gortner's affections, though we don't find out that he's a total psycho until his National Guard regiment is called into action. He's one creepy guy, and he has a fantastic death scene, which I replayed over and over again. Perhaps weirdest of all is Walter Matthau's cameo as a drunk guy in the bar in which Kennedy drinks his sorrows away; Matthau, not credited as himself, is decked out in the most garish '70s clothes imaginable, including a great red pimp hat. His dialogue consists solely of raising his shot glass and toasting various celebrities, like Spiro Agnew and Peter Fonda. After the quake, we see him one more time amid a throng of people who are holed up in the lobby of the Wilson Plaza. He does a hilarious drunken jig and then falls into the crowd, to the applause of those watching.

As you would expect, each of the central characters is introduced before the real action begins; this is where the movie bogs down a bit. It's fine that Geneviève Bujold's character is an aspiring actress on her way to an audition; does she have to force Heston to read over her lines with her after she explains in excruciating detail what the scene's about? George Kennedy's first scene is also a hoot, as he chases a speeding driver through the streets of L.A. And when you watch Richard Roundtree wipe out after his first attempt to ride his motorcycle over the rickety wooden track he's built, please note that his stuntman actually did lose control driving through the loop, and the filmmakers decided to leave it in.

The first indication that there's gonna be trouble in a seismic sense comes at the beginning of the movie, when one of the caretakers at the dam overlooking L.A.

drowns in an elevator shaft after a small tremor. After that, a young student at the seismology institute thinks he's found evidence of a huge quake coming within the next 24 hours, but is this enough proof to evacuate the city? In the meantime, we see our star-studded cast doing their normal everyday things, and as the events in their lives that day come to a head, the earthquake strikes. In fact, it hits just moments after Heston and his wife have a vicious argument in which he tries to leave. When she demands to know where he's going, he snarls, "Anywhere! A bar!!!" But of course you know that at some point in the film, with tragedy unfolding before them, they will reaffirm their love for one another. After all, is the creepy little Geneviève Bujold really going to satisfy a man like Charlton Heston? No, the garish, loud, drunken Gardner is more his match.

Then the earthquake hits. All of the earthquake sequences in this film are extremely loud, and I love the fact that the filmmakers used an audio gimmick to enhance the entertainment value, especially one with a name as William Castle-esque as Sensurround. Sensurround required theaters to have little subwoofers hidden all over in order for the bass energy to radiate deafeningly. In fact, this film won the Academy Award for Best Sound, in spite of the terrible dialogue looping, and it also won for Best Visual Effects.

The scenes of destruction are impressive. Buildings collapse, cars and trucks careen from highway overpasses, explosions tear the pavement apart, and lots of people die violently. People teeming in the streets are crushed by falling concrete, wood, and stone, or are sliced up by flying glass. Others fall from skyscraper windows or are left perched on their balconies as their houses on stilts crumble down the sides of hills. The devastation is so great that only a few buildings are left standing, with the rest of L.A. in flames.

Earthquake does, however, contain one of the cheapest-looking visual effects in the history of movies: During the quake, a crowd of people cram into an elevator at the top of a skyscraper. As they descend, the cable breaks, sending the elevator crashing down. Over a grainy freeze-frame of the bodies lying in a heap, with overly theatrical screaming on the soundtrack, great big blobs of bright red animated cartoon blood come flying toward the camera. The sudden apparent contempt for the audience on the part of the filmmakers makes this moment so very special.

If you're wondering about the dam, well, don't worry; they have to save something for the aftershocks. Wilson Plaza is where both Bujold and Gardner end up, along with Bujold's injured son. Lorne Greene is trapped in his skyscraper office when the quake hits, and he heroically saves a great many people before succumbing to smoke inhalation and a heart attack, illustrating the disaster movie rule that the more lives you save, the more likely you'll be killed for your trouble.

When the big aftershock hits and the dam finally breaks, Heston and Kennedy are in the final stages of rescuing 70 or so people from the Wilson Plaza parking garage and having them climb to safety up from an underground tunnel. As water rushes into the tunnel, a bunch of poor saps are washed away, but Kennedy and Heston hold on tight. As Bujold watches from above, Ava Gardner loses her grip on the ladder (when the guy above her steps on her foot!) and falls into the roiling water. Heston, having to choose between survival and Bujold or certain death and Gardner, lets go of the ladder and falls into the water, where he and his estranged wife drown.

Earthquake succeeds in unleashing maximum carnage while ensuring that audiences get the most Heston for their bucks. This is a lavish, very expensive-looking movie that, in spite of some silliness and pacing problems, is very entertaining and well made. It is by no means a great action or suspense film, but because it embraces the disaster movie philosophy with such gusto, it's a lot of fun. (As a side note, there is a longer, 1977 TV version that contains some previously unseen footage.)

Most Spectacular Moment of Carnage
Only three of the central characters die, and none expire particularly violently. So, I pick the woman on the street during the first quake who, hearing her friend cry out, turns to help her and is rewarded with a window falling on her head and enormous shards of glass impaling her through the face. This film is also notable for having a truck full of cows crash off a highway overpass. **(MR)**

The Night the World Exploded (1957)

Columbia Pictures   64 minutes

AT YOUR OWN RISK

DIRECTOR: Fred F. Sears

WRITERS: Jack Natteford, Luci Ward

CAST: Kathryn Grant, William Leslie, Tristam Coffin, Raymond Greenleaf, Charles Evans, Frank J. Scannell, Marshall Reed, Fred Coby, Paul Savage, Terry Frost

Those who lived to tell the tale remember that the day began with fragile, breathtaking beauty. The temperature was cool, in the low 50s. The air, mountain pure, even downtown. It was a day unreal enough to serve as a setting for the birth of the world—or the death of it.

No, it's not a weather report. Just a goofy rambling (and there are many) from the beginning of *The Night the World Exploded*, a silly B-movie sci-fi disaster flick that tries to combine earthquakes, volcanoes, and an end-of-the-world scenario all into one really short movie, with almost no money to do so properly.

Our leads are seismologist Dr. David Conway (William Leslie), his lovely female assistant, Laura "Hutch" Hutchinson (Kathryn Grant), and the older Dr. Ellis Morton (Tristam Coffin). The three, working together in a large movie studio made up to look like a lab, have developed a new, unproven instrument to measure and identify earthquakes. It's called a pressure photometer, and it's the noisiest invention in film history. Doctors Leslie and Coffin have to yell to deliver their lines over the spinning, clunking instrument (actually, it kind of looks like one of those gizmos used to hold bingo chips). Maybe it's because of this, and the fact that Leslie is so absorbed in proving the photometer's value to the world, that he fails to realize that the plucky Grant is in love with him.

But that's enough of the subplots. An earthquake strikes, buildings fall (courtesy of the World War II stock footage archives), and newspapers spin across the screen, informing the audience that thousands are dead because, frankly, that's just too damn expensive to show. Our narrator returns, overseeing the devastation and cleanup. It's explained that the earth has shifted off of its axis by three degrees, which will cause even more quakes! The governor sends the three leads off to a deep cavern with only two park rangers in tow (I guess the governor's budget was tight that month) to discover the cause of this shift and save the earth.

After the equipment is set up in a "pit" within the cavern—apparently one of the deepest points in the earth—Grant suggests she come down into the pit to help. Of course, everyone says she is too valuable to lose, although at this point, I hadn't seen her do anything to suggest this. In the meantime, Leslie, who is now clearly trying to win her heart, makes several insulting and sexist comments. That'll win her over!

What follows is a baffling sequence in which a rock-collecting park ranger discovers a strange new stone in the cave. He proudly shows it off to the doctors, who smile and humor him. Then, the rock promptly explodes and blows up the ranger's cabin, killing him and leaving nothing but smoke and ashes. Sometime later, Leslie concludes that this rock is the "112th element," and that it is pushing itself to the surface of the earth and causing explosions when it warms up. He flies to Washington and demonstrates his theory by calmly leaving one of the rocks out on a steel table to explode in a room full of the world's leading scientists. Leslie continues that they have nothing to worry about, however, because the rock melts steel two stages before it reaches its exploding point. The rock burns through the table and lands in a bucket. Leslie pours water on it, cooling and diffusing it. He never does explain what the following two stages would have entailed.

Our hero then demonstrates the effect of this new discovery on the earth (as if the world's leading scientists haven't figured it out yet) by placing a rock within a globe and hanging it from a tree in the desert. It explodes into dust. Despite the film's title, this is the only time the world (or in this case, a globe) actually explodes in the film. And it happens in the afternoon. Perhaps *The Afternoon a Globe of the Earth Exploded* would be a more appropriate moniker for this film.

In an even more ridiculous scene, Leslie, the other doctors, and officials use a government supercomputer called the Datatron to figure out how much time the earth has left. Amazingly, the Datatron takes in any information on a subject, analyzes all data, and answers any question. Which leaves one wondering, number one, why didn't they ask the Datatron what was causing all the earthquakes in the first place, and number two, how could they stop more from happening? Instead, they learn that the earth has only 28 days and 4 hours before it's completely obliterated. And everyone involved seems surprisingly calm about this. And that's because they have a plan.

More WWII bombing stock footage and more narration (is this supposed to be the voice of God? Who the hell is narrating this?) explain that the governments of the world drop water bombs (they sure don't look like "water bombs" to me), creating new riverbeds overnight, with the purpose of preventing the rocks from exploding. All our heroes can do now is wait. The final day approaches and the group becomes concerned by a call from a sheriff in Vegas. How he got their number, I don't know, but as he leans back in his seat, he calmly explains that an enormous volcano has risen from the ground and is likely to erupt (the smoking volcano is visible in the window behind the sheriff). Poisonous gas also happens to be leaking from it.

Leslie and Grant hop onto a plane (I use the term *plane* loosely; it's a set of a plane's cabin, with folding tables and chairs) bound for Vegas for the less-than-thrilling climax. They determine the only way to stop the volcano eruption is to blow up a nearby dam and cool the volcano off with water. Against Leslie's wishes, Grant helps him plant the explosives inside the dam, and both escape before it blows up. It's not particularly tense. But this is the highlight of the film's special effects; the water crashes down, flowing through a tunnel (a particularly nice shot), washing houses away (hope they remembered to evacuate the area), and putting out the volcano.

The writing and performances are awfully hokey, and most of the visual effects are poor. But, to be honest, it's difficult to dislike these late-'50s disaster films. They're so endearingly silly that one can forgive a lot. At least they're mercifully short. And that's more than can be said about many of today's bloated disaster films.

Most Spectacular Moment of Carnage

After a Greek news anchor reports that most of the earthquakes have been of a minor nature, the film cuts to a shot of a small shack on the side of a hill. Rocks tumble down, crushing the shack. Before you can say, "Is that supposed to be the news studio?" there is a cut back inside to the screaming anchor. Studio debris falls on him from above, crushing and, presumably, killing him. (**GK**)

The Rains Came (1939)

Twentieth Century Fox   103 minutes

RECOMMENDED

⚠

DIRECTOR: Clarence Brown

WRITERS: Philip Dunne, Julien Josephson (based on the novel by Louis Bromfield)

CAST: Myrna Loy, Tyrone Power, George Brent

The Rains Came, one of the earliest full-blown epic disaster films on record, harkens back to the days when men had pencil-thin moustaches and pulled the waistbands of their pants up to their armpits; to the days when women were shot in such soft focus that anyone viewing the film immediately ran outside of their local theater and made an appointment with their optometrist. And this film is truly no exception.

The film is set in the town of Ranchipur, India, in 1938, despite the fact that there seem to be no Indian actors anywhere. Our hero, drunken painter and ladies' man George Brent, casually pelts monkeys with rocks from his veranda using a slingshot. His best friend is a local Indian surgeon, played by the very un-Indian Tyrone Power. There's a lot of talking in the first 45 minutes of the film as the melodrama is slowly set up. Nearby is a local mission, where a forward young girl, played by Brenda Joyce, happens to be obsessed with Brent.

He visits the mission and Joyce, and she tells him how badly she wants to escape her parents and their "phony life." Actually, one can't blame her. All of the upper-class characters in this place are more than a little pompous. We also learn that she (along with many other characters in the film) is British, despite an accent that suggests Southern California more than England. Before being able to say much more to the girl, Brent is shuttled off to the Royal Palace for a party with His Royal Highness of India and the Maharani, who happens to chain-smoke and play a mean hand of poker. We meet Lady Esketh (played by Myrna Loy), Brent's old flame, who is now married to a wealthy aristocrat. Why should we care about any of these people? I honestly have no idea.

When the topic of monsoon season is brought up, Brent explains to the naive, sheltered Loy how things really are in India, because as an aristocratic painter, he's in touch with the people. Loy soon discovers Tyrone Power and is instantly smitten.

In no time Lady Loy is summoning Power to attend to her sick husband and escort her around the tourist sites at Ranchipur. Power walks her by a group of musicians and translates the love song for her like he's reading a medical textbook. Loy listens, enraptured, eyes fluttering. By this point anyone waiting for the disaster promised is mighty frustrated, having been forced to watch soap opera theatrics for almost an hour. Fortunately, things take a turn for the better very quickly. Buildings fall as an earthquake hits in the middle of the monsoon; rubble crushes many of the terrified subjects who are running down the town streets. The ground beneath them cracks up as the earth breaks apart. A dam cracks open, and a tidal wave sweeps over a bridge. All of this is shown onscreen with elaborate special effects that, frankly, look very convincing.

Loy's husband meets a nasty fate onscreen as his estate is taken down by the waves. We cut to the next day, where the rain is still coming down, and the characters wade through impressive, half-submerged sets of the town buildings. Brent, trapped at his home with Loy, is greeted by Joyce, who has canoed herself through the storm. With a plague now rampaging, the Maharani orders all to do their parts, and she declares "a state of emergency," which by now is painfully obvious and probably should have been stated much earlier. Brent, who magically appears at the palace after being stranded at his estate, is promoted, and he becomes the Maharani's personal aide. He calls on Joyce to assist him, and she gushes to the unimpressed Loy about the night before, when Brent passed out on top of her after swimming through the storm. "I never wanted the night to end," she reveals, despite (or, maybe because of) the fact that Brent was unconscious the entire time.

The music cues really swell at this point, and all of the characters profess their love for one another. Unfortunately for viewers, now that the disaster has passed, the interest level really begins to drop. Loy volunteers at the hospital where Power is, and the two have many melodramatic exchanges, with the town awash in flames behind them. Power walks over to patients and puts his hand on their heads, turning to Loy and telling her that "this doesn't really help much." Bet the patients feel great when they hear the doctor say that out loud!

At least there are some more wide shots of the burning, rubble-filled town to keep us interested—and, of course, a slow and protracted death scene near the end. Despite my complaint that the plot line closely resembles something out of *General Hospital*, the film is extraordinarily well made, and there are some great camera moves that are quite advanced for their time. The film deservedly won the 1939 Academy Award for Best Special Effects.

Most Spectacular Moment of Carnage

Myrna Loy's husband dies memorably. With water pounding through his second-story windows, the aristocrat's abused butler threatens him. A wave crashes in, and a shutter door is blown off of its hinges, crushing the husband underneath. The waves then take down an entire wall and sweep the butler to his demise. **(GK)**

San Francisco (1936)

MGM   115 minutes

AT YOUR OWN RISK

☢

DIRECTOR: W. S. Van Dyke

WRITER: Anita Loos (based on a story by Robert E. Hopkins)

CAST: Clark Gable, Jeanette MacDonald, Spencer Tracy, Jack Holt, Jessie Ralph, Ted Healy

San Francisco starts on New Year's Eve 1905, a mere four months before the famous earthquake that actually rocked San Francisco. This is primarily a musical melodrama, if such a thing is possible, leaving the quake and effects themselves to the end. It's still a generally entertaining film, though it might seem a little long for today's audiences. Clark Gable, decked out in a tuxedo for most, if not all, of the movie, stars as Blackie, a rapscallion entrepreneur, outspoken atheist, and owner of the Paradise, a cabaret/saloon on the seedy Barbary Coast. We know this movie is set in the Barbary Coast because characters continually say it to one another in the first 10 minutes: "Your saloon is the best on the Barbary Coast"; "The Barbary Coast is the best place in the whole world." I later expected one of the characters to mutter, "This is the best earthquake the Barbary Coast has ever seen."

With the setting firmly established, a young Mary Blake (played by Jeanette MacDonald) arrives at the Paradise. She's a small-town girl dreaming of a singing career. After warbling out a number that can only be described as "of its time," Gable, impressed by more than just her singing, hires the woman for his show. His motives become a concern to his childhood friend, boxing Catholic priest Spencer Tracy, who possesses a mean right hook and uses it on Gable in an early scene. Gable is continually at odds with his friend and his focus on morality.

Despite being described by all he knows as a disreputable businessman, Gable is good friends with others in the Barbary Coast community (perhaps because, as we're told, he has a good heart, deep down), who convince him to help them push for fire regulations and, later, to run for office. Gable seems an unlikely candidate. While giving a speech on "fire laws," a member of the crowd sarcastically asks who's sponsoring his campaign. Gable jumps off the stage and punches him in the face, to the cheering crowd's approval (who tell him, "You were swell!"), before building his speech to a creepy fever pitch.

Meanwhile, MacDonald delivers the first of many renditions of the title song, "San Francisco" (at a volume so loud it made me believe that her head might explode at any minute), while continuing to fend off Gable's advances. Personally, I think her aversion to Gable's character, Blackie, is due to the fact that he has a habit of referring to himself in the third person. "Blackie's gotta be number one, boy!" he exclaims, or "Blackie doesn't like it!" to express disapproval.

Later, Tracy shows up and accuses Gable of exploiting MacDonald and selling her mortal soul to the devil. Still in need of anger-management counseling, Gable's response is to knock out the priest. Tracy is hard to figure out, since he continually describes his friend as a good person deep down, then chastises him for his behavior. Also, after leading MacDonald to another romantic interest, he probes her as to whether she's really happy without Gable. I wasn't sure just what this priest wanted.

Finally, the earthquake hits. There are some impressive effects for their day, as walls and balconies fall inside the theater as MacDonald is singing, while the panicked crowd tries to escape. MacDonald disappears, leaving a disheveled Gable to dig through the wreckage, removing bricks exceptionally quickly in an undercranked (fast-motion) shot as he tries to find her. The street splits in half at one point, and various characters fall in between the cement blocks. Dynamite is brought in to blow up the buildings and stop the numerous fires. Gable continues to search the streets while this is going on, leading to several humorous shots of the dejected antihero wandering around with his head down as buildings are razed and tumble to the ground closely behind.

Does Gable find MacDonald? Will MacDonald's makeup even be smudged when he finds her? Will Gable suddenly find God and drop to his knees in prayer? You'll have to wait until the finale, and another musical number, as the entire population of San Francisco sings "The Battle Hymn of the Republic." I doubt this is how most people would react to losing their homes, but I suppose the filmmakers felt compelled to end the movie on an "up" note.

Regardless of my nitpicking, *San Francisco* is reasonably entertaining and is recommended for fans of classic film. Nominated for Best Picture and Best Actor Oscars, it won an Academy Award for Best Sound.

Most Spectacular Moment of Carnage

This film is quite old, so onscreen violence is kept to a minimum. During the aftershock, there are many sequences that are cut together very tightly for their day, including the street breaking up and people falling down into the fault. At one point a superimposed silhouette of a woman (one of the few visual effects that fails) falls from a third story window. It's all fun to watch. **(GK)**

After the Shock (1990)

Paramount Pictures   92 minutes

AT YOUR OWN RISK

Gary Sherman, director of some entertaining low-budget '80s horror and action flicks, realistically re-creates the Oakland/San Francisco earthquake of 1989 for TV audiences. The movie deals mostly with the collapsed Nimitz Freeway and the rescuing of those trapped in a dilapidated apartment complex. The filmmakers cut actual news footage of the disaster with their own scenes shot on video to create a documentary feel, and they add to the sense of realism by not scoring any of it. Whether or not this is a good thing is debatable. Starring Jack Scalia, Yaphet Kotto, Rue McClanahan, and Scott Valentine. **(GK)**

Deluge (1933)

RKO Radio Pictures   70 minutes

RECOMMENDED

Deluge is a movie that, unfortunately, no one can see right now, but it's of incredible importance. This film, directed by Felix E. Feist and starring Sidney Blackmer and Lois Wilson, is the first studio-produced narrative disaster picture. It features an earthquake that wipes out the West Coast and unleashes a tidal wave that threatens to finish off New York. The film was released with the tag line "Earth is doomed. Only a few will survive!" It's uncanny how little the marketing of this genre has changed in over 70 years. Let's hope that some restoration work is being done on the title so we can finally see this classic. **(GK)**

Shattered City: The Halifax Explosion (2003)

CBC   174 minutes

AT YOUR OWN RISK

This $10 million miniseries is epic by Canadian standards. It depicts the most dev-astating disaster in Canadian history: the Halifax explosion of 1917. For those who aren't up on Canadian history, a large ship carrying TNT crashed and detonated in the harbor, causing the biggest man-made boom in the world before Hiroshima, rocking much of the city, and killing roughly 2,000 locals. The series has its moments, par-ticularly the depiction of the explosion itself, and the sets of the devastated city are excellent. Unfortunately, some of the subplots are ludicrous, such as the one in which a German conspiracy to crash the ship and detonate the TNT is revealed. (The sabo-teur suddenly decides that killing is wrong and tries to stop the disaster.) The main story line is also slow; some of the performances are overbaked; and the movie is not-so-subtly infused with post-9/11 allusions and politics that are inappropriate for a story set during World War I. Watch carefully and you'll see Graham Greene and Pete Postlethwaite briefly. (**GK**)

RARE, OBSCURE, AND LESS IMPORTANT TITLES

The Big One: The Great Los Angeles Earthquake (1990) Made-for-TV

The Chain Reaction (1980)

The Day the Earth Moved (1974)

Earthquake in New York (1998) Made-for-TV

Ekipazh (1980)

Epicenter (2000) Straight-to-video

Miracle on Interstate 880 (1993) Made-for-TV

The Pennsylvania Miners' Story (2002) Made-for-TV

Quake (1993) Straight-to-video

DISASTER MOVIES' GREATEST STARS

It seems like just about every actor in Hollywood has appeared in at least one disaster movie. Incredibly, it is not uncommon for an actor to appear in four or more such films. Actresses have been a little wiser; many have chosen to appear in only one or two notable disaster flicks (in many cases, a smart career move). This section gives a brief overview of the great actors, directors, and even producers who have devoted themselves to at least several films in the genre.

Irwin Allen

Producer/writer/director extraordinaire, the late Irwin Allen may be single-handedly responsible for resurrecting the disaster film in the '70s. His love of the genre prompted him to develop, produce, and, in some cases, direct several of the most famous disaster films ever made. Also a respected television producer, Allen often worked disaster film elements into episodes of his series, and he introduced us to the made-for-TV disaster movie (Allen's TV disaster movies can be easily identified: he liked to punctuate their titles with an exclamation point).

Disaster Film Titles
The Poseidon Adventure (1972)
The Towering Inferno (1974)
Flood! (1976) Made-for-TV
Fire! (1977) Made-for-TV
The Swarm (1978)

Beyond the Poseidon Adventure (1979)
Hanging by a Thread (1979) Made-for-TV
When Time Ran Out . . . (1980)
Cave-In! (1983) Made-for-TV

Other Notable Films / TV Series
Voyage to the Bottom of the Sea (1961)
Lost in Space (1965–1968) TV series
The Time Tunnel (1966–1967) TV series
The Wrecking Crew (1969)

Henry Fonda

This famous and talented actor appeared in a surprising number of disaster films late in his career, usually in the role of the president or an admirable and important figure of great regard. Unfortunately, he was clearly doing it for the money, and many of the late-'70s films that he appeared in were the worst the genre had to offer. Oh well!

Disaster Film Titles
Rollercoaster (1977)
The Swarm (1978)
City on Fire (1979)
Meteor (1979)

Other Notable Films
The Grapes of Wrath (1940)
12 Angry Men (1957)
How the West Was Won (1962)
Once Upon a Time in the West (1968)
On Golden Pond (1981)

Morgan Freeman

While most actors today are (intentionally or not) steering clear of accepting too many roles in disaster pictures, Oscar winner Morgan Freeman doesn't seem to be afraid of the genre, and he leads the pack of today's disaster movie actors. His appearances in these films are probably an attempt on the producers' parts to raise the quality of their productions with Freeman's talent and presence. He raises the quality of any production by just walking through the frame. (But even Freeman couldn't save *Deep Impact!* Eeegghh!)

Disaster Film Titles
Outbreak (1995)
Hard Rain (1998)
Deep Impact (1998)
War of the Worlds (narrator) (2005)

Other Notable Films
Clean and Sober (1988)
Glory (1989)
Driving Miss Daisy (1989)
Unforgiven (1992)
The Shawshank Redemption (1994)
Se7en (1995)
Million Dollar Baby (2004)

Ava Gardner

Ava Gardner holds the prize as disaster movie queen, appearing in three such films during the '70s and one in the '50s, all of varying quality. Compared to George Kennedy, this may not seem like a lot, but few actresses have appeared in as many disaster movies.

Disaster Film Titles
On the Beach (1959)
Earthquake (1974)
The Cassandra Crossing (1976)
City on Fire (1979)

Other Notable Films
Show Boat (1951)
The Night of the Iguana (1964)

Charlton Heston

The hands-down, all-time greatest disaster movie star. Sure, he's appeared in such classics as *Touch of Evil* (1958) and *Ben-Hur* (1959). But when you think of '70s disaster films, you can't help but think of Heston first.

Disaster Film Titles
Skyjacked (1972)
Earthquake (1974)
Airport 1975 (1974)
Gray Lady Down (1978)
Solar Crisis (1990)
Armageddon (narrator) (1998)

Other Notable Films
Planet of the Apes (1968)
The Omega Man (1971)
Soylent Green (1973)
Midway (1976)
True Lies (1994)

Jerry Jameson

Although director/producer/writer/editor/crew guy Jerry Jameson has had a diverse career in TV and film, a quick glance at his resume might lead one to believe that this man specialized in nothing but disaster flicks—and, in truth, no one has directed as many disaster pictures as Jameson has. (In 1974, in particular, he should have been given the Academy Award for Hardest-Working Disaster Movie Director.) His contributions to the genre may be spotty in quality, but they are almost never boring. (Even *Superdome* [1978] features an all-star cast, but unfortunately that movie, which is about an assassin, does not qualify as a disaster film. In case you're interested, *Superdome* was parodied on *Mystery Science Theater 3000*.)

Disaster Film Titles
Heat Wave! (1974) Made-for-TV
The Elevator (1974) Made-for-TV
Hurricane (1974) Made-for-TV
Terror on the 40th Floor (1974) Made-for-TV

Airport '77 (1977)
Raise the Titanic (1980)
Starflight: The Plane That Couldn't Land (1983) Made-for-TV
Fire and Rain (1989) Made-for-TV

Other Notable Films / TV Series
Superdome (1978) Made-for-TV
Jerry Jameson also directed numerous episodes of *Hawaii Five-O*, which makes him cool in my book.

George Kennedy

George Kennedy will likely go down in history as the king of the *Airport* movies. Playing "regular guy" Joe Patroni, he essayed what is probably the most famous and enduring disaster movie character of all time. In fact, he has the distinction of being the only returning cast member of any of the *Airport* films. Kennedy appeared in the original *Airport* and in every single sequel. He was finally given the lead in the last (and ill-fated) film of the series. I admire his determination to stick with a concept until the bitter end. I also like his Breath Assure commercials.

Disaster Film Titles
The Flight of the Phoenix (1965)
Airport (1970)
Earthquake (1974)
Airport 1975 (1974)
Airport '77 (1977)
The Concorde: Airport '79 (1979)
Virus (1980)
The Jupiter Menace (main narrator) (1981)
International Airport (1985) TV

Other Notable Films
The Boston Strangler (1968)
The Delta Force (1986)
The Naked Gun: From the Files of Police Squad! (1988)

Leslie Nielsen

We all know Leslie Nielsen for his great comedy work, but few realize that Nielsen is also a disaster movie veteran. The fact is, for 10 years he appeared in several memorable disaster movie roles.

Disaster Film Titles

The Poseidon Adventure (1972)
...And Millions Die! (1973)
Day of the Animals (1977)
City on Fire (1979)
The Night the Bridge Fell Down (1983) Made-for-TV
Airplane! (1980)
Airplane II: The Sequel (uncredited, in flashback sequence) (1982)
Cave-In! (1983) Made-for-TV

Other Notable Films

Forbidden Planet (1956)
Viva Knieval! (1977)
Creepshow (1982)
The Naked Gun: From the Files of Police Squad! (1988)

William Shatner

William Shatner's disaster movies were mostly made-for-TV affairs (and are therefore, unfortunately, difficult to find), but his work in *Kingdom of the Spiders* and *Airplane II: The Sequel* is pure gold. If he hadn't already had his *Star Trek* franchise keeping him busy, he could have become a disaster film superstar—the genre would have suited his unique acting style well.

Disaster Film Titles

Horror at 37,000 Feet (1973) Made-for-TV
Perilous Voyage (1976) Made-for-TV
Kingdom of the Spiders (1977)
Crash (1978) Made-for-TV
Disaster on the Coastliner (1979) Made-for-TV
Airplane II: The Sequel (1982)

Other Notable Films / TV series
You need to ask?

Shelley Winters

OK, so she only appeared in two disaster films, but who can forget her Oscar-nominated performance in *The Poseidon Adventure*? Besides earning our respect for her roles in some classics of the cinema, we like her for those cheesy horror and exploitation films she did in the '70s, too (remember *Whoever Slew Auntie Roo?*). What a bizarre career!

Disaster Film Titles
The Poseidon Adventure (1972)
City on Fire (1979)

Other Notable Films
Lolita (1962)
Cleopatra Jones (1973)
The Tenant (1976)
Tentacles (1977)
The Portrait of a Lady (1996)

Honorable Mentions

Ernest Borgnine (who has appeared in at least four disaster films, three of which were Irwin Allen productions); writer Stirling Silliphant (in addition to the screenplays of numerous classics, he wrote four Irwin Allen disaster flicks); and Ned Beatty (who has popped up in at least four disaster movies himself). (**GK**)

Fun with Snow

Snow, while prominently featured in many disaster films, rarely takes center stage. There are many reasons for the lack of frosty titles. One, snow is cold. Nobody likes shooting in subzero temperatures. For movies about volcano eruptions, production crews get to take off for warm, exotic locales. There's nothing exotic about snow, nothing at all. And I should know, because I've lived in it for most of my life. If someone asked me to film a disaster movie, snow would probably be the last thing that I'd want to shoot. Plus, what's interesting about it? What can you do with snow? An asteroid, sure: you can fire rockets at it, drill into it, blow up cities with it, all kinds of stuff. Snow? Well, you can send an avalanche shooting down the side of a mountain, and then what? Get out the shovels—it's over.

Anyway, despite these problems, there are films that have attempted to put snow on center stage and milk whatever they can from it. Bundle up and check out a few of these titles. **(GK)**

The Accident (1983)

CBC/Trans-World Entertainment   103 minutes

AVOID AT ALL COSTS

DIRECTOR: Donald Brittain

WRITER: Bill Gough

CAST: Fiona Reid, Terence Kelly, Frank Perry, Esther Hockin, Anne Anglin, Laura Bruneau, Errol Slue, Charmaine Boyde, Michael Hogan, Timothy Webber

Not content to leave the disaster genre behind with the bewildering *City on Fire*, Canadian filmmakers tried once again with the made-for-TV movie *The Accident*. One thing that can be said of this film: it certainly doesn't hide the fact that it's Canadian. After all, only Canadians would try to set a disaster film at a hockey arena in a small town. This picture is character driven and doesn't even try to mimic more spectacular, expensive American features. The actors are all average-looking, which might add to the realism, but it makes love scenes difficult to endure.

Something about Canadian cinema that everyone should know: Canadian films often follow a standard formula. The characters are typically ineffectual (they're often complete losers) and events spin out of control around them. By the end of the film, after not doing much of anything, our heroes are usually worse off than they were at the beginning. And *The Accident* is no exception.

The movie opens to a Zamboni clearing the ice in a small arena while a saxophone blares the hilariously inappropriate-sounding theme, "When Winter Comes Too Soon." I half expected to see a couple undressed and making out in the middle of the rink, and it wasn't until the end of the movie, when the theme is reprised, with lyrics, that I realized why this music is used at all.

The characters (a family who runs a local variety store, a child and his grandparents, a divorcée and her two daughters) are quickly introduced before they're shuttled off to the arena. Just 10 minutes into the film, the roof caves in and crashes down on the spectators, the majority of whom are small children. Although there is no on-screen violence, the ensuing sequences depict the store owner/father digging through the rubble and trying to get his kids out. There are some nasty shots of kids on stretchers, tied to splints, and so on, being taken onto ambulances.

I was surprised at how quickly this film was moving along and thought that, per-haps, when the characters arrived at the hospital, I would see some flashbacks that would reveal just what had happened. Sadly, from this point on, each parent or guard-ian introduced loses a child, and the remainder of the story focuses on their struggles to go on living and on philosophical and theological debates about their lives. This leads to the most entertaining subplot, in which the grandfather of a victim ques-tions his faith and vows to find out what happened and why. After turning against a hunk of wood in his workshop and pounding it in fury with a hammer, he announces, "I'm planning on finding my own answers down here . . . I'm going to do my own inquiry!" This inquiry involves walking around and inside the arena with a clipboard, taking notes, snapping photographs, and building an elaborate wooden mock-up of the arena girders to test his various theories about how the roof caved.

Another woman takes her frustration out on her friendly horticulturalist neighbor by sabotaging his backyard greenhouse. The wife of the store owner is particularly de-spondent; she tells people on the street how easily their children can be killed if they aren't watched more closely. Strangely enough, she's also been having an affair with a traveling salesman (who must have seduced her with his enormous moustache). The husband never finds out, and the wife ends the affair amicably. Most of the time these characters walk around like zombies and stare blankly into space before randomly ex-ploding at family members.

This film may present a realistic picture of how people might react to such a hor-rible situation, but it sure isn't exciting or interesting for an audience to watch. After a while, I was only watching to see if I recognized any locations and to spot references to *The Muppet Show* and *The Electric Company*, shows that I used to watch as child.

Don't trust what it says on the back of the video box: "Many of the players and onlookers are hopelessly trapped in the debris. Some are killed instantly. Others stand a chance of survival, if only they can be rescued in time . . . it will touch your deepest emotions as you witness the bravery of the victims and those who risk their lives to save them." I'm still not sure what film they're referring to.

This movie is interesting (for about five minutes) as a nostalgia piece for Canadians like me. I remember corner stores looking like this when I was a kid, and my dad taking me to the local arena in the bitter cold to watch minor-league hockey.

But seeing that you're more than likely not Canadian, I can't think of any reason to check this one out.

Most Spectacular Moment of Carnage
There's nothing at all that's spectacular about this film. The cave-in occurs quickly, but all we see are some falling girders and plaster, which are quickly overtaken by dust. The shots of the kids being taken out, bloodied and lying on stretchers, are disturbing, so I guess that wins. **(GK)**

Avalanche (1978)

New World Pictures   91 minutes

AT YOUR OWN RISK

© Concorde/New Horizons Corp.

DIRECTOR: Corey Allen

WRITERS: Francis Doel, Claude Pola, Corey Allen

CAST: Rock Hudson, Mia Farrow, Robert Forster, Jeanette Nolan, Rick Moses, Steve Franken, Barry Primus

Produced by low-budget king Roger Corman, I expected *Avalanche* to be an entertaining cheesefest. Corman and the disaster-movie format would seem to be the perfect match. And indeed, they are. The film doesn't reach the heights of exploitive violence I'd hoped it would, but it's still really funny. Sadly, as much as I like a Corman picture, he's notorious for cutting corners during production. So while you get the requisite breast shot, a little bit of gore, and a few violent deaths (which, unfortunately, you have to wait way too long for), you also have to put up with workmanlike camera set-ups, a poor script, and substandard special effects. But that's still OK.

The film is set at a winter resort. There's a grand-opening celebration, so naturally the resort is chock-full of celebrity athletes. And, in typical disaster-movie soap-opera fashion, they're all sleeping with each other. In fact, it becomes difficult to remember just who's sleeping with whom. Many of these characters aren't very likable. The "groovy" downhill skier and his panicking, flaky girlfriend are particularly irritating. After enduring her nervous breakdown at the breakfast table, you'll want her to die first. This may also be the first disaster film to have been edited with a chainsaw: there's a lot of cutting between stories at inappropriate and disorienting times.

Rock Husdon overacts to the point where I considered his character to be mentally unstable, and Robert Forster's just too good to be in a movie like this. But the film is a must-see if you've ever wanted to see stars Hudson, Forster, and Mia Farrow disco, or if you've ever wondered what a smashed Hudson screaming "Aloha!" at a party would sound like.

When the avalanche finally hits, the fun starts. Of course, it occurs during the middle of the lineup of sporting events, which include a bizarre snowmobile event that makes *Death Race 2000* look timid. I couldn't help but ask myself what the hell was going on when athletes began kicking each other, flying out of their snowmobiles, and crashing into trees. Stunts for the sake of stunts, I suppose. Not that I'm complaining.

But back to the avalanche. Most people are simply buried in the snow. This includes, in an unintentionally hilarious sequence, the resort chefs. Not a single staff member had been seen up to this point; yet all of a sudden, chefs are being bounced around the kitchen, dropping cakes, and knocking over pots and pans. A gas leak makes it even worse. After all this goofiness, the chefs are blown around the kitchen by the resulting explosion.

The special effects range from passable to poor, except for an exceptionally well-executed ambulance crash. It loses control, plunges off a bridge, and lands in the icy waters below before exploding. (I'm not sure how a vehicle half submerged in water can explode, but I'm just happy something's happening!) If nothing else, this film certainly isn't boring.

Most Spectacular Moment of Carnage

Chefs being mangled are always fun to watch, but a news reporter's exit takes the cake. He's hanging precariously from a ski lift with a young boy when rescue workers arrive. The rescuers manage to catch the boy in a large net, but the reporter is not as lucky. He is electrocuted and falls, and, sadly, the rescuers don't catch him. He lands in the snow and ice with a thud. Whoops. (**GK**)

Avalanche Express (1979)

Twentieth Century Fox   87 minutes

AT YOUR OWN RISK

DIRECTOR: Mark Robson

WRITER: Abraham Polonsky (based on the novel by Colin Forbes)

CAST: Lee Marvin, Robert Shaw, Linda Evans, Maximilian Schell, Joe Namath, Horst Buchholz, Mike Connors

Despite the fact that it's from the director of *Earthquake*, it's debatable whether *Avalanche Express* qualifies as a disaster movie. It has only a 10-minute sequence, smack in the middle of the film, involving any sort of avalanche. Other than this, it's really just another poor action/spy thriller. I guess the producers wanted to hop on the disaster bandwagon and sucker a few more people into the theater.

The plot involves a Russian defector, played by Robert Shaw in his final film role, and the attempts by Maximilian Schell's evil character to stop the defector from delivering information about a secret weapon to the CIA. There's a lot of dull spy stuff here, with secret tapes being handed off from person to person, vehicles being switched to throw villains off the scent (and this is the first half hour . . . yawn!), globe-trotting to Switzerland, and so on. It's up to agents Lee Marvin and Linda Evans (playing Marvin's daughter? Nope, she's his girlfriend, in an unbelievably dopey romantic subplot) to protect Shaw.

Our heroes ride a Milan–Rotterdam train with the hopes of drawing Schell out and stopping his fiendish plot. Instead, they are attacked by a team of soldiers following Schell's orders and armed with machine guns. Marvin and the gang fight the team off. By now you really begin to feel sorry for all the other (unseen) passengers on the train. They didn't ask for this!

At this point in the film, villain Schell seems to think that creating an avalanche that will overturn and drown the train in snow is the simplest way to get rid of Shaw. I accepted his questionable logic, because at least the film was finally picking up. The avalanche is the most interesting and tension-filled sequence in the film. The train passes through the snowy Alps and the explosive charges are set. As the avalanche tumbles down toward the train, a village is visible is in its path. What will happen to the village, and more importantly, the villagers? Of course, the village is destroyed, leaving many innocent bystanders dead. But the filmmakers cut away from this violence, including Schell's death (we can only assume he dies; we don't actually see it) by torpedo. I'm sure you're wondering at this point what our heroes are doing firing torpedoes, but believe me, it's not half as interesting as you think.

The only reason to watch this poor man's *Mission: Impossible* is to see ex-football great Joe Namath try his hand at being an action hero. He does a decent job, and he earns points for a great death (see below). Everyone else looks like they're thinking about doing their laundry.

Most Spectacular Moment of Carnage

During the final battle on the train, good ol' Joe Namath struggles with a female agent, who is holding an armed grenade. Rather than throw her overboard, Namath chooses to grab the woman and jump off with her (probably not the best way to handle the situation). They explode as they fall from the train. Strangely, nobody reacts much to Namath's particularly unpleasant death. **(GK)**

The Day After Tomorrow (2004)
Twentieth Century Fox   124 minutes

AT YOUR OWN RISK

DIRECTOR: Roland Emmerich

WRITERS: Roland Emmerich, Jeffrey Nachmanoff

CAST: Dennis Quaid, Jake Gyllenhaal, Emmy Rossum, Dash Mihok, Jay O. Sanders, Sela Ward, Ian Holm, Perry King

Did you know that there even was such a thing as a "paleoclimatologist"? One would think this job might involve reading a lot of old *Farmer's Almanacs* and studying smelly old graphs. However, in this flick, things are decidedly different. Dennis Quaid stars as Jack Hall, a paleoclimatologist who spends the first five minutes of the film performing superhuman leaps, globe-trotting, and explaining and debating his findings in conferences with dignitaries from around the world. Who knew that being a paleoclimatologist could be so exciting?

Of course, our hero has a brilliant son, Sam, played by Jake Gyllenhaal. The two have a strained relationship. Instead of spending "quality" time with Gyllenhaal, Quaid is busy jumping over canyons of ice and retrieving large metallic cylinders that apparently will prove his global-warming theories (as if the simple fact that an ice shelf the size of a city fell off of Antarctica isn't evidence enough). It also can't be cheery when your dad believes that a climate shift will bring the earth into another ice age and wipe out much of the planet as we know it. (How would global warming bring the earth into another ice age, you ask? Global warming causes the vast polar ice caps to melt. Apparently, the melting of polar ice lowers water temperature around the world and can block the Gulf Stream. The Gulf Stream influences the climate, keeping temperatures in North America and Europe warm. A rise of cold-water levels would lead to radical climate shifts, storms, and so on, eventually resulting in a temperature drop worldwide and another ice age.)

Gyllenhaal is so upset by all this that he takes a trip to Manhattan with his schoolmates to compete in a Scholastic Decathalon and impress the girl of his dreams. Do these kinds of Scholastic Decathalon really exist? No time to ponder that just now, as our story quickly shifts to New York City. Perhaps Gyllenhaal really does believe his dad, and he knows that his chances of losing the Scholastic Decathalon will drop dramatically once the northern hemisphere is covered in ice and most of his competition is deceased.

Before long, twisters are ripping Los Angeles apart, and choppers in Scotland are crashing to the ground, killing inconsequential characters who have been introduced simply to die. This is not a bad thing, as the effects are good and the sequences are punchy and well edited. Before long, in the film's best sequence, a tidal wave crashes through Manhattan, submerging the city, causing New York even more traffic woes, and posing a significant problem in terms of finishing the Scholastic Decathlon. Gyllenhaal takes refuge with his friends in a library, deciding to wait to be rescued.

Meanwhile, Quaid's scientist buddy Terry (played by Ian Holm, who is sadly underutilized in one of the film's obviously manipulative subplots) tells Quaid to "save as many as you can." To Quaid, this seems to translate to "Don't think about anyone else and go save Gyllenhaal, even if it means sacrificing your coworkers and friends." At least his climatologist buddies seem to be low-key about dying horribly violent deaths while joining him in the long, subzero-temperature walk from Philadelphia to Manhattan. Thankfully, Quaid himself already proved himself able to accomplish Herculean tasks early in the film, so there is no doubt he'll reach his son and save the day, with or without their help. That is, if his son hasn't become a frozen chunk of ice or been torn apart by a group of computer-generated wolves stalking him. (Yes, the wolves look hokey. It is understandable that working with real wolves or dogs is a pain for filmmakers, but still, I wish they would have at least tried to use a real animal in some of the shots.)

In the end, your enjoyment of *The Day After Tomorrow* may depend on your love of the genre itself. Make no mistake, this film is a complete throwback to disaster films of yesteryear, with one important exception: most of the big stars don't die. And attacking the "science" in this film is pointless, as we understand early on that this flick isn't going make a lot of sense. People haven't plunked down their hard-earned cash to watch a Discovery Channel program about climatology. Still, the second half of the film, which deals with a large group of cold-front hurricanes freezing survivors, is a bit of a stretch. At this point anyone can see that the creators have written themselves into a corner and can't find a logical way out. When these cold fronts approach, ice literally chases the characters around buildings and landmarks as they race for nearby sources of heat. I'm not entirely sure how this would save them, and it seems that neither are the filmmakers. Their only recourse is to cut away before the end of these sequences, then reveal that several characters have miraculously managed to survive a 150-degree temperature drop by sitting next to a small stack of burning books, or by hiding next to a deep fryer at a local Wendy's.

As with similarly structured films like *The Day After*, *The Accident*, and *Threads*, the biggest problem lies with the fact that the big "money shot," or impressive cataclysmic event, happens early or midway through the film. After seeing cities devastated in the most spectacular ways possible, it's kind of difficult to get excited about watching the characters struggle to survive amid the rubble. This film does its best to keep things as exciting as possible, and it succeeds to an extent, but it can never completely overcome its cardboard characters, story holes, and ridiculous situations. I think it's a better film than *Independence Day* (which was also directed by Emmerich), so if you loved that, you'll appreciate this. Otherwise, approach with caution.

Most Spectacular Moment of Carnage

A reporter is crushed by a large billboard. A giant block of hail crashes down on a cop's head and comically knocks him out of frame, presumably to his death. A spectacular tidal wave sweeps through Manhattan, washing away hundreds of New Yorkers. But my favorite moment of carnage doesn't even involve a death. During a bit of turbulence on an airplane, a runaway beverage cart speeds recklessly down the aisle and almost (what a missed opportunity!) decapitates star Jake Gyllenhaal. **(GK)**

Shackleton (2002)

A&E Network Studios   184 minutes

RECOMMENDED

DIRECTOR: Charles Sturridge

WRITER: Charles Sturridge

CAST: Kenneth Branagh, Eve Best, Embeth Davidtz

ABLE CREW NEEDED FOR ANTARCTIC EXPEDITION!

Facilitate well-intentioned though slightly loony financier Ernest Henry Shackleton's dream to cross the Antarctic continent! Prepare for agonizingly cold temperatures, incredibly small quarters, ever-decreasing food rations, frostbite, and the eventual onset of scurvy. Please note that the possibility of your small ship becoming locked in the ice is high, as is the likelihood that, upon movement of the floes, the ship will sink, leaving you stranded in the coldest place on Earth for nearly two years. But who knows? You may return home alive, if you're lucky! All so you can say you did it—or, well, that Shackleton did it!

Who could resist that offer? None but the sane. I'm a Canadian, and why anyone would want to travel anywhere colder than it is here is beyond me. Still, thanks to great location shooting and good performances from the cast, this impressively mounted miniseries does a reasonable job of conveying Shackleton's passion for the mysterious continent, and more importantly, for saving his crew later on.

Branagh provides an effective portrait of a flawed yet sympathetic and eventually heroic explorer. However, the filmmakers obviously thought that Shackleton's rocky home life and infidelities would be of some interest to audiences. They aren't. That's why the first half of this miniseries tends to drag. You might even mistake the opening hour for an incredibly pompous, drawn-out episode of Masterpiece Theatre. Skip ahead to the crew gathering in Buenos Aires and start the film from there, and you won't miss a thing. Then enjoy the real story, as well as the impressive scenery and cinematography, which almost—I say almost—make you want to visit the starkly beautiful continent. The vistas (the movie was actually shot in Greenland and Iceland, which stand in for Antarctica) are as visually striking as one would hope for and worth the price of a rental alone.

The effects are surprisingly good as well, including a sequence in which the ship starts to sink and a photographer risks his life trying to salvage what few film canisters he can before it collapses into the ocean.

Should you rent the DVD, be sure to check out the bonus features, which include two fantastic documentaries on the Antarctic and the many dangerous explorations to the region in the early 1900s. They're as good as, if not better, than the miniseries itself, and they give viewers a complete picture of the Antarctic, of Shackleton's journey, and of the man himself.

Most Spectacular Moment of Carnage
Frostbite does some serious damage to some of the crew members, and there's nothing more cringe-inducing than seeing one of them lose a few digits to the cold during a makeshift amputation sequence. Yeow! **(GK)**

Vertical Limit (2000)

Columbia/Tri-Star   124 minutes

AT YOUR OWN RISK

DIRECTOR: Martin Campbell

WRITERS: Robert King, Terry Hayes

CAST: Chris O'Donnell, Robin Tunney, Scott Glenn, Izabella Scorupco, Bill Paxton, Nicholas Lea, Alexander Siddig, Robert Taylor, Temuera Morrison

Vertical Limit (also known as *Maybe It Isn't Such a Good Idea to Carry Nitroglycerin Up a Mountain* and *Now It's Your Turn to Hang Off a Cliff Ledge*) is pure '70s disaster movie cheese at it finest, and it certainly gets off to a rollicking start. Chris O'Donnell stars as Peter Garrett, a climber who likes to hang precariously in front of what is clearly a green-screen (a monochromatic screen, usually green or blue, that actors perform in front of. Later in the film production process, a background scene is added to the shot). O'Donnell, his sister Annie (played by Robin Tunney), and his father carry on soft-voiced conversations about music trivia as they climb, hundreds of feet apart, up the side of an Arizona rock face. Almost immediately, the strap holding the family together breaks, dumping two other climbers to their deaths and leaving the three hanging for dear life.

O'Donnell's father insists that he's weighing the other two down, and that they should cut him loose. Naturally, O'Donnell doesn't feel like this is the right thing to do, which results in an amusing screaming fit from the father. Tragically, the father is eventually cut loose and does fall, disappearing into the horizon. In most movies today, this would be enough, but I give these filmmakers credit for following the '70s disaster movie tradition: they cut to the ground below and give us a fairly tight shot of Dad's body crashing to the ground with a loud, dusty thud.

Fast-forward to some time later. A guilt-ridden O'Donnell has given up climbing mountains and devoted his life to nature photography in the Pakistani wilderness. Nearby, Tunney (who is now a famous and celebrated mountain climber) is helping billionaire Bill Paxton prepare to climb K2 as a publicity stunt for his airline. O'Donnell finds Tunney, which leads to a scene involving several awkwardly long stares at each other. In fact, this is a movie full of excessive pauses and stares, with all of the actors looking a tad confused, almost as if they've forgotten their lines, or like there's something going on between them that is more than just a family squabble. There's also an elaborate party scene at base camp, where climbers of various nationalities are introduced. These include a pair of annoying British climbers whose job is to provide comic relief, a Pakistani mountaineer who is devastated over the loss of his brother on Paxton's previous climb, and, most amusingly, Scott Glenn as Old Man Winter. Well, not exactly. Glenn portrays a scraggly, bearded, somewhat crazy loner named Wick who lives on the side of the mountain, where he searches for the remains of his wife, who was also lost four years ago on Paxton's last climb.

Paxton, portraying the daredevil billionaire as pure evil, pushes Tunney and the other characters to climb to the top despite the poor weather, resulting in their becoming trapped on a frozen ledge inside a cave after an avalanche. From this point on, the snowed-in Paxton spends most of his time gritting his teeth and staring at the other two climbers in an over-the-top manner. Down below, O'Donnell must be absolutely thrilled at this opportunity for redemption, and, against the protestations of others who wisely believe there's no point in risking the lives of even more people to attempt a hopeless rescue, he assembles a ragtag group to attempt the climb. He does this in dangerous conditions, knowing that they have only 36 hours before edema sets in and Tunney and the others die. These climbers require an experienced leader, which leads them to the grumpy Glenn.

I'm not exactly sure why anyone would be in a big hurry to recruit and follow the instructions of a burned-out, crazed mountain climber, but they are, and they do. Glenn actually wants to kill Paxton, whom he correctly believes is responsible for the death of his wife. It's especially funny when one considers that Glenn could easily just refuse the mission and let Paxton die, but instead chooses to climb K2, risking his life and the lives of others so that he can throttle Paxton himself.

From this point on, there are incredibly elaborate action scenes, and while they aren't for a second anything less than preposterous, they are not boring. The six climbers decide to take nitroglycerin along with them so that they can blow an opening through the ice and snow. Yes, that's right, not only are these characters leaping from helicopters and climbing mountains, they've also got large explosives strapped to them. This leads to all sorts of problems, as characters slip and slide on the ice. In fact, it's all a big comedy of errors as characters are blown sky-high after mishandling the nitro in various ways.

Yes, this flick is as cheesy and dopey as many of the cheesiest and dopiest of the '70s disaster films. It's good for a lot of laughs, but they're mostly at the film's expense. At least it's not dull.

Most Spectacular Moment of Carnage
There's a good, high body count and many elaborate deaths. Three people are killed by avalanches, three fall incredible heights to their deaths, another is stabbed in the neck with a syringe full of air, and two more are blown to smithereens when their explosives accidentally go off. Whoops! **(GK)**

RARE, OBSCURE, AND LESS IMPORTANT TITLES

Anything to Survive (1990) Made-for-TV

Avalanche (1969)

Avalanche (1994) Made-for-TV

Avalanche (1999) Straight-to-video

Into Thin Air: Death on Everest (1997) Made-for-TV

Ski Lift to Death (1978) Made-for-TV

Snowbound: The Jim and Jennifer Stolpa Story (1994) Made-for-TV

Hot Molten Lava

Ever since I was a kid I've had a strange souvenir in my possession: a small bag of ash from Mount St. Helens, which erupted on May 18, 1980. I don't know where I got it, but I've always had it. Basically it's just a small bag of dirt, and I was only six years old when the volcano erupted and I didn't live anywhere near it, but it still touched my life in some way. Thank you, Bunker Hill Souvenirs of Kellogg, Idaho!

To think that, even today, the inner depths of our planet Earth are still molten and churning is bizarre and unsettling. A volcanic eruption is actually a beautiful sight to see, a fascinating display of nature's raw fury (only it's not so beautiful to watch your house melt). For obvious reasons, the volcano is a popular element of the disaster genre. Sometimes these movies feature a small, quiet town nestled at the foot of a volcano, and you wonder: are these people just stupid? I mean, when the volcano erupts and destroys these small, quiet towns, are we supposed to feel sad? No, we're supposed to find it all so very exciting, but in the back of my mind I'm thinking, *hey, looks like you people picked the wrong neighborhood.* Now, in some volcano movies, the volcano itself pops up unexpectedly where there never was one before, and while that's highly unlikely, at least it's an entertaining idea.

There probably won't be any notable volcano movies made for some time to come, since that wad was basically blown back in 1997, so if you're into watching lava flow, you'll have to stick with what's already out there or tune into the Discovery Channel. Or you could move to Washington State, where Mount St. Helens has been rumbling again, proving that when no one's making volcano movies, nature fills the void. Nonetheless, while there's nothing wrong with all the asteroid movies, and the tornado movies, and the terrible (or, sometimes, perfect) storm movies, they pretty much can't compare with the pure destruction of a volcanic eruption. Sure, an earthquake rips the ground open, but a volcano just blows the whole damn place up, and that's pretty final. So prepare yourself for the ultimate battle: stupid humans vs. death-dealing volcanoes! It's a shame the movies themselves kind of suck. **(MR)**

The Core (2003)

Paramount Pictures   135 minutes

RECOMMENDED

⚠

DIRECTOR: Jon Amiel

WRITERS: Cooper Layne, John Rogers

CAST: Aaron Eckhart, Tchéky Karyo, Richard Jenkins, Hilary Swank, Bruce Greenwood, Alfre Woodard, Stanley Tucci, Delroy Lindo, D. J. Qualls

There's nothing quite like a goofy, old-fashioned, end-of-the-world sci-fi premise, such as in *Crack in the World, The Night the World Exploded,* and the more recent, unabashedly late-'50s and early-'60s-inspired *The Core.* Make no mistake, the film is no classic, but it at least seems to be aware of its predecessors, and it does its best to throw in everything but the kitchen sink to please you. Including lots of lava. Lots and lots of it. The flick even manages to incorporate the crashing of a space shuttle into the plot, leaving me with the surreal feeling that I was watching a disaster film within a disaster film.

Early on, a university professor studies recent unusual phenomena and comes to the natural conclusion that the earth's core has stopped rotating. This leads to many questions; I'm not sure that people with PhDs should refer to periodicals like *Fortean Times* as accurate scientific journals (why not have them check out *National Enquirer* while they're at it?). But before audiences are given any time to ponder this, the story moves forward and it's revealed that the planet is in mortal danger.

Naturally, a diverse, ragtag band of eccentric characters, including NASA pilots, a weapons expert, a physicist, a computer hacker, and so on, are recruited to save the world by drilling to the planet's core and detonating a nuclear weapon. This process is explained in many scenes in which characters stand by a chalkboard, pie graph, or diorama (you get the idea) and explain the science as slowly and simply as possible to let us all understand it. In the '50s, films were sometimes composed almost entirely of scenes like this, along with stock footage that was interspersed at the appropriate moments. It's amusing to see such scenes return in *The Core*, but at least this time the film has stronger actors who can sell these concepts with some dramatic flair. The scenes also feature some goofy technical terms and dialogue, including corkers like "We've got full rotation!"

Interestingly enough, the inner core of the earth ends up looking a lot like outer space. The special effects are decent, the weaker ones looking better on the small screen than they did at the theater. The film's saving grace is the cast, which is excellent. The actors manage to make their characters likable. Tucci's character, Dr. Zimsky, is borderline over-the-top, but in a film about drilling to the center of the earth, that's to be expected.

Much of the movie features elaborate suspense sequences involving the avoidance of giant diamonds and flaming lava while drilling down, as well as the occasional repair job performed outside of the ship. All of this is done well, with a reasonable amount of wit. So, while *The Core* is imperfect and at times pushes our suspension of disbelief, the film is an agreeable-enough addition to the genre, and it's worthy of a minor recommendation.

Most Spectacular Moment of Carnage
There's a painful-looking death by crushing, and another poor guy is cooked alive in his suit. This is all unusually nasty stuff for a film with a PG-13 rating. And, of course, one can't forget the tragic suicides of hundreds of British pigeons in Trafalgar Square. But a sequence that includes the destruction of San Francisco, in which drivers on the Golden Gate Bridge are burned before their vehicles burst into flames and topple off of the collapsing bridge (resulting in the flaying of several unfortunate fish) wins the prize. This movie isn't kind to animals, come to think of it. (**GK**)

Dante's Peak (1997)

Universal Pictures   112 minutes

AT YOUR OWN RISK

DIRECTOR: Roger Donaldson

WRITER: Leslie Bohem

CAST: Pierce Brosnan, Linda Hamilton, Charles Hallahan, Jamie Renée Smith, Jeremy Foley, Elizabeth Hoffman, Grant Heslov

For some reason, in the late '90s two movie studios felt the irresistible urge to rush two volcano movies into production at the same time. But we're all the luckier, as I don't believe it's possible to exhaust the endless possibilities of this particular topic. *Dante's Peak* beat the Tommy Lee Jones vehicle *Volcano* to theaters, and as such it was the more successful of the two, though it isn't the better film (of course, that's not saying much). The advertising campaign promised an adventure of explosive proportions, but in reality the film merely crawls inch-by-inch through the motions like so much spent volcano ejaculate—er, lava.

Pierce Brosnan stars as a very handsome volcanologist who visits the small town of Dante's Peak to check out the rumblings of a long-dormant volcano that looms over the town. Of course, this is all very personal to him, as a few years earlier his wife was killed as they tried to escape from a volcanic eruption. He is met by the town's mayor, Linda Hamilton, who also runs a restaurant and who spends a lot of the movie in an apron, raising her young daughter and son without the aid of a husband. We know her son is cool because he wears baggy pants, hangs out with long-haired boys, and has a wallet chain. After exchanging some longing glances with Brosnan, Hamilton believes his assertion that the volcano is about to explode, but she's the only one. No one wants to scare off the rich developer who wants to sink a lot of money into the town—a town that, at the top of the film, is given an award for being named the second-safest town in America. Now that's what I call irony!

Of course, we know the volcano is going to explode. We know this because in movies like this, the hero is always right. We know this because the day Brosnan arrives, two young skinny-dipping lovers are boiled alive as they frolic in the local hot springs. We know this because all scientific readings actually indicate there will be no eruption. And we know this because we saw it happen in the trailer. And when the volcano does go up, it goes up with a bang. This is where the movie becomes what we've been waiting 45 minutes for it to become: a special-effects extravaganza. But this doesn't really add up to much, because there's hardly a movie out there anymore that isn't in some way a special-effects extravaganza. In this case, we're talking about an extended eruption sequence that deftly mixes convincing live-action and model photography with good computer animation, but so what? We knew it was coming, and we probably had a pretty good idea of what it was going to look like.

Now, I liked the collapsing buildings and bridges, and the black ash storms are nice, as are the lava flow sequences, but the movie never really got my heart pounding. Why? Well, part of the problem might be that this is a far too warm and fuzzy disaster movie. Only a handful of people actually get killed, and never in graphic ways. We're never treated to the sight of bodies being crushed or burned or anything. There aren't even any corpses lying around after the carnage (unlike the 1997 Sylvester Stallone vehicle *Daylight*, which fills the screen with charred remains—now we're talking!). This movie seems far more interested in destroying land and property than it is in killing townspeople. The tiny town itself is completely obliterated, but all of its residents seem to have gotten out alive, and the viewer eventually realizes that carnage isn't what this movie's about. Rather, we're just supposed to get a charge out of all the explosive mayhem on a purely technical level, as if visual effects are all that matter. Bloodless disaster movies that offer only pyrotechnics and not much of a body count are, more often than not, staggeringly boring, as more and more concessions are made by the filmmakers in order to soften the film's edge and make it suitable for as wide an audience as possible. I mean, in this movie even the dog survives, in a most improbable way. (But of course that's a given, to be fair—dogs never die in disaster films.)

On a basic level, the movie tries to be a throwback to the great disaster movies of the '70s, but those movies generally were brutal; no one was safe, no matter how famous they were. People had to die, and in increasingly violent and surprising ways, or there would be no sense of real jeopardy (and precious little exploitative schlock value that made these films what they were). And while they ostensibly promoted the effects as the star, at a time when really convincing visual effects were much more difficult to create, these films were far more bloodthirsty. *Dante's Peak* is a disaster flick for the whole family, and that's just not any good.

There are a few things I did like about the film, though on a strictly cheeseball level. As a hero, Brosnan is manly yet gentle, and he has many pensive looks within his acting range, but he's not all that bright. He takes on the mantle of savior to Hamilton and the tykes, but he keeps leading them into incredibly dangerous situations from which he has no way to get them out. First the lake of acid, then across the lava flow, and now into the mine shaft, where they'll all be crushed to death! The lake of acid was my favorite, though they missed the opportunity to show corroded bodies floating around, or even the dog's corroded body, which is what I would have done. The mine shaft scene is pretty claustrophobic, and the movie does earn points for lingering unusually long on a creepy shot of Brosnan's broken, jutting arm bone. The physical art direction is convincing, what with the town blanketed in thick ash and leveled to the ground and all. But at its core, *Dante's Peak* is a fairly hollow and empty experience, and it's not even quite bad enough to be satisfyingly goofy.

Most Spectacular Moment of Carnage

The moment that sticks with me is really one of unintentional comedy, in which the aforementioned young couple frolicking in the hot springs are boiled when underground eruptions cause the water to become superheated. It's a humiliating death for them, as they were skinny dipping, and once dead, they float to the surface upside down, their asses sticking out of the water for all to see. Amazingly, someone is able to identify them to police solely by looking at their rear ends. This raises a lot of questions that, sadly, go unanswered. **(MR)**

The Last Days of Pompeii (1959)
United Artists   100 minutes

AT YOUR OWN RISK

DIRECTOR: Mario Bonnard (Note: much of the film was actually directed by Sergio Leone, who is uncredited)

WRITERS: Sergio Corbucci, Ennio De Concini, Luigi Emannuele, Sergio Leone, Duccio Tessari (based on the novel by Edward George Bulwer-Lytton)

CAST: Steve Reeves, Christine Kaufman, Fernando Rey, Barbara Carroll

The classic novel gets yet another treatment in this action/gladiator/disaster flick, which was filmed in Italy. Actors and voiceover artists dubbed the dialogue into English, making the film much funnier. Steve Reeves stars as Glaucus, a Roman centurion returning home to Pompeii after years in battle. "You would never think that a volcano would mean anything to a man. Yet how many times, in the heat of battle, have my thoughts flown to her," his traveling friends comment to him. Much of the dialogue is delivered in similar flowery prose, which seems out of place with the temperament of a centurion, but of course that makes it all the more entertaining. Characters in this film also seem to spontaneously burst into laughter together at things that aren't very funny.

Sadly for Reeves, things are not going nearly as well in Pompeii as one would hope. Gangs of hooded Christian assassins are terrorizing the locals. It isn't long before Reeves arrives at his homestead and finds that the same group of assassins has killed his father. So what to do? Reeves remedies the situation in true action-movie style by getting really drunk and chopping a table in half with his bare hands. He later gets himself into a brawl with a sinister local centurion. This results in an odd fight scene (odd mostly because everyone around watches in silence as the two struggle, and there doesn't seem to be any ambient sound in the background; only the loud "slaps" of the punches connecting).

The somewhat thick Reeves finally gets a clue and learns that Pompeii's high priest is responsible for the troubles. He decides to leave town and tell a consul of his discoveries, but he is attacked and shot with an arrow by the assassins. He manages to survive and stumble his way humorously to his destination before collapsing and unnecessarily pulling the tablecloth off of an ornately decorated table. After a speedy recovery, Reeves decides to deal with the problem personally. This results in action scenes in which Reeves dispatches the villains one by one with his sword. Later he wrestles a crocodile, a lion, and several gladiators, seemingly to break the monotony of killing the same thing day after day.

By this point, I was ready to write this movie off as a gladiator film, but the volcano does erupt. Unfortunately, the effect looks more like an earthquake than anything else, as panicked crowds run through the streets, many waving their hands in the air as to emphasize the terror that's going on around them. There are some decent shots of buildings, beams, and pillars falling on the crowds. The only character who appears unfazed is Reeves, who casually enters a collapsing structure and rescues a small child, hands him back matter-of-factly to his mother, and rejoins the evacuees. The lava itself is kept offscreen. All that is shown is a single tight shot of black liquid running down the street. I guess I was supposed to imagine that a massive amount of lava was flowing behind the crowds. The filmmakers attempt to make up for this by showering as many shots as they can with falling sparks. The end result, while not ineffective, looks like a crowd of peasants running through a steel plant. At one point the ground even opens up on the characters, and a few tumble in. Sadly, this effect was achieved much better in the earlier film *The Rains Came*.

There's no doubt that a film like this would have played best to toddlers as a Saturday matinee. As for the rest of us, we could do better. Interestingly enough, second unit director and cowriter Sergio Leone would later move on to make some of the best westerns of all time. Like the other major *Pompeii* adaptations (1913, 1935, 1984), this title is difficult to find on DVD.

Most Spectacular Moment of Carnage
During the chaotic earthquake—I mean volcano—sequence, a brick wall falls on a hapless Pompeii citizen. Other than that, most of the violence is kept offscreen. (**GK**)

Volcano (1997)

Twentieth Century Fox   107 minutes

RECOMMENDED

© Twentieth Century Fox

DIRECTOR: Mick Jackson

WRITERS: Jerome Armstrong, Billy Ray

CAST: Tommy Lee Jones, Anne Heche, Gaby Hoffmann, Don Cheadle, Keith David

Oscar-winning actor Tommy Lee Jones is as reliable as ever in this uneven but often entertaining disaster flick about a volcanic eruption in downtown Los Angeles. Though how such a thing might be possible is explained only in extremely broad strokes (and hand gestures), the film nonetheless chugs along at a reasonably quick pace and obscures its inherent implausibility with lots of visual effects.

Jones, as the director of the office of emergency management for the city of Los Angeles, is the guy you call when disaster strikes, as it often does in L.A. He's a tough but lovable workaholic who always gets the job done at the expense of other things in his life. This character isn't much of a stretch for Jones, but he's so good that he makes you forget that you've kind of seen this before.

When a series of earthquakes tears open fissures beneath the city, causing the La Brea tar pits to erupt in flames and spew lava all over Wilshire Boulevard, Jones teams up (and trades quips) with his second-in-command, Don Cheadle, and perky university seismologist Anne Heche in order to prevent further death and destruction. Cheadle is a great actor, but for some reason, in marked contrast to the intensity of some of his other performances, here he underplays his role to extremes. His monumental underreactions are hilarious, as he's never remotely fazed by the epic proportions of the devastation unfolding before him. Though his stalwart cool is meant to establish his character as reliable under pressure and worthy of command, most of the time it's merely comical as he cracks jokes and remains expressionless while L.A. is destroyed. As for Heche, there's no sexual tension whatsoever between her and Jones, which is probably for the best, even though the film has all the elements in place for them to fall passionately in love: she's single (ahem) and he's divorced, though he does have a whiny petulant teenage daughter.

As lava flows down Wilshire, engulfing everything in its path, Jones gets caught right in the middle of it, as he's the kind of guy who goes to work even while on vacation. He immediately takes control of police and firefighters and supervises the hasty construction of a "dam," made from concrete highway dividers and abandoned cars and trucks, so that they might stop the advancing flow. It occurred to me that it might not be desirable to drop a tanker truck into the path of hot lava because the gas tanks would likely explode, but that never happens, so I guess it's not that big of a deal.

Once the dam successfully stops the lava flow and an enormous fleet of helicopters douse the inferno with water, Jones thinks his problems are over, but Heche believes that more lava is quickly moving underground through the subway tunnels and will erupt right at the Beverly Center, which of course is across the street from the hospital where all the injured have been taken to receive medical care, including Jones's daughter, who was mildly scalded by some flying lava. It's also the site of a brand new 20-story crappy scale model—um, I mean, condominium building—which has not yet been opened to the public. It doesn't take a genius to figure out what's probably gonna happen here, as otherwise the movie wouldn't lavish a single moment on the building's developer, who by some amazing coincidence happens to be the boyfriend of the doctor who rescues Jones's daughter and takes her to the hospital.

But back to the subway line for a moment. Though it is still under construction, parts of it have been completed and are in use, and of course this means that there's a train full of people trapped underground in the path of the killer lava. The film suggests that it is the subway construction that has weakened the fault lines, causing the eruption, not to mention the fact that the tunnels themselves provide pathways for the lava to flow from one place to another. There actually is an underground subway system in Los Angeles, which I believe was built only to provide additional locations for action scenes in movies (it has popped up in *Lethal Weapon 3* and *Speed*, to name but two). Even though the events in *Volcano* are unlikely to occur in real life anytime soon, it never seemed like that great an idea to build a subway in L.A., as it certainly isn't the most geologically stable region in the world. But then, I'm not an engineer, so what do I know?

Anyway, once Jones and Heche arrive at the Beverly Center, they realize that blasting a trench in the street to divert the lava into the drainage canal that leads to the ocean won't work due to the slant of the landscape. Again, some hand gestures in the general direction of a map of some kind with lines all over it suffices as explanation. However, Jones gets the brilliant idea to blow up the condominium building so that when it collapses, it will force the lava flow into the canal. In the film's most preposterous sequence, a demolition crew sets explosives in the building and on the ground so that the building will fall in exactly the right spot to divert the lava into the trench that they're blasting out of the ground at the same time. A demolition such as this would take weeks of planning and days of physical preparation by a team of experts. A job this big could never be pulled off in less time than it takes to watch an episode of *Charles in Charge*, but in this movie the job gets done in less than 20 minutes!

The demolition goes as planned, the building collapses, the trench is blown out of the pavement, and the lava flows into the canal and out into the ocean. Thank goodness they had a whole 20 minutes to pull it off; imagine the rush if they'd only had 15. And how handy it was that they had all those plastic explosives, fuses, and detonators lying around!

And if you're still not entirely sure just what kind of movie you're watching, there's the scene in which, as the city lies in rubble and Jones starts cracking jokes again, Randy Newman's "I Love L.A." blasts on the soundtrack as the camera reveals the newly born Mount Wilshire, spewing smoke into the air.

This movie even finds time to make maudlin pleas for racial unity, as if this kind of message is at all appropriate in such a film. I see a movie called *Volcano*, I wanna see some crap get blown up, and that's all. And it doesn't matter that the central character is trying to save lives when the movie as a whole takes bloodthirsty pleasure in having people die in horrible ways. Besides, part of the fun of these movies is watching all attempts to save people fail miserably. *Volcano* wants to have it both ways, and that's more than a little manipulative. There is no place in this ridiculous volcano movie for moral statements about humanity, and this is certainly not the kind of movie people look to for moral guidance!

Still, at times the film provides effective thrills and some degree of humor. The fire and lava effects are excellent, though some of the miniature model work is extremely crude and obvious. The camerawork is often not particularly subtle (witness one scene when, to depict Tommy Lee Jones's horror, the camera pulls rapidly into his face not once, but *twice*, as he grimaces in shock). But the fact that this movie lays it on thick ultimately doesn't detract from my enjoyment of it; after all, *Volcano* was nominated for a Razzie for Worst Reckless Disregard for Human Life and Property.

Most Spectacular Moment of Carnage

When some poor sap tries to save the unconscious driver of a subway train that's trapped in the path of flowing lava, he learns the disaster movie's hardest lesson: never be a hero. Clutching the driver as he stands in the doorway of the train, with lava all around him and his feet already burning up, he leaps into a pool of lava and somehow finds the strength to toss the guy to safety as he melts away, screaming. "Hey, you're welcome, pal." **(MR)**

Volcano: Fire on the Mountain (1997)

Davis Entertainment   88 minutes

AVOID AT ALL COSTS

DIRECTOR: Graeme Campbell

WRITERS: Craig Spector, Steven Womack

CAST: Dan Cortese, Cynthia Gibb, Brian Kerwin

A made-for-TV movie released around the time of *Dante's Peak* and *Volcano*, this unspectacular disaster flick is competent and has passable effects (except for one section), but it really fails on a coherent story level.

Set in Angel Lake, California, near the Sierra Mountains, the film opens with a pair of newlyweds who decide to ski down a closed-off slope. After a brief earthquake, the ground cracks open, emitting a glowing red light, and the two promptly fall in. At State Geological Survey headquarters, heroic geologist Dan Cortese reports to his superior his prediction that a mountain near the Angel Lake community will erupt. He is scornfully told by his boss that the last time they evacuated a town on his hunch, nothing happened. This is spoken as if it was a bad thing that a devastating volcanic eruption did not take place. Cortese leaves immediately to investigate for himself, irritating Angel Lake's mayor. It doesn't take long before Cortese is found wandering on restricted property by mountain patrol officer Cynthia Gibb, who pulls out an automatic gun before promptly handcuffing and arresting him. I never knew that officers of the mountain patrol packed heat and carried handcuffs with them. Amazingly, as it turns out, Cortese is Gibb's ex-boyfriend. Will the two resolve their differences and get back together before the end of the film? Does a bear poop in the woods?

Of course, the mayor doesn't believe that the strange disappearances of skiers, the random tremors occurring almost daily, the poisonous gas that almost killed most of his mountain crew, and a red glow coming from the mountain mean anything. Even Cortese's very scientific use of a jelly donut to explain how a volcano works (by squeezing it) fails to impress and is only a waste of a delicious pastry.

When the lava hits, incredibly unbelievable events follow, including an obnoxious teenage boy discovering a pregnant woman and delivering the baby. After a cutaway to another scene, the mother returns, seated calmly with the child wrapped up in her arms, in no discomfort whatsoever.

At State Geological Survey headquarters, characters report that Cortese has predicted an even bigger quake and explosion to come. The only one who doesn't seem aware of this is Cortese himself. The climax involves an avalanche that is set off to stop the flow of lava and save the town. Believe me, it's not worth the wait.

Most Spectacular Moment of Carnage

There's little of interest happening here, with a total body count of three. A nasty businessman's death is, I suppose, the most violent, but it's also the most incomprehensible. With the lava flowing down toward him, the man deems it appropriate to rush outside and grab a snowmobile. After taking off, the climactic avalanche and lava hits and he is sent flying off of the vehicle, never to be seen again. No one in the film seems the least bit upset by this and the incident is quickly forgotten by all, because nobody really liked him anyway. **(GK)**

When Time Ran Out... (1980)

Warner Bros.   143 minutes

SO BAD IT'S GOOD

DIRECTOR: James Goldstone

WRITERS: Carl Foreman, Stirling Silliphant

CAST: Paul Newman, Jacqueline Bisset, William Holden, Edward Albert, Red Buttons, Barbara Carrera, Valentina Cortese, Veronica Hamel, Alex Karras, Burgess Meredith, Ernest Borgnine, James Franciscus, Pat Morita

Read carefully: Paul Newman plays Hank, a drilling foreman searching for oil in Hawaii. Alex Karras plays Newman's work friend Tiny. Karras is a big, strong man who, aside from assisting Newman (mostly by just standing around with his arms crossed), is obsessed with cockfighting and wants to defeat nearby bar owner and cockfighting rival Pat Morita. Newman is a partner of real estate developer Bob, played by James Franciscus. Franciscus owns the Hawaiian island and the resort that most of the movie is set on, thanks to his deceased father, who grew sugarcane there and became very wealthy. His father's friend Shelby, played by William Holden, is also a partner and developer. Holden desperately wants to marry his secretary, Jacqueline Bisset, but sadly, she is in love with Newman, with whom she had a relationship many years before. Holden also has a daughter, Veronica Hamel, who is married to Franciscus. Unfortunately, Franciscus is cheating on Hamel with a local Hawaiian girl named Iolani—Barbara Carrera—who is engaged to the hotel's manager, played by Edward Albert. Little does Albert know, but he is actually the illegitimate son of Franciscus's father, and therefore half owner of the island. Besides choosing not to inform anyone of this, Franciscus refuses to acknowledge the possibility that a local volcano that constantly emits smoke may be ready to burst. This may pose a danger for thief Red Buttons, who has stolen some bonds and traveled to this resort on the lam from pesky New York cop Ernest Borgnine. Also in danger are Burgess Meredith and his wife, who happen to be retired circus performers who specialize in high-wire walking.

Still with me?

Did I mention that there is an erupting volcano in this movie? After this ridiculously complicated setup, it's amazing that there's any time at all to get to the good stuff into this disaster flick, which would be Irwin Allen's last epic. I can completely understand why it was made, seeing as how it presented a paid vacation to Hawaii for all involved in its production. But as you can imagine, this film ends up being utterly hilarious.

As these endless plot threads are introduced and slowly develop, scene after boring scene unfolds. Karras speaks directly to his rooster before setting the animal down in the ring for its fight to the death with Morita's prized chicken. This is a marked contrast to the low-key Newman (maybe he's hoping no one will notice him in this film) as the voice of reason. After finding oil, Newman notes the strange change in pressure and reports it to his greedy partner, Franciscus. They head up to a large scientific lab that's been built on the top lip of the very active volcano. Why would anyone spend millions of dollars to do this? Probably so Franciscus, Newman, and other scientists can ride the observation car, which lowers itself from an arm inside the volcano. The car has a glass bottom, so all of the characters can watch the volcano's lava bubbling beneath their feet. That would seem to me to be its only purpose, except for the fact that it will obviously result in an elaborate action sequence in which the glass floor breaks. And of course this does happen, causing more personal and professional conflict between Newman and Franciscus.

Newman decides to relax from his near-death experience by going on a beachside picnic with ex-flame Bisset. Romance blooms, allowing us to hear both a syrupy love theme and Bisset proclaim, "I don't need any wine, you get me drunk!" Over an hour into the movie, just as I began to think that maybe I was watching the wrong tape and had been given some kind of daytime soap opera episode instead, the eruption finally occurs. The volcano effects could not look more horribly phony if they had tried. But, I must give the filmmakers some credit here. In spite of the cheesy effects and the fact that none the film makes any sense from this point on, many people die and all hell really does break lose, making this movie hysterically entertaining.

The ground shakes, causing the airport runways to crack up, power lines to fall, and a red sports car to fly off of the road, roll down the side of a hill (with a dummy visible inside), and explode at the bottom. The science lab breaks off of its foundation and quickly tumbles down the mouth of the volcano, killing all inside. Buildings in the village begin falling apart. And worst of all, Karras's prizewinning rooster gets loose. Karras runs down the middle of the street chasing the rooster in circles while the camera shakes and other villagers run around with their arms raised, screaming in panic. Their reactions are no doubt due to the large tidal wave that crashes down on the island, killing the rooster and the heroic Karras, who at least did everything he could to save his feathered friend before drowning. At this point, I had to the stop the movie and laugh for a full five minutes before I recovered.

Back at the resort, Franciscus insists that everything is just fine and nothing much has happened. Holden argues once again with Franciscus and lets him know that he "doesn't buy it." This is a brilliant assumption, considering that the volcano is clearly visible from all around, spewing out rocks and lava. Strangely enough, Borgnine (the New York cop) and Buttons (the criminal) instantly become close friends. Burgess Meredith's character, Rene, even remarks, "Those two remind me of [wife] Rose and myself a long time ago." Unless Meredith's wife is actually a man, this comment makes little sense and leaves a lot of unexplained subtext.

The film's longest sequence involves evacuees attempting to cross a rickety bridge, with fallen boards, rising flames, and a river of lava flowing underneath. Newman tests the bridge by walking across it unbelievably slowly. Upon arriving safely at the other side, he actually turns around and walks slowly back across the bridge to tell the others that it's passable. Newman, they were watching you the entire time! I think they got the idea. Finally, Meredith is put to good use as he promptly grabs a long bamboo shaft for balance, hoists a kid on his back, and walks the remaining metal skeleton. Describing this sequence just doesn't do it justice. You simply won't believe your eyes.

Shockingly, this film was nominated for an Oscar (for Best Costume Design), so someone on national television actually had to use the words *When Time Ran Out* and *Academy Award* in the same sentence. If you're in the mood for something bad and *The Concorde: Airport '79* is out (like that's ever going to happen), this demented disaster movie is a hoot to watch, so grab yourself some nachos and give this cheesefest a chance.

Most Spectacular Moment of Carnage

Alex Karras's demise is painfully funny, but I'm even more impressed with those who fall into the lava. Whenever this happens, there's an overhead shot of the character spinning backward in slow motion. Behind them is a cheesy, out-of-scale special-effect shot of flowing lava. Pat Morita in particular gives us a great expression and scream while he performs a slow backflip and is presumably incinerated into the molten red liquid. **(GK)**

Krakatoa, East of Java (1969)

ABC Pictures   131 minutes

AT YOUR OWN RISK

First things first. Krakatoa is west of Java. That bit of nonsense from the geographically challenged filmmakers should give you a sense of what to expect from this goofball opus. The plot revolves around a pearl-salvaging operation next to the volcano in question. It stars *Deep Impact*'s Maximilian Schell, Diane Baker, *Meteor*'s Brian Keith (as a drug-addicted diver who spends much of the movie locked up in a cage and hung over the ship), and Sal Mineo. Visually impressive, it is an expensive production that boasts some nice scenery. The eruption effects are weak, however. The end of the picture is where all the action is, as the group must sail a course off of the island and avoid a large tidal wave that follows. Best viewed as a laugh with friends, otherwise the very corny subplots, inane dialogue, slow setup, and lengthy running time will destroy your will to finish watching. A box-office failure at the time, it was reportedly rereleased, again to box-office failure, after Irwin Allen's films started to make a killing in the early '70s. Amazingly, it received an Oscar nomination for its special effects. (**GK**)

The Last Days of Pompeii (1935)

RKO Radio Pictures   96 minutes

RECOMMENDED

From the producing and directing team of *King Kong* (1933), Ernest B. Schoedsack directs Preston Foster, Alan Hale, and Basil Rathbone in an adaptation of the classic Sir Edward Bulwer-Lytton novel. The story had been told before in a little-seen Italian silent film from 1913, but this was the first major studio effort. This is another very important early title that I had thought would never see the light of day. But, good news for film fans, this title is included in the DVD special edition of the original *King Kong*. Be sure to check it out. **(GK)**

St. Helens (1981)
Parnell Films   95 minutes

AVOID AT ALL COSTS

Art Carney faces off against Mount St. Helens and loses. In spite of receiving a few positive reviews in some circles, there's nothing remarkable about this snore-inducing title. I could barely keep my eyes open through it. While the stock footage of the eruption is impressive, the special effects are not, making the climactic explosion, well, less than climactic. Not worth your while, trust me. **(GK)**

RARE, OBSCURE, AND LESS IMPORTANT TITLES

The Last Days of Pompeii (1913)

The Last Days of Pompeii (1984) Made-for-TV

THE BEST DISASTER MOVIES NEVER MADE

Following is a list of movies I think someone really ought to make. They might not currently be in development or production, but given attempts by studios to milk every conceivable disaster concept, it may not be long until *Space Volcano* becomes a reality.

Atomic Lava

Balcony!

The Basement Was Flooded

Brownout

Brush Fire

The Burning of Julio Iglesias's House

Calamity in the Salt Mine

*The Day the Earthquake Nearly Destroyed the Negative of William Friedkin's
    Blue Chips*

The Denver Refueling Incident

The Extremely Tall Building That Did Not Catch Fire

The Flaming Veranda

Hail Storm!

High-Pressure System!

I Remember Magma

It Rained for 20 Minutes

Killer Coriolis

Lava O'Clock

The Lemurs Advance

The Mall Roof Collapsed

Mild Tremor

Mushroom Cloud Boogie

Night of the Fruit Flies

The Plane That Landed Safely

Power Failure!

Raise, Then Drop, Then Raise Again, Then Drop the Titanic

Runaway Streetcar

Snow from the Sun

Space Volcano

Terror in the Lobby

They Nuked Shreveport

Thirty Seconds: The Night the Subway Went Dark

The Tide Rolled In

The Toothpaste Eruption

The Uneventful Cruise

The Virus Goes Bananas

The Wakita, Kansas, Chamber of Commerce Presents: Tornado Alley—
A Fine Place to Live

(MR)

Sinking Ships

Ah, the sea! The ocean air, the marvelous wonder of gazing out into the horizon, water surrounding you on all sides. The sun shining down on you. The thrill of the open vista and being alone with the elements. And then, the sudden realization that the water below must be pretty cold, and if something should happen, you're pretty much helpless. In the history of disaster films, no other event has influenced so many films as the tragic sinking of the *Titanic*. For all of you kids out there who don't know any better, James Cameron was by no means the first filmmaker to tackle that story, nor will he be the last. You only have to go back a couple of decades or so, and you will discover such hidden '80s gems as *Raise the Titanic* (go on and rent it, kids, I dare you!). Funny thing, though: most of the filmmakers felt the need to spruce up what they must have considered boring subject matter with various schemes and subplots onboard the doomed vessel. I find it hilarious that, with each and every film, those involved claim it to be more accurate than the last. Don't believe them; take the films for what they are. These are all melodramatic disaster films and very fictionalized accounts of the historic event in question. (*A Night to Remember* comes the closest to representing reality).

If all of these films were accurate, consider all of the things that must have been going on during the ship's brief voyage. Forbidden upper class/lower class romances, affairs, and love triangles, illegitimate children being disowned and reclaimed, suicide attempts, two concurrent plots to steal jewels on the ship, byzanium (a deadly, made-up mineral) being guarded in steerage, a rape, a shoot-out . . . hey, no wonder no one saw the iceberg coming! If you're really interested in true accounts of the sinking of the ship, read a book. Any attempt to take any *Titanic* movie seriously or as a factual document of history will result in you looking incredibly naive. And for those of you who are sick of it all (and believe me, after watching several of them in a row, I was), take solace in the fact that not all of the films included in this section are specifically about the *Titanic*. Many were only inspired by it (just kidding). There are even a couple of sunken submarine films for those interested. So hunker down for "Sinking Ships," or "All Things *Titanic*," featuring some of the longest movies presented in this book, or anywhere else on the planet, for that matter. **(GK)**

Beyond the Poseidon Adventure
(1979)
Warner Bros.   115 minutes

SO BAD IT'S GOOD

Before her fate is sealed by the deep, the superliner Poseidon will reveal one last secret...

© Warner Bros.

DIRECTOR: Irwin Allen

WRITER: Neslon Gidding (based on the novel by Paul Gallico)

CAST: Michael Caine, Sally Field, Telly Savalas, Peter Boyle, Jack Warden, Shirley Knight, Shirley Jones, Karl Malden, Slim Pickens, Veronica Hamel, Mark Harmon

Irwin Allen attempts to capitalize on one his biggest hits with this sequel to *The Poseidon Adventure*. This time, though, the cheese quotient is off the scales. The story, if you want to call it a story, picks up immediately where the original leaves off. A helicopter has presumably lifted the survivors of the original "adventure" away to safety. Looters Michael Caine, Sally Field, and Karl Malden (just how did this sailing team meet up?!) discover the *Poseidon*, which is still upside down, and is now, for some inexplicable reason, completely deserted. It's almost as if the marines, rescue teams, and media have all lost interest, thinking, "Aw, just let it sink. Let's go home." Regardless, our heroes meet up with yet another salvage ship, an evil salvage ship, this one led by a sinister Telly Savalas (the casting just keeps getting better and better, doesn't it?) claiming to be a doctor. So, he's a doctor who tends to patients on his boat at sea? Regardless, they all agree to board the ship.

Unfortunately, many of the lead characters in this sequel aren't particularly likable. As good an actor as Michael Caine may be, there's little he can do to sell his role as a gruff tugboat captain. I must admit, I do love the bizarre casting in these '70s disaster flicks. How did Allen decide that Caine was perfect actor for this part? Sally Field, who serves as the plucky comic relief, is so grating that you wish something, anything, would fall from the ceiling (or the floor, in this case) and stop her incessant whining. And yes, her character also serves as Caine's love interest. Caine affectionately calls her "monkey" throughout the picture. I couldn't figure out why. Using a primate term instead of, say, the more usual "sweetheart" doesn't sound very affectionate, does it?

As the ludicrousness builds, eight survivors are discovered. They include a blind man and his wife, a Texan drunkard (played by the great Slim Pickens), an angry and argumentative passenger (Peter Boyle), and a fashion model/double agent. Oh, and it's revealed that Malden's character has little time before he drops dead from cancer. Basically, they're a bunch of people who have no business being on the same boat, and they're used ineffectually in an attempt to heighten the melodrama.

Not only are the characters preposterous, but this time, the *Poseidon* sets look a little phonier as well. And there's little to draw your attention away from them. Thrill as the entire cast, one by one, climbs up a ladder. The running time of this sequence alone: 10 minutes. Ten full minutes of people climbing ladders! With no imminent danger involved. There aren't any raging waters pouring in, or fire—just a ladder going up. Now that is some serious padding. It might have been clever if the characters in this film discovered some of the bodies of characters from the previous film. But that doesn't happen either.

Anyway, as it turns out, Savalas is actually looking for plutonium hidden on the ship (did these guys read the script of *Raise the Titanic*?). And before you can say

"That's the stupidest thing I've ever seen in my life," Caine and the passengers are in a machine-gun battle with Savalas and his goons on the various ship decks. They fight, some escape, and some die elaborate deaths.

Despite this goofiness, the film is oddly engrossing (except for that 10-minute ladder sequence), is nicely shot, and does have some entertaining moments. I know it's not a good film, but by the climax I kind of found myself enjoying it. Maybe it was because I was so busy laughing at most of it. This is one you'll want to watch for all of the wrong reasons, but you have to be in right frame of mind.

Most Spectacular Moment of Carnage

A goon is unexpectedly chopped with an ax by fashion model Veronica Hamel. Veronica Hamel, ax murderer. Go figure. (**GK**)

Gray Lady Down (1978)

Universal Pictures   111 minutes

AT YOUR OWN RISK

DIRECTOR: David Greene

WRITERS: James Whittaker, Howard Sackler (adapted by Frank P. Rosenberg from the novel *Event 1000* by David Lavallee)

CAST: Charlton Heston, David Carradine, Stacy Keach, Ned Beatty, Ronny Cox, Rosemary Forsyth, Michael O'Keefe, Christopher Reeve

Gray Lady Down concerns the rescue of a downed nuclear submarine, which is captained by Charlton Heston. Charlton Heston is a great genre movie actor. Despite the destruction of an entire city (in *Earthquake*) or the plight of a damaged aircraft (in

Airport 1975), Heston manages to chew more scenery than any special effects department. And that's good, because without him, this would be one hard movie to sit through.

It's the last mission of the captain's career. As a fan of the genre, I knew disaster would strike within moments of learning this fact. Heston doesn't help matters by celebrating his retirement with the crew. And so, nearby, a Norwegian freighter loses its radar and crashes into the sub (those damn foreigners are always causing problems!). What happens to the freighter is never explained. But the sub does crash, perching itself on an ocean shelf, while water pressure threatens to finish the survivors off. The producers manage to use actual footage of a sub rising, which helps to add some realism. And some of the effects are OK, although there's a lot of obvious miniature work and the requisite stock footage.

There aren't really any bad guys in this film. After all, the characters are all trapped American officers. The film emphasizes that with "Americans" working "together" as a "team," any problem can be overcome. Unfortunately, some of the suspense is lifted because of this.

Things are a little different on the surface. Maverick designer David Carradine is called in by navy official Stacy Keach to clear rubble that's covering the sub by using an experimental minisub, the DSRV. When Carradine arrives—grouchy, disobeying orders, and with comic relief in the form of Ned Beatty in tow—Keach is less than impressed. Who wouldn't be? Bickering ensues. Yet, as usual in these films, the two learn to work together and make sacrifices for the sake of the sub.

Sadly, there's a great deal of repetitiveness from this point on. Carradine takes the DSRV down to the sub a total of four times, and each time his character solves a problem, another one emerges. This gets dull really fast. Eventually a daring rescue is attempted (à la *Airport '77*) using explosives and air pressure. Carradine and his sub are crushed while valiantly rescuing Heston. Besides Carradine (who bites it offscreen as the DSRV implodes), there are some notable fatalities in this film. Many sailors, who are locked off from the rest of the sub, drown as seawater fills the compartments. During the crash itself, crew members are burned and blinded by steam, knocked into posts and poles, and thrown around the sub—it's almost as if they were the cast of the original *Star Trek* series. And much of this film's ridiculous dialogue is made entertaining by the actors' (in particular, Heston's) deliveries. There's nothing funnier than seeing a frustrated Heston yell "I need propulsion!" or growl "All I know is I'm beginning to feel like a one-legged man at an ass-kicking contest!" as crew members look on in confusion.

While the film is reasonable as a time waster, all and all it feels like some kind of recruitment film for the U.S. Navy.

Most Spectacular Moment of Carnage
Cox sends Heston out of one of the sub's flooding chambers, then locks the door and drowns as his friend watches through a window in the door. In true disaster movie fashion, Cox's body floats right by the window, in Heston's full view. D'oh! (**GK**)

Juggernaut (1974)

United Artists   109 minutes

RECOMMENDED

© United Artists Corporation

DIRECTOR: Richard Lester

WRITER: Richard DeKoker

CAST: Richard Harris, Omar Sharif, David Hemmings, Anthony Hopkins, Shirley Knight, Ian Holm, Clifton James, Roy Kinnear, Freddie Jones, Roshan Seth

Juggernaut is a compelling suspense thriller that both embraces and transcends the genre it wants to bust. The luxury liner *Britannic* is on its way from England to America with 1,200 people aboard. It encounters storm activity shortly after embarking on its voyage, but captain Omar Sharif expects this and the malfunctioning gyroscopes (which keep the boat from rolling) to be the biggest problems he'll encounter. Little does he know that a brilliant mad bomber, who calls himself Juggernaut, has placed seven explosives contained within ordinary-looking metal drums throughout the ship. They will explode at daybreak the following day if $500,000 is not paid. Payment will ensure that the method of defusing the complicated bombs will be surrendered. Of course, the bomber also warns cruise line manager Ian Holm during a phone call, any preliminary attempt to defuse or move the bombs will set them off.

The bomber then demonstrates his seriousness by remotely detonating a small explosive on the top of the ship. (In one of the film's few flashes of inappropriate silliness, only one of the passengers seems particularly concerned about the explosion, not to mention the fact that this explosion doesn't appear to damage or cripple the ship in any way). The disguised voice on the phone sounds a lot like Richard Harris, but it can't be Harris, since he's the captain of the British bomb squad. I'm not sure if the voice is supposed to sound like him or not, but it's definitely disconcerting.

Scotland Yard detective Anthony Hopkins, whose wife and two children are aboard the *Britannic*, gets to work hunting down all known renegade bomb experts in England, while Harris and his team prepare to be flown out to the ship, since it is Her Majesty's policy not to negotiate with terrorists. Instead, they want Harris's team to defuse the bombs in spite of the fact that they have been warned that the devices are complicated and delicate. However, Harris is certain he can handle it. He and his team end up parachuting from the plane into the water, but when a rescue team sets out in a small boat to pick them up, storm conditions wash the rescue team overboard, resulting in the drowning death of one of Harris's crew (obviously not a very important member, as he's never mentioned again).

After swimming with great difficulty to the rescue boat, Harris and his team get to work, but not before Harris has a little drink. Personally, I think that he worked alcohol into his performance so that he could drink while acting and not just in between takes, though it never impairs his performance except for the scene in which he's got so much booze in his mouth that he has to stop talking and swallow before he can continue. Also, I'm not sure if it's particularly wise to smoke a pipe while defusing a bomb, but he does that, too.

By this time the passengers have been informed of the situation, and instead of panicking, they simply resign themselves to the sad reality that they will soon be fish food. This is undoubtedly the most polite, well-behaved group of passengers that a bomb-laden cruise ship has ever carried. No one goes nuts and tries to jump over-board, or causes a scene, or even says anything rude. They just mope about, play Pong, and generally hold their emotions in check—even the blustery American, who seems inspired by the British stiff upper lip. Having been sealed off from the rest of the ship by the emergency doors, for their own safety, the passengers even decide to throw a costume ball at the same time that Harris and his team work on defusing the bombs.

While this is happening, Hopkins's young son decides to take a walk around the ship in his pajamas and look for something to eat. He ends up in the ship's bowels, while one of the ship's crew—Roshan Seth, in a bizarre performance—is sent to look for him. It is never explained why Seth speaks to some people in a halting East Indian accent and to other people in a perfect British accent, even though, once he finds the kid, the kid notices and comments on this very thing. However, Seth doesn't get a chance to respond because, as he prepares to lead the boy away from the bomb-defusing activities nearby, Harris and his team, oblivious to their presence, close the emergency doors, sealing them inside a potentially dangerous area. Seth calls the con-trol room and, in a panic, the doors are opened. At that moment one of the bombs explodes, killing the guy who was working on the bomb and sending a fireball through the corridors toward Seth and the boy. Though the boy escapes unharmed, Seth gets charred when, in an apparent nod to slapstick comedy, the poor guy slips on a puddle of water and is engulfed in flames.

After this tragedy, Harris gives up and turns to booze for comfort, this time swig-ging right from the bottle. (I'm sure these drinking scenes were tough for Harris to pull off.) However, Sharif implores him to continue trying to defuse the bombs, even though at the same time in London, Hopkins, having failed to find the culprit, advis-es Holm to pay the money to avoid further loss of life. Eventually Harris, now nicely toasted, agrees to go back to work. He handles one bomb while one of his team mem-bers handles another as Harris communicates each step over the radio for the other guy to perform, the idea being that if Harris messes up and gets blown to smithereens, the other guy will know what not to do and will be able to continue.

As it happens, it is the other guy who slips up and gets incinerated. This explo-sion causes a leak in the ballroom where the costume ball is taking place, and there are some enjoyable shots of people in silly outfits screaming and running about. Most of the water is coming from the sprinkler system, however, and not from a breach in the ship's hull. None of the explosions have seriously damaged the ship, and it occurred to me then that if they just detonated every bomb one by one they'd probably be all right, as that approach, wasteful to human life as it is, so far seemed to be working. But none of that will be necessary, as a botched money drop leads to the London cops finding Juggernaut, who is forced to reveal to Harris exactly how to defuse the rest of the bombs. There are some interesting twists to the story involving the identity of the bomber and the instructions that he gives to Harris that I'm not going to reveal here but that heighten the considerable suspense of this climactic conclusion.

Aside from some odd moments of incongruity (likely courtesy of director Lester, who is not known for great seriousness), Juggernaut is nonetheless a clever thriller with a unique British slant on the disaster genre. There are only a few concessions to the viewer looking for '70s disaster cheese, but they are there, and they serve to make Juggernaut an interesting and unusual picture.

Most Spectacular Moment of Carnage
The movie is free of graphic, theatrical death scenes, aside from Roshan Seth's deadly pratfall, which gets my vote. **(MR)**

K-19: The Widowmaker (2002)

Paramount Pictures   138 minutes

AT YOUR OWN RISK

DIRECTOR: Kathryn Bigelow

WRITER: Christopher Kyle

CAST: Liam Neeson, Tim Woodward, Lex Shrapnel, Harrison Ford, Donald Sumpter

K-19: The Widowmaker, which is vaguely inspired by true events, is a frustrating flick. While nicely shot, it suffers from some pacing problems, and the central characters make so many horrible choices that I eventually lost any sympathy for them, particularly because their situation could have easily been diffused at various points. Not to mention the fact that this film more or less consists of characters staring intensely at gauges and welding pipes for over two hours. Not the most ideal way to kill that kind of time, if you ask me.

Harrison Ford plays the captain of *K-19*, a brand-spanking-new nuclear submarine and the pride of the Soviet Union. There are no smiles from this captain, and his character is one of the least likable in the actor's repertoire, as he continually drives his crew to exhaustion with unnecessary training exercises during the ship's maiden voyage. The more rational (at least, until the last 20 minutes or so) executive officer, portrayed by Liam Neeson, spends much of the first half of the movie at loggerheads with Ford, so the two spending their screen time together scowling and bickering. In the meantime, the crew is introduced in typical disaster movie tradition, with particular focus given to the young and inexperienced reactor officer. As soon as he is shown kissing his fiancée goodbye, with dramatic music booming in the background, you know his time onboard will not end pleasantly. The same goes for many other crew members, who may as well have "future radiation casualty" painted across their foreheads.

For nearly 60 minutes, Ford barks at the crew and puts them in mortal danger, causing physical damage to the men and to the ship itself while blaming the officers for any failings. The film gets bogged down here, only jumping to life occasionally due to some interesting camera work, including footage shot as the camera moves through the narrow passageways of the sub. But still, a little of this goes a long way, and I certainly got the idea that Ford had a death wish at least 10 minutes before the film thought I did. He is so unrepentant that he never becomes forgivable at a crucial moment later in the film.

Before you can say *Gray Lady Down*, condensation forms in the core reactor, and all are forced to deal with the possibility of a core meltdown and nuclear explosion. For the next 30 minutes, rational solutions are offered and rejected. Cue the overblown music and character sacrifices you picked out earlier in the film. Radiation levels increase, soon contaminating everyone within the sub. Naturally, Ford allows them to bake for a while.

And just try to figure out the climax. The nasty captain is given a lesson in how to give orders in a more tactful way, and from this point on the crew comes to love him. The film had completely lost me by the time of the military court martial, where he is described by an officer as a great guy and that "it would be an honor to sail under his command again." Yeah, because being unnecessarily exposed to radiation and having your skin blister and peel off between vomiting spells was so much fun the first time.

This is followed by an even more preposterous reunion in which Ford makes a speech to the "comrades" and hugs are shared. After nearly killing his crew unnecessarily, not to mention causing a nuclear disaster, it's hard to see why any "comrades" would buy into this. In fact, it seems downright hypocritical. Let me state that I understand the ideals that the film is trying to promote—working together despite differences, forgiveness, and self-sacrifice—I just don't think it does a good job of selling them. Instead of emoting, had Ford received a serious ass-whooping as an old man by those aged crew members still living (a credit reads that 27 eventually died of radiation poisoning) at the film's close, I might have been inclined to think better of this movie. Alas, that didn't happen.

Most Spectacular Moment of Carnage
The effects of radiation take their toll on the crew, particularly those doing welding within the reactor core. There's a lot of blistering skin and vomit, but it's displayed in a PG-13 kind of way. Another crew person is set alight, and yet another has his fingers crushed during an exercise gone awry. **(GK)**

The Last Voyage (1960)

MGM   90 minutes

HIGHLY RECOMMENDED

⚠

DIRECTOR: Andrew L. Stone

WRITER: Andrew L. Stone

CAST: Robert Stack, Dorothy Malone, George Sanders, Edmond O'Brien, Woody Strode, Jack Kruschen, Joel Marston, George Furness, Tammy Marihugh

I give full credit to the writer and director of this exciting "Sinking Ship" film—he sure knows how to start a movie. After a short narrative passage about the *Claridon*, a 38-year-old ship making one of its last voyages across the ocean, the first shot is a close-up of a note reading "Fire in the engine room." From here until the final credit crawl, it's nonstop action, mass panic, and hysteria. This is one of the fastest-paced disaster films of its era, and it doesn't waste a lot of time creating personal turmoil and melodrama among its passengers. The main problem to be resolved is the sinking ship, not (thankfully, for once) the troubled love lives of its passengers.

Robert Stack is quickly introduced as he enjoys a game of bingo (and who wouldn't enjoy a good game of bingo with Robert Stack?). He stars as a family man taking his wife and daughter to Tokyo to start a new job. What job would be taking them all the way to Japan? There's no time for this detail, because down below, the fire is quickly swelling. The ship's captain, George Sanders, is unconcerned and insists on not warning the passengers of any danger, fearing a panic. The engine room chief hurries in to try and release the pressure, but fails and is blown up in an enormous blast. Later, a character states that there "isn't enough left of the chief to scoop up." No time for tears in this movie, I suppose. This spectacular explosion rips through the ceilings, creating a giant hole from the engine room through several different decks and all the way out through the top of the ship. This all occurs before the opening credits have even finished rolling.

Stack races around the debris and narrowly misses being crushed by a piano falling from above. He discovers his wife trapped in the wreckage that was once their cabin. Pinned under a large piece of debris, she is unable to move, and she spends most of the movie yelping in agonizing pain. Come to think of it, this movie has a lot of offscreen wailing and many a sound of death throes from its crew and passengers.

Worst of all for Stack, his daughter is trapped in a corner of her cabin room, with a large hole from the explosion preventing any passage out. Stack tries to scale the debris and get around to his daughter using a creaky wooden board laid across the hole. After realizing that he is much too heavy to cross, Stack tries to convince his daughter to crawl to him. Naturally, she is crying and doesn't want to move, prompting Stack to yell at her in such a way that would terrify even me. There are many exceptional overhead shots used during the sequence to give a sense of depth.

Meanwhile, Sanders, who is perhaps one of the most deluded captains in screen history, refuses to evacuate the ship, maintaining that nothing serious is wrong. The bulkheads begin flooding and spilling water, but even this has no effect on him. In spite of the fact that he is surrounded by utter chaos, he insists that "I've never lost a ship and I'm not losing this one!" Stack finds some passengers who are willing to help try to rescue his wife, which gives him the opportunity to urge them to "get some beef into it!"

Apparently, none of these men have enough "beef," and they make little progress. There's some disturbing stuff as the wife contemplates suicide and later begs a crew person to kill her. She should know better than to count out Robert Stack. Finally, with the ship tipping into the ocean, the captain admits that there might be a problem. Panic ensues, and there are some incredible shots of the boat sinking into the ocean and passengers racing across the deck as it sinks (a real ship was lowered into water to create the effect).

There's some amusingly dated dialogue (one elderly passenger snaps for no particular reason, "Beat generation, bah!" at a crew member), but it's all entertaining stuff. And the film isn't overly melodramatic. There is thankfully little weeping from the characters (except for the daughter, who's continual screams do become annoying). Things happen to Stack and he deals with them quickly, as best he can, without resorting to any monologues. Early in the film, he even says that he won't say "I love you" to his wife because it sounds corny, and that he'd much rather show her. Then he grasps her. Now that's a hero anyone can root for. The sets are large and ornate; the filmmakers were more than likely trying to emulate and draw comparisons to *Titanic*.

The Last Voyage deservedly garnered an Oscar nomination for Best Special Effects. While you can easily see how some of the effects were done, they are still exceptional, and they even top the more sophisticated effects in many '70s disaster movies. For a film that is well over 40 years old, *The Last Voyage* still manages to entertain as an involving and exciting film.

Most Spectacular Moment of Carnage
Sanders finally gets his comeuppance when one of the ships large smokestacks collapses through his quarters, crushing him. But the best death occurs early in the film, during the original explosion, which sends an obvious dummy of a dinner guest flying several feet into the air, to the shock of those around. **(GK)**

A Night to Remember (1958)

Rank Film   123 minutes

HIGHLY RECOMMENDED

⚠

DIRECTOR: Roy Baker

WRITER: Eric Ambler (based on the book by Walter Lord)

CAST: Kenneth More, Ronald Allen, Robert Ayres, Honor Blackman, Anthony Bushell, John Cairney, Jill Dixon, Jane Downs, James Dyrenforth, Michael Goodliffe, Kenneth Griffith, Harriette Johns

Of all of the various incarnations that have been filmed before and since, this version of the events surrounding the sinking of the *Titanic* is likely the best. Filmed in black and white, the picture also combines black-and-white stock footage of the actual ship. Unlike many other *Titanic* movies, this film is devoted to following the facts as closely as possible (at least as the facts were known at the time). There is no family struggle or love story set against the backdrop of the ship sinking.

The main character in this version is Second Officer Kenneth More, who is quickly introduced, as are several passengers who are from either wealthy or impoverished backgrounds. At least this version doesn't focus on the uppity, first-class passengers as most *Titanic* films do, probably because it affords filmmakers the opportunity to display the grandeur of the ship's large dining rooms and main staircase. In this version, both the exceptionally well-realized first-class quarters and the lower decks are shown. There's even a "jigging" scene (pre-dating Kate and Leonardo), in which lower-class passengers request a number from the musicians.

Out on the ocean, the ship the *Californian* is introduced. Its wireless operators spot and begin reporting icebergs. Much attention is paid to wireless operators and the messages sent (and not sent) between them in this movie. The film supposes that, because so much of the *Titanic*'s wireless operators' time was spent sending messages for the passengers, that distraction was the main factor in the sinking. The wireless operators in the *Californian* are also shown listening in on messages sent by passengers, and they are told not to interfere by sending their own messages. In the process, important information about the icebergs that was to be transmitted between the two ships never arrived. This is the only version of the film that I have seen that pays this much attention to the *Carpathia* and the *Californian*, two vessels that were in direct contact with the *Titanic*.

More characters are introduced, and although little backstory is given, there is enough to understand their predicaments. The disaster itself occurs very early in the picture. Just 30 minutes in, the ship hits the iceberg, and from this point on, viewers see the captain, crew, and passengers dealing with the rapid sinking of the ship.

Perhaps the only uncomfortable laugh viewers might experience results from the actions of the watchmen of the *Californian*, just 10 miles from the *Titanic*. Intercut with scenes of the water flooding into the *Titanic* and the passengers fighting for their lives is a shot of the *Californian*'s crew. The *Titanic* sends off several visible distress flares, and the crewmen stare blankly, saying, "Wonder what a ship like that would want to fire rockets for?"

As the passengers realize the seriousness of their predicament, there are many tearful good-byes as husbands hurry their wives onto the lifeboats. As in every other *Titanic* movie ever made, two elderly passengers are introduced, with the wife refusing to leave her husband. But the filmmakers show the third-class passengers fighting and struggling their way up through the hallways and chained gate doors to the first class decks, only to find most of the lifeboats gone. While scenes like this exist in James Cameron's 1997 version, *Titanic*, in *A Night to Remember* such scenes are not used solely as a backdrop to tell another fictional story. This version shows the fates of actual passengers in greater detail, through sequences adapted from accounts by surviving passengers who were interviewed by Walter Lord.

The sets topple to their sides, and water rushes onto the decks. Some passengers are crushed by heavy machinery, while others take panicked dives from the main deck to the ocean below. They crash into the water with loud, very painful-sounding splashes. Tragically, even the ship's pastries aren't safe, as numerous shots show bread and other baked goods crashing off the baking racks to the floor (or wall, by this point) of the ship.

Many of the characters are killed off at this point. After the ship sinks, Second Officer More swims to a capsized boat and takes control, ordering the panicked survivors to stand in a straight line so they don't tip the boat. This was an image I remembered from reading the book as a child.

It's hard to make fun of a film like this. It's well paced, despite being 123 minutes long, and the tone remains serious without seeming dated or campy. As for the special effects, they are for the most part effective (the wide shots of the ship are obvious miniatures, but most of the other water effects still look good). I could see the influence that this version has had on many later adaptations, and in some cases there are shots that are almost identical. This film stills retains a lot of the power it had when it was originally released.

Most Spectacular Moment of Carnage

The filmmakers do their best to shock the audience as the ship goes under. A young couple, who are earlier given advice by the ship's designer on how to survive a sinking vessel, do well enough to climb off the ship and swim out without getting hurt. However, one of the ship's smokestacks collapses, coming down right on top of the screaming couple. (*GK*)

The Poseidon Adventure (1972)

Twentieth Century Fox   117 minutes

RECOMMENDED

⚠

DIRECTOR: Ronald Neame

WRITERS: Wendell Mayes, Stirling Silliphant (based on the novel by Paul Gallico)

CAST: Gene Hackman, Ernest Borgnine, Red Buttons, Carol Lynley, Roddy McDowall, Stella Stevens, Shelley Winters, Jack Albertson, Pamela Sue Martin, Arthur O'Connell, Eric Shea, Leslie Nielsen

If you were trapped on a capsized ocean liner and had to fight your way through the sinking, upturned ship toward possible freedom, or more likely, ignominious death, I doubt you'd look back on the experience as much of an "adventure"; more likely you'd sue the shit out of the cruise line and seek therapy. However this was the '70s, and this was Irwin Allen, and according to him, any tragic event was ripe for plundering for entertainment's sake, and it's a good thing he felt that way or audiences wouldn't have had the star-studded action extravaganza that is *The Poseidon Adventure*.

It doesn't take long for the viewer to discover that the gigantic cruise ship S.S. *Poseidon* is a doomed vessel, for the movie opens with a title card that reads: "At midnight on New Year's Eve, the S.S. *Poseidon*, en route from New York to Athens, met with disaster and was lost. There were only a handful of survivors. This is their story."

And then Irwin Allen begins to lay it on real thick. Viewers find out, as the ship is tossed and turned by high winds and 35-foot waves, that the vessel is top-heavy due to the fact that it has not yet taken on enough ballast. Knowing this, the representative of the ship's management demands that they nonetheless move at full speed to avoid missing a deadline, thereby preventing them from taking on further ballast. To top it off, the ship is named after the Greek god Poseidon, who, as the captain explains, is the god of the seas, storms, tempests, earthquakes, and other miscellaneous natural disasters. Not to mention the fact that this is the *Poseidon*'s final voyage.

Sounds like a trip worth taking, huh?

The first act of the film introduces the characters that matter; as we all know, everyone else in the movie, none of whom are big Hollywood stars, are just dead meat from the get-go, and their stories aren't important. We are left to speculate upon which of the big stars being paraded before us will die as well, and how violently. The cast of stars is very tasty indeed, and the thought of any one of them dying horribly is enough to keep one's interest, er, afloat.

Gene Hackman, fresh off *The French Connection*, plays an angry, nearly defrocked priest on his way to a remote mission in Africa, banished because he likes to tell people not to pray to God to solve their problems. He expresses his intensity by yelling a lot. Ernest Borgnine is a New York detective who flips out at the slightest provocation and who doesn't seem to know how amazingly ugly he is. He expresses his intensity by yelling a lot. Leslie Nielsen is the ship's captain, a stolid man of action, yet he's willing to compromise his sense of duty just to save his own ass. He expresses his intensity by yelling a lot. You know, I still find it hard to take Leslie Nielsen seriously in pre-comedy roles; I know that's unfair, because he put in decades of solid dramatic acting before switching gears in 1980, but I still can't look at him in anything non-comedic without picturing him pulling eggs out of someone's mouth.

Roddy McDowall plays a waiter or something, and apparently he's a really great one, because everyone seems to know his name. Shelley Winters and Jack Albertson play a married couple on their way to Israel to see their grandson for the first time. You know that one of them is definitely going to die because they're on their way to see their grandson for the first time, and they keep talking about it and talking about it. Winters put on 35 pounds for the role, and she's suitably enormous. Red Buttons plays a lonely, unmarried haberdasher who speed walks for fun. Though he seems meek and powerless, he will prove to be heroic later, though the girl he's trying to save (Carol Lynley, playing a rather annoying singer) is so intent on not saving her life that you sometimes wish he'd just leave her there. Stella Stevens plays Borgnine's wife, an ex-hooker whose greatest fear is that someone on the ship might actually recognize her from her days as a streetwalker. Finally, teenager Pamela Sue Martin and precocious preteen Eric Shea play brother and sister traveling alone on their way to meet up with their parents. In the classic tradition of Wil Wheaton on *Star Trek: The Next Generation*, it is Shea who, to a large extent, saves the day, though you will want to pound him for constantly reminding everyone of all the privileged rich white-boy things he's done in his life, like surfing in exotic locales.

The movie chugs along for almost exactly 30 minutes before the sub-sea earthquake hits, which sends a 400-foot wave crashing down on the *Poseidon*. Leslie Nielsen is the first star to die, as water fills the control room. Then, the boat begins to turn over, leading to the famous scene in the ballroom where all the passengers and most of the crew who'd been celebrating the new year now find themselves hanging on for dear life as the room turns upside down. At first it looks very much like the actors are simply straining along with a tilted camera, but upon closer inspection it does appear that the set was actually tilted, as most of the stunt work of people sliding down the floor or hanging off of bolted-down tables is very realistic, as are the sets in general.

In any case, many deaths occur in this scene, though only a few are pictured, and none of the big stars are killed. I quite like the hapless guy who gets crushed by a grand piano, though I'm sure many prefer the cool shot of the guy losing his grip on the table bolted to what is now the ceiling and falling to his death. There's also a giant Christmas tree bolted to the floor that falls from its moorings into the crowd of survivors below and crushes a man as it collapses on its side. Much to my delight, no one helps the man or even reacts in any way to his misfortune.

Hackman appoints himself leader at this point, since the only thing most of the survivors want to do is sit there and wait to be rescued. However, Hackman wants to climb! He's sure that they'll be rescued if they beat the rising water to the propeller shaft, where, as know-it-all Eric Shea explains, the hull is only one inch thick. Since, as Hackman points out, one inch is "one inch thinner than two inches," that's where he decides to go. All the big stars agree to go with him, yet they cannot talk any of the other passengers into coming along.

Hackman and company use the Christmas tree to climb out of the ballroom and into the bowels of the ship. Buttons has to convince Lynley to leave the corpse of her dead brother, the guitarist in her band, behind and climb to safety. In movies like this, it's always a relief when the band dies, for that ensures their annoying song—in this case, a little ditty that promises "there's got to be a morning after"—is never heard again during the movie. Anyway, as the last of them climbs the tree to relative safety, a ballroom wall collapses, filling the room with water, and they all take one last look at the room of drowning people before continuing on their way. Hackman gives a look of tragic concern, though there's also a trace of "I told you so."

Once our remaining heroes reach the next deck, they discover that there are other survivors marching about in eerie silence. I'm not sure where they came from, since I thought everyone was in the ballroom, but oh well. None of them want to follow Hackman, who is certain that they're going the wrong way, toward the end of the ship, which is sinking fastest. His small crew agrees to give Hackman 15 minutes to find a way to the engine room or they're turning around and joining the others, but not before a teeth-gnashing argument between Hackman and Borgnine. The two of them together can rid a room of all scenery, and they're in fine form in this picture. Hackman goes on his way, leaving the others to forage for supplies. Meanwhile, little Shea walks into a bathroom full of upturned urinals and still finds a way to take a leak.

Hackman returns just in time, informing everyone that he's found a way to the engine room, and they follow him just as a wall of water rushes in, threatening to wash them all away. They find that the pathway Hackman found leading to the engine room is now completely flooded, meaning they will have to swim it. Hackman ties a rope to himself and goes first, but halfway through his swim he's trapped by a fallen chunk of metal. It is then found out that Shelley Winters's character used to be a top swimmer in her youth, and that she can hold her breath for minutes on end. She dives in after Hackman, who by this time has been holding his breath much longer than is humanly possible, I would think, and, after rescuing him, the both of them continue to the engine room, which sits above the water. Winters then chooses that particular moment to have a heart attack and die, and she milks it for all it's worth. Quite a nice scene, really. Borgnine appears suddenly, and Hackman sadistically sends him back to get the others, meaning that he will have made the trip three times. They all then end up climbing a rickety catwalk leading to a door that will take them to the propeller shaft. Unfortunately, as they climb, further explosions rock the ship, and Stella Stevens takes a swan dive off of the catwalk, landing hard on the steel girders below, and in a pool of fire to boot.

Borgnine, having witnessed this, gets really pissed. He angrily blames Hackman for his wife's death, seemingly ignoring the fact that she was knocked off of a rickety catwalk by an explosion. Hackman, seeing that the explosion has also set off a valve that is now blocking the doorway with blazing hot steam, decides that it's a good time to sacrifice himself, so he leaps through the air and grabs onto the metal wheel that turns the valve on and off. In an amazing feat of stamina, he hangs on for dear life while at the same time attempting to turn the wheel and shut off the steam. Then, unfortunately, he lets go and dies.

Now, the movie doesn't unfold in real time, but it seems to have very few lengthy temporal gaps. Nevertheless, as they finally emerge from the ship, the survivors are welcomed by the sight of a beautiful day and a rescue helicopter. So . . . they started to climb right after midnight, and now it's morning? Honestly, I don't think it could have taken them five or six hours to reach the propeller shaft, especially when you consider that the ship only has three hours of emergency power and the lights are still on when they get to the engine room. I suppose the sun rises really early in that part of the world. Also, I don't think it's recommended to land a helicopter on top of a sinking, exploding ship. But what do I know, right?

The Poseidon Adventure may have some laughable moments and lapses in logic, but in all fairness, it's a really entertaining movie with genuine suspense. The production design is superb, and it is evident that this was a very physically strenuous film to shoot. It deserves its place in disaster movie history, and though you may chuckle at times, it is never anything less than solid action entertainment. The Poseidon Adventure took home Oscars for both Best Original Song and Special Achievement in Visual Effects.

Most Spectacular Moment of Carnage

The movie is fairly bloodless, and I've already made mention of the most memorable deaths. However, though Shelley Winters's death is not particularly violent, she doesn't escape entirely unscathed. As Hackman holds her dead body and weeps, he suddenly spits all over her face, and that's enough to make anyone cringe. **(MR)**

Raise the Titanic (1980)

Twentieth Century Fox   115 minutes

AVOID AT ALL COSTS

DIRECTOR: Jerry Jameson

WRITERS: Eric Hughes, Adam Kennedy (based on the novel by Clive Cussler)

CAST: Jason Robards, Richard Jordan, David Selby, Anne Archer, Alec Guinness, M. Emmet Walsh, J. D. Cannon, Norman Bartold

How can anyone possibly make a disaster movie this dreary? You would expect a $30 million epic of this magnitude to actually be interesting. Adapted (poorly, one hopes) from Clive Cussler's bestseller, the plot concerns a Cold War-era race between American and Russian agents to find the made-up mineral byzanium. Why would anyone want this? To make the deadly byzanium bomb, of course. What does a byzanium bomb do? Beats the heck out of me. The U.S. government tells our heroes it's for a top-secret defense project. Whatever the case, viewers will soon learn that the only place to find byzanium is at the bottom of the Atlantic (good choice of mineral, guys! Isn't that something you should have thought about during the design phase of the project?), stored on the *Titanic*.

Our two unlikable heroes, Richard Jordan as the "man of action" and David Selby as the scientific "thinker" (he likes to drop model boats of the *Titanic* into tanks of water to try to determine the real vessel's location), waste time hypothesizing and searching for the whereabouts of the ship. All the while, Jason Robards expounds on the political importance of finding the mineral before the other guys do. What follows is a competition between Robards and Selby to see who can have the longest, most boring expository sequences in the film. It's a toss-up.

As if this isn't dry enough, there's also a love triangle subplot: Selby's reporter girlfriend, played by Anne Archer, was once involved with Richard Jordan's character. Thankfully, this story line is abruptly dropped without any resolution an hour into the film. Just as the audience is about to nod off for good, the *Titanic* is discovered. But by this point, I didn't care. What are supposed to be incredible moments of discovery, like when Jordan finds a smokestack in the ocean, just aren't all that exciting. If it blew up, or maybe if aliens swam out of it, that would be exciting. Neither of those things happens.

To make a really long story short, the *Titanic* is raised and tugged into New York Harbor for the film's "money shot." And guess what? It looks like a big model. Wherever they claimed to put that $30 million, it couldn't have been into special effects. Maybe they spent it on the underwater photography, although those scenes all looked so murky I'd have a lot of trouble believing that.

After Jordan and Selby finish thumping around on the ship's decks like they're in McDonald's Playland, they discover the vault they're looking for, resulting in a preposterous anticlimax. Oh, and as for the resolution of the political intrigue with the Russians, they're scared away by a sub and two air force jets that fly overhead. Huh? And what will the government do now with the historic liner? One assumes it'll be left in the harbor as a new tourist attraction.

What might be most interesting for those watching the film today is catching the historical inaccuracies (which, naturally, no one could have known at the time). I mean, tugging the *Titanic* into New York is ridiculous enough. Knowing today that the ship was split into parts makes it all the more preposterous. Nobody in the film seems remotely interested in the historical significance of finding the *Titanic*, either. The search for byzamium (like anybody cares) takes center stage. All the characters come off as just a bunch of jerks.

The film garnered several Razzie nominations upon its release, which should come as no surprise to anyone who's seen the movie. If you ask me, this film is a greater weapon than any byzanium bomb could have even been! ZZzzzzzzz.

Most Spectacular Moment of Carnage
There's nothing in this movie that even remotely approaches spectacular. There is an undersea mishap in which a Starfish Sea Probe goes too deep, floods, and implodes, killing three. It's hard to see. **(GK)**

S.O.S. *Titanic* (1979)

EMI   97 minutes

AT YOUR OWN RISK

DIRECTOR: William Hale

WRITER: James Costigan

CAST: David Janssen, Cloris Leachman, Susan Saint James, David Warner, Ian Holm, Helen Mirren, Harry Andrews, Beverly Ross

This little-seen British made-for-TV movie is yet another interesting if unspectacular take on the *Titanic* sinking. After the opening credits began to crawl across the screen in a style similar to those of the late-'70s TV movie *Hurricane*, I began to worry. But, thankfully, the film production value here is much better than it is in that film. And it has a solid cast.

Ian Holm portrays White Star Line chairman Ismay with some humanity, unlike all of the other versions of the story, which always seem to present him as a complete and utter moustache-twirling scumbag from the moment he's introduced. As his character leads the viewer through the ship, a few things are shown that no other versions have bothered to, like a working exercise room. OK, so a couple of guys bouncing a ball and riding primitive exercise bikes is nothing spectacular, but after viewing four or five of these films in a row, I'll take anything off of the beaten path.

David Warner and Susan Saint James play second-class passengers and school-teachers Laurence Beasley and Leigh Goodwin. Their romantic escapades are the most refined and awkward captured on film since those displayed in *Remains of the Day*. Most amusing is the fact that David Warner typically portrays mad scientists, crazy persons, and villains in horror films, and to see him playing a shy, genteel schoolteacher seems odd, to say the least. He and Susan Saint James pull it off well, however, even though it does become something of a chore to sit through after a while. "We're both cautious," Saint James remarks, which may be the understatement of the millennium.

It's obvious that this production doesn't have as big a budget as some of the other versions, but the filmmakers do a decent job of covering it up. There is rarely any use of wide shots on deck, and cameras seem to be placed low and angled upward most of the time. The film thankfully avoids cutting back to cheesy shots of the *Titanic* at sea like other adaptations, which was probably due to the lack of money needed to produce such a shot. Incoming water is shown sparingly, but it eventually builds as the ship starts to sink. Finally, as passengers are taken to the lifeboats, the water begins flooding through empty cabins. All of this actually works to the film's benefit.

There's a minor subplot involving some third-class passengers who make their way up to the second-class deck. After reaching the first-class dining room, they all pause to admire its beauty. Almost all of the *Titanic* films have a scene like this late in the movie, so it will have little impact if you've seen it many times before. Hilariously, an armed security guard appears and, thinking they are "looters," gives them all a gruff talking to. Not much of what he says makes any sense, but the fact that anyone listens to his rant is amusing. In the end, the women are allowed to pass, while the men stay to await their fates.

If you like stories of unrequited love in true British fashion, this might be your movie. It is an agreeable little title.

Most Spectacular Moment of Carnage

The violence is kept to a minimum, and most of the action occurs when the ship sinks. Passengers jump over the rails in panic; others are blown over the side of the ship; some are shown trapped as the waters flood the hallways inside the ship. But my favorite shot involves a runaway piano, which is for some reason on the main deck. It knocks a few people around as it slides down into the ocean. **(GK)**

Speed 2: Cruise Control (1997)

Twentieth Century Fox   125 minutes

AT YOUR OWN RISK

DIRECTOR: Jan de Bont

WRITERS: Randall McCormick, Jeff Nathanson

CAST: Sandra Bullock, Jason Patric, Willem Dafoe, Temuera Morrison, Brian McCardie, Michael C. Hagerty, Colleen Camp, Lois Chiles, Bo Svenson, Glenn Plummer, Tim Conway

As hard as this sequel tries, it just doesn't live up to the entertaining, fast-paced original. Once again, there's a mode of transport speeding out of control. The difference is that this time it's a boat. The bus in the original allowed the characters to interact within a tight space on heavily populated streets. There was danger around every corner, and none of the passengers could get off the bus. The sea, of course, is much less populated, and in this film people disappear and reappear on various levels of the decks without explanation. None of this helps in terms of building tension.

The film opens with a driver's examination sequence. As Sandra Bullock takes her road test, she actually causes accidents. This is strange, considering that she seemed to be a fairly capable bus driver in the first movie—at least she was able to stay on one side of the road. Even stranger is the fact that instructor Tim Conway chooses not to stop her or tell her to pull over. I assume that this is all supposed to be hysterically funny, but starting the movie with Bullock's glib reactions to hitting objects and almost killing other drivers doesn't sit well.

Meanwhile, Bullock's new boyfriend, Jason Patric, is involved in an elaborate police chase. The two cars cross paths amid the chaos, upsetting Bullock when she spots him driving a police car. Apparently, up until this point Patric had lied about his job, but he is really a "suicide squad" LAPD cop, whatever the heck that is. Fortunately for him, Patric suddenly pulls out a pair of tickets for a Caribbean cruise and calms the upset Bullock. Does he always carry expensive cruise tickets with him on special assignments? Did he pick them up during the chase?

On board the cruise ship is one creepy dude named Geiger who is out to steal valuable jewels. Played by Willem Dafoe, this character is supposedly dying from copper poisoning (a bizarre condition I've never heard of), and he regularly dumps slugs all over his body. He's also a computer whiz and a maniac who has hidden many explosive devices within the golf clubs and balls that he carries around the liner. Also introduced are several typical bickering couples, a deaf girl, a cruise photographer, an annoying bellhop, and the band UB40, who are busy playing their famous brand of easy-listening reggae in the dinner hall. Before long, Dafoe takes control of the ship via his various computers, and he uses sensor controls to give the impression of fire in the boat.

Dafoe shuts the boat down and declares that all have 15 minutes to evacuate the liner. The parents of the deaf girl board a lifeboat despite the fact that they can't find their daughter. I'm not a parent, but I don't believe that I would do that. Unfortunately for those getting on the final lifeboat, Patric bickers with the first officer about what's happening long enough for time to run out and the boat to get stuck and hang precariously above the water.

Actually, all that follows seems to be Patric's fault. By standing on the boat and arguing, he puts the remaining passengers back on the ship and their lives in danger. Just because he's a suicide squad cop doesn't mean *everyone* has to be. He could have hopped off and dealt with the situation himself, or perhaps even got on the lifeboat and alerted the authorities. After all, one of these rich fat cats must have a cell phone on them! By allowing Dafoe to steal the goods and leave, the authorities could have boarded and evacuated any stragglers and shut the ship down. But of course, if Patric did the smart thing, there wouldn't be a movie.

Patric also has an interesting way of trying to stop the ship. He begins by racing down to the engine room, smashing a monitor, and randomly pressing buttons on the control panel. He is quickly advised that this is a bad idea, so instead he begins flooding the engine room with water to slow the ship. There is a series of misadventures when Patric and Bullock find and retrieve passengers on the ship, like the little girl who has almost drowned by the waters Patric has allowed to flood in. All of this action is shot in a shaky, handheld style that could not be more irritating. To all of the filmmakers who think that shaking a camera adds a degree of realism to the film: it doesn't. All it does is make us aware of the camera. It also makes it impossibly hard to figure out what's happening. You're spending all of this money on sets, effects, and pyrotechnics, and we can't see any of it!

While Patric has to deal with the aftereffects of rashly flooding the engine room, the ship heads toward the densely populated St. Martin Harbor. At one point a water-skier crashes into the side of the boat with a painful thud. This leads to a spectacular crash in which the cruise liner smashes through some boats (one even explodes) and plows through the dock into the town. Panicked crowds run as the ship takes down every building in its path. The sequence is well shot and does look amazing, although it is drawn out for nearly 10 minutes. And again, there are silly gags as people react in completely unrealistic ways. Despite efforts to show people running away, there can be no doubt that at least some of the folks in these structures have been killed, and that makes the humor all the more misplaced.

This problem with tone that plagues *Speed 2* continues to the end, when, back in Los Angeles, Bullock takes yet another driving test with Conway. As the car speeds away, the movie fades to black, and we hear the sound of screeching tires and a loud crash. Again, this is supposed to be hilarious, but it only left me with the impression that Bullock and her driving instructor had been killed by a large truck. The performances are fine and the film is technically impressive, but there are too many plot holes and too much inappropriate humor. Most importantly, the movie can't sustain our suspension of disbelief enough to make it enjoyable. This film won a Razzie for Worst Remake or Sequel.

Most Spectacular Moment of Carnage

Willem Dafoe's death is incredibly elaborate. He crashes his plane into a large flag-pole (at least, that's what I think it is) on a nearby tanker. Gas leaks out and the plane explodes, blowing up not only Dafoe, but also the entire tanker. Dafoe seems to find this incredibly funny, and he dies with a huge grin on his face. Despite this, the most disturbing moment might really come when Patric gets seasick. Get ready for a dandy shot of him lying in bed next to a pail of vomit. **(GK)**

Titanic (1953)

Twentieth Century Fox   93 minutes

AT YOUR OWN RISK

⚠

DIRECTOR: Jean Negulesco

WRITERS: Charles Brackett, Richard Breen, Walter Reisch

CAST: Clifton Webb, Barbara Stanwyck, Robert Wagner, Audrey Dalton, Thelma Ritter, Brian Aherne

Anybody who thought James Cameron's *Titanic* went overboard in the romance department needs to take a look at this 1953 version, which is interesting enough and was very well shot and produced for its day, but it plays more like a domestic drama than a disaster movie. I can understand why it was awarded an Oscar for Best Writing, Story and Screenplay, since all anyone in the movie seems to do is talk.

The film opens with menacing shots of the iceberg that will sink the ship, and a title card explaining that "all general navigational data on the sinking of the ship has been taken and adapted verbatim." Not only does this not make much sense, but it's an easy claim to make, considering that the movie pays little attention to "general navigational data"; in fact, it's never referred to again, and the events surrounding the sinking of the ocean liner are used only as backdrop to the main story.

Barbara Stanwyck plays Julia, a rich socialite on the run from her estranged husband. She boards with her young son and her beautiful but stuck-up daughter. Other characters are introduced, including Thelma Ritter, who is clearly essaying the role of Molly Brown. The sets, including the giant dining room, a lounge, the engine room, and the main stairway, are quite impressive, as is the filmmaker's attention to detail.

The film cuts back to land and Stanwyck's husband, who bribes a ticket off of the father of an immigrant family and boards the ship. Once out at sea, he comes up from the lower decks to the first-class area and confronts Stanwyck, who, as it turns out, has secretly tried to steal the children away from Paris and their boorish father to America. There, she believes, they can grow up normally and not be spoiled and obnoxious for the rest of their lives, like their father. Stanwyck even correctly describes her daughter as "an arrogant little prig." And for her son, she states that there will be no more horse-drawn carriages; he will have to walk to school. This is all well and good, but it sounds strange coming from a glamorous socialite dressed up in a fancy party gown. If she really felt this way, why didn't she buy second- or third-class tickets? Regardless, I suppose she has the right idea, and she is the most sympathetic character up to this point.

Aghast at what he discovers, the husband storms away to the lounge for what must be a 36-hour poker marathon. While all of this is going on, there's an incredibly funny romantic subplot developing, in which a young passenger named "Gifford" (or just "Giff," to his friends), played by Robert Wagner, pursues Stanwyck's daughter. Another one of Stanwyck's reasons for leaving her husband is to save her daughter from an arranged marriage to some "toad" back in Paris. Stanwyck likes Wagner, and she wishes her daughter would meet and marry someone less pretentious and upper-class than the Frenchman. Someone more like Wagner, who wears a turtleneck with a giant "P" on the front signifying his college, Purdue. Wagner tells the daughter of his adventures on the tennis squad and that he is on his way home with the team after losing a tournament with Oxford. Wagner also has a fondness for smoking pipes and wearing sports jackets. Seems like a real salt-of-the-earth type, doesn't he? Despite the fact that this guy seems no less pretentious than anyone else, at least he is friendly and upbeat (so upbeat that he might even be on uppers). Naturally, he wins the heart of Stanwyck's daughter with his ruffian charm, at one point even teaching her "the hottest jig the kids do."

You start to hope, while all of this is happening, that the ship might actually be sinking, and that none of the characters have just noticed it yet. I was half expecting to see some other passengers running through the background screaming while Stanwyck and her husband have yet another argument about yet another "inexcusable breach of etiquette." But, alas, there's still no sinking going on.

Finally, with little more than 20 minutes left in the movie, the ship strikes the iceberg. The effects are acceptable, but unspectacular. In wide shots the boat looks like a model. These shots are also used much too frequently, as if to remind audiences that this is the *Titanic*, in case anyone has forgotten. However, later shots of lifeboats being lowered into the water from what must be a two-story set are impressive. There are several long, tearful farewells. Most amusing is Wagner's; he says his goodbye to Stanwyck's daughter, then attempts to free a tangled lifeboat and falls into the ocean face first.

While the film definitely has merits, it's a little too dated and slow for today's audiences, and the melodrama is a bit too over-the-top for my tastes.

Most Spectacular Moment of Carnage

The film is very tame, the sinking of the *Titanic* itself is short, and no one dies onscreen. Wagner's fall is the best stunt, but a drunken priest's death is the most amusing. After hearing an explosion below deck, presumably from the engine room, the priest is warned not to go down there "for God's sake!" He announces that he must go down for that very reason, takes two steps inside, and is presumably blown to smithereens as another explosion sounds and smoke and debris come up from below. **(GK)**

Titanic (1996)

Hallmark Entertainment 173 minutes

AT YOUR OWN RISK

⚠

DIRECTOR: Robert Lieberman

WRITERS: Ross LaManna, Joyce Eliason

CAST: Peter Gallagher, George C. Scott, Catherine Zeta-Jones, Eva Marie Saint, Tim Curry, Roger Rees, Harley Jane Kozak, Marilu Henner, Mike Doyle, Sonsee Ahray

This TV miniseries may as well be called "Harlequin Romance's *Titanic*." At two and three-quarter hours, it's just too much soap-opera romance for a guy to take.

First, the movie introduces an Irish nanny who's clearly got mental problems. She has nightmares about the upcoming trip, is visibly nervous, and emits a general strangeness. Despite these obvious drawbacks and against all logic, Harley Jane Kozak sees this nanny as a fitting choice to look after her children. Kozak eventually decides that the nanny's behavior is inappropriate, but her doltish husband asks to give her a second chance.

There's also a young "thief" with somewhat limited stealing skills. After snatching a passed-out passenger's ticket, he boards the vessel and is greeted by a snarky, snarling purser, played by Tim Curry, who feels that the thief would be his perfect partner in crime. Why the purser would need a hand to enter an empty cabin, steal a tiara, then hide and recover it later is beyond me.

While this is going on, we also become embroiled in a "forbidden" romance between the happily married Isabella Paradine—Catherine Zeta-Jones—and her long-lost ex-boyfriend, Wynn Park, played by Peter Gallagher (the actor, not the '70s watermelon-squashing wacky comedian). *Ham* is the operative word for these two every time they share a scene together. Between the various melodramas, there are brief sequences in the wireless room involving the iceberg warnings. George C. Scott, who plays Captain Smith, seems to spend much of the movie walking around the ship and talking to the lead characters as their relationships progress in a manner not unlike a grizzled Captain Stubing from *The Love Boat*. He even allows characters to wander the bridge and steer the ship around for their amusement.

The thief steals a tuxedo and strolls among the upper-class passengers before he falls in love with a young Danish woman in steerage class, who is traveling to Minnesota with a group of religious converts. There are numerous scenes of this romance, intercut with Zeta-Jones's and Gallagher's love scenes, between the fade-outs to what were commercial breaks when this flick aired on TV (I started hoping that there would be some commercials on the tape to break up the monotony). The pacing of the movie is extraordinarily slow, and the ship doesn't even hit the iceberg until the 80-minute mark (which, presumably, would be at the end of the first night). Zeta-Jones sends off a wireless message to her husband telling him of her plans to run away with Gallagher and marry him. This is especially interesting considering the fact that she has nothing bad to say about her absentee husband, whom she describes as a proud but extremely kind man.

In a fairly tasteless scene, the purser decides to rape the young Danish girl, which leads to a break in his partnership with the young thief. The thief concludes that stealing from people is a bad thing, and he rushes up to help the young girl to the lifeboats. Despite the fact that they are both third-class passengers, they are allowed through the gates to the main deck above. The thief sends her off, then trips himself and falls off of the boat and into another lifeboat (shades of Robert Wagner in a previous *Titanic* adaptation).

Tim Curry, who by this point is overacting to the level of a stand-up comic, grins devilishly, wraps himself up in a long black sheet, and poses as a woman before jumping into a lifeboat undetected. After the young Danish woman recognizes him, he immediately pulls a gun. Hilariously, after he is bashed in the head with a boat oar, Curry contorts his face to make a comical, cartoonish expression. Before the audience has the chance to see the stars and tweeting birds spin around Curry's head, he collapses into the icy water and dies.

The melodramatic score swells by this point, as those left behind on the ship (including Gallagher) meet their fates. The ship's sinking is shown through a series of unimpressive dissolves, most of which involve close-ups of splashing water and trays, cans, and other objects overturning.

The visual effects are poor, with the *Carpathia*'s arrival in New York taking the dubious honor of worst digital effect shot in this production. The main deck of the ship was clearly built inside of a studio, and the whole thing seems like it was very quickly slapped together. The miniseries managed to garner a couple of minor Emmy nominations, but it's not really worth bothering with, I'm afraid.

Most Spectacular Moment of Carnage

The whole movie is really quite tame; the most disturbing event occurs when the young thief pulls a dead passenger into the lifeboat and showers him with kisses, for some reason thinking him to be his young Danish sweetheart. Creepy. (**GK**)

Titanic (1997)

Paramount   194 minutes

HIGHLY RECOMMENDED

⚠

DIRECTOR: James Cameron

WRITER: James Cameron

CAST: Leonardo DiCaprio, Kate Winslet, Billy Zane, Kathy Bates, Frances Fisher, Gloria Stuart, Bill Paxton, Bernard Hill, David Warner, Victor Garber, Jonathan Hyde, Suzy Amis

Titanic holds the distinctions of being not only the longest disaster film reviewed in this book and the most expensive film production ever (to date), but also of being the highest-grossing film of all time (at least, as of 2005) and the most critically successful disaster film ever made. It swept up 11 Oscars for Best Picture; Best Director; Best Cinematography; Best Art Direction-Set Direction; Best Costume Design; Best Music, Original Dramatic Score; Best Film Editing; Best Effects, Visual Effects; Best Sound; Best Effects, Sound Effects Editing; and Best Music, Original Song.

The film starts at present day, with salvager Bill Paxton attempting to discover a lost jewel (referred to as the "Heart of the Ocean") from a necklace that he believes to be locked away in a safe inside the wrecked ship. There's some haunting footage of the actual ship under water, which was shot by Cameron himself.

To Paxton's disappointment, the necklace isn't found, but watching a news report about the operation is an elderly survivor named Rose—played by Gloria Stuart—who knows what became of it. Rose is flown in and spins her tale to the salvager—and the audience—for the next three hours. I suppose this part is realistic, as anyone who has a grandparent can relate to their telling ass-numbingly long stories that seem to have no end. Well, at least hers is about something interesting.

Rose as a privileged young girl is played by Kate Winslet. She is traveling with her fiancé, Cal, played by Billy Zane, and her extremely stuffy mother, played by Frances Fisher. Socialite Winslet is sick of the "endless parade of parties and cotillions, yachts and polo matches" (aren't we all?). Cue the first shot of artist/transient Jack Dawson, played by Leonardo DiCaprio, and his buddy, Fabrizio, who win steerage tickets in a card game and rush to make it on the ship just as it sets sail. (DiCaprio's buddy has gotta reala thicka Italian-accent, and he disappears soon after getting onboard, but reappears later to meet his end ina reallya nasty waya when he getsa flattened lika pizza by a smokestack.)

The film quickly focuses on the story of Winslet's and DiCaprio's forbidden love, which begins when DiCaprio foils her suicide attempt. As the two become closer, DiCaprio proudly shows off his sketches of one-legged prostitutes, teaches the art of spitting, and shows her how to hang over the rails of large ocean liners. It should be noted that the deck of the *Titanic* is barely populated in many of these scenes, which doesn't make a whole lot of sense, but it isn't anything that you would notice unless you had just watched four other *Titanic* films. Most of these movies really fall off of the rails when they put so much emphasis on melodrama and not enough on the story of the boat itself, but in this case it serves to prove just how talented the performers are that I wasn't bored by it.

Meanwhile, the shifty Zane and his henchman Lovejoy, played by David Warner (in his second major *Titanic* film), are in possession of the famed jewel, and Zane tries to offer it to Winslet as a gift. He forbids Winslet to see third-class passenger DiCaprio. Naturally, she runs off with Leo. Winslet convinces DiCaprio to sketch her in the nude (not that it should take much convincing), and the two consummate their love.

Finally, the story of the boat comes to the forefront, with two watchmen looking for icebergs. Unfortunately, they're distracted by the sight of DiCaprio and Winslet kissing outside on the main deck. The film actually suggests that, because these guys were busy watching DiCaprio and Winslet make out, they didn't see the iceberg in time. Therefore, DiCaprio and Winslet are indirectly responsible for the *Titanic* sinking! Regardless, this silliness is quickly forgotten as the ship hits the iceberg, which tears a hole along the vessel's starboard side.

The remainder of the film involves our heroes trying to make their way from the lower to the upper deck as the water pours in from all around. The effects are spectacular. Not only do the wide exterior shots of the ship slowly sinking look phenomenal, but there are also spectacular shots of water crashing through doors and flooding the beautifully ornate interior sets. In particular, there's a thrilling sequence involving a long hallway, DiCaprio, Winslet, a father and his child, and a powerful wave of water.

The two eventually make it back upstairs and face off with Billy Zane. Zane, who is particularly upset at this point, brandishes a gun. It's amazing that Cameron manages to maintain our suspension of belief at this point. As far as I've read, at no point during the actual sinking of the actual *Titanic* was a passenger chasing people through crowds of evacuees and firing loaded weapons at them. But this director shoots and cuts action exceptionally well, and the last hour of the movie moves at an extremely brisk pace, remaining exciting to the end.

The sinking itself is chilling. Passengers slide down the side of the boat as it tips upward and breaks in half. Unlike in other versions, swimmers are shown being sucked back into the boat as the water crashes through the windows. All of this is horrifying and extremely well executed.

Unfortunately, Kathy Bates's Molly Brown, a character who in all of the other versions takes charge of a lifeboat and sweeps back to pick up passengers, is ineffective in this movie, and she's simply told to sit down and "shut up."

The story ends back in the present day with the teary-eyed salvagers, though it's a wonder that no one responds, "Well ma'am, that's fine and all, but that's not what we asked you." The incident involving the tossing of the jewel back into the ocean is one that I've never really understood, since the necklace itself seemed to hold little significance to Winslet and DiCaprio, and its monetary value could likely feed a starving nation. Regardless, many people are moved by this, and as the old woman lies down (presumably for the last time), Cameron manages some haunting visuals of the ship and the characters who lost their lives on it.

Yes, despite my jokes, this is an exceptional film, and I can understand why it was so successful. Every demographic is appealed to, from teenage girls (who came to see DiCaprio) to *Titanic* history buffs to disaster film buffs. This resulted in a take of over $600 million domestically and more than $1.2 billion around the world.

Most Spectacular Moment of Carnage
As the rear of the *Titanic* stands up and bobs, characters hanging on for dear life, but fall. Not only do they fall an incredible distance, but they seem to hit various railings and other objects on the way down. Most horrible and painful-looking is a man who jumps off of the boat and bounces off the ship's propeller on the way down before landing into the icy water with a loud splash. **(GK)**

Sub Down (1997)
USA Pictures   93 minutes

AVOID AT ALL COSTS

Those who thought *Gray Lady Down* was an underappreciated masterpiece will certainly have more ammo after watching this loser. Stephen Baldwin, Gabrielle Anwar, and Tom Conti play scientific geniuses studying the effects of global warming while on a naval submarine under the Bering Strait. After an accidental crash between two subs, the crew must fight fire, a lack of power and oxygen, and a bad script. Conti attempts to get to the surface in his own mini-sub but is killed when it depressurizes, leaving our two remaining heroes to pilot the nuclear sub to the surface. They do, just in time to watch whales splashing around. This still doesn't explain how they plan to signal anyone of their distress in the middle of ice-covered Arctic waters, but you won't care by this point. You'll just be happy that it's over. Directed by "Alan Smithee," the pseudonym used when a director is too embarrassed with the final product or has had disagreements over the film with producers. In any case, it may as well translate to "really bad movie." **(GK)**

Voyage to the Bottom of the Sea (1961)
Twentieth Century Fox   105 minutes

RECOMMENDED

Although director Irwin Allen wouldn't fully establish his disaster movie formula for another decade, the seeds of it can be seen in this disaster movie masquerading as a sci-fi adventure flick. Stars Water Pidgeon, Joan Fontaine, Barbara Eden, Peter Lorre,

Robert Sterling, Michael Ansara, and Frankie Avalon (who croons the title theme) make up the nuclear submarine crew who must save the world from a "ring of fire" that threatens to burn up the earth. They must do this by launching a nuclear rocket and pushing the flames into outer space. That is, if they aren't eaten by the giant squid along the way. While the tidal waves and fires that are supposedly occurring around the world aren't shown, the film does have everything else genre fans could hope for, including an end-of-the-world scenario, goofy scientific explanations of what is going on and how to stop it, characters who must make sacrifices to save the mission, romance, a musical theme, and even elaborate deaths—including a character who is radiated and then eaten by a shark. With impressive effects and nice CinemaScope widescreen photography, this Saturday-matinee-with-popcorn flick is a lot of fun. **(GK)**

RARE, OBSCURE, AND LESS IMPORTANT TITLES

Atlantic (1929)

Brittanic (2000) Made-for-TV

Final Voyage (1999) Straight-to-video

Killer on Board (1977) Made-for-TV

Morning Departure (1950)

Perilous Voyage (1976) Made-for-TV

The Ship That Couldn't Stop (1961) Made-for-TV

Survive the Savage Sea (1992) Made-for-TV

Titanic (1943)

Titanic: The Animated Movie (2001) Straight-to-video

Voyage of Terror (1998) Made-for-TV

DON'T BE A HERO: THE DISASTER MOVIE'S HARDEST LESSON

If you're ever caught in an earthquake, or a flood, or a volcanic eruption, or if you happen to be trapped in a tunnel or are otherwise caught in the middle of any cataclysmic scenario, remember this one important tip for survival: never help anybody. It's one of the perverse delights of disaster movies that those people who try to be heroes generally end up seriously injured or dead. And how big a movie star you might be has absolutely no bearing on your chances of survival, especially if you're surrounded by other movie stars vying for attention. Unless you happen to be a dog, the odds are not in your favor. To wit:

In *The Poseidon Adventure*, Shelley Winters makes a dangerous underwater rescue when Gene Hackman gets trapped underneath a heavy piece of metal; after saving him, she promptly dies of a heart attack. Later, Hackman risks his life to shut off a steam valve, allowing everyone else to escape before he falls to his death below. In *The Towering Inferno*, Robert Vaughn desperately tries to stop a crazed Richard Chamberlain from possible death when Chamberlain grabs onto a harness on a cable strung between that building and a nearby one and pushes himself out the window; Vaughn tries to pull him back, but they both end up falling to their deaths moments later.

In *Earthquake*, heroic Canadian Lorne Greene, in spite of his age and his prodigious smoke inhalation, refuses to leave his office until he's helped everyone else escape, and then he himself is finally rescued, only to die later of a heart attack. You're welcome, Lorne. In the same film, Charlton Heston crawls through collapsing rubble to rescue a bunch of people trapped in an underground parking garage, and once he's done this, he's swept away by a torrent of water, never to be seen again. In *Juggernaut*, one member of a bomb squad, on his way to defuse a series of explosives on a cruise ship, is killed before he even gets to the ship, and others are blown to bits later on when their defusing efforts go awry.

In *Miracle Mile*, Anthony Edwards tries to warn everyone of the impending nuclear disaster as well as save Mare Winningham from certain death. Unfortunately, over the course of the film he gets held at gunpoint several times, is forced to jump from a speeding truck onto a freeway off ramp, nearly gets hit by a car, is shot at, survives a nuclear blast, crashes into the La Brea tar pits in a crippled helicopter, and finally, as he drowns, is incinerated by another nuclear explosion. Was she worth it, Anthony? In addition, the pilot of the helicopter ends up dying along with Edwards and Winningham only because he came back to save them as he had promised to do. Big mistake!

In *Tornado!*, L. Q. Jones unwisely ventures back into the storm to try to hammer an important scientific instrument into the ground, and he is soon gone from this world. In *Independence Day*, Randy Quaid is forced to go on a suicide mission when his fighter jet's missile won't launch and he's humanity's last hope. His death leaves his three children orphaned. In *Daylight*, Sylvester Stallone is about to finally escape from the tunnel, but he ends up trapped once again with no way out because he tries to rescue a dog. He's not killed, of course, but he is forced to find an even more complicated and dangerous escape, and he nearly drowns as a result.

In *Volcano*, a heroic guy leaps into a trapped subway car, which is slowly being engulfed by lava, in order to save the unconscious driver; he manages to throw the driver to safety but ends up dying horribly when he leaps from the train into a pool of lava. In *Titanic*, Leonardo DiCaprio insists that Kate Winslet, and not he, float to safety on a chunk of debris, ensuring that he will freeze to death within the hour.

In *Armageddon*, man of steel Bruce Willis, after busting his ass to save Earth from a runaway asteroid, ends up being the only person capable of setting off a nuclear explosion, which will destroy the asteroid and him with it. In *The Perfect Storm*, a rescue helicopter trying to save a family trapped on a boat in the storm ends up crashing, eventually leading to the drowning death of one of the pilots.

If, with these examples, I can save even one life by inspiring someone not to lift a finger to help someone else, then I've done my job. **(MR)**

Big Space Rocks

Movies about big space rocks have always had dramatic potential. What cataclysmic events would be caused if a meteor struck Earth? How would the characters try to avert destruction? What crazy stuff would people do knowing that the end of the world was fast approaching? The subject matter has always been ripe, but to be honest, I haven't been satisfied with the results so far. I mean, if you were to think of your favorite disaster movies of all time, do any of them involve comets or asteroids? I think the problem is that, in some cases, there's too much plot leading up to five minutes of special effects at the end. In others, there's too much action and not enough plot (which isn't as severe a flaw, because at least it's fun). No, the perfect balance hasn't been struck yet. Not that this should sour you on all these titles; you might enjoy some of them anyway. Just don't expect the best that disaster has to offer, OK? (**GK**)

Armageddon (1998)

Touchstone Pictures   151 minutes

AT YOUR OWN RISK

DIRECTOR: Michael Bay

WRITERS: Jonathan Hensleigh, J. J. Abrams

CAST: Bruce Willis, Billy Bob Thornton, Ben Affleck, Liv Tyler, Will Patton, Steve Buscemi, William Fichtner, Owen Wilson, Michael Clarke Duncan, Peter Stormare, Keith David, Udo Kier, Charlton Heston (narrator)

From the hyperactive director of *Bad Boys* and *The Rock* comes *Armageddon*, a film that harnesses just about every visual effects technique ever devised to bring you the supremely indifferent experience of watching really good actors squander their talents while cracking unfunny jokes and ducking explosions. While it's not a total pooch screw on the level of *The Avengers* (1998) or *Lost in Space* (1998), *Armageddon* nonetheless numbs the mind with nonstop action supporting the flimsiest of material.

Right off the top, the words *produced by Jerry Bruckheimer* ought to tell you a lot. Too much isn't nearly enough for this guy. And director Michael Bay brings his trademark sledgehammer-like touch to every scene. He's of the mind that the more you move the camera unnecessarily and the faster you cut scenes without regard to pacing, the better your movie will be! The script was cobbled together from the work of more than seven writers above and beyond those credited, including, amazingly, Robert Towne, whose previous work includes *Shampoo* and *Chinatown*. And one of the film's many producers is none other than Gale Anne Hurd, who is partly responsible for some of the best action movies ever made (including *The Terminator* and *Aliens*), but this isn't one of them.

The basic plot of *Armageddon* is this: an asteroid the size of Texas is heading toward Earth, and the only way to stop it is to send a drilling crew out to the asteroid to plant a nuclear device deep inside of it. NASA enlists the help of the best oil driller in the world, Harry Stamper, played by Bruce Willis. He brings in his crew of roughnecks to back him up. That's it. That's what supports two-and-a-half hours of visual effects.

The picture is lengthened by unconvincing moments of romance between Willis's daughter and the youngest, best-looking member of his crew—Liv Tyler and Ben Affleck, respectively—which of course Willis disapproves of. So much so that after catching them in bed together, Willis chases Affleck with a loaded shotgun and shoots at him, blowing holes in his own oil rig. I understand that audiences are supposed to think this is funny, and that it's critical in terms of getting the audience to understand that Willis is a hotheaded cowboy; a man just crazy enough to take the job of saving the planet. Yeah, OK.

I think the only reason Tyler is in this picture is so that the filmmakers could secure the use of the Aerosmith songs that underscore dramatic moments. I also think anyone who's ever heard an Aerosmith song understands that only a very special kind of film dares to underscore a dramatic moment with the rock stylings of Steven Tyler. However, such a musical decision fits well with the overblown score by Hans Zimmer clone Trevor Rabin. If you need big, broad action music without a single shade of subtlety, I guess it's good to know where you can go to find it.

We all know that in a movie like this, the asteroid is obviously not going to collide with Earth, but some degree of devastation is expected. So there are numerous scenes in which major cities are leveled by smaller pieces of rock that have broken away from the huge, bilious mass of gas and rock and ice heading our way. New York City is the first to get a taste of the action; its skyscrapers are ripped apart, and cars and bodies are thrown about. Even the Empire State Building is toppled. But the story is not about those poor New Yorkers, and after this initial scene of carnage, the filmmakers never go back there. In fact, no one ever mentions it again, as if it never happened.

Singapore gets hammered next, followed by Paris, and somehow it doesn't seem like a big deal, like it's all going to be OK. The aftermath of these tragedies is never shown because it's all merely icing on the cake of action that is being whipped up before us. None of those people really matter, just like you, the viewer, don't really matter: you're just one of millions of people whom the producers of this film want to suck money from. All of the characters that I was supposed to care about are merely rote depictions of empty personalities; there's no human core. It's all for show, and this lack of soul gives everything a mechanized feel. Make no mistake: this movie is about special effects and explosions and manufactured emotions, and all of the very talented actors have the same glazed look in their eyes. They can't believe they're actually in this movie, and that they have to say the things they have to say.

After what seems like hours of rock montages, meaningless comedic moments with each character, and chemistry-free romantic interludes between Tyler and Affleck, it's finally time to blast these guys into outer space, in a new space shuttle design that allows for real Han Solo–type maneuvering. Two shuttles are sent up, carrying drilling equipment, a huge space Jeep called an armadillo, the drilling crew, and some NASA astronauts. The brilliant plan is for both shuttles to dock with the Mir space station, where they'll refuel and continue on their way.

This plot contrivance, however, is merely an excuse to destroy the Mir, allowing its sole inhabitant, played by Peter Stormare, to join the drilling crew and help save the day with broad bits of comic relief. Stormare is a very good actor, but here he is given little to work with, not to mention the fact that until Stormare's appearance, the otherwise great Steve Buscemi is meant to be the film's comic relief. But it is consistent with this film's need for excess that every character brims with one-liners and dry sarcasm. Clearly unhappy to be a part of this picture, Buscemi sleepwalks through his role in a stunned daze. He's given little to do, and we are given little justification for his odd behavior. When he goes nuts and commandeers a machine gun (more on that later) for no apparent reason, Will Patton is forced to proclaim, by way of explanation, that he's come down with "space dementia," which ends all further conversation on the subject.

But before this happens, the crew has to land on the asteroid. In a very confusing and badly choreographed sequence, the shuttles are caught in a terrible rock storm surrounding the asteroid, and one of the shuttles is ripped apart and crashes miles from the landing site. In classic Michael Bay style, it's very difficult to figure out exactly what's going on and to whom it is happening. Though Bay obviously understands film technology, he doesn't understand how to utilize it to tell a story. He's a technician, not a storyteller, and his disregard for maintaining narrative and visual cohesion sends all of his carefully planned pyrotechnics into a bustling tailspin.

Affleck survives the crash, but several other peripheral members of the drilling team meet their makers (including Owen Wilson, looking very much like Trey Parker in BASEketball). In addition, it just so happens that the bulk of the crew, including Willis, was in the other shuttle, which set down safely. With the help of his new Russian friend, Affleck uses the armadillo to find his way to the rest of the crew. For some reason, the armadillos are tricked out with machine guns, which naturally raises the question of what it is, exactly, that they think they might find out there in space that would necessitate the use of machine guns. In any case, I was almost hoping some horrible space monster would suddenly appear, because that would have been the only way in which this shamelessly outrageous movie could have been made more so.

As the movie continues, and the crew's attempts to drill the full 800 feet in the time allotted prove fruitless, it's time for the requisite scene in which it's discovered that the government has a backup plan. This plan involves remotely detonating the warhead as a last resort—without informing the drilling crew. Either the crew gets out in time or they all die, and of course, one of the NASA crew members (William Fichtner, twitchy as ever) is in on it. He even pulls a handgun on Willis at one point, prompting Buscemi to exclaim, "A gun in space?" as if they had not already fired off a few rounds. But Willis talks Fichtner out of allowing the detonation to happen, and drilling continues, until a sudden quake destroys their drilling equipment. Cue Ben Affleck, who arrives on the scene to finish the drilling. Everything seems to be going wonderfully until it is discovered, of course, that the nuclear bomb they are to plant in the asteroid has been damaged and can only be detonated manually, meaning someone has to stay behind. Guess who?

Yes, I'm sure you can figure it out. Willis makes the ultimate sacrifice so that Affleck can marry his daughter and listen to Aerosmith records. It is as if their burgeoning, youthful love represents everything on Earth that Willis is trying to save, except of course for most of New York, Singapore, and Paris. I guess I'm not supposed to worry about that, only about whether or not Tyler and Affleck will ever see each other again so that they can caress one another awkwardly in the setting sun and play with animal crackers while Affleck shows off his amazing ability for mimicry and Tyler giggles. If ever a film has milked the contrived suspense of a foregone conclusion, it's this one.

The acting talent in this movie is considerable. As the NASA official in charge of the mission, Billy Bob Thornton radiates confidence and integrity, even as he utters ridiculous dialogue before a constantly roaming camera. It must have been mindboggling to costar in a movie that likely had a bigger catering budget than the entire budget for *Sling Blade*. Tyler and Affleck are both very good actors, but they have little to do here but spout clichés and look good. Will Patton looks really confused the whole time, and I hardly blame him. Udo Kier even makes an appearance, which was certainly welcome. There's also an ominous voiceover from Charlton Heston, in which he informs us that a huge asteroid has hit the earth before and that it will happen again. (Perhaps it was Heston who suggested that they bring machine guns into outer space with them.) And as for Willis, I like the guy, and he does a good job. The only reason he comes off looking bad after all this is because as an actor he is capable of more, and he doesn't really need to take the gigantic paycheck to make obviously manipulative, mercenary movies like this.

Armageddon is an exercise in endurance, and it's the best example you'll find of an action movie so caught up in selling itself to you at every moment that it is devoid of any real humanity. If robots watched movies, they'd love this one. We humans should look elsewhere.

Most Spectacular Moment of Carnage

The scenes of mass destruction are handled in such a way that I felt distanced from the deaths. Actually, there aren't any really cool deaths to speak of. If pressed, I'd vote for the scene in which the second shuttle, trying to land on the asteroid, collides with bodies flying from the damaged first shuttle, but that's stolen outright from *Starship Troopers*, so *Armageddon* loses even more points for not finding a cool way to dispatch people on its own. **(MR)**

Asteroid (1997)

NBC   120 minutes

AVOID AT ALL COSTS

DIRECTOR: Bradford May

WRITERS: Robbyn Burger, Scott Sturgeon

CAST: Michael Biehn, Annabella Sciorra, Zachery Charles, Don Franklin

This is a reedited, two-hour version of the two-night, roughly three-hour miniseries
that premiered on NBC. After an amusing opening in which a truck explodes in the
first minute (all right! Action already!), star Michael Biehn is introduced. He's a federal
emergency management official who not only has organizational and office skills, but
who also finds the time to save helpless people from burning houses while out in the
field. Annabella Sciorra is an astronomist/love interest who discovers a large asteroid
heading directly for Earth. Good news, one thinks. Things are really getting off to a
quick start. Unfortunately, as fragments of the asteroid crash down, too many uninteresting characters (including a group of doctors in Dallas and a firefighter in Kansas
City) show up, their lives to become intertwined in various (and sometimes ridiculous) ways.

 This indeed is a fairly fast-paced and competently put-together made-for-TV movie, perhaps as a result of the reediting (the fat has been trimmed). However, it also
suffers from some leaden, flat dialogue. And, of course, many of the situations are
unbelievable. As the first fragment hits Kansas City, a mere 15 minutes in, Biehn's
character decides to drive into the abandoned city. Why? So that he can rescue two
firefighters whose vehicle has broken down during a last-minute check to ensure that
the city has been evacuated (although one wonders why they would do a last-minute
check with an asteroid bearing down on them in the first place. Whom do they expect
to find?). In the movie's best scene, the fragment hits a dam, causing a nasty tidal
wave to flood the city. Biehn tries to outrun the rampaging floodwater in his truck as
a horrendously fake miniature of the city is washed away behind him. Amazingly, the
miniseries version of this flick was nominated for an Emmy for Outstanding Special

The Great Entertainment Adventure of Our Time!

TWO YEARS IN THE MAKING...
PRESENTED AT A COST
OF $15,000,000.

THE COUNTERAGENT

THE COUNTESS

THE RIGGER

THE CAPTAIN

THE SMUGGLER

THE GESTAPO

THE EX-SPY

THE CHEAT

George C. Scott

A ROBERT WISE PRODUCTION

"The Hindenburg"

Also Starring **Anne Bancroft** as the Countess Co-Starring WILLIAM ATHERTON
ROY THINNES · GIG YOUNG · BURGESS MEREDITH · CHARLES DURNING · RICHARD A. DYSART
Music by DAVID SHIRE · Based on the book by MICHAEL M. MOONEY · Screen Story by **RICHARD LEVINSON & WILLIAM LINK**
Screenplay by **NELSON GIDDING** · Directed by **ROBERT WISE**
THE FILMAKERS GROUP · A UNIVERSAL PICTURE · TECHNICOLOR ® PANAVISION ®

DISTRIBUTED BY CINEMA
INTERNATIONAL CORPORATION

Original sound track available Exclusively on MCA Records & Tapes

DANTE'S PEAK

EXPLODING SOON

www.dantespeak.com

YOU WILL PAY ME 1½ MILLION DOLLARS BY DAWN OR THE WORLD'S GREATEST LUXURY LINER WILL RIP OPEN LIKE A CAN OF SARDINES AND 1200 MEN, WOMEN, AND CHILDREN WILL DIE. GOOD DAY. —JUGGERNAUT

BRITANNIC

Only one man to save 1200 lives! | His ship is at the mercy of Juggernaut! | He feels the full fury of Juggernaut! | He has minutes to find Juggernaut! | The Captain's woman: she too must submit! | For the first time he faces the truth! | Just one last chance to become a hero!

"JUGGERNAUT"

THE GREATEST
SEA ADVENTURE IN HISTORY
HAS JUST BEGUN!

DAVID V. PICKER presents **RICHARD HARRIS · OMAR SHARIF** in "JUGGERNAUT"
A RICHARD LESTER Film with DAVID HEMMINGS · ANTHONY HOPKINS · SHIRLEY KNIGHT
IAN HOLM · CLIFTON JAMES · ROY KINNEAR · Executive Producer DAVID V. PICKER · Associate Producer DENIS O'DELL
Written and Produced by RICHARD DeKOKER · Directed by RICHARD LESTER

PG

United Artists

74/273

TITANIC...
THE GREATEST SEA DRAMA IN LIVING MEMORY

THE RANK ORGANISATION PRESENTS WITH PRIDE

KENNETH MORE IN
A NIGHT TO REMEMBER

From the book by Walter Lord   Screenplay by Eric Ambler

Produced by William MacQuitty

Directed by Roy Baker

ONE
TINY SPARK
BECOMES
A NIGHT
OF BLAZING
SUSPENSE

The tallest
building
in the world
is on fire.
You are there
with 294
other guests.
There's no
way down.
There's no
way out.

THE TOWERING INFERNO

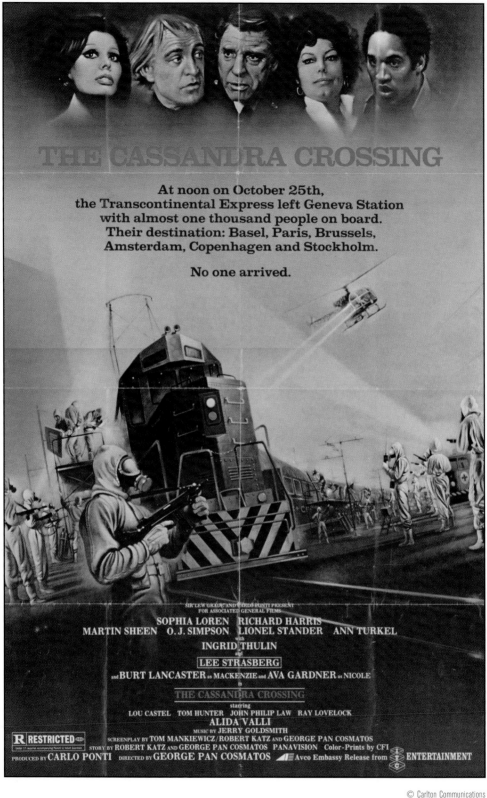

THE CASSANDRA CROSSING

At noon on October 25th,
the Transcontinental Express left Geneva Station
with almost one thousand people on board.
Their destination: Basel, Paris, Brussels,
Amsterdam, Copenhagen and Stockholm.

No one arrived.

SIR LEW GRADE AND CARLO PONTI PRESENT
FOR ASSOCIATED GENERAL FILMS

SOPHIA LOREN   RICHARD HARRIS
MARTIN SHEEN   O. J. SIMPSON   LIONEL STANDER   ANN TURKEL
with
INGRID THULIN
and
LEE STRASBERG
and BURT LANCASTER as MACKENZIE and AVA GARDNER as NICOLE
in
THE CASSANDRA CROSSING
starring
LOU CASTEL   TOM HUNTER   JOHN PHILIP LAW   RAY LOVELOCK
ALIDA VALLI
MUSIC BY JERRY GOLDSMITH

R RESTRICTED
Under 17 requires accompanying Parent or Adult Guardian

SCREENPLAY BY TOM MANKIEWICZ/ROBERT KATZ AND GEORGE PAN COSMATOS
STORY BY ROBERT KATZ AND GEORGE PAN COSMATOS   PANAVISION   Color-Prints by CFI
PRODUCED BY CARLO PONTI   DIRECTED BY GEORGE PAN COSMATOS   Avco Embassy Release from ENTERTAINMENT

ด่วน
มาถึงไทยแล้ว
ภาพยนตร์ที่มีผู้ชมมากที่สุด
ภาพยนตร์ที่ทำเงินสูงที่สุด
พริบตาเดียว ทุกอย่างย่อยยับสิ้น
ไม่มีเสียงร้องของชัยชนะ..ไม่มีเหรียญตรา..นอกจากความวินาศถาวร
เดอะ เดย์ อ๊าฟเตอร์
นิวเคลียร์ล้างโลก
THE DAY AFTER

© MGM

A WILD SCIENCE FICTION NIGHTMARE.

A living, crawling hell on earth.

KINGDOM OF THE SPIDERS

A LARRY WOLNER - MICKEY ZIDE Presentation

WILLIAM SHATNER

co-starring TIFFANY BOLLING · WOODY STRODE · ALTOVISE DAVIS and introducing

LIEUX DRESSLER · DAVID McLEAN · NATASHA RYAN · MARCY LAFFERTY · Produced by IGO KANTOR and JEFFREY M. SNELLER · Executive Producer HENRY FOWNES
Screenplay by RICHARD ROBINSON and ALAN CAILLOU · Directed by JOHN BUD CARDOS · An ARACHNID Production · A DIMENSION PICTURES Release

PG PARENTAL GUIDANCE SUGGESTED SOME MATERIAL MAY NOT BE SUITABLE FOR PRE-TEENAGERS

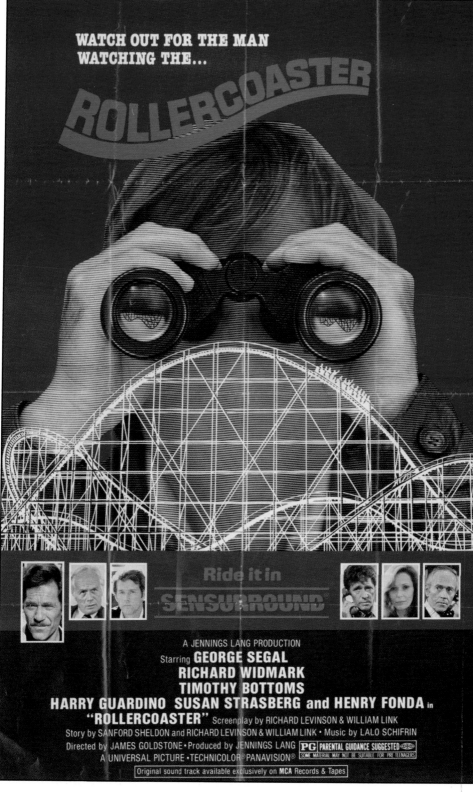

WATCH OUT FOR THE MAN
WATCHING THE...

ROLLERCOASTER

Ride it in
SENSURROUND

A JENNINGS LANG PRODUCTION
Starring GEORGE SEGAL
RICHARD WIDMARK
TIMOTHY BOTTOMS
HARRY GUARDINO SUSAN STRASBERG and HENRY FONDA in
"ROLLERCOASTER" Screenplay by RICHARD LEVINSON & WILLIAM LINK
Story by SANFORD SHELDON and RICHARD LEVINSON & WILLIAM LINK • Music by LALO SCHIFRIN
Directed by JAMES GOLDSTONE • Produced by JENNINGS LANG PG PARENTAL GUIDANCE SUGGESTED
A UNIVERSAL PICTURE • TECHNICOLOR • PANAVISION® SOME MATERIAL MAY NOT BE SUITABLE FOR PRE-TEENAGERS
Original sound track available exclusively on MCA Records & Tapes

THE SWARM is coming!

MICHAEL CAINE · KATHARINE ROSS · RICHARD WIDMARK · RICHARD CHAMBERLAIN · OLIVIA DE HAVILLAND · BEN JOHNSON · LEE GRANT · JOSE FERRER · PATTY DUKE ASTIN · SLIM PICKENS · BRADFORD DILLMAN · FRED MacMURRAY as Clarence · and HENRY FONDA as Dr. Krim

IRWIN ALLEN's production of "THE SWARM"

Produced and Directed by IRWIN ALLEN Screenplay by STIRLING SILLIPHANT Music by JERRY GOLDSMITH

ORIGINAL SOUNDTRACK ON WARNER BROS. RECORDS AND TAPES.
Read the Signet Paperback

From Warner Bros.
A Warner Communications Company

STYLE B

78 0037

© Warner Bros., Inc.

H·G·WELLS'

THE War OF THE Worlds

COLOR BY **TECHNICOLOR**

PRODUCED BY **GEORGE PAL** · DIRECTED BY **BYRON HASKIN** · SCREEN PLAY BY **BARRE LYNDON** · A PARAMOUNT PICTURE

Visual Effects, although those who nominated it must have been at the refrigerator while this scene was on. Naturally, our hero survives and saves the firefighters.

But the worst is yet to come. When the bulk of the asteroid is destroyed (via an elaborate series of laser beams mounted on air force fighter planes and shot into space; I'm not really sure why it needed to be done this way, as that seems unnecessarily complex and prone to failure, but I'll let it slide. After all, failure is what I want!), the various fragments pummel the earth, and in particular Dallas, where Sciorra's father and son are currently residing. The impact is rendered using computer technology and miniatures, with a panicked crowd blue-screened into the foreground. And, as expected, the result is very cheesy. The remainder of the film mainly concerns Sciorra's search for her family. Yawn. On the positive side, the climax involves a nifty rescue on top of a building that is sliding into the asteroid's crater.

The main problem with watching a made-for-TV disaster movie is that, sadly, there aren't going to be many elaborate or spectacular deaths. And this is the case with *Asteroid*. Nor is there the money to really depict the things an audience expects in a disaster film. And this movie's all-American message of "just trying to help people, that's what it's all about" (yes, a character actually says this) in times of chaos is beyond hammy and forced. This TV movie also has a noticeably bad TV-movie-of-the-week kind of score. I suppose this is a passable time waster, but it does not contain a believable and engrossing story to make it anything special.

Most Spectacular Moment of Carnage

Not much in the way of big deaths. Ninety minutes in, Sciorra's father falls a flight down through the wreckage of a hospital, at which point a metal girder falls on his legs. (GK)

Deep Impact (1998)

Paramount   121 minutes

AT YOUR OWN RISK

© Dreamworks and Paramount Pictures

DIRECTOR: Mimi Leder

WRITERS: Bruce Joel Rubin, Michael Tolkin

CAST: Robert Duvall, Téa Leoni, Elijah Wood, Vanessa Redgrave, Morgan Freeman, Maximilian Schell, James Cromwell, Ron Eldard, Jon Favreau, Laura Innes, Mary McCormack, Richard Schiff, Leelee Sobieski, Blair Underwood, Dougray Scott, Gary Werntz, Bruce Weitz, Besty Brantley, O'Neal Compton, Rya Kihlstedt, Denise Crosby, Kurtwood Smith, Charles Martin Smith (uncredited)

The first of 1998's two big "giant space rock" movies to be released was *Deep Impact*, a touchy-feely disaster flick that has a great cast but that becomes more and more irritating as it goes along. *Armageddon* may have been as stupid as a bag of hammers, but at least it knew it was dumb (I hope). I'm not sure what *Deep Impact*'s excuse is.

The movie opens in Richmond, Virginia, when a brainy young student, Elijah Wood, discovers a comet while taking part in some kind of late-evening or early-morning astrology club assignment. (Why any teenager would be doing any sort of schoolwork outside the hours between 9:00 a.m. and 3:00 p.m. is beyond me.) This discovery is relayed to a pizza-scarfing astrologist, who realizes the severity of the situation and attempts to warn others. He races out to his Jeep and speeds down a winding road as he tries to dial out on his cell phone. Perhaps he is calling to order another pizza for pickup, because I'm not sure why he'd really need to leave his post. I mean, it's not as if the comet's hitting tomorrow. Before he can order another pie, he's hit by a truck and sent down a ravine, the car exploding as it flips. Maybe realizing that not much would be occurring in the next hour, the filmmakers tried to give us this explosion to keep us interested.

It's a year later, and driven CNBC reporter Téa Leoni is following up on a story about the secretary of the treasury, who has resigned unexpectedly. Scene after scene follows as Leoni becomes embroiled in this story, not fully realizing that it has to do with a giant comet speeding toward Earth. Unfortunately, the audience knows, and we have to sit through 20 minutes of investigation before the president, played by Morgan Freeman, must announce the news to America. A more apt description of Freeman's role would be that of a narrator who pops up every so often to fill the audience in on what is happening. He tells the public that he has also informed all of the scientifically backward nations of the world (who apparently would have no way of figuring this out for themselves) that a giant comet will hit the world within one year.

Many scenes involving Leoni and her divorced parents, played by Maximilian Schell and Vanessa Redgrave, follow. Still unable to get over the breakup of their marriage, Leoni goes to meet each of them separately. She is particularly incensed by Schell, who is remarried to a woman only two years older than she is. The arguments between Leoni and Schell go on throughout the whole movie, until the audience wants to literally slap Leoni and tell her to get over it already!

Back in Virginia, Elijah Wood, teenage astronomer, has become a full-blown celebrity, and he is told by one of his peers at an assembly that "famous people always get sex." Yeah, and high school students who are famous for discovering imminent disaster-inducing, Earth-destroying comets would likely get their asses kicked by students, too. Probably most disastrous for the lusting Wood is that the whole sex prophecy does not turn out to be true.

The *Messiah* (there are a lot of biblical references here), a shuttle sent to drill a hole into the comet and set off nuclear devices, is introduced. The shuttle astronauts are for the most part arrogant and unlikable, except for Robert Duvall, who is continually shunned by the others. In fact, I was left thinking that maybe these people deserve to be hit by a comet. Naturally, there are problems during the drilling mission, and one of the astronauts is shot into the atmosphere by explosive gases, while another is blinded. The charges are detonated, but they have no effect; they just break the comet into two pieces, one small and one large.

President Freeman informs us that a "Noah's Ark" of sorts has been dug; it's a cave deep under the ground in Missouri. He announces that a random draw will determine which citizens will be allowed inside, and that those selected will be telephoned immediately. The fact that most of the people seem to be away from home and watching the broadcast in large, public places mustn't have dawned on Freeman. The president declares martial law, then tells the public "I believe in God" before offering an on-air prayer for survival (something that I, for one, wouldn't want to see my world leader do).

Naturally, the brainy Wood and his family are chosen to go, but his neighbors and dream-girl Leelee Sobieski are not. Wood proposes to Sobieski and the two are married, which allows her family to come along. The whole marriage between the two kids is supposed to be sweet, but it really doesn't comes off as much more than a horny kid doing anything to "get some."

Leoni then learns that her mother has killed herself, and she decides to sit on a park bench in the middle of a rain shower. Her father drives by, finds her, and reveals that his frightened bride has just left him to be with her mother. "How does it feel?" she snaps back at him. "I feel like an orphan!" At this point, I wanted the father to hit the gas and run the daughter down, but sadly, this didn't occur.

Up in space, the crew members decide to sacrifice themselves and take out the larger of the two pieces of comet. But, of course, not before each astronaut is given the chance for an extended and tearful farewell with their families. The astronauts have really strange, borderline-creepy things to say to their loved ones, like "I'll be haunting you."

Finally, the comet hits the ocean and forms a 100-foot digital tidal wave, which sweeps through Manhattan, submerging it. The effects, which can only be described as coming from the School of Good Enough, only last for a minute or so. All of this New York carnage seems especially strange considering that most of the movie takes place in Virginia and Washington, D.C. The wave also crashes through Missouri, but—preposterously—several folks survive, and they speak of rebuilding the country to its former glory.

So what's the moral of this story? Maybe living in California (whose citizens were no doubt unaffected and spent the running time of the movie surfing and rollerblading) isn't such a bad idea after all. My criticism of this film notwithstanding, *Deep Impact* was very successful, earned some nominations for Blockbuster Awards, and won some statues from other, equally respectable sources.

Most Spectacular Moment of Carnage

There isn't a lot to choose from here, because the tidal wave is really all there is. I'd have to say the winner is probably the scene in which the enormous wave finishes off Leoni and Schell, because at least it closes the book on one of the film's most annoying storylines. **(GK)**

Meteor (1979)

American International Pictures   105 minutes

SO BAD IT'S GOOD

DIRECTOR: Ronald Neame

WRITERS: Stanley Mann, Edmund H. North

CAST: Sean Connery, Natalie Wood, Karl Malden, Brian Keith, Martin Landau, Trevor Howard, Richard A. Dysart, Henry Fonda, Joseph Campanella

I was very surprised and happy to learn that low-budget king Samuel Z. Arkoff was behind the scenes of the seemingly big-budget *Meteor*. Arkoff, whose company American International Pictures has been responsible for producing and releasing some of the cheesiest sci-fi, teen, and horror pictures of the '50s, '60s and '70s, is the next best thing to Roger Corman. With such big stars, one expects a maverick like Arkoff to give us a real show, utilizing the bigger budget while still getting down and dirty with spectacular death scenes and other more exploitative elements.

The movie does get off to a slam-bang start. As goofy Superman-esque opening credits roll, each name is scored with a booming dah-dah-dah-dum. The movie won an Oscar nomination for Best Sound. Apparently, all you needed to do to get a Best Sound nomination in 1980 was crank the volume up. A foreboding voiceover starts up, while stock footage of the solar system is displayed. But the grade-six science lesson ends abruptly.

Suddenly, the action cuts to the sea and Dr. Paul Bradley, played by the always-entertaining Sean Connery. Connery hooks up with Karl Malden, who grimly tells Connery about a horrible accident that's caused a meteor threat, all with a long and now unnecessary flashback that left me wondering why didn't the filmmakers didn't just open the movie with this sequence to begin with. At this point, the filmmakers dote on long shots of a probe (a sign of things to come) floating in space for endless amounts of time. Was I supposed to be admiring the wonderful miniature work or something? Remember all of the endless shots of the *Enterprise* in the original *Star Trek* movie? Well, it's just like that, only worse, since here the filmmakers opt to use cheap models.

Naturally, there is one huge honking meteor out there. Malden informs us that an enormous, five-mile wide chunk of it will hit the earth in six days, with many smaller chunks arriving in the meantime. Connery agrees to meet with NASA officials to discuss how to deal with the problem. At this point we still have no idea what type of doctor Connery is (he could be a dermatologist, for all I know), why his input is so important, or why he's so grouchy all the time.

Cut to Switzerland, where B-movie queen Sybil Danning appears as a female skier walking through a small village. Moments later, a meteor fragment hits the top of a nearby mountain, causing a devastating avalanche. Skiers are swept under the wave of snow. Bleachers, skiers, snowmobiles, and even a lodge all get taken out. But even this was not satisfying to me; I had the feeling that I'd seen it all before. Indeed, I was right. Samuel Arkoff actually used footage from Roger Corman's *Avalanche* and inserted it into the scene. All that is new is Sybil Danning, who runs into a church that collapses on top of her under the weight of the snow.

Also lame is a tidal wave that slams Hong Kong. Panicked crowds run, stealing apples and paintings. The camera focuses on one particular man rushing to find his wife, baby, and dog. The wave hits and washes them away, along with a communication center. Why is this important? Maybe the filmmakers figured that it's the little stories that add meaning. No, it's just stock footage.

In case you're still interested, Connery and Malden are shipped off to "meteor headquarters," for lack of a better term. It's an underground base next to an old subway station under the Hudson River in New York, hidden under the American Telephone and Telegraph Company. Malden cleverly comments that "nobody would think of putting their most important emergency striking power under the busiest city in the world." Indeed, because it's a terrible idea. Regardless, Connery grunts in agreement.

After dozens of agonizingly long shots of rockets in space, the climax arrives. There are explosions, rubbles falls, and before you can say, "Great idea, Malden, building a base under a city!" the exit to the building is blocked. The characters have to hurry out through a subway tunnel, extending the pain of watching this stink bomb for another 10 minutes.

In summation, I was hugely disappointed with this yawnfest. When I was a kid I had a couple of T-shirts with press-on designs. One of my favorites was my Fonzie shirt. But my absolute favorite was an orange shirt with a press-on picture of the poster artwork from this movie, with the title, *Meteor*, in bold letters. It pictured dozens of rockets about to strike the giant rock. (I can't remember if it had Sean Connery and the other celebrities' heads along the bottom, but I hope it did.) There is actually no shot like this in the movie, and that makes me angry. This terrible flick should be viewed as an example of how not to make a disaster film.

Most Spectacular Moment of Carnage

Well, it's the avalanche, but as I said, the scene is stolen from the film *Avalanche*, so does it still count? It'll have to, I guess. **(GK)**

Meteorites! (1998)

Paramount   89 minutes

AT YOUR OWN RISK

☢

DIRECTOR: Chris Thompson

WRITER: Bart Baker

CAST: Tom Wopat, Roxanne Hart, Darrin Klimek, Pato Hoffman, Marshall Napier, Amiel Daemian, Leo Taylor, Vanessa Steele

Direct-to-video disaster films can really annoy me. Every week some knuckleheads are knocking out some low-budget quickie. Not that *Meteorites!* is a bad film; in fact, it's much better than most of the straight-to-video titles out there. It's just that it's completely unnecessary—capable and passable, and also entirely forgettable and unimpressive.

Meteorites! is a disaster film for the whole family: kind of a "Li'l Meteor," for lack of a better description. A retired bomb diffuser, played by Tom Wopat, is asked to assess the damage after a meteor falls and causes random explosions. His wife, played by Roxanne Hart, is a science teacher who seems to be everywhere except teaching in her classroom. Also introduced are their high-school-aged son and daughter. Of course, this means that a large chunk of the movie is going to deal with the angst of its teen-age characters. And what problems they have! While the daughter struggles with the question "Will I win the Miss UFO beauty pageant?" the son must ponder the even more pressing issue of "Will I get laid during the Miss UFO beauty pageant?" All the while you'll be asking, will the meteors just hit the Miss UFO beauty pageant already? On the positive side, at least these kids aren't overly whiny and angry.

Meanwhile, we are treated to scenes that depict the leads' lack of detective skills. By the time Wopat and Hart figure out what's happening, they face the usual resistance from the sleazeball town mayor. He's in the habit of paying thugs (who, despite their best efforts, look about as threatening as my grandmother) to rob his own home so he can collect the insurance money. The main tough guy is later scared off and runs away like a schoolgirl when Hart's character brandishes a Taser on him.

Things go crazy as the meteors fall. The film picks up some momentum at this point, as people become trapped and must avoid the falling rocks. A hospital is hit, trapping three characters (one of whom dies by electrocution); there's a car crash; and a festival Ferris wheel falls amid the chaos. These scenes are well filmed, and the effects are decent, but there's no real conflict or tension. We know that things will work out just fine, the family will be reunited and behave as if nothing horrendous has just occurred to their small town. This is strictly for those desperate for a disaster flick.

Most Spectacular Moment of Carnage

In an attempt at light humor, the filmmakers have a tabloid reporter look into the sky to see a meteor bearing down on him. All that remains after the hit are the reporter's smoking boots, which I can only assume is supposed to be hilarious. **(GK)**

When Worlds Collide (1951)

Paramount   81 minutes

RECOMMENDED

⚠

DIRECTOR: Rudolph Maté

WRITER: Sydney Boehm (based on the novel by Edwin Balmer)

CAST: Richard Derr, Barbara Rush, Peter Hansen, John Hoyt, Larry Keating

Produced by George Pal (who would later bring us the superior sci-fi classic *The War of the Worlds*), *When Worlds Collide* is a fun, heavy-handed, Oscar-winning sci-fi disaster epic depicting the end of the world. Based on a premise that would later be recycled in films like *Deep Impact*, the movie tells the story of a star on a collision course with Earth and how humans choose to deal with their impending demise.

The movie opens with a big explosion, albeit under the title credits. Like most disaster films of the '50s, there are less-than-subtle allusions to the Bible, and the first major image shown is of the good book. A voiceover intones, "And God looked upon the earth, and behold, it was corrupt; for all flesh had corrupted his way upon the earth. And God said, 'I will destroy them with the earth'" while an angelic choir sings in the background.

After the Bible studies finish, the story moves to South Africa and hero Dave Randall, played by Richard Derr. Derr is a "cool-cat ladies' man," and the first shot of him shows Derr piloting his two-seat airplane while making out with a young female passenger. What's even more amazing is that he doesn't seem to be looking out the window, or have either of his hands anywhere near the steering wheel. Now that's my kind of hero! Derr, known for his secrecy, is assigned to deliver a special top-secret piece of luggage (which is chained to his wrist so as not to arouse suspicion) to New York, to a Dr. Hendron, played by Larry Keating. Come to think of it, our lead is basically a glorified FedEx delivery man.

Amusingly, all of the brilliant scientific minds in this movie can't keep their mouths shut.

After stepping off of the plane, Derr quickly leaves his female companion. Keating's assistant, played by Barbara Rush, arrives to escort Derr to Keating. She begins blurting out information in a taxi, until she finally reveals, "I haven't the courage to face the end of the world." (I hoped for a reaction shot or a spit take from the cab driver at this piece of information, but sadly, it never occurred.) Apparently, Zyra, a planet revolving around a large star, is rapidly approaching. It will pass the earth, causing tidal waves and earthquakes, before the star itself—the interestingly named Bellus (which sounds like a gastrointestinal disorder, not a star)—will destroy the world completely within a year. Of course, no one believes these claims, and the scientists are ignored by the United Nations. Derr believes Rush, however, and of course romance soon blooms between them.

Enter John Hoyt, the most evil, wheelchair-bound billionaire since It's a Wonderful Life's Mr. Potter. With his and other investors' funding, the doctor agrees to build a "Noah's Ark" rocket ship to Zyra, where the 45 humans drawn to win a place onboard will land and continue the human species (at least, one would assume, until Zyra crashes into some faraway planet in another galaxy).

There are many montages of the ship being built and of people working, and stock footage of cities around the world being evacuated, until the first series of disasters hit "at one o'clock, the hour of doom!" Sure enough, there's an earthquake, volcanoes erupt, bridges fall, and trees and cities catch fire. A tidal wave washes away a small shack, and then in the next shot sweeps through New York City. It's all done with obvious miniatures, but it's entertaining regardless. There's a great shot (or should I say, painting) of the flooded city, half sunk and flanked by a couple of capsized tankers.

Unfortunately for the heroes, much of their work on the spacecraft is ruined, and a large crane falls on several of the workers. Seeing as how these people knew this was all going to happen well in advance, it's amazing that no one thought to prepare for this eventuality. And, with time running out, this only leaves days to make repairs and prepare the launch. None of this is helped by a panicked voice on a loudspeaker, which urges the workers, "Please rush! There are seven days left; we're falling behind schedule. Make it up! Hurry!" No doubt this is the real reason that the workers revolt in the last few hours. With Bellus on the horizon, events lead to a final scuffle.

I love the interiors of the rocket ships in these types of movies. Every movement seems to be controlled by the flip of an abnormally large switch. They may as well just have two switches with the words Take Off and Land printed on them. The rocket takes off like a rollercoaster flying off a set of giant rails, heads into the sky, and arrives at Zyra. The shots of the surface of Zyra are most amusing, because they've been animated. As the group stares off into the horizon of their new world, I expected Looney Tunes characters to jump into the landscape and greet them.

In all, *When Worlds Collide*, is a silly but entertaining sci-fi disaster film. I recommend seeing it if only to see what Oscar-winning special effects looked like in 1951.

Most Spectacular Moment of Carnage

The mass scenes of destruction are well realized for their day, but there aren't any on-screen deaths. The best moment of carnage comes from a surprising source. Sick of his irritating boss, Hoyt's assistant pulls a gun and threatens to kill him. His plan backfires when the invalid suddenly pistol-whips him from between his legs and goes back about his meeting with Keating. Was I to believe that Hoyt has been packing heat under his blanket the whole time? **(GK)**

The Apocalypse (1997)

Columbia   97 minutes

AVOID AT ALL COSTS

The Apocalypse is yet another in a growing series of direct-to-video travesties. Every time I sit down to watch one of these I cringe, anticipating the worst. And that's what I usually get. To put it bluntly, this movie is a chunk of poop. Stars Sandra Bernhard, Cameron Dye, Frank Zagarino, Michelle Anne Johnson, Lee Arenberg, Merle Kennedy, Matt McCoy, and Laura San Giacomo. As an added bonus, the film features irrelevant *Hamlet* references and is surprisingly pretentious. **(GK)**

Tycus (1998)

Paramount   94 minutes

AVOID AT ALL COSTS

Despite the depiction of a tornado blowing through the streets of New York City on the front of the video box, Tycus is actually a chunk of a comet on a collision course with the moon. It's explained that the ensuing explosion will cause numerous natural disasters. Low-budget, straight-to-video production is exactly what you get, and even the great Dennis Hopper (who isn't the lead, but a supporting character) doesn't get a chance to really act crazy the way I like him to. There are shots of exploding volcanoes, panicked crowds, comets, and so on. But unfortunately, they're all shots that have been ripped off from other movies (the *Dante's Peak* influence is particularly noticeable), so what's the point? You know what you're in for if you rent this one. **(GK)**

RARE, OBSCURE, AND LESS IMPORTANT TITLES

The Day the Sky Exploded (1958)

Planet on the Prowl (1966)

Now That's a Fire!

When I was a little kid, a kerosene heater in my house exploded one night, engulfing the living room in flames. I would have slept through the whole thing if my sister hadn't woken me up and pulled me out of bed. The house didn't burn down or anything, but I do remember the flames burning across a wall of my house, and I remember the enormous heat that came from it. As a matter of fact, it melted a large dish of candies and destroyed our TV, making it impossible for me to view any disaster movies that week. OK, maybe I'm carrying this story well past the point of being interesting, but the point is that fire can be quite frightening, and many of us can relate to characters who face one. Fire also looks great on film. Frankly, I'm amazed that more disaster films haven't been devoted to the subject. It should also be noted that s'mores (chocolate and toasted marshmallows on graham crackers) would be an appropriate viewing snack for these flicks, although I discourage the building of a bonfire in your living room. **(GK)**

City on Fire (1979)

Twentieth Century Fox International   106 minutes

AVOID AT ALL COSTS

DIRECTOR: Alvin Rakoff

WRITERS: Jack Hill, David P. Lewis, Céline La Frenière

CAST: Barry Newman, Susan Clark, Shelley Winters, Leslie Nielsen, James Franciscus (as Jimbo!), Ava Gardner, Henry Fonda, and a bunch of really bad Canadian actors

> *"What you are about to see could happen to any city, anywhere."*
> —Opening credit

So, I suppose that a 500-acre refinery might be built right in the middle of my city by a cost-cutting mayor. And maybe there'd be a mentally unstable worker there who's just been fired. Let's say he runs around the refinery with a maniacal grin on his face, turning every switch and knob that he sees; you know, just for the heck of it. Of course, no one notices this, or sees his behavior as strange. Then, in the process, he could release flammable chemicals into the surrounding city. And maybe there'd be a couple of guys in the city doing some welding who would accidentally set the chemicals (and themselves) ablaze. This fire would spread, engulfing the whole city. It could happen in anybody's town, right?

That's just the beginning of the preposterous coincidences in this inept, Canadian-made disaster movie wannabe. It's the same old story. A lot of characters are brought together during the course of a raging fire in the city (though the majority of the action takes place within a hospital surrounded by the fire). Some live, some die. Only it's never been done quite this poorly before. Shot in what can only be described as "Brown-O-Vision," the entire film seems to have a brown tint to it. It is also inanely scripted, badly acted, and filled with subplots that don't make much sense. For instance, there's the newsroom subplot. Every so often, the film cuts away from the blaze to alcoholic anchorwoman Ava Gardner bickering with news director James Franciscus. Do these characters really need to be in the film? Of course not. They're just famous actors who seem to have been written into the movie.

The fire itself involves a series of cheeseball effects, like undercranking the camera to produce the look of a fast-moving fire. Just make sure you don't look at anything else within the frame, like the grass, or you'll see it moving at three or four times its normal speed. And let's not forget the painfully overwrought score.

I'm not ruining anything by saying that the characters trapped in the hospital eventually rescue themselves by wrapping up in wet towels and running down a flame-engulfed street. All the while, firefighters douse them with more water from their firehoses and create a fountainlike pathway for them to maneuver their way to safety. For some reason, as soon as these people get to the end of the block, they are no longer affected by the flames, smoke, heat, and danger just a few feet behind them. And, apparently, the next block is unaffected by the raging fire.

On the plus side, there are some spectacular deaths and some nasty burns. (In one hilarious moment, a nurse screams in terror as she sees a burn victim. Would that be professional protocol for this situation? I'd feel really great about my chances if I were the patient.) Shelley Winters appears as a nurse, and she is crushed by a falling wall. And watch for a dramatic scene outside the hospital with Susan Clark and Leslie Nielsen (whose character, introduced as a jerk, actually survives and manages to be somewhat heroic). In the midst of their most important moment together up to this point in the film, the camera focuses not on the actors, but instead on a shot of a patient in a wheelchair next to them, and the patient is relieving himself. I'm not kidding.

All of the shots seem to last a few beats too long. Watch in excitement as Barry Newman, our hero, goes through the entire process of making a milkshake, and then . . . drinking it . . . slowly. Thrill as our part-time stalker, full-time moron saboteur Herman Stover (played by Jonathan Welsh) sets the plant on fire and then goes to buy himself a suit. Why did the filmmakers waste minutes of screen time showing this? The movie even has a bad, tinny sound mix, and it sounds like a lot of the dialogue was looped.

Unfortunately, fire chief Henry Fonda must also deliver a hammy and preachy message to the audience at the end of the film. "All it takes is one man. Could be anybody. Your neighbor, my neighbor. One man to destroy a city." Yeah, there's one to grow on. Actually, it took several people (some mentally unstable), all doing idiotic things, to cause this fire, so even the message loses all impact. Fonda promptly leaves the room (no doubt to collect his paycheck and get out of there), followed by the rest of his team. Apparently, nobody needs to do their jobs anymore.

This is one bad, bad movie.

Most Spectacular Moment of Carnage
A photographer runs into his burning apartment to secure some juicy tabloid shots. He catches fire and runs out of the building, engulfed in the flames and burning up fast. As if this isn't enough, he's then plowed down by a car as he runs into the street. Good stuff. **(GK)**

The Day the Earth Caught Fire (1961)

British Lion-Pax   94 minutes

AT YOUR OWN RISK

DIRECTOR: Val Guest

WRITERS: Wolf Mankowitz, Val Guest

CAST: Janet Munro, Leo McKern, Edward Judd

This isn't your typical disaster film. For one, it's in black and white. Second, there aren't any major stars in it. Third, it's British, which means you should expect a lot of chatting. All this results in an interesting, thought-provoking, well-produced film that's entertaining but a little too talky at times for my taste. And, unfortunately, it breaks a cardinal rule of disaster films with its misleading title.

The film begins in an empty, desolate London. These images are well shot, in stark black and white, and are quite eerie. Edward Judd plays our hero, Peter Stenning. He walks through the empty streets to his newspaper office in London, where he begins to spin a tale (or, more to the point, write an article, not that it looks like it's ever going to be printed at this point). Apparently, the earth is on a collision course with the sun, and the only hope now rests in a series of nuclear blasts to set the planet off its doomed course.

A flashblack takes us back 19 days earlier into the hectic newsroom. Judd is a surly, divorced (with a son he never sees), hard-drinking, and generally unpleasant news reporter who, despite his credentials, seems to do little reporting of the news. He's the kind of character who cracks unfunny jokes, and then grouses when his co-workers do it because he feels they aren't taking him seriously. Amid all this witty newsroom banter, it seems that the stories of the day all relate to earthquakes, floods, and sun rashes. Judd's assigned to do a story on sunspots, and no sooner is he given this task then he gets into an argument with the Met office (which provides England with weather and climate information) switchboard operator/love interest Jeannie, played by Janet Munro. She slaps him across the face when he comes to get a press release in person. You just know at this point they'll be making love within a half hour of screen time.

Back in the newsroom, science editor Leo McKern (who is Judd's best buddy, and who is busy writing the sunspot article for Judd, who is too busy flirting with Munro) learns of a nuclear test. It seems the Americans and Russians have both tested weapons at exactly the same time, creating the biggest jolt the earth has taken since the ice age. Protesters scrap with pronuclear folks during a demonstration when suddenly, a solar eclipse appears in the sky. That's definitely not a good sign.

More trouble arrives when a heat wave hits England, causing a hot mist to cover the city. Transportation via buses and the subways are shut down, leaving the city in a panic. Planes are rerouted! Actually, nothing spectacular happens, although again, the effect of a city covered in mist is achieved well. This strange circumstance leaves Judd and Munro (who meet up at a carnival) to navigate through the fog. Naturally, they end up back at her apartment. His advances are refused. He turns to booze for comfort. Back at the newsroom, it is explained that one-third of the globe has been paralyzed by unusual weather. McKern explains his suspicions to the other reporters: that the nuclear tests have knocked the planet closer to the sun. Everyone in the newsroom stops what they're doing the minute this guy has anything to say, like he's the authority on everything.

As things get mistier outside, things get even mistier inside as Judd explains to Munro that he used to be a writer until his marriage and drinking problems forced him into a newspaper job. His sob story works, and he finally scores. Outside, a cyclone ravages London, blowing people around, breaking windows, and flipping cars. A man's (model) boat is flipped in the raging waters. Although they're obviously faked, many of the miniature effects are well executed. And at least the film is finally getting down and dirty.

Things heat up again when Munro discovers the obvious—the planet has been tilted 12 degrees off its axis, changing its weather patterns, and it is now heading directly for the sun. Judd makes the social faux pas of using this information, which he was told in confidence, to write a front-page story on the crisis. Munro looks none too pleased as she is taken into custody by the British government for leaking information. I'm supposed to root for this guy, right?

Now comes the disaster. Stock footage of floods, snowstorms, and brushfires across the planet are mixed with tight shots of panicking crowds around the globe. As a famine hits, the filmmakers use stock footage of cows dropping dead from the heat. Due to the famine, young punks form "water gangs" and stalk the streets, rioting, playing trumpets and horns like Sgt. Pepper's Lonely Hearts Club Band, and abusing the locals. This leads to an entertaining confrontation between Judd and a gang. Time is running out, and the world's only hope is to set off more nuclear blasts in an attempt to knock the earth back on its axis.

And, most importantly, Judd decides to give up drinking. Personally, I have a bit of a problem with end-of-the-world movies in which the characters suddenly give up their vices, like drinking or smoking. Frankly, it doesn't make any sense to me. It's like being diagnosed with cancer and *then* giving up cigarettes. If you're going to die anyway, you may as well smoke like a chimney, especially if it relaxes you. Not so in these kinds of movies. The characters want to spend the last hours of their lives in miserable torment.

Toward the end of the movie, the filmmakers cut to some great footage of various cities. There's a particularly nice shot of the Thames—it's completely dried up, the soil is cracked, and ships lay about on the dirt. As Judd finishes his story and pontificates on the fragility and beauty of life, the camera pans to two papers ready to go to the presses. One says, "World Saved"; the other, "World Doomed." It's a clever, almost eerie shot, but it does raise the question: if the blast doesn't work, why bother printing the "World Doomed" edition of the paper? Who's gonna be around to buy it?

The ambiguity of the ending, while effective, also leaves me with another problem. As I'm sure you, too, must be wondering by now, why is the film called *The Day the Earth Caught Fire*? The earth doesn't actually catch fire at any point in the film. That's false advertising! Disaster flicks shouldn't cheap out when they promise something like that in the title. *Avalanche, Earthquake*, and even *Flood!* delivered what they promised. So why, then, can't the earth catch on fire? Hell, even in the film *Santa Claus Conquers the Martians*, Santa Claus actually does conquer the Martians! So you see, I don't think that I'm asking too much here.

Most Spectacular Moment of Carnage

There isn't much in the way of carnage in this film. But I think the best moment comes toward the end, when Munro is attacked in her apartment by the rampaging "water gang." Judd races to the apartment to rescue her. Upon his arrival, he beats the hell out of them (it's about time he did something in this movie), punching one punk into the elevator shaft, who falls several floors to his death (offscreen, of course). **(GK)**

Fire! (1977)

Warner Bros.   98 minutes

RECOMMENDED

⚠

DIRECTOR: Earl Bellamy

WRITERS: Norman Katkov, Arthur Weiss

CAST: Ernest Borgnine, Vera Miles, Patty Duke Astin, Alex Cord, Donna Mills, Lloyd Nolan, Neville Brand, Ty Hardin, Gene Evans, Erik Estrada

Another Irwin Allen spectacular, this one set in a small Oregon town facing a growing forest fire. Ernest Borgnine stars as the likable, always-grinning Sam, a wealthy local lumberyard owner who is deeply in love with lodge owner Martha Wagner, played by Vera Miles. Borgnine, a man who typically appears exactly the same no matter what year it is, manages to sport a hilarious retro look in this movie (as do most of the actors); he's decked out in great '70s fashion, including a loud jacket and a cowboy hat. Miles runs this lodge in the middle of a forest, and although she doesn't seem to do a heck of a lot there, it's a given that her life will soon be in peril and that Borgnine will have to come to the rescue.

But there are other stories to set up and introduce along the way, including that of the fire itself. There's a group of convicts working in the forest. One of the convicts is an Indian named Frank, who is played by Erik Estrada. Estrada's so scary, chipmunks flee in terror when he approaches (literally). Just 10 minutes in, the fire starts. The convicts and the warden are battling the flames, and there's a great shot of one of the men on fire, screaming as he runs through the camera frame. Allen certainly doesn't waste any time before getting down to business. The fire is briefly stopped, and the warden reports that there's no danger—but of course the fire, which is smoldering as the men leave, is not really extinguished.

This poses problems for many people in the small town. Unfortunately for local teacher Harriett, played by Donna Mills, she's decided to take an entire class out on a field trip to collect leaves. As the fire builds, a little girl wanders off into the woods. In a matter of just a few shots, the fire grows exponentially to an enormous size. "I'll come back for you!" Mills screams before driving off with the other kids. Good thing she got all of the parents to sign those field trip release forms! Most entertaining is a pair of doctors, featuring a heavily mustached, ascot-wearing Alex Cord and his soon-to-be ex-wife, Patty Duke Astin. Cord is an actor I'm not particularly familiar with, and in this film he has the most unusual delivery I've seen in some time. He says every line extremely slowly, using a voice that's almost as deep as Barry White's. It's particularly humorous in their first scene, when the script forces the character to repeat himself. "Hey . . . I love you. I . . . love . . . you," he says, stretching those three words out as much as humanly possible. I actually had the time to fix myself a sandwich while the line was being delivered.

After seeing smoke, the couple decides to hang around just a little longer to help out, as the fire builds to a frenzied inferno. The elderly town doctor decides to drive to the lodge to assist, and the filmmakers cut to stock footage of a bear in a forest, then back to the road, where a bear appears. The doctor decides that the best way to deal with a bear standing in the middle of the road is to drive his car off of the side of the road into a large tree stump and flip the vehicle over. He does this perfectly, breaking his right leg.

Meanwhile, the story returns to Estrada, who's in the most lax state prison camp imaginable, where convicts stand around and play pool all day. He walks into his sympathetic warden's office and volunteers to help fight the fire, with the intent of escaping into the flames and catching a passing train (or, I should say, stock footage of a passing train).

The flames move toward the lodge, much to Borgnine's concern. He also heads out there. Upon his arrival, Borgnine, along with Cord, takes up the task of finding the little lost girl. With the help of a helicopter pilot, they rescue her. But the fire blocks their return to the lodge. This means that the children, the teacher, the doctor, Duke Astin, and Miles are trapped inside. There are some impressive shots of the fire burning, and there's a wonderfully elaborate death scene. At one point, a firefighter scales a tall tree to its top, where it is burning. After a cutaway, the fireman is shown awash in flames and falling past camera, screaming all the way down. A flaming tree falls right on top of him and also flattens a convict.

Borgnine uses all of his equipment to attempt to rescue those trapped inside the now-flaming lodge. Hopping into his Jeep, he attempts to lead them to safety. Unfortunately, in true disaster movie fashion, his great heroism results in his spectacular demise. As for convict Estrada, while waiting to catch his train he discovers the crashed helicopter and blinded pilot and is faced with a moral dilemma.

Most of the characters are brought safely back to the lumber mill just in time for the climax, which involves a large propane truck that is about to explode and blow up said lumber mill. Again, in true disaster film tradition, love blossoms between the two doctors amid the rampaging fire, and they talk of setting up a practice together. This is all fine and dandy, except that I had also been treated to shots of the city on fire by this point, and I wondered if there was indeed a town left to practice in. Lastly, Miles somberly remembers Borgnine via a last-minute flashback of many of his scenes, including his elaborate death. Not exactly an upper of an ending, but I'm not complaining.

The fire scenes are well staged and the film moves at a fast pace, is entertainingly cheesy, and, most importantly, is never boring. As TV disaster films go, this is one of the most amusing.

Most Spectacular Moment of Carnage

Poor Ernest Borgnine. He plays the nicest character in the film yet he dies the most graphic death. While leading the lodge occupants to safety, a large tree falls in the middle of the road. The flames surround them, and Borgnine decides to push the debris off of the road and an escarpment with his Jeep to clear the way. He succeeds but, naturally, the Jeep catches fire, too, and it rolls down the escarpment in flames before finally exploding. (GK)

Firestorm (1998)

Twentieth Century Fox   89 minutes

SO BAD IT'S GOOD

DIRECTOR: Dean Semler

WRITER: Chris Soth

CAST: Howie Long, Scott Glenn, William Forsythe, Suzy Amis, Barry Pepper

Apparently, there are only 400 firefighters trained to parachute into blazing forests that are inaccessible to ground crews. They're called smokejumpers, and ex-gridiron star, Fox NFL Sunday broadcaster Howie Long is one of them. In fact, when *Firestorm* begins, he is almost immediately shown parachuting in to save a family in distress. Their house is on fire and the daughter trapped inside, with flames surrounding the entire area.

Long plays Jesse, a man who seems to have magical powers. This is the only way that I can explain someone parachuting to the ground and whipping out a running chainsaw from his backpack. After sawing down a nearby tree, the chainsaw disappears and is magically replaced in the next shot with an ax. It may be implied that these items are with every smokejumper as they hit the ground, but where do they keep them? A chainsaw is a rather large and protruding object that would be noticeable. And is it wise to keep something next to you in a forest fire that is powered by gas? Anyway, Long heroically runs in with his smokejumper buddy, Scott Glenn, and rescues the girl. Trapped by a fire wall (or so it is described by the characters, otherwise no one would know what the hell was going on), Glenn gets injured when a large camper explodes, flies through the air, and lands on his leg. All looks lost, until a plane dumps a red liquid and suffocates the flames. An amusing way to start a movie, yes?

The film has no time to ponder or answer any questions, only to show slow-motion shots of the heroic Long walking out of the flames with Glenn and the child. This may actually be the last heroic deed Long completes in this film. Back at the smokejumpers' training camp, Long grills and trains a motley assortment of firemen, including Jonathon Young, a wacky, moronic guy who keeps dropping his ax inches away from Long's head. Long always seems to just shake his head, finding all of this funny.

Nearby at the high-security Wyoming State Penitentiary is the villain, a convict played by William Forsythe, who looks like a cross between Jesus Christ and a member of the Allman Brothers Band. Somewhere out in the forest is $37 million that the convict stole before his arrest. Forsythe's elaborate escape plan involves being sent on a bus along with some other convicts to help fight a fire that Forsythe arranged to have an associate set. Forsythe enlists the help of a small gang of cronies (including *Battlefield Earth*'s Barry Pepper) to overtake the officers in a gunfight. Amazingly, this plan goes off without a hitch. The convicts and cops left alive are locked up in the bus together as a raging forest fire closes in. Even the wacky firefighter Young manages to get himself trapped on the bus, an impressive feat, mostly because I couldn't figure out where he came from, and it didn't make any sense for him to be there in the first place.

Forsythe and his cronies pose as Canadian firefighters (who have just happened to wander into Wyoming) and accidentally run into Suzy Amis, who is trying to escape the fire. As it turns out, Amis is devoted to carrying the eggs of a rare species of bird to safety. Long finally arrives to assess the situation, parachuting in via a really cheesy green-screen effect, and leads the convicts and woman to a nearby trading post. The action begins as Long and one of the convicts, a large, ex-pro wrestler, duke it out. Despite getting a few good shots in, Long is hit over the head repeatedly with a canoe and loses the fight. He is only saved when the wrestler tries to leave the burning cabin and is shot dead. By the end of the picture, Forsythe, unwilling to share the loot, will have picked off all of his convict friends one by one (shooting one dead, pushing another off a cliff), in essence doing Long's job for him.

Long pulls himself up and escapes the trading post on a motorcycle. At this point, the villains have a truck to drive and Amis in tow as a hostage, which leads to a ludicrous chase through the forest in which Amis is rescued. My favorite moment in the film occurs at this point, when Long pulls out a running chainsaw from his magician's bag and, without even turning around, tosses it over his head. The spinning blade lands in the windshield of the van. Batman doesn't have this many gadgets!

Our leads Long and Amis, who are now being chased by Forsythe and one other convict, hide in a makeshift hut built from tree branches. Luckily, Amis has military training and can build makeshift huts. She can also start a distress fire, something that Long seems completely incapable of. But before long, poor Amis is kidnapped again. Glenn appears and explains that two fires are approaching, and that when they collide a "firestorm" will occur, killing everyone in the vicinity. Thank goodness Forsythe has already taken care of that problem.

Reaching the lake just before the firestorm, Long confronts Forsythe and a "surprise" villain that isn't particularly surprising. (It's Scott Glenn, the only character who isn't accounted for during the course of the action, plus he's retiring, doesn't have much money, etc.) Long also takes the opportunity to make a cowardly dive into the lake while Amis is being attacked. By now the firestorm occurs, in the form of some goofy effects of the entire skyline bursting into flames. It looks almost ridiculously apocalyptic.

As for the bird eggs, despite tumbling off a cliff, being shot at, having been surrounded by intense heat and flames, and being submerged, they hatch safely. You should be getting the point by now that this movie is as stupid as a bag of hammers, and I haven't even recounted all of the insane, unbelievable events that occur.

I like Long, and he has a great, confused expression throughout the proceedings, almost like he can't believe he's in a movie. Unfortunately, since the release of *Firestorm* he seems to have been sent back behind the desk of *Fox NFL Sunday*, where his colorful commentary is well suited and much more appreciated. Who knows, maybe he's just waiting for a better script.

Most Spectacular Moment of Carnage
After taking an ax in the chest, Forsythe still refuses to die, and he is killed only when a hole is fired through a boat, his head is pushed through the hole, and the firestorm singes his face off. It is barely visible, but it's hysterical anyway. **(GK)**

In Old Chicago (1937)

Twentieth Century Fox   96 minutes

RECOMMENDED

© Twentieth Century Fox

DIRECTOR: Henry King

WRITERS: Sonya Levien, Lamar Trotti (based on the story "We the O'Learys" by Niven Busch)

CAST: Tyrone Power, Alice Faye, Don Ameche

Based on the events surrounding the Great Chicago Fire of 1871, *In Old Chicago* is an entertaining classic that really manages to impress in its last 20 minutes, when the fire burns out of control. The film tells the tale of the O'Leary family and opens in 1854 with the tribe on its way to Chicago. One gets a sense that Chicago would be much better off had this family never made it there, as fights and strange accidents seem to plague them throughout the movie.

After arriving in the city, the young O'Leary boys decide to help a group of ladies out of their carriage. Naturally, one woman falls into the mud, staining her dress, but the boys' mother insists that she can get the stain out. There's a funny close-up of the mother's hands washing the dress as time marches by. Years are superimposed across the screen, finally stopping in 1867, giving the impression that the mother has spent 13 years washing this particular dress. But no, over this time she has begun a successful laundry business from her farm. Her now grown-up son Tyrone Power has become a powerful and popular, though slightly shady, figure in the community, while his brother Don Ameche has emerged as a respectable and moral lawyer. Little brother Tom Brown seems to have found his purpose in life as "comic relief" for the family. Our first introduction to him is in the family barn, getting romantic with the Swedish cow milker/family hand June Storey. Storey rarely says more than "Ya!" with the thickest of accents.

It's very strange that in the '30s, filmmakers felt compelled to insert musical numbers into their films (actually, now that I think about it, that was the case in the '70s, too). One gets the impression that if the world ended in one of these films, the characters would go out singing and dancing as the earth opened up on them. When Power enters a local saloon owned by acquaintance Brian Donlevy, he gazes upon cabaret singer Alice Faye. Power falls instantly in love with Faye, and I was forced to watch her sing a couple of musical numbers. There's a good five or six numbers in all, as a matter of fact, which seems entirely unnecessary. Anyway, the smitten Power wants Faye as his girl, and he also would like open his own establishment with her in "the Patch," a seedy area of Chicago.

So how does Power show his deep love and affection for Faye? Take note. In the '30s, courting rituals seem to have involved hiding in the female's mode of transportation. If the male was thrown out, he should have then followed her to her apartment and hide inside. When she arrived, the male was to greet and court the woman by jumping out from behind a curtain, chasing her around the room with a wild look in his eyes, and wrestling her to the ground. At this point she should have been totally enraptured and kiss him. For all of you out there who might be willing to give this a try, unfortunately, unless you're Tyrone Power, behavior like this will likely get you labeled with the nasty title of "stalker," and it will also get you arrested.

Power's brother Ameche is running for mayor. Unfortunately for Power, Ameche's mayoral plans include cleaning up the Patch, which he claims is a terrible fire hazard (hint, hint). When Ameche wins, one of his first duties as mayor is to tell his brother to get out of the Patch or he will be prosecuted. Ameche is also upset that Power hasn't asked Faye to marry him yet. The hesitant Power complies, asking to marry Faye on the spot. After this, he happily tells his brother that he only did it to avoid prosecution. Again, not a smart thing to say. This results in one of the best scenes in the movie, a brawl between the two brothers. Ameche hits his brother so hard that Power flies backward across the room and into the door (the effect is undercranked so it looks sped up). Power hits back, sending Ameche in the other direction, flying over his own desk. This continues as each of the actors delivers a single blow, which results in the other actor throwing himself across the room.

Back at the farm, Mom accidentally leaves a lighted lantern next to a cow. This results in the fire that makes up the last 20 minutes of the film. The fire footage looks great, and there are some great wide shots of panicked crowds running through the streets of fire, people jumping from buildings, and fire wagons racing down the streets and almost getting into accidents themselves.

The mob, with the approval of Power, thinks that Ameche started the fire to clear out the Patch, and they set out to kill him. Clearly, if there's anyone that they should lynch, it's Ameche's mother. Unfortunately, Power begins to feel some guilt when he learns the real reason for the fire, and he races through the streets to stop the mob before they kill his brother (which apparently would have been acceptable had Ameche been the one who'd started the blaze). All of the brothers meet up and face the mob. In the chaos, Ameche is shot. Power's goon heroically picks him up and attempts to carry him to safety, but the building explodes and, in a stunning wide shot, falls right on top of the two men. Meanwhile, there are effective shots of a kerosene factory exploding and drenching the city in flames, and there are some really incredible shots of the city in flames in the background.

When you think about it, from the beginning, all the O'Learys have done is bring corruption, death, and fire (along with affordable laundry service, admittedly) to the city of Chicago. Mother O'Leary speaks eloquently (well, not really) about both the family and the city moving on, rebuilding, and continuing to thrive despite the odds. Yeah, lady, it's easy to make a speech about rebuilding when you're the one who burned the city to the ground.

Don't get the wrong impression. I enjoyed this movie and I highly recommend it. It runs a reasonable 96 minutes, and it doesn't outstay its welcome. In fact, I can safely say that it ranks as my favorite '30s disaster film. The story takes some unexpected turns, the effects are spectacular for their day, there are screaming crowds and shots of panicked, rampaging cattle (!), and there's even some onscreen carnage. So if you want to see an old disaster flick, I'd say that this is the one. The box for this film says it was released in 1938, but it won two 1937 Academy Awards (hmm?), for Best Supporting Actor and incredibly, Best Assistant Director. Go figure.

Most Spectacular Moment of Carnage
Although I really like the opening death and the fight between the brothers, Brian Donlevy's demise takes the cake. At one point during the fire, cattle free themselves from a dairy plant and race down the flaming streets of Chicago. Donlevy tries to hang on to the side of building, but he falls and is trampled to death by bulls. If there were a raging fire burning through my city, that would be the way I'd least expect to die. (**GK**)

Last Night (1998)

Alliance/Rhombus   95 minutes

RECOMMENDED

⚡

DIRECTOR: Don McKellar

WRITER: Don McKellar

CAST: Don McKellar, Sandra Oh, Roberta Maxwell, Robin Gammell, Sarah Polley, Trent McMullen, Charmion King, Jessica Booker, David Cronenberg, Tracy Wright, Callum Keith Rennie, Karen Glave, Arsinée Khanjian, Geneviève Bujold

Last Night is a darkly humorous comedy about the end of the world as seen through the eyes of various Torontonians. Unlike in most other disaster films, in this movie there is no question that the world will come to an end (in roughly six hours, to be exact), and these Canadians are well aware of that fact. The film never explicitly describes just what is about to destroy the world. It takes place during the last "night," yet the streets are bright, like on a sunny summer afternoon, so I assume that the planet is on a collision course with the sun and will likely be incinerated.

Everyone seems to have accepted their fate and, with little time left, most just want to get together with their loved ones, and maybe attend a big end-of-the-world party at Nathan Phillips Square. Everyone, that is, except for Don McKeller, whose wife has died from a long illness. As the film begins, he attends a family meal, where he argues with his comically unstable mother over her decision to hold a "Christmas dinner." It's certainly not Christmas, but the mother insists on putting up the tree, giving out stockings, cooking a large turkey, and staying happy. After being chastised for being late, McKeller responds, "The world is ending tonight at midnight; that's keeping me pretty occupied." Despite the fact that he lives alone, McKeller doesn't want to spend his final hours anywhere but in his apartment.

Unfortunately for him, it won't be that easy. After leaving the dinner, he discovers a dejected Sandra Oh sitting on his front step. Oh, who was out to get a bottle of champagne for the big event, has had her car upturned and now has no way of getting home. Using McKeller's phone to call her husband, she gets nothing but the answering machine. As her panic builds, the mildly annoyed McKeller relents and tries to help her find a ride home. In the meantime, an oddball assortment of characters intersect. This includes a gas company representative (played by director David Cronenberg), who is calling up every customer in the city and calmly going about his last day of work as if it were any other. There's also an old high school acquaintance of McKeller's who is putting on a concerto at 11:00 P.M., and another friend who has rejected spending the last hours of his life joining a prayer circle with his stepmother in Mel Lastman Square (you probably have to be Canadian to find this reference funny). Instead, he has chosen to devote his remaining time to fulfilling every sexual fantasy he can think of. He keeps a detailed list written on his kitchen walls, and he marks off every sexual task as it is completed. All this seems very wacky, but in fact the humor is low-key, and it works effectively.

As the hours quickly pass, McKeller and Oh slowly open up to one another. McKeller complains that everyone wants to "hook up" on the last night, and he later explains that he is avoiding it because "I don't want to risk having bad sex today." Many more strange situations follow, including a scene in which McKeller's friend makes a pass at him and another in which McKeller and Oh try ineffectively to hotwire a car. There are also intermittent cutaways to a newscaster covering the end-of-the-world party. At one point the broadcast shows the world's largest guitar jam, which is occurring in North York and is led by Randy Bachman (the legendary Canadian guitarist whose band, Bachman-Turner Overdrive, is famous for the song "Takin' Care of Business").

As the final hour passes things heat up, and some characters are attacked and assaulted by gangs and frightened citizens. The characters really open up to each other, until the poignant final moment of the film, which is scored to the tune of "Guantanamera." There are no reprises or lucky twists of fate for the characters in this film, although the movie still manages to end on a humanistic note. I really appreciated the different tone, deadpan humor, and polite nature of the characters, who, even as the world ends, retain their mostly friendly dispositions.

Last Night won a pair of Genie Awards (Canadian Oscars) for Callum Keith Rennie as Best Supporting Actor and Sandra Oh for Best Actress. Since its release, the picture has won and was nominated for numerous film festival awards. There are no big effects or explosions, but that's all a part of the film's unusual charm. What do you know? Sometimes good films actually do come out of Canada.

Most Spectacular Moment of Carnage
This film is subtle and low-key, and there isn't very much onscreen violence. Citizens do attempt to overturn a streetcar at one point, and David Cronenberg meets his fate

rather violently: after being threatened at home by a frightened young man with a shotgun, the film cuts back much later to Cronenberg, shot dead and spread out in a pool of his own blood. (GK)

Terror on the 40th Floor (1974)

MetroMedia   100 minutes

AVOID AT ALL COSTS

DIRECTOR: Jerry Jameson

WRITERS: Edward Montagne, Jack Turley (story)

CAST: John Forsythe, Joseph Campanella, Lynn Carlin, Anjanette Comer, Laurie Heineman, Don Meredith, Kelly Jean Peters, Pippa Scott

Clearly intended as a quickie, low-rent *Towering Inferno* rip-off, *Terror on the 40th Floor* (also known as *The Blazing Tower*) is an incoherent snoozefest that, even at a mere 85 minutes, plays as if it were in slow motion. The DVD box lists this film's running time as 100 minutes; clearly quite a bit of material is missing from the version I saw. Nonetheless, I was relieved to be spared from those surely riveting extra 15 minutes.

It's some big corporation's Christmas party, and everyone's getting all tanked up, but top executives Forsythe, Campanella, and Meredith are really more interested in making some time with a few of the pretty young women back in Forsythe's office. Soon the party ends and everyone goes home except for our aforementioned group of execs and their "girlies." (For some reason there is one more woman in the group, this one not a nubile young thing and not the object of anyone's affections.) The security guard, thinking everyone has left, locks the office from the outside. Oblivious, Forsythe and friends continue to party, thinking that they can leave any time they want. Forsythe is married, but that doesn't stop him from coming on to one of the chicks, who he tries to impress by showing her rare books and taking her to the boardroom, where she seems to be aroused by the fact that many key corporate decisions had been made there. Campanella, on the other hand, having plied his conquest with expensive champagne, seems not to want to bed her; instead, he wants her to give him access to the top-secret personnel files. As for Meredith, he's all for hot sex immediately in his office.

While this is happening, a maintenance worker is down on the 12th floor, fixing a faulty heating unit and swigging from a bottle of booze. When he accidentally knocks a bucket of water onto the floor and the machine he's working on starts sparking, he's shocked to witness a fire suddenly erupt all around him. Of course, when he steps on the fire to try to put it out, he becomes engulfed in flames. At that moment the security guard happens to come by, and he tries to help the guy out. This is hilarious, because it's is clear that a stunt double is being used for all the wide shots of the guy on fire, while the regular actor is seen in medium shots and close-ups, and he is quite clearly not on fire. And yet, the film cuts back and forth with no regard to continuity.

Moments later the fire department arrives, even though no alarm has been heard going off and no one has been seen calling it in. The firefighters, of course, think the building is empty aside from the now-dead maintenance worker and injured security guard, so they get to work trying to fight the fire that has already spread up to the 19th floor. Even though the fire department has brought a fleet of trucks and other emergency vehicles with them, all loudly blasting their sirens and flashing their lights, the partygoers see and hear nothing.

After a series of firefighting sequences, which I believe to be stock footage provided by the Los Angeles Fire Department, Campanella is revealed in the file room, angrily reading a memo about himself in which he is not described lovingly. After Don Meredith walks in on this, Laurie Heineman, the woman who let Campanella in, decides to go home, but she stops when she sees smoke in the hallway near the elevator. Then a bizarre cut occurs in which it appears that quite a bit of footage is missing, because suddenly everyone knows about the fire and is trying to escape through some sort of heating duct or something, which won't open. In addition, Forsythe now has a wound on his bandage-wrapped hand, everyone's sweating like pigs, and the lights have been shut off. Also, Campanella at one point apologizes to Forsythe for having said something rude, but what it was I do not know. This creates a wonderful sense of complete randomness, and this feeling pervades the rest of the movie, which never completely makes any sense again.

Heineman suddenly starts to go nuts. She runs around screaming, and every time someone tries to help her she just gets crazier, until finally she runs through a glass door and collapses on the floor, bleeding profusely. Then, the three men decide to try to use the elevator shaft to get down to the floor below, as they can't seem to break the lock on their office door. (And by "can't," I mean they do not even try, just as they do not try to pick up the phone and call anybody. Perhaps these things happened in the footage that was cut, but who knows.) It is at this point that people start having strange flashbacks in which they lament the failures of their lives. I can't begin to tell you how bizarre it is to witness a disaster movie, especially one that doesn't really make any sense to begin with, resort to unrelated flashback sequences to kill time. The older woman, saddened by a picture on the wall that's impossible to discern, flashes back to a recent conversation with her boyfriend, in which she reveals to him that she's pregnant and he reacts by telling her to get lost.

Campanella also has a flashback in which he recalls himself at a swanky buffet restaurant with his daughter. He and his wife have separated, and his daughter blames him, his love of booze, and his many unrealized promises for the future. She leaves in a huff without touching any of her food, and the flashback comes to an end. As it happens, he's the guy chosen in a coin toss to be the one lowered into the elevator shaft by a fire hose tied around him. Once lowered, he eventually manages to crank the doors on the floor below open, but before he can climb out of the shaft, he somehow slips out of the hose and falls, screaming, to his death.

Now it's time for Forsythe's flashback, and it consists of an argument with his wife over her crazy habit of mentioning their dead son. Meanwhile, a guilt-ridden Meredith has broken a window and is lapping the air up. He doesn't get a flashback, by the way. For the next little while, not much happens other than shots of firemen putting out fires and the occasional shot of one of our trapped partygoers gasping for air or looking pensive or something. Finally a helicopter is sent up, and a rescue team is dropped onto the roof while the chopper scans the windows with a searchlight to find survivors. Once they're found, everyone is helped into the chopper and brought to safety—and just at the last minute, too, for as they leave the 40th floor is engulfed in flame. This is all about as exciting as watching an instructional video on how to retile your bathroom.

Once on the ground, the pregnant woman is met by her lout of a boyfriend, who agrees to reconsider his position on the impending abortion that he formerly supported. And of course Forsythe reconciles with his wife, and after a final shot of the building with gigantic flames shooting out of the top windows, the film thankfully comes to a close.

There is hardly a moment of actual terror or suspense in this movie. The filmmakers' insistence on trying to wring contrived emotional content out of ridiculous flashbacks, and their failure to introduce any other level of action or drama, makes the entire viewing experience one of boredom and curious strangeness. In fairness, the only version currently available has footage missing, but I'm quite sure that watching the even longer version would not have lessened the movie's horribleness. Vic Mizzy's unbelievably inappropriate musical score doesn't help either. Though the dated social mores and funky music are sort of funny for a while, there is no good reason to spend an entire 85 minutes watching this piece of crap when you could easily be doing something more valuable with your time, like shooting smack.

Most Spectacular Moment of Carnage

As you now know, out of our group of central characters only Campanella buys it. Luckily the filmmakers do throw in a shot of an obviously fake dummy falling down the elevator shaft, contorting horribly as it hits everything it can on the way down, with shrieks of pain added on the soundtrack. Nice. **(MR)**

The Towering Inferno (1974)

Twentieth Century Fox/Warner Bros.   165 minutes

HIGHLY RECOMMENDED

⚠

© Twentieth Century Fox and Warner Bros.

DIRECTOR: John Guillermin (action sequences directed by Irwin Allen)

WRITER: Stirling Silliphant (based on the novels *The Tower*, by Richard Martin Stern, and *The Glass Inferno*, by Thomas N. Scortia and Frank M. Robinson)

CAST: Steve McQueen, Paul Newman, William Holden, Faye Dunaway, Fred Astaire, Susan Blakely, Richard Chamberlain, Jennifer Jones, O. J. Simpson, Robert Vaughn, Robert Wagner

Richly deserving of its 1974 Best Picture Academy Award nomination, Irwin Allen's *The Towering Inferno* is a fantastic suspense/action movie that, unlike that same year's *Earthquake*, doesn't resort to obvious exploitation. Now, I'm happy that *Earthquake* was so bloodthirsty and violent, but I'm much happier that the makers of *The Towering*

Inferno took the material seriously and made a large-scale action film with humor, suspense, and drama that even today enthralls the viewer. And best of all, if you're still looking for over-the-top disaster movie thrills, it's got that too.

It begins with a small electrical fire in a storage room on the 81st floor, and for hours, no one even notices it. It turns out that many of the electrical systems are shorting out, and this is of great concern to architect Paul Newman, who designed the building to exacting specifications. He has now come back from a vacation to discover that his boss, William Holden, and Holden's son-in-law, Richard Chamberlain, have cut corners to save costs. However, not even his indignation can stop the massive gala that will be held that night at the top of the tower to celebrate the building's opening to the public. As celebrities of the stage, screen, and political scene arrive for the party, Newman scrambles to prevent further electrical overloads. By this time, the fire in the storage room has gotten completely out of control, and it isn't long before security chief O. J. Simpson sees smoke pouring into the hallway on his security monitor. Simpson immediately calls the fire department, while Newman goes to check out the fire. Faced with this nightmare scenario, and with one of his engineers already burned badly, Newman tries to convince Holden, up on the 183rd floor, to evacuate the party, but of course Holden will have none of it.

Enter the San Francisco Fire Department, led by chief Steve McQueen, who brings his men inside and quickly takes over. He's extremely professional, to the point that he doesn't seem remotely daunted by the task of fighting fire in a building of this size. Still, he's unable to prevent the fire from mysteriously spreading throughout the building and eventually causing massive explosions. As the fire spreads from floor to floor and tenants are evacuated, it becomes very dangerous for the partygoers above to take the elevator to safety. This is a result of the failing emergency systems, which may cause the elevator to stop on a floor where the fire is raging. (Which actually happens to an unlucky group of people who ignore the warning and cram into the elevator; they're all burned to a crisp when a fireball explodes into the opening doors.) Therefore, everyone will have to be evacuated by the very slow "scenic elevator" on the outside of the building, but that ceases to be an option when the power fails. The next chance would be helicopter evacuation from the roof, but high winds make that next to impossible. Taking the stairs is also out of the question, as smoke and fire fill the stairwells, not to mention that there's a constant threat of explosions.

Newman eventually makes it to the party (after saving two kids, including Bobby from the *Brady Bunch*) and, as McQueen prepares to set up shop on the roof of a neighboring building, Newman rigs the scenic elevator with a "gravity break." This means that the elevator will drop slowly but not be able to return. And you know what that means, disaster fans. Among the 12 people he sends down are his girlfriend, Faye Dunaway, and Jennifer Jones, the object of big-hearted con man Fred Astaire's affections. But of course there's an explosion, which tears a hole in the side of the building next to the elevator as it descends, knocking Jones out of the elevator to certain death below.

Meanwhile, McQueen has set up a system of cables that will carry people, one at a time in a metal, chair-like harness, to the roof of the building next door. Though it's a slow, unbelievably terrifying process (and one that, in real life, at that height and in those wind conditions, would be a spectacularly short and deadly ride), it is successful. At least it is until Newman is informed that the fire will engulf the room in 15 minutes, but that it will take three more hours to evacuate everyone who's left. A drunken, cowardly Richard Chamberlain suddenly jumps onto the chair harness, and a few others try to join him as well by hanging on for dear life. That's when Robert Vaughn tries to stop them by grabbing hold of the chair. But instead of Vaughn pulling them all back to safety, Chamberlain forces the chair, with Vaughn still hanging on, down the cable and away from the building. Moments later they all lose their grips and fall to their deaths. It's always fantastic in one of these movies when two stars die at the same time.

Anyway, McQueen's got his plate full, what with the fire and the explosions and the general chaos, not to mention the continuing, dangerous evacuation from building to building, and he's forced to add one more task to the checklist: saving the people in the scenic elevator, which is now hanging precariously. And, of course, he can only do this by being hoisted up there by helicopter and jumping on the roof of the elevator and hooking it onto a cable hanging from the helicopter . . . well, you get the idea. Once this heroic deed is done, he's informed (by a dead-serious Dabney Coleman) that he's got to go blow up the water tanks on the floor above the partygoers, as this will probably douse the flames, though it may kill a few people in the process. One supposes they could have done that hours earlier, but then Richard Chamberlain would probably have survived, and that's not any good.

So back into the building he goes, teaming up with Newman to strategically place plastic explosives to blow out first the floor, then the gigantic water tanks. Since there's no way for him to leave the building once he's done this, he and Newman go back to the party and tie themselves down. Five minutes later the tanks explode, sending a gigantic, torrential flood down into the room. There are some casualties (bartender Gregory Sierra, for one), but overall the scheme proves to be successful, and the water flows down the stairwells and elevator shafts, dousing the fire as it goes. I'm not sure how everyone got down to the lobby after this, as none of the characters are shown taking the stairs or the elevator, both of which I think would have been impossible tasks, but oh well.

The Towering Inferno is the quintessential (and most famous) Irwin Allen production in that it is of an enormous scale and it features a huge, all-star cast. However, what also sets it apart is its high-quality script, taut direction, lavish production design, and cinematography, as well as another great score by John Williams (who also scored Earthquake that same year), and extremely restrained, realistic performances by Steve McQueen and Paul Newman. I see The Towering Inferno as the blueprint for all of the best action films that have followed it (if not in content, then in tone). The film won Oscars for Best Cinematography, Best Film Editing, and Best Music, Original Song ("We May Never Love Like This Again"). The Towering Inferno proves that sometimes, when a disaster film takes itself seriously, both the audience and the film community will, too.

Most Spectacular Moment of Carnage

This movie features one of the most famous, amazing death scenes in disaster movie history. As the fire spreads, Robert Wagner and his secretary finish up their illicit tryst in his office and prepare to leave. They open the door to find that flames have engulfed the next room. Wagner wraps a wet towel around his head and, still suave as hell, tells her he'll be back with help soon. The moment he steps into the other room, he bursts into flame and begins to flail wildly as he runs around. The scene sadistically goes on and on until finally he crashes through the window and plummets to his death. And if that's not enough, the secretary ends up ablaze as well, and she takes a header out the window just like her doomed lover. Second prize goes to Jennifer Jones's death scene, in which, after falling from the scenic elevator, her body hits an overhang on the side of the building with a sickening thump, then twirls back over the side and keeps on going. **(MR)**

Inferno (1998)

Viacom Productions   90 minutes

AT YOUR OWN RISK

This made-for-TV movie depicts the chaos caused by a solar eruption. As the heat wave is sent from the sun to the earth, temperatures rise and create problems for an out-of-work doctor, a *Baywatch*-esque lifeguard and romantic interest, a teacher and a student, a greaseball tow truck driver, and an army general. Their paths all cross as they attempt to work out an elaborate love quadrangle and endure temperatures rising above 140 degrees. Nothing spectacular here (no one bursts into flames or anything), but the film boasts reasonable production values, panicked crowds, and an onscreen drowning. Stars James Remar, Stephanie Niznik, Daniel von Bargen, Anthony Stark, Kathryn Morris, Jonathan LaPaglia, and Antwon Tanner. Directed by Ian Barry. **(GK)**

Solar Crisis (1990)

Trimark   112 minutes

AVOID AT ALL COSTS

Yikes, another Alan Smithee film means a "disaster film" in the most literal sense. A solar flare threatens the earth, causing riots, locust swarms, and other disasters. Not that any of this was visible in the film; the viewer is just told this is happening. An international team must detonate an antimatter bomb to prevent the flare from striking the planet. The story of three generations—a grandfather, a father, and a son (Charlton Heston, Tim Matheson, and Corin Nemec, respectively) is emphasized but never brought to a satisfactory conclusion. In fact, nothing much happens at all in this flick besides a lot of dull scenes with talking heads. At least Jack Palance is entertaining as he chews up scenery, grunts, laughs maniacally, and delivers lines that make no sense whatsoever. You know you're in trouble when a movie opens with a rolling crawl explaining what's happening, and then cuts away to another scene with yet another rolling crawl. Full of jarring cuts and scenes that end before they come to any conclusion, the movie has a generally unfinished feel to it. The whole thing is just god-awful. *Solar Crisis* went straight to video in North America after producers decided it was unreleasable as a feature film. Also stars Annabel Schofield and Peter Boyle. **(GK)**

RARE, OBSCURE, AND LESS IMPORTANT TITLES

Ring of Fire (1961)

THE MOST RIDICULOUS DISASTER MOVIE CONCEPTS EVER

Some of the more unusual disaster movie concepts originated in the '70s and early '80s. It must have been hard to continue making the same films about raging fires, erupting volcanoes, and meteors crashing to Earth, and producers and filmmakers must have felt compelled to come up with new ideas. They came up with some pretty wonky ones, too, such as sinkholes, interstate car crashes—there was even an entire film devoted to people trapped in an elevator! Unfortunately, while many of these films sound incredible in a "so bad they're good" kind of way, they aren't available on VHS or DVD yet, so you'll have to wait to check them out. Sorry.

Burning Rage (1984)
A made-for-TV movie about a raging coal fire burning beneath a small mining town, starring Eddie Albert, Carol Kane, and Tom Wopat. Filmmakers were really grasping at straws by 1984.

Catastrophe (1978)
The fact that it has an impressive-looking poster depicting various calamities is about the best that can be said about this project. William Conrad narrates stock footage of real-life disasters. Meant to fool '70s disaster movie fans out of their hard-earned dough.

Cave-In! (1983)

Poor Irwin Allen. After bombing with his last three disaster pictures at the theater and seeing the genre completely dry up, he still produced and aired this made-for-TV movie. From the limited information available, I gather it is about a group of people trapped in a cave, hopefully (but not likely) with a grizzly bear. Stars Leslie Nielsen and Ray Milland.

Condominium (1980)

A three-hour-plus miniseries about the residents of a condominium who are struggling to endure rising utility rates and a hurricane. With Barbara Eden, Steve Forrest, Ralph Bellamy, and Dan Haggerty.

The Elevator (1974)

This made-for-TV movie features a group of people (including James Farentino and Roddy McDowall) from various backgrounds who are trapped inside a skyscraper elevator. I was trapped inside of an elevator for 90 minutes when I was 12 years old. It was the most boring experience of my life. I'm not sure that this film is any different.

Hanging By a Thread (1979)

Made near the end of Irwin Allen's disaster movie career, this made-for-TV movie features Patty Duke Astin, game show host Bert Convy, Donna Mills, and Cameron Mitchell trapped in a cable car as it hangs precariously over a ravine.

Heat Wave! (1974)

For the love of God, break out the sunscreen! A routine summer occurrence is turned into a made-for-TV disaster movie. As far as disasters go, this would seem to be an easy one to avert—all you would have to do is stay indoors, turn up the air conditioning, and enjoy a cool, tasty beverage. Director Jerry Jameson churned out *Hurricane, Terror on the 40th Floor,* and *The Elevator* the same year, and this isn't much different, qualitywise.

Konchu Daisenso (1968)

A Japanese movie in which savage bugs turn on the population and attack. Cities burn and disaster strikes as insects take over the world. Never released in North America. (I wonder why?)

Lost! (1986)

What a lame title for a disaster movie! What the hell is this film supposed to be about? Being lost is something that can easily be remedied with the use of a map, or even by asking directions. This Canadian film is actually about an overturned cruise ship and the tensions that rise between the survivors, some of whom are religious extremists who want to die. This film was nominated for a couple of Genies (Canadian Oscars), but don't hold out much hope that it's going to be all that good.

Night of the Lepus (1972)

A very violent, absolutely incredible film that must be seen to be believed. I'm stunned that this hasn't been released on DVD yet. Stuart Whitman, Janet Leigh, and DeForest Kelley (*Star Trek*'s Dr. Leonard "Bones" McCoy) battle giant mutated bunny rabbits that are headed for the big city! Sometime the raging rabbits are filmed in slow motion to make them appear larger; sometimes terrible visual effects are employed; and occasionally, a man dressed in a bunny suit is used for close-ups to give us the impression of "giant" killer rabbits. The animals even race through a small town, destroying it and attacking the occupants. Hysterical.

Oil (1976)

In this Italian disaster flick (its original title was *Cuibul Salamandrelor*), an oil spill catches fire. Panic ensues. I think it might have been better had a city and its inhabitants been submerged in an unexplained tidal wave of oil.

On Hostile Ground (2000)

A made-for-TV movie about a killer sinkhole that threatens to devour New Orleans and ruin Mardi Gras. Yup, I couldn't believe it either. Stars John Corbett.

Smash-Up on Interstate 5 (1976)

A made-for-TV movie about a big, violent car accident, featuring Robert Conrad, Buddy Ebsen, Vera Miles, and Donna Mills. Tommy Lee Jones appears as an officer. The producers must have figured that it was cheaper to make a disaster movie about a traffic pileup than one about an earthquake.

Storm (1999)

This standard made-for-TV movie is only funny because of its lame title. Unlike, say, *earthquake* or *avalanche*, the word *storm* just doesn't inspire the same kind of fear. Usually when I hear that word it's in an innocuous sentence like, "Bundle up, there might be a storm coming in." Anyway, L.A. ends up in the path of a government-designed killer hurricane, and scientist Luke Perry is the city's only hope. *Hasta la vista*, L.A. With Martin Sheen.

Thirst (1998)

People with incredibly dry throats struggle to survive a muggy afternoon. Who sponsored this film, anyway, Coke? Just kidding, folks. Actually, the plot of this made-for-TV flick revolves around parasites infecting a town's water supply and making many people sick. This is a bad idea, as it's a bit difficult to visually depict the horror of a parasite menace in an exciting way. Frankly, I like my idea better. With Adam Arkin and Joely Fisher.

The Void (2001)

This low-budget, direct-to-video clunker starring Adrian Paul (of TV's *Highlander*) and Malcolm McDowell is about the formation of a black hole on Earth that threatens to suck the planet into oblivion. Yeah, I guarantee some suckage if you rent this one. (**GK**)

Really Bad Storms

We've had a lot of trouble with storms lately. As I write this, only days ago a tornado hit just a few blocks from my house, moving a school off its foundation and sending its roof floating away into the sky. No one was hurt, but it was pretty scary stuff. It seems only natural for filmmakers to try to capture the monumental fury and power of such forces of nature. There's just one thing that I don't understand about these films. Some of them feature "storm chasers," characters who believe that, yes, it is worth risking their lives to sit through, pass through, or even study a monumental force of nature up close and get themselves killed in the process. Seems to me that there's little that driving beside a funnel cloud can accomplish that meteorological satellites and radars can't. Then again, if these characters were smart, the movies wouldn't be as goofy, would they? So let's begin a comprehensive look at movies that feature Really Bad Storms. **(GK)**

Cyclone (1978)

100 minutes

AVOID AT ALL COSTS

DIRECTOR: René Cardona, Jr.

WRITERS: René Cardona, Jr., Carlos Valdemar

CAST: Andrés Garcia, Hugo Stiglitz, Carroll Baker, Arthur Kennedy, Lionel Stander

This *el lame-o* Mexican/Italian cheapie (which is also known as *Terror Storm*, *Ciclone*, and *Tornado*) is very bad in almost every possible way, and it's sleazy to boot. Set in the Caribbean, the film introduces three groups of people, each on a *Gilligan's Island*–esque tour boat, a fishing barge, or an airplane. Their lives are intertwined by the arrival of an unexpected cyclone.

At least there's no waiting. The storm hits almost immediately, flooding the island (or, more accurately, a miniature of the island—shots of this are mixed with stock footage). During the storm the plane crashes. Actually, the plane footage looks reasonable. Anyway, it crashes and the seats fly forward, crushing some passengers à la *Alive*. The survivors swim outside the plane as it (well, a model of it) begins to sink to the sea floor. It looks like the producers actually splurged and rented a tank and part of an aircraft for some decent-looking wide shots of the plane in the sea. Too bad they had to squander the money they spent and ruin it by painting the airline name, Carlber, in green, blocky, unevenly sized and spaced letters on the side of the plane. It was almost looking like they had a real movie there for a minute.

On to group number two. After the storm hits, the fishermen all jump off their barge and into a rickety lifeboat in the rocky waves (which doesn't seem like the smartest thing to do in the middle of a cyclone; I'd have taken my chances on the big boat). Group number three's tour boat loses its engine.

Thirty minutes in, the "cyclone" portion of the film ends. The survivors all meet up and struggle to stay alive on the tour boat. This might be an interesting scenario if any of the characters were developed, but they aren't. They're just a bunch of bad Italian actors (and Lionel Stander, who must have needed the money really badly) reading terribly scripted lines of an expository nature to cue the audience in to their obvious problems: "Water is necessary for survival." "The water must be rationed!" (Pronounced "ray-tioned" by these actors.) "But I want more!" This is typical of what passes for dialogue in the film. The filmmakers also opt for excruciatingly long shots (you'll wonder why the editor didn't cut away to something, anything) of what appear to be confused actors looking into the camera. Either the director was trying and failing to depict the internal drama of the characters in their doomed situation via the Kuleshov Effect (by intercutting expressionless shots of actors with the sea and each other to create various effects), or he was simply padding the running time. My pick is the latter.

Pure exploitation takes over when the plane crash survivors are either gobbled up by sharks, or, days after the storm (how hard could it be to find these people in now-perfect weather?), they run out of food and must find an alternative. Soon, people start panicking (check out Stander's Albert Einstein hair at this point—it's hilarious) and behaving badly. First, a fisherman grabs a woman's poodle, slits its throat, and then skins it. The poodle looks like rotisserie chicken by the time he's done. The gang then resorts to cannibalism, eating the flesh of the dead people on the boat. Obviously this is yet another exploitation of the events that occurred in the Andes some years before. The characters even mention that event as a means of rationalizing what they're doing. But those bodies were frozen. Thankfully, the filmmakers don't show the grisly details here, but one wonders how helpful eating warm, bacteria-ridden human flesh might be. Anyway, after seven days (seemed like seven years to me), two survivors sail off in the lifeboat to find help.

Just to throw another ridiculous element into the mix, a woman gives birth while stranded at sea. She and the baby seem fine despite the fact that they've received no medical attention or assistance. It's that easy to recover from childbirth! Finally, a fight breaks out, the boat sinks, and sharks try to gobble up everyone on board (aided by an inappropriate Lucio Fulci-esque, fast-paced keyboard dance track). The filmmakers cut between footage of people splashing around and sharks with pieces of bloody meat in their jaws. Help arrives, and some of the characters make it to safety, although these scenes are so ineptly filmed that it's almost impossible to identify who they are. I couldn't even tell if the baby made it. This is some pretty sick and sleazy stuff. Trust me, avoid this one.

Most Spectacular Moment of Carnage

Although the plane crash is passable, the painful expressions on the faces of those whose lives this film has touched (mainly me) might be the real tragedy. I'll never get those 100 minutes back. **(GK)**

Flood! (1976)

Warner Bros.   94 minutes

AT YOUR OWN RISK

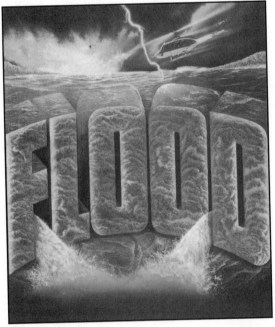

DIRECTOR: Earl Bellamy

WRITER: Don Ingalls

CAST: Robert Culp, Martin Milner, Barbara Hershey, Richard Basehart, Carol Lynley, Roddy McDowall, Cameron Mitchell, Eric Olson, Teresa Wright, Francine York

This hilarious Irwin Allen made-for-TV movie depicts the horrors brought on after a dam floods and breaks. Robert Culp stars as Steve Brannigan, a cool, laid-back helicopter pilot in the small town of Brownsville. As the film opens, Culp lands his helicopter with fisherman Roddy McDowall aboard at a lake on the other side of the town's dam. A husband and his pregnant wife—Cameron Mitchell and *The Poseidon Adventure*'s Carol Lynley—are introduced. McDowall's brief cameo is almost entirely useless; he never appears again, despite the fact that he is billed sixth.

Meanwhile, a young boy playing on the rocks of the dam nearly has his head taken off when the structure sprouts a leak and a large rock socks him in the cranium. On his way back from the lake, Culp discovers the boy, finally takes off the sunglasses that he has been wearing throughout the first 20 minutes of the film, and patches the kid up with a ridiculous red bandana that he's had tied around his neck. Culp decides the boy is fine, tells him to get checked out later, and leaves. At the airport, Culp mentions the boy's predicament and the leak in the dam to his soon-to-be brother-in-law, Martin Milner. The grumbling brother-in-law seems to do everything in this town. As the movie progresses, it turns out that he is not only an airport mechanic, but also town councilman and coach of a local boys' sports team. What a busy guy! Milner is also engaged to be married to a nurse, who is played by a youthful Barbara Hershey. The age gap between these two characters can only be described as disturbing.

Unfortunately for Milner, the town mayor (who is also the injured boy's father) does not take Milner's concerns seriously and refuses to drain the dam. He fears that it will ruin the lake and destroy the tourist trade that the town depends on. There's a lot of bickering between the two men until Milner, defeated by the council and certain that the dam will collapse, runs around town telling all of the boys he coaches to warn people to leave and board up their houses.

The dam finally breaks, in one of the movie's most entertaining bits: watch for the Tonka truck plunging down the miniature dam set (with dam worker Cameron Mitchell supposedly inside). There's a great moment where Culp must race across the frame and save a sandbag worker from being run over by an incredibly slow-moving bulldozer. The water pours through, the power goes out, and the town begins flooding (which is shown via stock footage), although water levels seem to vary from scene to scene. Naturally, the mayor continues to argue that all is well despite the rising waters. And, as if having a dead husband at the bottom of a dam isn't bad enough, Mitchell's wife goes into labor as the water pours in. Culp, Milner, and the nurse attempt a daring rescue operation in which Culp lands the chopper on top of the woman's house, climbs in, and frees her (her leg is hooked in a crossbeam; the water is up to her neck). The set actually looks good, and some expense must have gone into building it and flooding it with water.

But there are some jarring cuts that don't make any sense. Out of nowhere, the floodwater surrounds the local hospital to which many characters are being evacuated, yet minutes later Culp runs out of the building and sets off in his chopper to search for the young boy. Umm, shouldn't the helicopter be fully submerged by this point? It's also funny that while all of this is going on, Milner doesn't really seem to care about the injured boy that Culp abandoned at the dam; he just continues to mutter that the kid can take care of himself and that he'll be fine. Of course, he isn't fine; he's floating downstream and hanging on to the upturned trunk of a tree for dear life. More devoted to the boy's cause is Culp, perhaps because he wants his scarf back. Gritting his teeth, Culp later opens up to Milner with a politically incorrect, vague story from his youth about his kid brother trying to help a "half-wit greenhorn" and falling to his death. Apparently, Culp has held onto the scarf his dead brother wore ever since.

After that bizarre scene, Culp and Milner decide to blow up a bridge with dynamite and block the floodwaters. "Like popping the cork out of the bottleneck!" Culp grimaces, doing his best Cliff Clavin impersonation. Culp sees his scarf and runs back to try and save the boy before the bridge blows up (Milner can't be bothered, I guess).

This TV movie is amusing enough, and it has decent production values, but it doesn't really make a whole lot of sense, nor does it entertain as thoroughly as Irwin Allen's other TV movie, *Fire!* manages to.

Most Spectacular Moment of Carnage

The mayor's wife, frantic about the disappearance of her son, dives into the floodwater to rescue the boy, but the kid she's spotted turns out to be another child. The flailing boy makes it to the hospital safely, while the wife drowns unnecessarily in the process. **(GK)**

Hard Rain (1998)

Paramount   97 minutes

RECOMMENDED

© Paramount Pictures

DIRECTOR: Mikael Salomon

WRITER: Graham Yost

CAST: Morgan Freeman, Christian Slater, Randy Quaid, Minnie Driver, Edward Asner, Michael A. Goorjian, Dan Florek, Ricky Harris, Mark Rolston, Peter Murnik, Wayne Duvall, Richard A. Dysart, Betty White

So, what exactly is "hard rain," anyway? Is it a cross between rain and sleet? Rain that comes down so intensely that it hurts? Or is it an icy, solid rain? And what would possess anyone to call a movie *Hard Rain*? Frankly, just calling it *The Flood* (its original, working title) would have been much more appropriate.

In spite of this flaw, and the criticism that was heaped on the film upon its release, I found this big-budget, box-office loser to be quite enjoyable and, if you can shut your brain down for 90 minutes, I think you'll find it to be one of the more entertaining disaster films in recent years. Christian Slater stars as Tom, an armored-transport worker. A large cowboy-hat-toting Morgan Freeman plays the mild-mannered criminal Jim, who, along with his cohorts, is intent on robbing Slater's truck for its booty of three million dollars.

In an extremely grumpy performance, Edward Asner plays Uncle Charlie. Maybe it has to do with his character, or maybe Asner was mighty upset about being a film in which he was constantly showered with water. At least he doesn't have to worry about that for long, as he meets his demise at the hands of Freeman's band of looters as they attempt to rob Slater's truck. After seeing Asner's fate, Slater realizes that he, too, will be killed by the gang no matter what he does. That is, unless he hides the money from them and contacts the authorities.

The rest of the movie is a 90-minute chase, as the criminals pursue Slater through a series of elaborate, half-submerged waterscapes. Along the way, Slater crosses paths with other characters, including a shifty Randy Quaid, who is referred to only as "the Sheriff," and Minnie Driver as Karen, an art restorer working on an elaborate small-town church. She won't leave the church, claiming that she's put too much work into the stained glass windows to leave. So she is, apparently, willing to die. There's also a bickering old couple played by Betty White and Richard Dysart, as well as various deputies that naturally become involved in the money retrieval.

Of course, given the cash involved, characters in the film turn bad. There's some hilarious dialogue as "the Sheriff" growls, "For 20 years I've been eating shit—breakfast, lunch, and dinner. Well, tonight I'm changing the menu. From now on, everything I'm going to eat is gonna be shit-free!" Only Randy Quaid could deliver a cheese-drenched line like that and sell it. One nasty deputy decides that best thing to do during the flood is attempt to rape Driver, and he goes to the elaborate measure of first taking her home and handcuffing her to the stairway banister before attempting it. It's always fun to see alliances change during the course of a film, and this disaster flick has a couple such cases, including one in which Slater must team with Freeman to fight off the "anti-shit" Sheriff and his deputies. By now the dam has completely flooded, and a tidal wave of water begins to submerge the entire town as Slater attempts to rescue Driver from her house, which not only floods, but also separates from its foundation and begins to float away with the tide. This leads to an exciting final battle on the rooftop of the floating house.

But, as I mentioned earlier, the movie is far from perfect. There's an unintentionally funny slow-motion shot of a character throwing down a machine gun in disgust at the end of the movie. Is this intended to be an antigun statement? One can certainly understand the sentiment, but a silly movie like this really isn't the place for it. There are a few other minor problems. The last shot of the old couple shows them stranded in the branches of a large tree. For all I know, they could still be up there. The freeze-frame ending is also strangely abrupt. And some of the country bumpkin characters are just too stupid to be believable, although I suppose that I can't say for sure, as I've never been to Huntington, Indiana. Still, the movie is paced well, runs a tight 97 minutes, and is never boring. I liked the cinematography, the action sequences are well cut, the leads are likable, and the flooded-city set looks phenomenal. As good as digital effects can be (and they do attempt some digital effects in this film, which are noticeable), you can't beat using real water and flooding a real set. I appreciate the effort this film made.

In fact, take it for whatever it's worth, but I would go out on a limb and claim that this is, hands down, the best flood movie ever made.

Most Spectacular Moment of Carnage

There are some solidly spectacular deaths. Almost all of the characters stay alive long enough to get swept away and drown in the climactic tidal wave of floodwater. During a chase inside a school, one character is knocked off of his Jet Ski and flies headfirst into a glass trophy case. Another character takes a bullet through his eye socket. Another is electrocuted, convulses, and catches fire. Yet another is hit by a floating propane tank, which promptly explodes, sending his flaming carcass into the air. But the sheriff's death takes the cake. He narrowly avoids being hit by a motorboat as it flies in the air over his head, only to be hit in the face by the boat's spinning propeller. And, believe it or not, even that doesn't kill him. What a resilient guy! Finally, blood gushing down his face, he is eventually killed by a barrage of bullets fired by our heroes. **(GK)**

The Hurricane (1937)

Samuel Goldwyn Company   103 minutes

RECOMMENDED

⚠

DIRECTOR: John Ford

WRITERS: Based on the novel by James Norman Hall and Charles Nordhoff; adapted by Oliver H. P. Garrett; screenplay by Dudley Nichols and Ben Hecht (uncredited)

CAST: Dorothy Lamour, John Hall, Mary Astor, C. Aubrey Smith, Thomas Mitchell, Raymond Massey, John Carradine

It's interesting to note that even in the '30s, disaster movies were long. While most pictures of this era run about 70 to 75 minutes, many '30s disaster movies approach the two-hour mark (see *The Rains Came* and *San Francisco*). *The Hurricane*, by comparison, clocks in at 103 minutes, making it one of the shorter such titles of its day. This is not to suggest that this film *seems* long (actually, it moves along at a much quicker pace than its remake, the 1979 *Hurricane*), but to just point out what impressive spectacles these films were even as early as the '30s.

The plot revolves around the village hero, Terangi, played by John Hall, who is first mate on a trading ship. Described as "charming" in a sort of "wacky native way" by the French governor's circle of friends, Hall is the kind of man who likes to dive off the boat from the top mast, and he also has the unfortunate-sounding talent of "smelling a wind." Hall gives his character an unnecessarily thick Polynesian accent, but stereotypes like this were typical of the period, and at least the character is likable. He's engaged to his childhood sweetheart, Marama, played by Dorothy Lamour. After an elaborate marriage sequence, Hall and Lamour run along the beach together, each wearing a lei, and the sounds of ukuleles swell as the two canoe along the picturesque South Seas shoreline. Come to think of it, this picture starts out like an Elvis Presley movie.

Lamour is concerned about Hall leaving her so soon to set sail, but he explains that he loves the sea because, when he proudly wears his first-mate cap, "I'm just the same as a white man." (Of course, I waited in vain for someone to explain to Hall that he *is*, in fact, a white man, and that Lamour is very clearly a white woman, as well.) Lamour stows away onboard as the ship leaves dock, but after being told that her husband will lose his position if she stays, she casually leaps off the deck and into the water and swims to shore.

After arriving in Tahiti, things go very poorly for Hall, who is insulted and hit by a drunk in a bar. After retaliating, he is locked away in prison for six months, unable to see his wife. It turns out that Lamour is pregnant. Despite the doctor's, village chief's, local priest's, and other friends' protests to get Hall's wrongful conviction overturned, the stuffy French governor refuses, explaining that the natives have to abide by French law. Our hero is taunted and tortured by evil prison guards. The performance of John Carradine, as a detestable warden with an evil scowl, is alone worth the price of admission. There's a great montage as Hall, slowly going mad within the walls of his prison cell, makes escape attempt after failed escape attempt, racking up a 16-year sentence in the process. Despairing after eight years in jail, Hall attempts to hang himself; but in fact, his would-be suicide is an elaborate ruse. He breaks free and, in perhaps the film's most satisfying moment, hits the warden in the face so hard that it kills him. I'm not sure how this is possible, but it works within the context of the film.

On the run, Hall hides along the docks of Tahiti before leaping through a window into the sea and stealing a canoe. Lost in a storm, he is finally retrieved by a local priest. Obligated to turn him in, the priest asks Hall if he meant to kill the warden. The priest decides that "You've sinned, but others have sinned more against you." A heavenly choir chimes in, suggesting that even God agrees that a deathblow to the face was exactly what the prison warden deserved (frankly, I agreed, too). Hall is reunited with his wife and daughter, and the three plan to make an escape to a remote part of the island.

This all leads to an extended climax when the hurricane finally hits, washing the village away. In perhaps the most spectacular scene, the waves crash through the walls of the nearby church, killing the helpful priest and most of the praying villagers. Any film by director John Ford is worth watching, and while he is still most famous for his westerns, his experience with action scenes really helps the film, particularly the hurricane scenes. They are quite exciting and tightly cut. In the end, *The Hurricane* is, surprisingly, one of the most action-packed of the '30s disaster films, and it is definitely recommended. The movie won an Oscar for Best Sound Recording.

Most Spectacular Moment of Carnage

Time to cancel those South Seas ticket reservations. During the hurricane, many locals tie themselves to the trunks of large trees. This proves unsuccessful for the most part, and there are several shots of villagers being uprooted and swept away. **(GK)**

Hurricane (1974)
ABC   74 minutes

AVOID AT ALL COSTS

☠

DIRECTOR: Jerry Jameson

WRITER: Jack Turley (based on the novel by William C. Anderson)

CAST: Larry Hagman, Martin Milner, Jessica Walter, Barry Sullivan, Michael Learned, Frank Sutton, Will Geer, Lonny Chapman, Patrick Duffy

I am amazed that this made-for-TV movie is supposed to be based on a book—a book that was actually published, and that actually sits on bookshelves somewhere—because the plot seems to be thrown together as an afterthought. Were there detailed descriptions of stock footage seemingly borrowed from the National Weather Board in the novel? How about paragraphs that describe characters reacting to random shots of floodwaters, tornadoes, and stormy clouds? It's only minutes into the movie that grimy old footage of the above appears (don't worry if you miss any of this footage; you'll see it over and over and over again), as it is revealed that Hurricane Hilda is building in the Gulf of Mexico. We know the hurricane is building because typewritten "weather bulletins" saying that very thing periodically scroll across the screen incredibly slowly, no doubt to pad the running time of this film.

First to be introduced is a group of air force pilots on a dangerous mission to drop beeping metal cylinders (I'm guessing that they're tracking devices) into the eye of the storm. They talk a lot and use lots of fancy terminology, such as "quadrants," "vectors," and "UHFs," which mean absolutely nothing to me. I think I was supposed to be impressed with this technobabble. Next, there's Larry Hagman and his wife, Jessica Walter, who are not only doing some recreational boating in the eye of the storm, but also are running low on gas. There are some hilarious sequences later in the movie when shots of the characters in the boat are intercut with stock footage of tidal waves. And there's crusty Will Greer and Michael Learned, who appear in Hurricane Weather Headquarters Central (wherever the hell that is). Surrounded by reel-to-reel recorders, they make cheeky jokes and act more concerned about the ramifications an incorrect prediction will have on their careers than the deaths of people such a prediction would cause. Geer, the resident expert at this institute, frowns upon Learned, blathers endlessly about "the boy who cried wolf," and speaks against her use of scientific data to predict storms. I suppose he prefers to lick his thumb and stick it out the window of the institute to check for high winds.

Don't expect anything special from this one. It's generally a snoozefest, complete with uninteresting characters and situations. The only mildly amusing sequence involves the drunken neighbor of a young couple. He invites them to some kind of "storm party." The husband, played by Patrick Duffy, wants to leave before the house is totaled, but he also doesn't want to offend his blitzed host. What to do? Ah, it's only a hurricane. Staying behind for another drink or two won't hurt, right?

In true '70s tradition, the opening credits list Michael Learned, Frank Sutton, and Will Geer as "special guest stars." Beats me how actors can be credited as "special guest stars" in their own movie.

It goes without saying that the producers were really cutting corners here. The stock footage is terrible, and it doesn't come close to matching the newly shot footage. When a special effect is required (such as when Hagman and Walter are stuck on a boat in the eye of the storm), it's substandard. And yes, that is the actual black-and-white footage of the *Minnow* from *Gilligan's Island* (although it was stock footage to begin with, I'll forever associate it with the show) that is used, twice, to depict Hagman's ship in the storm. A note to the producers: guys, if you're going to use stock footage, make sure that if the film's in color, so is the stock footage. Otherwise, it's really noticeable. 'Nuff said.

Most Spectacular Moment of Carnage

The air force plane catches fire and explodes, killing all onboard. Unfortunately, this is never depicted, because that would have been far too expensive. It's just implied with an abrupt cut. There's only one notable death in the film, and it isn't particularly violent. The drunken neighbor's party ends tragically when his house is leveled. A window breaks, rain pours on the surprised guests, the ceiling cracks, and plaster falls. The host awakes to see the wreckage and his wife's body being carted away. "I'm sorry, honey!" is all he can muster. **(GK)**

Hurricane (1979)

Paramount   120 minutes

AVOID AT ALL COSTS

DIRECTOR: Jan Troell

WRITER: Lorenzo Semple, Jr. (based on the novel by James Norman Hall and Charles Nordhoff)

CAST: Jason Robards, Mia Farrow, Max von Sydow, Trevor Howard, Dayton Ka'ne, Timothy Bottoms, James Keach

Hurricane is a $22 million (that was a lot of money back then) remake of John Ford's *The Hurricane,* brought to you by Dino De Laurentiis. Shot by famous cinematographer Sven Nykvist, at least it looks pretty, and the Bora Bora location adds some flavor. But those are about the only positive comments that can be made here. The film feels like a poor attempt to fuse disaster-film elements with a Harlequin Romance novel. In spite of being made a full 40 years later than the original, this version is actually more melodramatic than its counterpart.

The tale is set in Samoa in the 1920s on a U.S. Army base, which is run by stodgy, bored-looking general played by Jason Robards (and you'll be as bored as Robards's character appears, too, after 120 minutes of this). He wears a permanent frown, is mean to the natives, and keeps a tight military rule on the island. The bulk of the movie, though, deals not with Robards's excessively grumpy character, but with a "forbidden love" affair between the local Samoan chief, played by Dayton Ka'ne, and Robards's daughter, played by Mia Farrow.

Curious about the natives' free and exciting lifestyle, Farrow goes off to stay with them and paint them. The next thing you know, she and Ka'ne are making out in front of the Samoan sunset, with Farrow delivering stilted dialogue and making declarative statements like, "Just love me!" Of course, Robards wants no part of this melodrama (he's too busy chewing scenery in his own subplot), and he orders the chief arrested and brought to prison on the trumped-up charge of performing an illegal native ceremony. This leaves the lovers no option but to run away into the jungle to forage together and start a new life.

It's at this point that the film turns into a big-budget *Blue Lagoon*, with painfully long montages of the two lovers swimming together, canoeing together, and laughing together. This probably would make a great travelogue video for the Samoan tourist board, but I wanted action by this point, and *Hurricane* didn't even seem to want to deliver this. In the original film, the filmmakers knew enough to cut away from this stuff as quickly as possible and get right to the action. Unfortunately, the people behind this version didn't know any better.

The low point occurs when the chief decides to seductively wash and kiss Farrow's feet (while purring "Later I'll put some lemon on it") in a particularly romantic scene. Why would anyone want to see this? Often, when viewing a really bad movie, there comes a certain point when you know that the film cannot recover. A friend of mine even likes to yell out "Pull the goalie!" during this moment. All of you readers should use this terminology too, the next time you watch a bomb like this. It's a good analogy. And in *Hurricane*, the feet-sucking scene is the definite goalie-pulling moment. Actually, the goalie should be off of the ice and driving away from the arena by this point.

But enough with the hockey references. Before long, the young chief is arrested and detained on a ship. During a hilarious escape the chief strikes an officer, knocking him off the side of the boat. The officer falls into the water five feet below and dies. I suppose they just don't make those tough navy sailors like they used to. They can't even swim anymore. And it must've been some right hook. Once again, a knockout punch is something that a movie made in the '30s can usually get away with, but this is just too ridiculous a stunt to pull in a modern film.

Finally, after 90 painful minutes of weepy violins and melodrama, the hurricane arrives. It blows a lot of straw buildings apart. Whoopee. During the climax, things get a little more interesting, as the large navy ship docked nearby starts toppling in the storm. In the film's most entertaining scene, a furious Robards wades over to the ship and attempts to push it upright himself before being swept away by the storm. A lot of soldiers, natives, and other characters are killed by the hurricane. The village ends up half submerged, and the navy ship actually crashes through the village church (a decent special effect, but it comes way too late to help this film). Love's grand, isn't it? Just stick to the original.

Most Spectacular Moment of Carnage

Robards's strongman death takes the cake, and there are a couple of other good deaths during the climactic storm. Also, watch for the chief's jealous girlfriend. She commits suicide by jumping into the waves and crashing into the sharp coral reef. Ouch! **(GK)**

Night of the Twisters (1996)

Atlantis/MTM/Family Channel/PorchLight Entertainment   90 minutes

AT YOUR OWN RISK

⚠

DIRECTOR: Timothy Bond

WRITERS: Sam Graham, Chris Hubbell (based on the novel by Ivy Ruckman)

CAST: Devon Sawa, Amos Crawley, John Schneider, Lori Hallier, Laura Bertram, David Ferry, Helen Hughes, Jhene Erwin

Let me first warn all movie renters out there that *Night of the Twisters* is wholesome family entertainment, and that equals no fun for guys like me, who really want to see actors like John Schneider get sucked into a tornado. Like many family films of its kind, the plot focuses on a teenager (this one lives in Blainsworth, Nebraska) and how his entire family manages, through love and courage, to survive the storm. Not just any storm, but several "anticyclonic" (which sounds like something that might be in my car engine) twisters, which apparently are particularly nasty and unpredictable.

Early on, teenage lead Devon Sawa and his buddy end up alone at Sawa's home when the first twister strikes. Sawa has a somewhat strained relationship with his stepfather (John Schneider), but of course, it's nothing really serious, and most of their arguments are over why the teenager has forgotten to walk his grandmother's dog. Adding to the strain is the fact that Schneider's store is in dire financial straits, and he's just been denied a loan. However, this bankruptcy subplot is forgotten almost immediately, and whether or not Schneider's store was foreclosed remains unknown. Maybe the storm blew it away and saved everyone the trouble.

Some of the on-set effects in the farmhouse, such as the cupboards shaking and stairs cracking up, are well done. So are many of the outdoor shots of debris from the wrecked homes and towns. But the digital shots of the tornadoes themselves look terrible. Really terrible. This is particularly true during the climax, as a twister chases the family truck down the expressway. The computer-generated shots look absolutely hilarious. Anyway, Sawa rescues his baby brother, then drives his pal and his pal's sisters to safety before searching for his stepfather and grandmother. He finds his grandmother, who is completely batty and who gives a long monologue on angels, as well as Schneider, who is pinned under a truck (something that never would have happened to Bo or Luke Duke!). It's an interesting scene, if only because we get to see Schneider try to act from the shoulders up. Despite being a family film and having a low body count, there are a lot of characters who get maimed and tortured, something that I would have thought might be even more disturbing for families to watch than outright deaths.

Night of the Twisters is certainly passable, but it's lacking the nastier qualities that I like in disaster flicks.

Most Spectacular Moment of Carnage
No lives are lost onscreen, but there is quite a bit of destruction, and many of the family members get hurt. Perhaps the most painful-looking episode involves a flying trash can lid that hits Sawa's mother in the face, tearing a large gash on her forehead. (**GK**)

The Perfect Storm (2000)

Warner Bros.   126 minutes

AT YOUR OWN RISK

DIRECTOR: Wolfgang Petersen

WRITER: William D. Wittliff (based on the book by Sebastian Junger)

CAST: George Clooney, Mark Wahlberg, Diane Lane, John C. Reilly, William Fichtner, Bob Gunton, Karen Allen, Mary Elizabeth Mastrantonio, Allan Payne, John Hawkes, Christopher McDonald, Dash Mihok, Josh Hopkins, Michael Ironside

The Perfect Storm tells the supposedly true story of a group of down-on-their-luck fishermen, focusing primarily on Captain Billy Tyne, played by George Clooney, and Bobby Shatford, played by Mark Wahlberg. Against all logic, they travel far from the coast of Massachusetts into the Flemish Cap deep in the Atlantic Ocean, and in doing they so come across one of the worst storms in history.

When the movie opens you get the impression that the filmmakers will strive to do justice to the real people and an amazing true story. Perhaps they tried too hard. Despite the fact that the first half of the film is devoted to developing these characters, I never managed to connect with them. They are shown hanging out at the bar, and members of their families are introduced. A conflict between two fishermen, played by William Fitchner and John C. Reilly, is also established, and they spend the rest of the movie shouting at one another. Clooney, Wahlberg, and the rest of the people playing the fishing crew are excellent actors and they have some humorous moments, but the film still resorts to obvious disaster film tactics to try to gain sympathy. The characters are forever talking about what they're going to do when they get back home to their wives and families. In this type of film, as any moviegoer knows, that's the surest sign that a character will be dying.

Clooney's character isn't particularly likable. In fact, he's kind of crazy, and he leads his crew into the storm despite their protests and numerous warnings. It doesn't help that Clooney's also saddled with some less-than-brilliant lines. At one point he even growls to his crew that they're going out there "because that's where the fish are!" Just try to keep a straight face when you hear that one.

At this point the filmmakers really must have taken some liberties with the story. These guys have the worst luck! Besides their not being able to catch very many fish, a shark jumps onboard and bites Wahlberg (he recovers amazingly quickly, and is running, swimming, and jumping around the boat in the following scenes), while Reilly gets himself caught on a fishing hook and almost drowns. Inadvertently, these men appear to be the most inept fisherman ever to hit the sea. And after almost an hour, you really do want the storm to take these characters out, which certainly doesn't do justice to the real people involved; those men couldn't possibly have behaved like these guys.

But at least by this point the real reason to watch the film kicks in, and that's to see the spectacular storm effects. There are terrific sequences involving the crew trying to cut loose an anchor, board up the windows, keep the boat from capsizing, and of course, attempt to ride a giant tidal wave. All of this action is very well shot and cut together, and for the last 30 minutes, the film gains some momentum.

But back on shore, overstatement reigns supreme, with the family members screaming, shouting, and acting more terrified than the sailors who are actually in the middle of the storm. At least Clooney, Wahlberg, and the others onboard have an excuse for screaming. They *have* to scream every line just to be heard over the waves that are pounding into them. Particularly amusing is television meteorologist Christopher McDonald, who appears in two exposition scenes solely to deliver exposition about the storm. His performance is unintentionally the funniest, and he's forced to gaze, baffled and perplexed, into his computer screen, his hair mussed, and mutter lines like "Oh my God. It's the perfect storm!" Diane Lane (as Wahlberg's girlfriend, Chris Cotter) and Mary Elizabeth Mastrantonio (as fellow captain Linda Greenlaw) try to chew up more scenery than the storm itself, and that's quite a feat.

By the time it all subsides, however, the audience is left rather indifferent. The fishermen and their boat go down under a huge tidal wave, and the movie ends with an overwrought eulogy spoken by Mastrantonio. (Watch, in the background, for Michael Ironside's reaction shot; he looked to me like he's wondering if it's too soon to call the insurance company and get some money back on his boat.) Mastrantonio emotionally speaks about her friend Clooney and states that "any man who sailed with him must have been the better for it." Excuse me? I'd like to know how any of these fishermen could possibly be any *worse* off for knowing him. They're dead! The speech is clearly intended to bring the audience to tears, but it's ineffective—maybe because, at this point, the audience might be asking themselves how much of this really happened and how much is overblown Hollywood speculation (a lot, I think).

So what does it all mean? Is the film supposed to be a tribute to the determination of the working-class fisherman? If so, why depict the captain and other characters this way? No, if anything, it's a tribute to the advancement of special effects. Yes, the storm is perfect, but the script . . . eehhghh.

Most Spectacular Moment of Carnage

There's some spectacular storm footage, and my favorite involves the boat flipping over. But the nastiest bit of violence occurs when Reilly gets his hand impaled by a large hook and is pulled into the ocean. The tip of the hook is visibly pointing out of the skin. Yeow! (**GK**)

Tornado! (1996)

Hallmark Entertainment and Von Zernick Sertner Films   89 minutes

AT YOUR OWN RISK

⚠

WRITER: John Logan

DIRECTOR: Noel Nosseck

CAST: Bruce Campbell, Shannon Sturgess, Ernie Hudson, L. Q. Jones, Bo Eason

Timed to air on the Fox network just prior to the theatrical release of the big-budget *Twister*, this fantastically stupid TV movie dares to put an exclamation mark after its title without delivering the requisite thrills and excitement. It's the story of a small group of meteorologists in Texas's Tornado Alley, led by scientist Ernie Hudson and "gifted" storm chaser Bruce Campbell, and their struggle to prevent their government grant from being revoked by Washington bean counter Shannon Sturgess. It's just that Hudson has finally finished working on his new scientific device, which will be dropped into the path of oncoming tornadoes in order to return valuable scientific information that might be able to save lives. This machine looks exactly like the ones used in *Twister*, except it's not designed to pop open and release little airborne devices into the storm; instead, it's just supposed to sit there and apparently not do anything, making it unclear exactly how it works.

Our little group of scientists is soon joined by U.S. government auditor Sturgess, and you immediately know that within 20 minutes she'll be getting right into the down-home Texas groove necessary to convince her not only to extend their grant, but also to fall in love with that irresistible Bruce Campbell. She's got a week to make her decision, and things aren't looking so good for them when she arrives, what with the skies clear and free of storm activity. So, there's plenty of time to enjoy Texas barbecue and get hammered down at the local watering hole! But what better way to get to know everyone, including the young nerdy assistant and Campbell's crusty old grandpa, who likes to dispense homespun wisdom while condemning the technological trappings of his grandson's team as inferior to a man's intuition when it comes to finding and predicting storms. There's even a conniving "villain," though he's not really much of a bad guy, just an obnoxious TV weatherman who likes to remind people that while Campbell is a "starter," he himself is a "finisher," and that's supposed to be some terrible insult.

After three uneventful days, Sturgess decides to leave, and she explains that her decision about the future of the research program was made for her before she even left Washington. In a preposterous bit of exposition, she reveals that, because the research suggests that global warming is the cause of the changes in weather patterns that lead to storm activity like tornadoes, the U.S. government is shutting down their little group because, according to the U.S. government, global warming doesn't exist, and they don't want anyone suggesting otherwise! Given that, I'm not sure why they even sent her all the way to Texas in the first place.

Of course, it's at that moment when a tornado hits nearby. Sturgess goes with the group to chase it down, only they're too late to do anything and the storm takes out a small town. This misadventure galvanizes Sturgess's emotional connection to Campbell, apparently, since she decides to stay for a while, but what is she waiting for? Why, the same thing that the audience is waiting for: the fabled F5 tornado that is bound to hit in the final act of the movie. And when it does, it seems that point zero is the front yard of the research center, meaning they don't have to chase this one down, and isn't that convenient? As winds pick up, Hudson and his crew bring his barrel-shaped machine outside to stick it in place with the aid of mechanical legs that shoot into the ground, but one of the legs isn't working, and the storm is getting closer, and Hudson tries in vain to hammer the leg into the ground. But really, the only person who can save the day is Grandpa.

Did I mention that he has a big secret? Yes, when Grandpa was a little kid he watched his mother get carried off to her death by a tornado. So, does he have a vendetta/death wish? Why, sure he does! He grabs the hammer and tries to bash the machine's leg into the ground, but he gets knocked out by flying shrapnel, forcing Campbell and Sturgess to go back out there. For some reason, instead of dragging this 70-year-old man back to the shelter, they tie him to the machine, and that's when the tornado hits them. Only, it doesn't seem to be that big a deal. An F5 tornado cuts a massive swath of destruction, but not this one. Sure, it rips shingles off of roofs, but when it passes directly over our three friends, it merely treats them to a little wind, and seconds later they're in the eye of the storm. Conveniently, Grandpa wakes up and keeps hammering the leg as Campbell and Sturgess return to the shelter. Grandpa then vanishes as the high winds return, and that's that. Well, he sure showed that tornado, huh? What I don't understand is how a guy in Tornado Alley with a storm chaser for a grandson would have to wait 65 years to find a storm to die in.

Anyway, his sacrifice has meant that Hudson's machine stays put. It returns valuable scientific readings, none of which I was made privy to, for in a movie like this, as long as everyone gets what they want and love blooms in Tornado Alley, the viewer need not concern himself or herself with less important things, like what, from a scientific perspective, it is that these people actually do. Unfortunately, the combination of a complete lack of insight into this subject, crappy visual effects, the constraints of a TV budget, and the thudding, obvious script makes it just about impossible for the viewer to feel any real excitement or suspense. On the other hand, I'd watch Bruce Campbell try to jimmy a locked car door with a coat hanger for two hours and be grateful for the experience.

Most Spectacular Moment of Carnage

Even though a whole town gets wiped out, I was not treated to the sight of even a single dead body. I was therefore forced to recall Ernie Hudson's extremely distasteful performance in *Penitentiary II*, which turned out to be more than enough to make up for this movie's lack of violence and potato salad. **(MR)**

Twister (1996)

Warner Bros./Universal Pictures   112 minutes

RECOMMENDED

DIRECTOR: Jan de Bont

WRITERS: Michael Crichton, Anne-Marie Martin

CAST: Helen Hunt, Bill Paxton, Cary Elwes, Jamie Gertz, Philip Seymour Hoffman, Lois Smith, Alan Ruck, Sean Whalen, Scott Thomson, Todd Field, Joey Slotnick, Jeremy Davies

Jan de Bont's *Twister* is a ludicrous yet entertaining action movie that stands as a prime example of how the art of screenwriting has taken a back seat to pyrotechnics and visual effects. The so-called "script," by Michael Crichton and his wife, is filled with embarrassing dialogue and obvious plot and character contrivances, but that seems to be the point, as the film wears its lack of substance almost as a badge of honor. However, as long as the viewer acknowledges that the joke at the film's core informs the entire structure of the movie, it is possible to appreciate this movie on that level, even as the self-reflexive irony collapses under its own weight.

Bill Paxton and Helen Hunt are a storm chasing couple in the final stages of a protracted divorce, but of course it's obvious immediately when Paxton's new fiancée (a polar opposite from Hunt's character in every way) shows up that, over the course of the film, they're gonna fall in love again. But of course they're not really *out* of love at all, and it's never entirely clear why they split in the first place. Apparently, Paxton left his wife and his storm chasing life for some reason, and he appears to be reluctant to return to those things, but really, he's not. This is the extent of what passes for character development in this movie.

But somehow, as *Twister* lumbers forward, it doesn't matter anymore that these characters are empty, that the story follows a rigid, predictable formal structure, or that the dialogue is outrageously bad. The viewer gets hooked into the overall thrust of the material, which is not subtle, but it works, damn it! *Twister* is structured as a sort of ever-expanding series of increasingly unbelievable events; therefore the audience's incredulity also grows, but, to be fair, as the action becomes more and more outrageous, the film also becomes more entertaining. Our storm chasers, in the span of approximately 24 hours, come face-to-face with twister after twister, each one bigger than the last. This culminates, of course, in a confrontation with the biggest and deadliest kind of tornado, the fabled F5, which is also the kind of tornado that, when Hunt's character was a child, pulled her father into its hungry jaws before her very eyes. Hilariously, one dares not even mention the F5 in her presence, as the term inspires hushed tones and even dropped silverware (as in, silverware that slips out of one's limp, shocked hand). Hunt is obsessed with chasing tornadoes, as she possesses a personal vendetta against them, not to mention a death wish of sorts.

Because she's the leader of a publicly funded crew, she struggles with rapidly diminishing funds and resources. Her team of kamikaze meteorologists are a bunch of ragtag weirdos, each one a different "type," yet each one also unsocialized in the same way. In an odd bit of casting, her team includes Jeremy Davies, Alan Ruck, Todd Field, and Philip Seymour Hoffman (in a role I'm sure Jack Black desperately wanted). They're up against not only Mother Nature, but also an opposing team of storm chasers who are "evil" because this crew is privately funded and they tool around in shiny black trucks that are loaded with high-tech equipment (not to mention the fact that they're led by a theatrical, glowering Cary Elwes). But what they don't have is Paxton's intuition, and the movie suggests that he's got a natural instinct for predicting storms and where they will go once they hit, something that no amount of computers and number crunching can replace. Elwes has also stolen Paxton's design for a device that, when dropped in the path of a tornado, will release hundreds of tiny sensors into the storm in order to return valuable data.

This machine is ridiculous, and it is never fully explained how it works, but they certainly do make a point of showing all the switches and flashing lights and other things it's festooned with. Not that those things help Paxton when he's hanging on for dear life in the back of a speeding pickup, being pelted with hail as he tries to turn the damn machine on. Instead of merely having an "on" switch, he's got to flip whole banks of switches to turn on all the flashing lights and beeping noises, and as a result of this time-consuming process, they fail to deploy the sensors in time.

Of course, this machine is called Dorothy, in case you needed another reminder that this movie is just one big dumb joke. Not only have Paxton and Hunt emblazoned that name on the side of the machine, but they've painted a picture of a young Judy Garland as Dorothy Gale on the machine as well. Do you get it now? Well, just in case you don't, Elwes's modified version is called "D.O.T." And hey, isn't that Judy Garland on the TV in that scene where the tornado is about to destroy the town of Wakita?

Thankfully, in no other way does this movie mirror the events that occur in *The Wizard of Oz*, though it is interesting to note director de Bont's inappropriate Stanley Kubrick references peppered throughout the film. I'm not sure how he got permission to use scenes from *The Shining* in the famous drive-in sequence, but what amazes me more was that, as Kubrick's horror masterpiece unspools on that big screen, neither Paxton nor Hunt, nor any of their crew, actually watch it!

So, here's the movie in a nutshell: Paxton's and Hunt's crew are the good guys because they're passionate, clever, and not a bunch of "corporate kiss-butts" (actual movie line), unlike the other storm chasers, who are evil because they drive black trucks and are, in fact, "corporate kiss-butts." However, as soon as Paxton shows up after a long absence just to get the divorce papers signed, all hell breaks loose, and suddenly there are tornadoes of all sizes and description coming, one after the other. And even though, in all their years of storm chasing, none of them (besides Hunt) has ever seen an F5, they all will before the film ends, and of course, after failing several times to get Dorothy to work, that, too, will happen, and just when the F5 strikes. Oh yes, and all of this excitement and adventure will bring Paxton and Hunt back together again. It's wonderful how things always tend to work out, isn't it?

I suppose you're between a rock and a hard place when you try to make a two-hour movie about tornadoes, since you're forced to cram the film with twister after twister just to keep the action moving forward. I could say that even while you're doing this, you could still pay some attention to character development, but then that wasn't the film they were trying to make here. *Twister* is unabashedly a technical exercise, and it's not the film you turn to for anything more. The defining line of the movie, for me, is spoken just after Paxton and Hunt have almost been killed chasing a tornado. They get back in the truck and Paxton says, "We're going again," as another tornado develops nearby. It's as if all they have to do to find a tornado is go and look around, and when you understand this, you will understand the simplistic but effective thought process behind this film.

Twister was nominated for two Oscars (Best Effects, Visual Effects; and Best Sound), and it won the Golden Raspberry Award for Worst-Written Film Grossing Over $100 Million (Jamie Gertz received a Worst Supporting Actress nomination for her performance in the movie.) It's really pretty rare for a movie to be honored as both the Best and the Worst in a given year's crop of films.

Most Spectacular Moment of Carnage
Since Cary Elwes is the closest this film comes to having a villain, it's no surprise

when, at the end of the movie, the driver of the truck he's riding in is impaled by a huge piece of flying shrapnel. The truck is then sucked into the air, tossed around a bit, and slammed to the ground, where it explodes in flames. Sharp-eyed viewers will note that there are at least two other people in the truck, one of whom appears to be Jake Busey. **(MR)**

BRIEF REVIEWS

Gold (1974)
Hemdale   120 minutes

AT YOUR OWN RISK

This is a decent thriller. Starring Roger Moore, Susannah York, Ray Milland, Bradford Dillman, and John Gielgud, the movie was shot in South Africa. It lags in the middle, but the opening cave-in sequence and the extended half-hour climax, which involves set a rapidly flooding gold mine, are tense and exciting. Director Peter Hunt is famous for his work on James Bond films, and his talent shows here. Do not watch the version that is currently available on DVD; it is badly cropped, poorly transferred, and horribly dim. Wait for a proper version to be re-released. Had the quality of the DVD version I saw been better, this film might have received a higher rating.

Tidal Wave (1975)
Concorde   82 minutes

AT YOUR OWN RISK

Released initially to huge success in Japan under the title *Nippon Chinbotsu* (which translates to *The Submersion of Japan*), Roger Corman bought the rights to this film, recut it, inserted scenes with Lorne Greene, and dubbed it. The results are undoubtedly awkward, though the special effects from the Japanese version are quite impressive. The rights have since reverted back to the original film's production studio, Toho, so the likelihood of finding Corman's version is extraordinarily slim. Film director Joe Dante appears briefly in the sequences shot in the United States.

RARE, OBSCURE, AND LESS IMPORTANT TITLES

Gale Force (1992) Straight-to-video

Tidal Wave: No Escape (1997) Made-for-TV

Triumph Over Disaster: The Hurricane Andrew Story (1993) Made-for-TV

Just a Little Radiation

Hello, and welcome to the most depressing chapter in the book. Focusing on movies that deal with nuclear threats, killer viruses, and bacteria-induced plagues, it could be subtitled Films That Take Themselves Much Too Seriously, or, Films That Involve Gradual, Painful Deaths.

Almost all of the nuclear-disaster films in this section date from the late '70s to the late '80s. I guess the threat of nuclear war loomed large on people's minds then. There are definitely some good films, but there are also some slow, tedious, overly preachy exercises as well. I suppose that preaching was the whole point of those movies, but these people should remember in the future that subtlety goes a long way. At least more recent ventures into the subgenre have been considerably sillier.

Virus/bacteria films are usually somehow more entertaining than nuke movies (with the exception of *Warning Sign*; that was just plain stupid), even though disease

259

is just as real a threat to the human race. Maybe it's because we haven't experienced the unpleasantness of a major plague in recent years, and therefore the concept seems more fantastic to us. These films do have much more potential to be over-the-top ridiculous.

Please note that while *The China Syndrome* (1979) is a good movie about a nuclear plant, it is not included in this book because no disaster actually occurs, and it fits more into the realm of thriller. *The Andromeda Strain* (1971) also lacks just a few too many elements to be included. **(GK)**

Atomic Train (1999)

NBC/Trimark   161 minutes

AT YOUR OWN RISK

DIRECTOR: David Jackson, Dick Lowry

WRITERS: D. Brent Mote, Phil Penningroth (segment 1); D. Brent Mote, Phil Penningroth, Rob Fresco (segment 2)

CAST: Rob Lowe, Kristin Davis, Esai Morales, John Finn, Mena Suvari, Edward Herrmann

This miniseries has surprisingly lofty aspirations in that it attempts to combine two elaborate disaster movies into one. Spread over two nights when it aired on TV, the first segment involves characters attempting to stop a runaway train carrying a nuclear weapon, while the second segment features attempts to disarm the weapon before it obliterates Denver, Colorado. It also wins some points for both having the train crash and the atomic weapon detonate, all of this despite the best efforts of lead NTSB train-wreck inspector John Seger, played by Rob Lowe. The first segment of the film is by far the most entertaining.

After opening with a hilariously pointless scene involving a near accident with a school bus full of children, our hero Lowe appears, as do his wife and *Brady Bunch*-style clan, which includes a teenage daughter and son from previous marriages. The wife's ex-husband is a cop who manages to find time to coach his kid's basketball team, mostly so he can berate his son's limited athletic ability. But the introductions are over rather quickly. Fifteen minutes in, we see a train that is running without brakes. Lowe, who is in the process of confronting his fear of heights, is called away from rock climbing to deal with the situation. Clearly it is amazing foresight on the part of his bosses to send someone who specializes in investigating train wrecks to try and prevent one. Perhaps they're well aware of the fact that Lowe will fail.

As it turns out, there's a decommissioned Russian nuclear weapon onboard the train. Even worse is the fact that our leads don't know exactly what will set off the bomb. With the "atomic train" speeding toward Denver, Lowe hangs from a helicopter and drops himself on a following train. He later leaps onto the atomic train itself, all so that he can attempt various other stunts (including scaling the side of the speeding locomotive) for the next hour of the film in a futile attempt to get the brakes working again.

There are some entertaining scenes as characters dangle over the rails and fall to their deaths. By this time Denver is in a state of panic, with looters and bad drivers littering the streets. Naturally, Lowe's family is separated all over the city, and they attempt to find each other amid the chaos. (This leads to an amusing sequence later when, reunited, the family stops at a busy gas station and discovers that an armed militia group has taken control of it. In broad daylight, with cars lined up everywhere to get gas, our gruff cop/ex-husband confronts the price-hiking militia group and manages to get involved in a full-scale shoot-out with them. Why any of these people would want to fire guns in and around gas tanks is beyond me.)

Back onboard the train, Lowe attempts to defuse the bomb. He fails, so he hurries to reunite his family and get the hell out of town. In come men dressed in the white biohazard suits I've come to expect from this subgenre. Unfortunately, Lowe's not there to assist them, and, through a series of comical errors, the nuclear weapon detonates.

As the impact of the blast hits there are some fun, cheesy shots of cars flying through the city streets, a woman screaming while being hurtled along with the vehicles, and, of course, Denver in flames. It's at this point that the already long miniseries begins to get tiresome. Like many other films of this sort, the real climax occurs when the nuclear weapon detonates, and all that follows drags by comparison. I suppose it's difficult to switch gears from two hours of jumping from helicopters and hanging off the side of an out-of-control train to scenes of characters wandering slowly through the destroyed streets, lost and confused. Government officials reveal that everyone who can get out of the city within 24 hours will likely miss the nuclear winter and thus not only survive, but also not suffer any complications from the blast. (I'm not sure if this is scientifically accurate, having sat through films like *Threads* and *The Day After*, but oh well.) Peole must evacuate on foot, since an EMP has knocked out power in all vehicles. Before long Lowe appears from nowhere to rescue his kids, somehow having telepathically determined their exact route and location.

Of course there are other characters in the film besides Lowe's family, but none of their stories are particularly interesting, nor do these subplots intertwine much. They're just your typical disaster movie supporting cast types, there to fill in some time. Overall, this television miniseries is passable, but unspectacular. If you feel you absolutely have to see it, just watch the first half. *Atomic Train* won the Golden Reel Award for Best Sound Editing (for TV).

Most Spectacular Moment of Carnage

There are some good, elaborate deaths in the film. Particularly enjoyable are the sudden, graphic deaths of the train operators. With every new challenge, one of them seems to slip off of the train and under its wheels. But the death of the ex-husband/cop wins the prize. Not only does he fall (a full story, onto his back) from a running motorcycle and become paralyzed, but the ladder that his son must use to climb up to safety then falls on top of him. As a result, the trap doors that he is sprawled on swing open, and the cop plunges another few stories into the darkness below and to his certain death. **(GK)**

The Cassandra Crossing (1976)

AVCO Embassy Pictures   129 minutes

RECOMMENDED

⚠

DIRECTOR: George Pan Cosmatos

WRITERS: Tom Mankiewicz, Robert Katz, George Pan Cosmatos

CAST: Sophia Loren, Richard Harris, Martin Sheen, O. J. Simpson, Lionel Stander, Ann Turkel, Ingrid Thulin, Lee Strasberg, Ava Gardner, Burt Lancaster, Lou Castel, John Phillip Law, Ray Lovelock, Alida Valli, Thomas Hunter

An interesting mix of disaster movie elements, including both a deadly virus and a train in peril, *The Cassandra Crossing* is fairly exciting and well paced. The film opens in Geneva, Switzerland, at the International Health Organization. An ambulance pulls up. Two men, carrying a patient on a stretcher, emerge from the vehicle and race into the enormous, yet barely populated, building. Suddenly, as all three men (including the guy on the stretcher) open fire on the guards inside and proceed to shoot up the complex, it becomes clear that they are actually some sort of terrorists. Two of these terrorists are shot dead by guards, who also manage to shoot a container holding highly contagious bacteria that, if released into the air, will cause a pneumonic plague. Among other things, the disease causes nasty red boils and lesions on the infected parties. The third terrorist manages to escape (but not before he's exposed to the bacteria), and he promptly hops on a train bound for Stockholm.

Enter Burt Lancaster, who has managed to swing a deal with the producers of this film to shoot all of his scenes within two rooms of the building complex. While the other actors fight the symptoms of the plague and embroil themselves in intrigue and machine gun battles, Lancaster plays a colonel who takes control of the situation by spending the entire movie staring into monitors and giving orders through a microphone. At one point, Lancaster loses contact with the train and even complains about not being able to reach anyone onboard. Maybe if you got up off your ass for a minute, left the building, and followed the train, you'd be able to, pal.

But I'm getting ahead of the story. Also on the train are leads Richard Harris and Sophia Loren. Harris plays a famous neurosurgeon. He's twice divorced from Loren, and she's just written a nasty, tell-all book about him. "There's a lot of love in it as well," Loren argues in Harris's train car (a setting that conveniently allows the actor the chance to walk around shirtless). The two continue to bicker before, inexplicably, sleeping together. Also onboard are a musically challenged soft-rock band, complete with their tone-deaf lead singer; an eccentric old man with a knack for stealing watches; and O. J. Simpson, as an undercover narcotics agent posing as a priest. In addition, there's a wealthy socialite, played by Ava Gardner, and her youthful, narcotics-trafficking companion, essayed by Martin Sheen (who's hilariously decked out in a red jacket and pants, a large scarf, and enormous sunglasses), not to mention a train conductor named Max. The role of the friendly Max is performed by Lionel Stander (who also appears in *Cyclone*), the actor who also played the role of Max the butler in the late-'70s / early-'80s television cheesefest *Hart to Hart*.

Lancaster informs us worriedly that the train must be contacted before the plague is spread among its passengers. He worries that, just by talking to others, an infected person could spread the disease. And, almost immediately, the infected terrorist begins infiltrating the passenger cars, playing with children, bumping into people, petting a dog, and even stumbling into the kitchen and coughing into the food. Lancaster does manage to get a hold of Harris and inform him of the dilemma, telling him to search for a "bloated, discolored, sweaty" suspect. Harris finds the man, and he and the other passengers proceed to try and unload him from the moving train onto a helicopter. The transfer fails, but the hound dog is taken off the train for medical attention back at the International Health Organization. "The dog is approaching coma," one of the doctors gravely declares as he stares at a monitor that shows the sleepy pooch, who's in a quarantined room. Meanwhile, all the infected (or soon-to-be infected) humans have been left on the train.

By this point, Lancaster doesn't want *anyone* to be let off the train, and instead he reroutes it to Poland, where an isolation camp is waiting. The train is stopped at a military checkpoint only long enough to receive the medical supplies requested by Harris, as well as a team of 42 machine-gun-toting, biohazard-suit-wearing officers, before moving out. Not allowing anyone off of the train, they shoot the kindly old man, who I naturally thought had been killed. But he pops again a few scenes later, only mildly perturbed by the bullet hole in his arm. By this point, 60 percent of the people on the train have become seriously infected. Not Harris, though. He seems immune to everything.

The characters soon learn that the train must pass over a rickety bridge known as the Cassandra Crossing. Sophia Loren must softly say the words *Cassandra Crossing* at least 20 times in the next five minutes of the film while discussing it. What's worse for the passengers headed for isolation is that they begin to recover from the disease. The scientific explanation of this has something to do with oxygen killing the cells of the bacteria, but it's wisely glossed over in favor of action. The passengers learn that the bridge is on the verge of collapsing, and that Lancaster intends to just let it happen. Director Cosmatos humorously cuts back to shots of the bridge more than three times, each time with an ear-blasting, menacing, ominous music cue. Really, how frightening can you make an inanimate object that is shot in broad daylight seem?

Harris enlists the help of O. J. Simpson and the cowardly Martin Sheen and stages a revolt, knocking out the soldiers, stealing their machine guns, and opening fire. In fact, Harris and Simpson kill more characters than the plague does, at one point even shooting a soldier in the face. Sheen attempts to redeem himself for his wardrobe with an elaborate plan involving climbing outside the train, scaling the side of it, and separating their passenger car before it crosses the bridge. Of course, he fails spectacularly. Several more missteps, sacrifices, and elaborately agonizing deaths follow, including a heroic leap that Harris attempts, which results in him falling off of the train and crashing to the ground below with a painful thud. The climax is incredibly gruesome, with disturbing but effective shots of passengers on fire and even bodies floating in the water. This makes the close of the film even stranger: two major characters react to the carnage with hugs and kisses; apparently, they're just happy to have saved, well, themselves, and perhaps half of the 1,000 passengers.

Most Spectacular Moment of Carnage

There are two equally shocking deaths. Coming in first place is rock-climbing '70s hipster Martin Sheen's: as he scales the side of the train, he is seen by an officer and is blasted with a machine gun. Sheen goes flying off of the side of the train and lands on the rocks below. A close second place: during the train crash at the film's climax, a steel girder crashes into a passenger car and embeds itself in the stomach of a surprised victim. Yeow! (**GK**)

Control (1987)

Coproduction: Alliance Entertainment, Cinecetta, Cristaldifilm, Les Films Ariane,
Radiotelevisione Italiana, Selena Audiovisuel
89 minutes

AVOID AT ALL COSTS

DIRECTOR: Guiliano Montaldo

WRITERS: Piero Angela, Jeremy Hole, Guiliano Montaldo, Brian Moore

CAST: Ben Gazzara, Kate Nelligan, Kate Reid, Burt Lancaster, Ingrid Thulin, Erland
Josephson, Cyrielle Claire, William Berger, Jean Benguigui, Andréa Ferréol, Lavinia
Segurini, Andrea Occhipinti

The back of the video box of this late-'80s nuclear paranoia film claims that it is "a
disaster movie," although I'm not so sure. Fifteen volunteers from various countries
agree to spend 20 days locked together inside an underground nuclear bomb shelter
in Frankfurt, Germany. They include a Canadian doctor, American newspaper journal-
ist Ben Gazzara, divorced disarmament activist Kate Nelligan, and Nelligan's son, as
well as a magician (who I wished would make himself disappear) and an Italian, sporting a two-day stubble growth and sunglasses that he wears all the time, who spends
the movie trying desperately, and failing, to look tough and intimidating. There's also
a racist and a famous model-turned-actress who claims that she needs the $10,000
(the amount each person is given to partake in this experiment) to pay for the services
of a press agent.

Frankly, there isn't much of note to say about this boring turkey. Nothing happens. Characters sit around in their bunkers and personal conflicts arise, and there's a
lot of arguing and fighting. It's like *The Real World: Underground Bunker*. Watch for a
deep, late-night conversation between the model and the doctor. Their eye-lines don't
match up, making it look like these two are sharing their innermost thoughts with
a nearby lamp. There's also a party dance scene with a teenage girl that is shot *very*
tastelessly. Toward the end of the movie, the characters are tricked into thinking that
a nuclear strike is about to take place. This leads to even more bickering, which drives
the model to attempt suicide and causes the team organizers (led by Burt Lancaster,

who's barely in the movie) to pull them out of the bunker. In the end, Gazzara can only conclude "There is no shelter from the bomb."

This was an Italian, Canadian, and French coproduction, so anyone who has seen it outside of these countries probably did so on cable or on home video. The score, by Ennio Morricone, and the major stars are good, but many of the other performances are not. Though its heart may have been in the right place, this laughable flick is most definitely not worth your while.

Most Spectacular Moment of Carnage
The entire movie is a train wreck. **(GK)**

The Day After (1983)

ABC Circle Films   126 minutes

AT YOUR OWN RISK

© MGM

DIRECTOR: Nicholas Meyer

WRITER: Edward Hume

CAST: Jason Robards, JoBeth Williams, Steve Guttenberg, John Cullum, John Lithgow, Bibi Besch, Amy Madigan, William Allen Young, Calvin Jung

The Emmy-winning (for sound editing and for special visual effects, anyway) *The Day After* was a controversial TV film in its day. Focusing on the devastating effects a nuclear war would have on the world, it depicts not only terrifying blasts and mushroom clouds, but also the picturesque nuclear winter and dandy effects of radiation that follow. As if that's not horrifying enough, it's announced, at the end of the film, that in all likelihood the movie has underestimated the effects of nuclear war.

The story is set in and around Kansas City, Kansas. As is the case in all disaster movies, characters of various backgrounds are introduced: Jason Robards and JoBeth Williams are doctors; John Lithgow is a science professor; and Steve Guttenberg is a student at the state university. While these characters are introduced, radio and news reports tell us about a growing crisis in Europe involving the Russians. Unfortunately, there isn't much more to say about the first 30 minutes of the film, because all anyone seems to being doing is watching or listening to the news. At least, as tension mounts, there are scenes involving rioters and looters in the streets and panicked shoppers clearing out supermarkets as air raid sirens blare.

The characters learn that war has broken out and that they have less than 30 minutes to get to their loved ones before the missiles arrive. Naturally, due to the blocked roads and panicking crowds, most of the characters get stranded, and an EMP causes all electrical instruments to die. Before the detonation of the nuclear weapon, there's a pretentious slow-motion shot of a white horse running. (There's a lot of this type of imagery, including Norman Rockwell–esque shots of families in parks and so on. I get it, already.)

Robards's character gets the closest look as the blast hits. All of this is graphically and frighteningly displayed, as mushroom clouds appear in the orange skyline. Buildings explode, people burst into flames, debris flies everywhere, and many people are vaporized. Viewers can at least be amused for this brief moment, as those who are vaporized glow for a moment, revealing their skeletons, just like some of those killed in The War of the Worlds. Some of the impact is also lessened by the use of stock footage of atom bomb explosions that anyone who's seen a movie has witnessed a million times before. The overall effect is frightening nonetheless. Robards survives, but he loses his wife and daughter in the blast. (Going back a few scenes earlier, please note Robards's daughter's enormous '80s glasses, which would not look out of place on Elton John, and the insane, almost tartan wallpaper pattern in Robards's kitchen.)

The remaining hour takes place mostly within a hospital, where the doctors uselessly attempt to save the lives of those survivors who were hit by the blast, while slowly becoming infected by radiation themselves (this is displayed with nasty burn makeup) and meeting their own fates. Many who don't die right away are shot dead—there are horrific scenes of firing squads wiping people out. Nobody's very happy or energetic after the blast, due to radiation sickness, and the helpless remaining characters are left with nothing to do (again, something that isn't particularly cinematic).

Even seeing Steve Guttenberg suffer the aftereffects of a nuclear explosion fails to be as amusing as I would have thought it'd be. I suppose this is a credit to the filmmaking, but frankly, this movie is just too damn serious.

Like *Control*, *Testament*, and *Threads*, this movie plays on audience fears and makes its point early on. After the blast, it's clear that no one's going to survive, so audiences then have to endure the hopelessness that follows and wait patiently for the credits to roll. At least if these films had been made in the '30s, there would have been a musical number thrown in. (Wow, I never thought I'd be requesting a musical number in a movie.) Instead, I just ended up looking at my watch and waiting for all of the characters to die their very, very slow deaths.

The Day After is certainly well made, and it did an exceptional job of depressing the hell out of me. It would have scared audiences in the '80s, but today the effects don't seem as impressive, and the film is too dated-looking and inaccurate. Perhaps the world leaders decided to reduce nuclear arms in order to spare us the agony of sitting through more of these films. Hey, whatever works.

Most Spectacular Moment of Carnage
The blast itself is certainly disturbing, but a *Gone with the Wind*-inspired shot of a gymnasium filled with citizens who are infected and dying of radiation is also effective. **(GK)**

Miracle Mile (1988)

Hemdale   90 minutes

RECOMMENDED

⚠

DIRECTOR: Steve De Jarnatt

WRITER: Steve De Jarnatt

CAST: Anthony Edwards, Mare Winningham, John Agar, Mykelti Williamson, Kurt Fuller, Denise Crosby, O-Lan Jones, Alan Rosenberg, Earl Boen

Miracle Mile is a very clever and visually inventive hybrid of drama and black comedy that I continue to find entertaining even after several viewings. Despite the constraints of its low budget, it manages to create a vivid, romantic environment in which recognizable things take on a different perspective under the light of its subject matter. Though it depicts a nuclear Armageddon, the film is filled with whimsy and imagination, and it draws the viewer into its stylized, absurdist world.

Anthony Edwards, still sporting a full head of hair, is a 30-year-old touring jazz trombonist who, while in L.A., meets the young Mare Winningham, who is surely a victim of '80s fashion (in this film, anyway) but is still a fine actress. They quickly fall for each other. After spending a day or so together, he has to get ready to leave town with his band, so they make a date to meet up at her place of work (a Bob's Big Boy-type establishment) just after midnight, when her shift ends. He goes back to his hotel and sets his alarm, but as he sleeps, the power in the hotel cuts out when a bird, having picked up one of his discarded lit cigarette butts, carries it up to the hotel roof and drops it on a power transformer or something. As a result, he sleeps in until almost 4:00 A.M., but after he wakes up he takes off for the restaurant anyway. She's not there, of course, so he calls her house and leaves a message on her answering machine. Moments later, as he's still standing outside, the pay phone rings, and Edwards answers it.

He hears the terrified voice (Raphael Sbarge) of a young man who thinks he has called his father. The man reveals that he's calling from a military base in North Dakota, where a horrible accident has occurred, causing nuclear warheads to be launched against Russia. He also says that within an hour and ten minutes, the Russian nuclear response will reach the United States. A confused Edwards only has time to reveal that the kid's got the wrong number before he hears the guy being shot to death.

Stunned, Edwards enters the restaurant, where he tries to convince everyone that what he's just heard might very well might be true. No one believes him until a power-dressed Denise Crosby confirms some of the story through her various high-powered contacts in the world of defense. As a result, everyone in the place immediately grabs as many supplies as they can, piles into a truck, and heads for the airport. Edwards however, decides that he must find Winningham, so he leaps out of the truck and onto a freeway ramp (after stealing a gun). As he recovers from this stunt, a car screams onto the ramp, nearly hitting him, and Edwards forces the driver, a very young Mykelti Williamson, to drive him to Winningham's apartment building (which requires them to turn around and drive back onto the freeway via the off ramp; there's a nice stunt here as a car, speeding off the freeway, nearly smashes into them).

Before they get there they realize that they need gas, and the only place open is a gas station that serves taxis. The owner, a great, laconic Eddie Bunker, is about to let them gas up (after extorting money from them and holding them at gunpoint) when, for some reason, the cops show up. Williamson, nervous about all the stolen electronic equipment in the trunk of his car, sprays them with gasoline. When one of the cops fires her pistol, she bursts into flames. Edwards and Williamson leave in the police car just as the gas station explodes, killing the other cops (and, presumably, Bunker as well).

They end up at Winningham's apartment building, and Edwards breaks into the place to find her out cold on valium. He carries her outside, but by this time Williamson has left to get his sister. So Edwards is forced to push Winningham in a shopping cart all the way to an office building on Wilshire, where Crosby was supposed to have arranged to have a helicopter waiting to fly them to the airport. When they arrive at the heliport, they find a helicopter but no pilot, so Edwards goes off to try to find one somehow. Desperate, he wanders into a late-night health club, where he actually manages to find a helicopter pilot, but when they leave the club he sees Winningham across the street, also on a search for pilots, so he sends the guy off to the heliport and runs after her. Moments later a police car loses control and crashes through the front window of a department store nearby. Edwards and Winningham venture inside to see what the hell's going on, only to find that it's Mykelti Williamson behind the wheel, with his sister next to him, and that both of them have been shot. As the sun begins to rise, they become aware that panic is about to set in on the streets of Los Angeles. The news is spreading.

Cars, station wagons, Winnebagos, all loaded with personal possessions, speed through the streets. In a matter of minutes, the sidewalks are teeming with people, the streets are frozen in gridlock, and violence erupts. Since this is L.A., there's the requisite looting, and as our two protagonists navigate this mob scene, they find people literally mugging and beating other people right in front of them. On the road, cars smash into each other, pedestrians are run over, and—my favorite—bicyclists are taken out as they smash into just-opened car doors. Edwards thinks he sees his pilot across the street, so he hands Winningham his gun and sends her back to the heliport. When he gets across the street and finds the guy, it turns out not to be the pilot, but just a guy trying to watch a TV in a store window, as the local news is reporting on the impending nuclear strike. With no more time to spare, Edwards is forced to leap from one car roof to another in order to get across the street. When one angry motorist begins to shoot at him, he immediately drops to the ground and crawls underneath the vehicles, passing dead, crushed bodies as he goes, and finally escaping into the sewer (with the gun-toting driver still chasing him). Once underground, he finds an exit that, fortunately, leads directly into the building he wants. He climbs out to find Winningham in the lobby, and they board the elevator. Before they get to the roof, an explosion rocks the building. When the doors open, they see that the helicopter is gone and that the sky has turned yellow. Soon they see missiles in the air, which is why it's a relief when the chopper returns. Once they're in the air, they watch as more missiles hit the earth. Yet, during the climax, Edwards and Winningham still manage to find some sort of poetic beauty in their final predicament.

While this film's formal structure might be too esoteric for many viewers, it would be a shame not to take a chance on this movie, as it is filled with great performances, interesting characters, and fine art direction and cinematography (it was nominated for numerous Independent Spirit Awards). Obviously, Anthony Edwards and Mare Winningham were never big box-office draws, but they're both perfect as two bright, happy, young people who have to come to terms with the end of life. Though their characters are quirky in particular ways, you may find yourself identifying with them in their quest for nothing more than to be together in a time of horrible crisis. Look for Jenette "Vasquez" Goldstein in a very small role about halfway through.

Most Spectacular Moment of Carnage

As people watch the local TV news cover the story, the newscast switches to a live feed of a reporter on the street in the middle of the rioting. A moment after he starts to talk, a guy in the crowd shoots him through the back right on camera, then shoots the cameraman! Oh well, it was probably the Fox network. **(MR)**

Outbreak (1995)

Warner Bros.   128 minutes

RECOMMENDED

⚠

DIRECTOR: Wolfgang Petersen

WRITERS: Laurence Dworet, Robert Roy Pool

CAST: Dustin Hoffman, Rene Russo, Morgan Freeman, Kevin Spacey, Cuba Gooding Jr., Donald Sutherland, Patrick Dempsey

From the director of *The NeverEnding Story* comes this brutally entertaining thriller, which apparently frightened the hell out of Roger Ebert, though I've heard he scares easily. Nonetheless, *Outbreak* is particularly notable for having the most Patrick Dempsey of any film in its genre, though how he got billing over Kevin Spacey will forever remain a mystery.

From the outset it's clear that this movie wants to thrill the audience at all costs, no matter how implausibly. If it didn't, would I be treated to the sight of Dustin Hoffman leaping out of a helicopter onto a Korean shipping vessel in the middle of the ocean, à la Alec Baldwin in *The Hunt for Red October*? While I enjoyed this film's "anything goes" attitude to a certain extent, I did find its overall combination of drama and action to be an uneasy one. I think this movie proves, among other things, that if you give the audience too much of what you think they want, you threaten to undermine the elements that inherently make a movie successful from a storytelling standpoint. Was a helicopter chase necessary in a movie like this?

It is 1967, and in a mercenary camp in Zaire a deadly outbreak of the Motaba virus is killing everyone in sight, so army officials Donald Sutherland (who replaced Joe Don Baker well into the film's production) and Morgan Freeman decide to blow the place up, thereby containing the virus outbreak while at the same time protecting it for themselves to use as a biological weapon.

Fast-forward 30 years: they've been covering this up all these decades, but now, with a fresh outbreak of a deadly virus in Zaire, the secrecy is about to unravel. See, Sutherland is Freeman's boss, and Freeman is Hoffman's boss and friend, and Hoffman is the head of the U.S. Army's infectious diseases laboratory, and, see, Hoffman is a really smart guy, and he likes to ask questions, and he never stops until he gets what he wants and, well, if he finds out about what his boss was up to back in the '60s, it could ruin Freeman's career!

Hoffman and his crew are sent to Zaire, where they collect samples of the virus and return it to the States, thinking that they've discovered something new. They have no idea—yet—that it is the dreaded Motaba virus. Oh, did I mention that Hoffman's ex-wife, Rene Russo, used to be a member of his team, but has since accepted the top position at the Center for Disease Control? Gee, I wonder if they'll fall back in love before the movie ends. I wonder if the CDC pays better than the army. Looks like divorcing him was the best decision she could have made, but really, you can tell she still loves him by the way she continues to make compromises for him, blah blah blah.

Anyway, after having seen the virus in action (it kills, messily, within 24 hours of infection), Hoffman tries to get his boss to send out an alert about Motaba, as he believes that, due to its unparalleled deadliness, it poses a threat to the United States, but Freeman refuses. He cites a list of examples of Hoffman's prior warnings about other diseases, all of which proved to be false and alarmist. Though Freeman is simply covering his own ass by trying to stop Hoffman in his tracks, it's still odd to hear him remind Hoffman of all his many mistakes after his earlier description of Hoffman as "the best" at what he does.

Meanwhile, in California, Patrick Dempsey manages to smuggle into the country a monkey from a research facility in Zaire, with plans to sell it to a pet store. Sadly, the shop owner doesn't want it, and Dempsey releases the primate into the forest, then boards a plane for Boston. By now, of course, both he and the pet-store owner have been infected, as the monkey is the virus's host, and once Dempsey lands in Boston he unknowingly sets out infecting others. Then some lab technician at a California hospital comically sprays infected blood all over his face when he sticks his hand into a spinning centrifuge, and let me tell you, when you're screwing around with Motaba, that's the last thing you want to do. The technician then goes to the movies and infects the whole theater before causing a scene at the concession stand. And now the virus is airborne.

Soon a small Northern California town is quarantined by the army, but Hoffman and his crew fly there against orders not to. Also on the scene, of course, is ex-wife Rene Russo. By this time, both the army and the CDC have traced the path of the virus to the point where they know that it hasn't spread beyond the town, and they therefore assume that it won't spread if they keep the town sealed off. They don't yet know that the virus has become airborne, though they're soon to find out. As if that weren't bad enough, a second strain of the virus has emerged, for no particular reason that I can see.

Of course it's obvious that Freeman and Sutherland have buckets of antivirus in storage, but they won't tell anyone for fear of revealing their terrible 30-year-old secret, so Freeman is forced to continue to stymie Hoffman at every turn. To make matters worse, Sutherland shows up and demands that Hoffman be arrested, all the while planning to bomb the town, just as they did in Zaire. He even gets presidential approval for the bombing, but not before hearing an over-the-top antibombing filibuster from fine character actor J. T. Walsh. I think it was written in Hollywood law somewhere that if you were making a movie back then, you were obligated to put Walsh into at least one scene, which is why he racked up a shockingly long list of credits before his untimely death.

Hoffman and company's research leads them to a Korean shipping vessel, which is the one that brought the monkey to the States. As it happens, Cuba Gooding, Jr., is not only a scientist, but also a fantastic helicopter pilot, and he and Hoffman steal a chopper and head out to sea to find the ship which is when Hoffman has to jump out of the chopper and onto the ship in an action-hero kind of way. While on the ship they find pictures of the monkey, which they later display on television after commandeering a live news program. By this time the monkey is living in the woods behind a house, and it has befriended the little girl who lives there with her apparently single mother.

What follows is a long action sequence in which a couple of attack helicopters, on Sutherland's orders, try to chase and destroy Hoffman, Gooding, and the monkey. They all get away, and once back at the lab, Hoffman and Gooding immediately begin to work on developing an antivirus for both strains of the disease by using the monkey's blood. But then they find out that the bomber plane has been deployed, and that in a few minutes, in spite of the fact that they believe they can produce a cure for the virus, the entire town's going to be wiped out. Hoffman and Gooding get back into the chopper to intercept the plane, and Hoffman pleads over the radio with the bomber pilots. Hoffman does a lot of pleading in this movie. Every time he wants to explain something to someone, he adopts a sort of childish, so-mad-I-might-cry expression and vocal delivery, which usually culminates in a series of sarcastic, rhetorical questions in which he shames the subject of his rant into doing what he wants.

Hey, guess what? Rene Russo's got Motaba! Yes, she pricked herself with an infected needle earlier in the film when trying to save an also-infected Kevin Spacey (yeah, he's in the movie, but has very little to do other than to make quips and look thoughtful). Hoffman and Gooding return to the hospital after their little aerial adventure, and Hoffman goes to see her and removes his protective helmet, exposing himself to the virus just so she can touch his face! Luckily for him, Gooding has managed to whip up the antivirus in record time, though it's never explained how that might be possible. And instead of giving the antivirus to the people who are closest to death, he loads Russo up with it, even though she's not been infected very long and she still looks relatively healthy (unlike Spacey, who's bleeding disgustingly; for some reason, the filmmakers never show what happens to him and give no indication of whether he lives or dies. It's always nice when a movie decides for the audience who, exactly, deserves their concern and sympathy).

While I clearly don't think that *Outbreak* is a great movie by any means, I must admit that it is so intent on entertaining the audience that it succeeds in spite of itself. It's too long and often silly, and the suspense generally feels contrived, but the fine cast raises the level of the material, as does Michael Ballhaus's cinematography. The movie is diverting enough that you forget that you don't care about any of these people until the film is over, and by then you're already hooked.

Most Spectacular Moment of Carnage
This movie's got a massive body count. So many people die that, at one point, an abandoned barn is filled with corpses and set ablaze. My favorite moment of bloodthirsty violence comes when a bunch of people in the quarantined town decide to try to escape in a truck. After ignoring repeated requests to stop, they are shot to death by an army helicopter, after which the truck bursts into flames. I guess just blowing out the tires or something and arresting the occupants wouldn't have been satisfying enough. **(MR)**

Panic in the City (1968)

United Pictures Corporation   96 minutes

AVOID AT ALL COSTS

DIRECTOR: Eddie Davis

WRITERS: Eddie Davis, Charles E. Savage

CAST: Howard Duff, Linda Cristal, Stephen McNally, Nehemiah Persoff, Anne Jeffreys, Dennis Hopper

The first thing that's wrong with this movie is the title. Only those poor souls who sit through the entire thing will know that there's not one scene depicting any sort of panic. However, there is a city. As the excruciating boredom of this film wore me down, I began to observe the bits of the frames around the actors, and I became fascinated by the old-fashioned cars and gas stations and supermarkets and all that kind of stuff. Sometimes, even a crappy movie can inadvertently serve as an anthropological document of a particular time in history (in this case, Los Angeles in the late '60s), and that can become far more interesting than what's happening in the film. Add to that the staggeringly awful, dragged-behind-a-car-for-six-miles picture quality of the version I saw (mastered and duplicated in EP speed!) and the perverse allure can be more clearly understood. I'm old enough to remember sitting in class in elementary school and seeing beat-up 16mm prints of educational films and the occasional G-rated feature. There's something about a faded, dirt-covered, improperly spliced viewing experience that, to me, captures the tactile, fragile nature of film, especially when the movie itself is a ham-handed relic that is so out of touch with reality that it was dated when it was made.

This movie was made in 1967, but it bears more of a resemblance to a 1950s atomic-age flick. Howard Duff stars as an agent (with the suspiciously named National Bureau of Investigation) who's looking into the bizarre case of a man found stumbling through the streets of Los Angeles, dying from intense exposure to radiation. The man is taken to a hospital, where it's discovered that the amount of radiation to which he's been exposed will kill him in a matter of hours. By the sound of it, he's more deadly to be around than a bucket of plutonium, yet they keep him in a regular room, with only an unlocked door between him and the rest of the hospital (but they do encase his clothing in lead!). According to a doctor, anyone who's been in the same room with him will have to be "decontaminated," but how, exactly, that's done is kept a secret.

It is eventually revealed that the man is a respected scientist who was working on a top secret project that turns out to be a terrorist plot to manufacture atomic bombs in private homes and hide them throughout the United States, for reasons unknown. It doesn't take us long to figure out what's going on, but an oblivious Duff seems unable or unwilling to put the pieces together. He's far too busy trying to awkwardly romance a young, vaguely foreign-sounding doctor who carries a Geiger counter in her purse while out on dates.

Anyway, as the boring plot unfolds, another very prominent scientist steps in to take the place of the first guy (who's now dead), under the watchful, twitchy eye of Nehemiah Persoff, the man in charge of this mysterious terrorist plot to nuke major American cities for no particular reason. I especially enjoyed the scene in which this scientist decides to hold a press conference to explain why he is leaving the school he teaches at, for he makes sure to loudly express his disdain for nuclear energy and all its potential dangers. If he was trying to raise all the red flags here, he succeeded. If you're a famous scientist (yes, this movie suggests that such a thing is possible) and your work is focused on nuclear energy, and you're going to go off and join up with terrorists to build atomic bombs because the last guy, who was also a famous scientist, died from exposure to radiation, and the, heh, National Bureau of Investigation is all over the case, would you make a public statement in which you proclaim that you're quitting your job? If I was that guy, I'd just quietly go on "vacation" rather than hold a press conference that's attended by a throng of oddly fascinated reporters. (Not to mention that no one ought to give a rat's ass what this guy does. Quit, don't quit, eat a candy bar, go to Mars, who cares? Who is he, a rock star? Ooh, he teaches at the university! Whatever he does is front page news!)

Besides, he ends up under police surveillance only because Duff, who's in attendance at the press conference, happens to see a woman skulking in the kitchen. He recognizes her as the same woman who came to the hospital to see the man dying from radiation under the guise that she thought he might be her husband, when really she's with the terrorist group. It seems that she only went to the hospital to find out the guy's room number so that she could pass that information along to Dennis Hopper, who ends up killing the poor sap. Duff somehow puts the pieces together and decides that this blowhard scientist is somehow involved in whatever it is that's going on, not that he knows what that is, of course.

Eventually, Duff starts to figure out what's up, due largely to the fact that this terrorist group needs parts for their bomb and they decide to have a local machine shop manufacture them. Duff manages to get a photo of these plans and confirms that they indeed can only be bomb parts, and the rest of the movie depicts him trying to figure out exactly where the bomb is being made. He resorts to dressing up as a telephone repairman and going door-to-door with a Geiger counter, looking for any unusual radiation. Amazingly, the device is not set off by the massive flood of deadly rays from the gigantic Zenith television sets found in these large suburban homes. Somehow he does manage to find the house in which our scientist is working on the bomb, but by this time a crazed Persoff has armed the weapon in an attempt to blow it up right there, again for no particular reason. Instead of exploding, the bomb, which is now highly unstable, begins to leak its radioactive contents.

I should point out that, as I watched this movie, I had decided early on that, due to its lack of suspense, action, panic, and violence, it was not suitable for inclusion in this book. However, something amazing happened in the last 15 minutes. It became exactly the film I had hoped it would be. After suffering through a staggeringly old-fashioned melodrama, with all evidence pointing to an equally dry conclusion, I was stunned when the movie quite suddenly became delightfully fatalistic. Duff enters the house, is (of course) exposed to deadly amounts of radiation (undoubtedly just like all the residents of that street, who've been asked to stay in their homes), and finds the bomb in the basement. Following this, he calls for a helicopter. Then, in a superhuman effort, he drags the heavy bomb across the basement floor, up the stairs, and out of the house. This is much more difficult than it sounds, as the bomb appears to weigh a ton, not to mention the fact that Duff is starting to physically collapse from the radiation, his skin breaking out into welts. Oh, did I mention he's also a pilot?

Well, he is. After rolling the bomb out into the middle of the road (ensuring at the same time that everyone standing around outside the house will soon die themselves), he attaches the bomb to the underside of the massive chopper and takes off for the ocean, where he plans to drop it so that if and when it explodes, it will be for the most part contained. This is, of course, a great plan. Sure, let's strap a highly unstable atomic bomb that is leaking radioactive matter and that might explode at any time to a helicopter being piloted by a guy drifting in and out of consciousness and fly it over the city of Los Angeles! He manages to make it to the ocean, where, instead of dropping the bomb into the water, he puts the chopper in a hover and (like many members of the audience, I'm sure) loses consciousness.

Then it's stock footage of a gigantic nuclear explosion, one so large that it would undoubtedly incinerate Los Angeles and the surrounding area instantaneously. If you look closely you will see that this actually shows an explosion that was detonated either on the surface of the ocean or underwater, but by this point who really cares. The explosion sends up a mushroom cloud of epic proportions. Millions of people are going to die!

However, according to the film, a nuclear explosion of that size, at that distance from the city of Los Angeles, would not actually obliterate everything in its path; amazingly, a shockwave does not rip across the city, turning buildings and people into ash. I prefer to think, though, that the breeze shown wafting in as the film draws to a close is loaded with deadly radiation, and that soon everyone will die, leaving only an eerie, deserted, corpse-filled city. It doesn't matter that the film suggests that everything's going to be OK and that disaster has been averted; anyone who sees this will know better, and that's what makes this final scene so fantastic. It is because of this that the film deserves mention.

Most Spectacular Moment of Carnage

The movie is almost devoid of notable violence. The very high body count that I know must result from many of this film's events is merely implied. So, you'll just have to make stuff up. Close your eyes and picture Howard Duff being impaled by a crowbar, or Linda Cristal driving to work and losing control when she reaches into her glove compartment for a tissue and accidentally drives off a twisty mountain road, taking a school bus full of children with her. See, it's fun! **(MR)**

The Plague (1992)

Coproduction: Compagnie Francaise Cinematographique,
The Pepper Prince Company Ltd., Oscar Kramer S.A., Cinemania, Canal+
105 minutes

AVOID AT ALL COSTS

DIRECTOR: Luis Puenzo

WRITER: Luis Puenzo (based on the novel by Albert Camus)

CAST: William Hurt, Sandrine Bonnaire, Jean-Marc Barr, Robert Duvall, Raul Julia, Victoria Tennant

This is one weird, pompous disaster movie. Based on the classic novel *The Plague* by Albert Camus, the film is set in South America. William Hurt, who can be an excellent actor, gives an overly pondering turn this time, as a doctor. As the film opens, he seems to be reading passages directly from the novel, and it sounds like much of the dialogue has been taken directly from it as well. Unfortunately for the audience, this does not turn out to be a good thing. The dialogue is strangely antiquated, and many of the conversations (particularly early on) don't make much sense, nor do they seem to go anywhere.

The story concerns a small group of characters who become trapped, either by choice or by fate, in the city of Oran after it is quarantined due to a plague outbreak. There's a French reporter/love interest for Hurt, a cameraman, and a local profiteer (played by Raul Julia), as well as wacko writer Robert Duvall. Nothing that occurs in the first 45 minutes seems to make any sense whatsoever, and many of the scenes end before any important information is communicated. When Julia and the French reporter discuss, in a local restaurant, the idea of leaving the city, Julia states that he doesn't want to go because it doesn't matter whether he catches the plague or not (suggesting that he already has a disease). He bursts into loud, spontaneous laughter, and the French reporter joins in, gets up from the table, and walks away to begin another strange conversation with other guests in the restaurant. End of scene.

As the situation within the city degenerates, this kind of stuff is intercut with Hurt's somnambulistic performance. There's a lot of slow line delivery, head scratching, and perplexed looks. He's acting on the inside, I suppose. Meanwhile, the cameraman videotapes and then speaks with a tarot-card-reading street performer, who tells him that he has been given the power to help heal those who are afflicted. Why the cameraman deemed the street performer worthy of filming when a plague is ravishing the city is beyond me, and I sure don't get why he would believe the performer's predictions. Nevertheless, he volunteers to help Hurt treat the sick and is immediately turned down. In fact, whenever any character offers to help out with treatment, Hurt looks annoyed and tells them to go away. Yet he always seems upset when talking to his superiors, claiming that not enough is being done. Anyway, he always grouses before relenting to the volunteers. In the cameraman's case, maybe Hurt does this so that they can wander the streets aimlessly and deliver non sequiturs to each other.

You wouldn't believe the dialogue in this movie. Conversations typically start with lines like "Every time I get into bed I remember that I am one day older." Earlier in the film, Hurt begins a conversation by talking about his last phone conversation with his sick wife. "We talked about our dead daughter," he explains, while I waited in vain for the reporter to respond, "Sounds like a fun conversation. Glad I missed it." Hurt gets riled up at certain points in the movie because the female reporter brings up the subject of his sick wife, yet he seems to bring it up so often himself that you wonder why he's so upset. These dialogue-heavy discussions of inner feelings end with resolutions like "There's a little bit of plague in all of us."

Not all survive past the climax, when Julia suddenly goes bonkers and begins randomly firing his rifle into the streets below his apartment. "It will always come back," he shouts meaningfully before he is taken away, and Hurt follows this up with his own fatalistic thoughts about the fact that the plague lies dormant "in furniture and linen chests, in trunks and handkerchiefs" before the credits roll. Makes you think, don't it? Not really, and that's the whole problem with this pretentious picture. The production value is good, and the film is interesting from a visual standpoint, but sadly, there's nothing else remotely entertaining about this movie.

Most Spectacular Moment of Carnage

The cameraman is fatally shot in the chest during Julia's rifle rampage; a priest who questions his faith commits suicide by lying in a pit with plague-ridden bodies while a bulldozer dumps earth on top of them; and a choirboy sings an earth-shattering final note as he dies from the effects of the plague, while the teary-eyed cast looks on. God, even the death scenes are pretentious in this movie. (GK)

Red Alert (1977)
Paramount   96 minutes

AT YOUR OWN RISK

© Paramount Pictures

DIRECTOR: William Hale

WRITER: Sandor Stern (based on the novel *Paradigm Red* by Harold King)

CAST: David Hayward, M. Emmet Walsh, William Devane, Ralph Waite (in a "special guest appearance," according to the opening credit), Adrienne Barbeau, Michael Brandon, Jim Siedow

Nuclear disaster movies like this one must be easy to produce. They always seem to take place in engine rooms and control booths, with a lot of pipes and steam. The only major expenses would be all the white biohazard suits everyone has to wear.

Almost all of *Red Alert* is set within these types of sets, in particular a nuclear plant in Minnesota. There are numerous shots of water dripping from one of the pipes. Immediately, a fluctuation in water pressure is discovered in the plant's main control room in Colorado. As in most films of this type, the control-room computers look hilariously frightening; it's amazing that a nuclear facility is controlled by a machine that barely looks capable of loading a game of Pong.

The film cuts to a house and its tenants—a nuclear plant worker and his extremely depressed wife. In a later scene, the wife pulls out a gun and kills herself. Seeing as I barely knew what was going on at this point, this all seemed completely bizarre, almost like I was watching a completely different movie, but it does all come together later. Our heroes, "security investigators" William Devane and Michael Brandon, are introduced, the cigar-chomping Devane screaming his first line at the top of his lungs. This is one of the most intense, angriest heroes ever in a disaster film, and he delivers his dialogue at an ever-increasing decibel level that would cause anyone's ears to bleed. All he wants to do, he says (emphasizing the first syllable to the extreme), is go "ffffishin'!" Even more intense is the "commander" of operations in Colorado, Ralph Waite, who is at odds with Devane and who grinds his teeth with every line. I imagine he had to spit out teeth after every take. This character doesn't just have a pickle up his butt; he's got an entire iron rod up there.

A small explosive goes off in the nuclear plant, setting off its computer's alarm and trapping 14 workers inside the exposed area. Detectives Devane and Brandon are called in to investigate. The film quickly turns into a mystery as the leads try to figure out what has happened. Sheriff Sweeney, played by M. Emmet Walsh, appears, informing the characters about the woman's suicide. It seems her husband, Jim Siedow (of *Texas Chainsaw Massacre* fame), is one of the men left behind in the containment room near the reactor. Devane and Brandon determine that sabotage may have been involved, and they dig up information about the worker. As it turns out, he has built several explosives, including an undetonated potassium bomb that may be planted in the quarantined area.

Word spreads and soon the entire city begins to clear out to the airports, while Brandon and Devane search frantically for the bombs. Walsh returns with an audio-cassette containing a confession by Siedow. After hearing one sentence, the angry sheriff fast-forwards the tape to the last sentence. The characters then walk away, choosing not to listen to it. What, they don't have 10 minutes to listen to the whole tape? Clearly, these characters suffer from attention deficit disorder. Yes, our heroes seem to want to do things the hard way.

Devane wants to enter the containment room, find the bomb, and rescue a man who is still alive inside the room (he is periodically heard moaning over the speakers—I'm not sure I want to know what he's *really* doing in there). After endless arguments about it with the commander, Devane decides to enter anyway, cleverly leaving his oxygen behind in the process. By this point it is implied that no radiation or contaminants have been released into the containment room. I guess we're supposed to figure this out by Devane's outfit—he's dressed in a white biohazard jumpsuit, but his wrists, neck, ears, and scalp are exposed. He also frequently pulls off his mask and yells at people in intense fury. Indeed, the bomb is located outside of the containment area, and the majority of what has happened has been the result of human and computer error, which resulted in the erroneous reporting of radiation. Just when you thought the screaming and yelling was finally over, the film manages to reach a new height. Devane screams that there is "no radiation, at least not enough to kill anybody!" while Waite looks about ready to spontaneously combust. Watch for his delivery of the line "You've got to stop that crane!" which is yelled at a level that no doubt caused permanent hearing loss to crew members and which will make your speakers at home explode.

The climax features the now-oxygen-deprived Devane jumping to the crane, hanging from it, and bouncing off of the reactor's door for a couple of minutes in an attempt to stop it from opening. Even Brandon gets in on the action. The sequence ends abruptly. If it weren't for the celebrating, I'm not sure I would have had any idea how things turned out. In the end, our hero celebrates by lighting a cigar in the containment room (which can't be a good thing, can it?). A passable film, it's perhaps worth watching to see Devane's and Waite's "subtle" performances.

Most Spectacular Moment of Carnage
After the initial explosion, one of the 14 workers catches fire, another is hit on the head by a flaming pipe, and a third is blown off of a ladder. Actually, this is some pretty violent stuff here for a network TV movie. Their dead bodies are shown lying about the containment room. (**GK**)

Robin Cook's Virus (1995)

Von Zerneck Sertner Films   90 minutes

AVOID AT ALL COSTS

DIRECTOR: Armand Mastroianni

WRITER: Roger Young (based on the novel *Outbreak* by Robin Cook)

CAST: Nicollette Sheridan, William Devane, Stephen Caffrey, Dakin Matthews, Kurt Fuller, Barry Corbin, William Atherton

After sitting through *Robin Cook's Virus*, there is no doubt in my mind that the book upon which it is based must be as astonishingly boring as this lifeless made-for-TV movie. "The virus is mankind's ultimate predator," reads the title card that ushers us into this lethargic "thriller." One could not be blamed for thinking at this point that the movie would actually have something to do with a deadly viral outbreak. However, this couldn't be further from the truth. After a brief prologue set in Zaire in 1976, in which a slew of villagers die from a mysterious illness (and a white guy stumbles through the jungle for no particular reason), the movie takes us to the present day and the Center For Disease Control in Atlanta, Georgia, where scientist Nicollette Sheridan has been toiling away in obscurity for three months. However, because she's sleeping with a high-powered doctor (William Devane, who says really romantic things to her like "You know, it's a good thing you didn't practice pediatrics; there'd be all these little boys having wet dreams all over Philadelphia"), she gets handed an assignment: go to Los Angeles and look into an unexplained and bizarre illness that has struck the head doctor of an HMO. And go she does, but not before attending a party where she meets another high-powered doctor, Barry Corbin, who can't help but loudly proclaim his hatred for HMOs to whomever will listen. I wonder if that will prove to be significant later.

A plane lands in Los Angeles, and she's on it. (Throughout the course of the film she flies to several different locations, and each time there is a shot of a plane landing. I assume this is because the filmmakers believed that if they didn't show that, the viewer might think that she walked from L.A. to, say, Atlanta.) Anyway, she arrives at the clinic and is promptly informed that, in addition to the one case she has been sent to look into, seven other patients have come down with the virus. She ends up taking a look at the nearly dead doctor with the mysterious virus and discovers that, in addition to the welts and bleeding and pus that are apparently associated with the Ebola virus (which, actually, is far less disgusting than what *really* happens to people when they get this virus), he has a bloody open wound on his head and a round welt on his back. She finds out that he was mugged a week earlier, and that's where the head wound came from. I guess no one thought it was odd that a week-old head wound was still bleeding.

She finds out that he had just come back from five weeks in Kenya, along with a monkey, which had bitten him. The primate is being held on the premises, so she goes to see the monkey and attempts a strange conversation with it as she prepares to gut it for testing. The monkey, oddly, never responds to her questions. The tests end up revealing that the monkey carried the Ebola virus, and this explains what killed the (by now, dead) doctor. This discovery opens the door for the repeated use of the phrase "The most deadly virus known to man!" In the meantime, Sheridan is mysteriously transferred out of L.A. and sent to St. Louis to look into another case of what may be Ebola.

Outraged, she goes to St. Louis and finds that the first victim among several in that city is not only also a doctor, but the head of an HMO to boot, and his corpse also has an open head wound and a strange round welt, and not only that, but he, too, was mugged a week before getting sick. However, he didn't go to Kenya and he was not bitten by a monkey. Sheridan decides that this is not just a coincidence, but rather the work of a killer who injects doctors with the Ebola virus in order to kill them, hence the round welt (which is, apparently, the mark of such an injection) on each man's body. Of course, this in no way explains why it was necessary to inject the first doctor with the virus after he was bitten by a monkey that carried the virus, but undoubtedly most viewers would be asleep by this time, so they would not question such logic.

(OK, I know what you're saying: the monkey was a diversion, and the test results that found Ebola virus in the monkey were meant to throw everyone off of the killer's trail. If this is so, then why would the killer think that no one would be the wiser after he mugs and kills the second doctor in precisely the same way as he did the first, with no monkey on hand as an alibi?)

Anyway, our heroine returns to Atlanta and finds that new outbreaks have hit Philadelphia, and then Atlanta itself. No one she tells seems to believe her story of a conspiracy, and she discovers that she's being set up as the thief of a vial of Ebola from the CDC. She does a little snooping and begins to make connections between a number of doctors involved with both the CDC and another installation in Atlanta that is set up to contain deadly viruses, though none of this ever really makes any sense. There's also a strange man following her, and before long he attacks her in her hotel room. He's intent on injecting her with the virus, but she ends up injecting him instead, and after that he is never seen again. Sheridan confronts Corbin and accuses him of masterminding this scheme to kill heads of HMOs with the Ebola virus. He confesses, then kills himself without ever explaining why he just didn't have them shot or something, like a normal person would do. Apparently he believed that hiring a killer with a clearly identifiable M.O., arming him with the Ebola virus, and having him kill only HMO doctors was the perfect crime, and that the threat of spreading "the most deadly virus known to man" was a small price to pay to ensure the closures of said HMOs.

As you can imagine, I was pretty pissed off by this point, since the widespread outbreaks that I thought would occur—nay, that *should* have occurred—did not. Everyone in the movie keeps talking about how deadly Ebola is, and how carefully people need to be when handling tiny vials of the stuff, yet the killer flies from city to city, carrying the virus and somehow manages not to contaminate himself or planeloads of people. In addition, the "outbreaks" that do happen claim a total of perhaps 40 people, even though the clinics don't quarantine the affected patients until they're forced to by the CDC. Not to mention that they never show any truly gruesome displays of slow rotting death. At the end of the movie, after Sheridan's name is cleared and she is given her job back, the CDC is relieved that the virus seems to have "mysteriously vanished," and everyone goes on their merry ways. The movie concludes with incongruously grim facts about how deadly the Ebola virus is, including the revelation that such viruses exist to fight off nature's greatest predator: humans. I'm not sure what that has to do with monkeys, or William Atherton, or anything else that happens in this movie, but if you're having trouble sleeping, this movie will really do the trick.

Most Spectacular Moment of Carnage
Sadly, the disgusting effects of the Ebola virus on what should have been thousands of innocent men, women, and children are never shown, in spite of the fact that the events that occur in the movie would undoubtedly lead to a very serious, widespread outbreak. However, for gruesome thrills, you can't beat the scene in which Sheridan, hiding in a morgue, must crawl over rotted corpses to escape. **(MR)**

Threads (1984)

BBC/Norstar   116 minutes

RECOMMENDED

⚠

DIRECTOR: Mick Jackson

WRITER: Barry Hines

CAST: Karen Meagher, Reece Dinsdale, David Brierly, Rita May, Nicholas Lane, Jane Hazlegrove, Henry Moxon, June Broughton, and lots of other British actors

This is a nasty nuclear war film designed to "one-up" the competition by being even grosser and more disturbing than all others. I can imagine what the tag line for this film might have been: "You thought *The Day After* was disgusting? Check this one out!"

The lack of big-name actors and the low-key acting style and camera work give the film a documentary feel. It opens with a shot of a spider weaving its web, while a stuffy narrator tells us that every thread that is broken by nuclear war affects another and another. And this picture goes to great lengths to show us just how. Set in Sheffield, England, in a community near a NATO target and a nuclear power station, the story concerns two young lovers, played by Karen Meagher and Reece Dinsdale. Meagher learns she is pregnant, and the two decide to keep the baby and move out of their parents' homes and into their own apartment. All the while, news reports inform us of a growing conflict between the United States and the USSR. The film has a jarring sound design; the sounds of air force planes (stock footage, by the way) are often used to cut into new scenes.

When protests build and get out of hand and newscasters report that armed conflict has taken place, things start going really mad. Locals attempt to leave the city, causing traffic jams. Supermarkets are cleared out, resulting in food shortages. Martial law is enforced and, worst of all (at least for the teenagers of Britain), nonessential phones are disconnected! Meanwhile, the narrator explains that government-appointed local officials have been assigned to take control and to stockpile supplies in case of an attack. Television entertainment becomes less exciting than it once was (but then again, I'm talking about the BBC here), as the only programs available seem to be foreboding emergency broadcasts explaining the details of how to bury a dead, irradiated family member.

The inevitable occurs when an EMP knocks all power out and a large mushroom cloud glows over the city. There's a flash, and suddenly cars crash through buildings and crowds run in panic. When the blast finally catches up to them, windows shatter, impaling glass shards into the faces of those nearby. There are more explosions, while onscreen text explains that the blast has killed two-and-one-half to nine million people. But the fun doesn't end there. There are more shots of members of Dinsdale's family, who don't reach safety in time, getting hit by the blast, and random shots of carcasses on fire, burning right down to the skeletons. There are even shots of writhing cats in the rubble of the street. What could possibly be more disturbing, you ask? How about vomit, and lots of it!

Radiation causes all the surviving characters who are not trapped under rubble to upchuck onscreen. The pregnant Meagher, who survives the blast in her parents' basement, gets a mild case of cabin fever and decides to run outside into the warm radiation, eventually finding her way to a zombielike mob at a hospital. Still reading? Again, if you thought that what you had seen previously was disturbing, there's even worse to come. Back in town, the rats are busy eating corpses on the streets and passing fun new diseases along to survivors. All of the characters die out at this point, with the exception of Meagher and Dinsdale's best buddy, who decides to move out to the country, get some fresh air, and, you know, maybe eat a raw, dead irradiated sheep carcass as well.

At this point, the film fades out and cuts to title cards that lovingly describe the ongoing aftereffects week by week, then month by month, and eventually, year by year. Meagher delivers her baby, a daughter, and much of the film now deals with their survival on a farm. Conditions revert back to those of medieval times, only without the delicious buckets of chicken and elaborate jousting-on-horseback displays; instead, we get only guttural *Planet of the Apes*-esque gibberish being spoken by sickly farmers. Now the film is really dragging, and every scene ends with an irritating fade to black. I began to wonder just where the film was going. Nowhere much, it turns out, except for a heartwarming scene in which a character gives birth—to a dead fetus. Yippee!

I suppose I'd have to say that this picture is the most effective of all the nuclear disaster films, given that I prefer the fun, silly disaster movies that make no sense over the other type of nuclear disaster films, which are often overwrought. *Threads* is the most disgusting and disturbing nuclear war film ever, so you might as well pick this as the one to see.

Most Spectacular Moment of Carnage

There are so many disturbing things that it's impossible to pick one. At first, I thought there was nothing more disturbing than seeing a grandmother after the blast, one eye burned shut and hair falling out of her charred scalp. But no! Later, in the hospital, the fantastic visuals include amputations and glass being pulled out of faces, as well as blood, dirt, and what appears to be pus running down the hospital hallway floors. Who wouldn't enjoy that!? **(GK)**

Virus (1980)
Toho Studios   115 minutes

AT YOUR OWN RISK

DIRECTOR: Kinji Fukasaku

WRITERS: Kôji Takada, Gregory Knapp, Kinji Fukasaku (based on the novel *Fukkatsu No Hi* by Sakyo Komatsu)

CAST: Chuck Connors, Glenn Ford, Olivia Hussey, George Kennedy, Masao Kusakari, Edward James Olmos, Henry Silva, Bo Svenson, Robert Vaughn, Sonny Chiba

Well, first things first. The reason you've never heard of this movie is because it was a Japanese production, made with a mostly Japanese crew in conjunction with the Tokyo Broadcasting Corporation. (Its original title is *Fukkatsu No Hi.*) Make no mistake though—the impressive cast includes huge stars from just about everywhere. *Virus* is a chopped-up version of the original movie, and unfortunately, it's the only one most people living in North America might have seen.

Storywise, things don't make a heck of a lot of sense. A rare virus that's being developed as a deadly weapon is stolen during an elaborate shoot-out at a snowed-in cabin in East Germany. There, a scientist has perfected a supergerm that can infect everyone unless the temperature drops significantly below freezing, at which point the germ stays dormant. Some time later, a rare form of influenza sweeps Japan and Eastern Europe, slowly making its way toward the United States. It almost seems as if the film is striving to be as "international" as possible by flipping back and forth, disjointedly, from nation to nation. Glenn Ford is introduced as the president, and Robert Vaughn and Henry Silva are also introduced. For 30 minutes the three of them debate and try to determine exactly what the virus is and why it was released. There's a lot of overacting going on, as Silva, playing a general, insists that it's a threat to the nation's security. As it turns out, the virus spares no one, and soon Ford and Vaughn are wrapped up in blankets, hacking and coughing their way to a slow death as the nation crumbles around them. There are some pretty nasty shots depicting this, with bodies littering the streets and other corpses being piled into heaps and set on fire. Silva, who is now for some unknown reason acting certifiably nuts, seems to be the only one who's unaffected, and he makes his way down to the war room beneath the White House, arming the nation's nuclear weapons and readying to fire them.

And suddenly, that's the end of Ford, Vaughn, and Silva. They never reappear in the film, leaving you to wonder why they were introduced in the first place. After seeing the death toll in major cities around the world superimposed onto images of each city, an entirely new movie starts. This one picks up in Antarctica, where the international teams stationed there learn that they are the last ones left alive on the planet. Team members include George Kennedy as America's team leader, Edward James Olmos (who sings at one point), and Chuck Connors as a British submarine captain. Don't worry. Connors doesn't even attempt an accent; he expects the viewer to just accept the idea that he's British. Anyway, as his character is introduced, the audience is too busy watching him blow up another submarine to care. Suspension of disbelief is also tested when we are informed that Olivia Hussey's character is Norwegian. She's discovered in Antarctica at a Norwegian base by a couple of Japanese team members after her husband and all of the other Norwegians have apparently gone crazy, committed suicide, and/or shot each other to death.

All together, the 800 humans left on Earth discuss what to do. The first major problem? Love, baby. Repopulating the species. Much is made of the eight females on the continent, and how best to "share" their services among the extremely "horny" men. I'm not making this up. It also seems that Hussey and Japanese scientist Masao Kusakari seem to be falling in love amid all of this. They exchange long, awkward glances before Hussey is taken away by another male who has "won" her in some kind of sex drawing. Fortunately for Kusakari, the man is distracted after discovering that a large earthquake may occur. This is bad new for everybody, as the residents determine that the earthquake will set off an automatic nuclear missile response in the United States (thanks to Henry Silva), which will trigger a response by the USSR, causing complete annihilation. Even Antarctica won't be immune, as there are missiles pointed in its direction, too (no doubt to wipe out the threatening penguin armies that may be amassing).

What to do? Why, send Bo Svenson to save the day! Svenson and scientist Kusakari are sent back to Washington to shut down the system before the earthquake triggers the rockets. After saying their farewells (the women are shipped off the continent for safety), our heroes inject an untested antidote for the virus into their abdomens, which involves a wonderful close-up of Bo Svenson's stomach. At this point, Kennedy, Olmos, and the other characters (except Connors, who has one more scene to complete) vanish from the story (again with the vanishing characters!), leaving Svenson and Kusakari to try to save the day in the third act.

Unfortunately, things don't go as well as expected, and they fail to shut down the system. Over the radio, Connors kindly thanks them for trying (although that's probably not what Connors's character would be thinking), then disappears from the movie without a trace. My guess is that everyone left in Antarctica is killed in the nuclear blast. At this point, I thought, wow, this may not be a good movie, but I'll give it some credit. There's an awful lot of disaster in this disaster movie. A killer virus is bad enough, but to actually wipe out the entire planet with nuclear weapons? That seems to be going above and beyond the call of duty.

But don't shed a tear, because the last 10 minutes of this film are perhaps its most ridiculous. Now deciding it wants to be some sort of art film, the story picks up four years later. Amazingly, from the ashes walks Kusakari, who has somehow managed to survive a nuclear blast at ground zero and come out relatively unscathed. He wanders along the barren landscape and ends up in a church, where he proceeds to have an imaginary conversation with a large crucifixion display. In a highly questionable move by the filmmakers, Kusakari doesn't speak; instead, his thoughts are captioned across the bottom of the screen. He arrives in the South American camp where Hussey and the other remaining women and children who were evacuated live. How he managed to walk across continents without the help of a map or even a compass, I'll never know. He greets Hussey, who races over and hugs him, before finally speaking the film's final words: "Life is wonderful." I'm not sure if this is supposed to be sarcastic or not. You be the judge. You can ponder it while listening to the soothing sounds of the movie's theme, "Toujours Gai Mon Cher," as its singer wails to us all that "it's not too late to start again."

Most Spectacular Moment of Carnage

There's a great deal of carnage early on, when we get a close-up of a man shot in the eye, mass suicides, heaps of bodies on fire, and streets littered with victims of the virus. But the most agonizing death belongs to Bo Svenson. After being toppled by falling cement and metal during an earthquake, he finds himself lying on the floor, impaled on a metal rod. His scientist buddy pulls the rod out, allowing Svenson to crawl around in agony for another scene before dying. (GK)

Warning Sign (1985)

Twentieth Century Fox   99 minutes

AT YOUR OWN RISK

DIRECTOR: Hal Barwood

WRITERS: Hal Barwood, Matthew Robbins

CAST: Sam Waterston, Kathleen Quinlan, Yaphet Kotto, Jeffrey DeMunn, Richard Dysart, G. W. Bailey, Rick Rossovich

"You've got fatalities there, Major. Don't tell me about yeast!"

So says small-town sheriff Sam Waterston to federal biological containment specialist Yaphet Kotto after the Bio-Tek Agronomics lab, somewhere in Utah, is locked down for unknown reasons. While the lab claims to be working on the harmless splicing of vegetable genes, scientist Richard Dysart and his team are really developing deadly biological weapons. And of course, as these things are bound to happen, something goes terribly wrong!

How it happens is quite comical, actually: a vial of deadly bacteria becomes stuck to the arm of Dysart's protective suit as he's comparing slides or something; neither he nor anyone else in the room notices the vial hanging from his arm as he walks around handing things to people. Finally, the vial drops on the floor (but doesn't break), and no one notices that, either. Eventually, G. W. Bailey steps on the vial, smashing it, but no one notices *that*. Now the virus has been released into the air, and anyone who's not wearing a protective suit has been infected. The standard decontamination procedure as one leaves the lab is apparently enough to eradicate all trace of the virus, except that Bailey's wearing contact lenses, and since you have to keep your eyes closed during decontamination, that's how he carries the virus out of the lab, which is exactly what I want!

As five o'clock rolls around and everyone's getting ready to leave, security guard Kathleen Quinlan (who also happens to be the sheriff's wife) receives a warning on her computer that indicates a contamination has occurred. Following standard procedure, she puts the building into lockdown, trapping most of the staff, including herself, inside the building. Those who had already made it outside don't seem to realize that there might be a very good reason to lock the building down, which is why, over the course of the film, they ignore safety procedures and make attempts to break into the building for no apparent reason. (I won't even mention those workers who decided they'd rather escape at the last possible moment than stay inside for the safety of others, making it seem as if these people either are unaware of or choose to ignore the standard protocol.)

What no one on the outside knows is that the virus to which some have been exposed is designed to be a biological weapon that first disorients the enemy, then makes them want to kill each other before finally dying. I'm not sure why it was necessary to make this weapon engage the "rage center of the brain," as a scientist puts it, thereby turning people into psychotic killing machines, rather than just create a virus that incapacitates and kills the enemy without any of that other stuff. But, as it happens, the effect this virus has on the workers in this lab doesn't fit the virus's description. Oh, it certainly turns people into killing machines, but they seem to have no interest in killing each other! Instead they lumber about like an army of zombies in a George A. Romero picture (except the Romero picture would be good), which certainly isn't what you'd want your enemies to be doing.

Meanwhile, Kotto and his team have taken charge of the scene. while a frustrated Waterston tracks down Jeffrey DeMunn, a scientist who used to work for the lab but who quit years earlier to continue his own extremely important work in the field of vegetable genetics. He knows the layout of the place, as well as the effects of the virus and the accompanying antivirus, which he helped to create and which doesn't work, for some reason. What's puzzling him is why Quinlan hasn't gotten sick while everyone else around her who is not in isolation has fallen ill. But Quinlan has bigger problems to worry about: a crazed G. W. Bailey and several others are intent on escaping from the building, and they need her access codes to do so. When she refuses to help, they grab an ax and start busting down the door. There's a truly incredible moment here in which, once the door's been opened, Quinlan points her gun at the crowd; in response, the guy with the ax throws it at her head, burying the ax in the wall inches from her face. Then Bailey comes over to calm her down as if this hadn't just happened.

Then there's a muddled sequence in which a bunch of soldiers enter the building and, for some reason, force Bailey and Quinlan and the others back into the same lab where the original exposure took place. Then they are forced to walk through an access corridor of sorts, where they meet up with Dysart and his drooling crew of maniacs. Of course, a slaughter ensues. Armed with only an ax and, um, sticks or something,

Quinlan and Bailey manage to overpower and kill the gun-toting soldiers. Following this, Waterston and DeMunn break into the compound for some reason. Once inside, they find Quinlan still healthy, while everyone else they come across has gone completely mad. DeMunn suddenly realizes that the reason Quinlan's not sick is because she must be pregnant; the higher levels of estrogen in her system have prevented her from falling ill. By this time, both Waterston and DeMunn have been exposed to the virus, as their paper-thin protective suits have ripped open as a result of their minor physical exertion, though only DeMunn develops symptoms; Waterston remains in top condition. Of course they need DeMunn to develop an antiserum, which he manages to do in a matter of moments even while drifting into unconsciousness.

Armed with inoculation guns (and so flush with manly power that Waterston can be heard saying "Clint Eastwood would love one of these!"—clearly an indication that he has seen very few Eastwood pictures), Waterston and DeMunn engage the crazy bastards who are still running rampant in the lab in hand-to-hand combat, finally inoculating each of them with the antivirus, except for Dysart, who blows his own head off with Waterston's gun after rambling for a few minutes about the failures of science. Then Quinlan somehow connects a huge tub of the antivirus to the building's sprinkler system, and soon the good stuff's raining down on everyone and everything. This seemed suspect to me; I didn't realize that merely spraying the serum at people would be enough to eradicate the virus from existence. When you go to the doctor for a flu shot, he doesn't just spray it in your face. You'd probably have a few questions for him if he did.

As a final act, Waterston hammers a sign to the front door warning people to stay out of the place. This, he believes, will "keep the kids out" (maybe this is the titular "warning sign.") Then everyone leaves, including the feds. Even though there's been a deadly viral outbreak. Even though the virus itself still exists in vials inside the lab. Even though there are probably some dead bodies still in there somewhere. Even though there was a massive cover-up that threatened many innocent lives. And even though no one can be entirely sure that the virus has been contained. No one does any tests to see if pumping the serum through the sprinkler system actually killed the airborne virus. Plus, as far as I knew at this point, Quinlan's unborn baby had also been pumped full of the stuff, having taken the proverbial bullet for its mother. I don't know if I was supposed to think that every last one of these people is a complete idiot, but that's my inclination, and I'll stick by it.

Warning Sign is well photographed (by Dean Cundey), and though Waterston seems to give off a Roy Scheider vibe and Quinlan generally behaves like a scared little girl, the acting is good. However, the film can't decide whether it wants to be a thriller or a cautionary tale or a horror movie or what, and since it doesn't add up to much of anything in the end, it seems like a big waste of time. This is made-for-TV material, not feature-film stuff, and *Warning Sign* pales in comparison to many other cinematic offerings of the same year. But it does have that great scene where they nearly take Quinlan's head off with an ax. I love that scene.

Most Spectacular Moment of Carnage
Did I mention I love the scene with the ax? I know it doesn't split her head open, but it comes damn close, and it made me laugh my ass off. I mean, how many movies are out there in which someone throws an ax at somebody's head? Not nearly enough! **(MR)**

Acceptable Risks (1986)

ABC Circle Films   92 minutes

AT YOUR OWN RISK

"I just love this place; isn't it perfect for us?" says Brian Dennehy's granddaughter earnestly, looking out from her backyard at a picturesque series of gray industrial smokestacks from a chemical factory just a few short miles away. Yeah, sure it is. Dennehy plays the factory's overworked manager, who, under pressure from his corporate bosses, increases chemical production at the facility and pays the ultimate price. Not a lot of action happens in the first hour, and instead the movie focuses on a subplot involving grandfather Dennehy falling for a young coworker and their relationship (we're spared any elaborate love scenes, though). Meanwhile, pressure grows in a chemical tank. Eventually the tank explodes, spreading deadly chemicals into the community. Of course, there are many shots of panicked people hacking and dropping dead in the streets. The abrupt final shot is a freeze-frame of Dennehy emoting over his tragically poisoned granddaughter. **(GK)**

Chernobyl: The Final Warning (1991)

Turner Home Entertainment   100 minutes

RECOMMENDED

Solid acting by Jon Voight and Jason Robards makes this one of the better made-for-TV disaster films. Voight plays a nice-guy doctor in L.A. who's brought into the USSR following the Chernobyl meltdown. Firefighters, battling blazing debris after the explosion, have been irradiated and now cling to life while helpful Voight and his medical team attempt bone marrow transplants to save them. While the film is low on action (after all, it's based on a real event), there is some very disturbing imagery of radiation and burn victims in the hospital sequences, and the movie effectively makes a plea not only against nuclear power, but also for disarmament and world peace, without sounding too preachy. In addition, there's some nice photography of the Red Square in Moscow. Directed by Anthony Page. (**GK**)

On the Beach (1959)
MGM/United Artists   134 minutes

RECOMMENDED

On the Beach features a great cast that includes Gregory Peck, Ava Gardner, Fred Astaire, Anthony Perkins, Donna Anderson, and John Tate. It is a slow but extremely well-crafted film about the aftermath of a nuclear war. Radiation has made the world uninhabitable, with the exception—for the time being—of Australia. A submarine captain, a lieutenant, a scientist, and other characters must deal with their own imminent deaths, which will come in a matter of months as the radiation cloud slowly approaches the continent. There's some hope, though, in a radio transmission picked up from San Diego, and the second half of the movie deals with a submarine voyage to discover just who is sending the messages. San Francisco and San Diego are shown during the voyage and are presented as ghost towns. Best of all, viewers get to see Fred Astaire take part in a spectacular "death race," filled with exploding cars and suicidal driving, days before the end of the world. This is a classic film that makes its point well and isn't as preachy as some of the later nuclear terror films. Directed by Stanley Kramer, it was nominated for two Oscars, for Best Film Editing and Best Music, Score of a Dramatic or Comedy Picture. The movie was remade as a miniseries in 2000. (**GK**)

The Stand (1994)

ABC   366 minutes

RECOMMENDED

This miniseries is a decent, Emmy-nominated (for its great makeup effects, as well as for its art direction and music) adaptation of Stephen King's novel of the same name. It gets a little wonky during its last segment, which features a bit too much in the way of Bible prophecies, self-proclaimed martyrs, and superimposed heads of characters floating in the sky for my tastes. Maybe it wasn't such a good idea to follow the source material this closely. Otherwise, there's a lot of good stuff here, as a super-plague infects and kills most of the population, leaving the survivors to band together in either a good-guy camp or a bad-guy camp. The cast includes Gary Sinise, Molly Ringwald, Jamey Sheridan, Laura San Giacomo, Ruby Dee, Ossie Davis, Miguel Ferrer, Corin Nemec, Matt Frewer, Adam Storke, Ray Walston, and Rob Lowe (who dies an explosively spectacular death, I might add). Written by Stephen King and directed by Mick Garris, it features tons of amusing cameos, including ones by Ed Harris, Kathy Bates, and many film directors. **(GK)**

Testament (1983)

Paramount   90 minutes

AT YOUR OWN RISK

Lynne Littman directs Jane Alexander, William Devane, Ross Harris, Roxana Zal, Lukas Haas, and Philip Anglim in this flick, which also features Kevin Costner, Rebecca De Mornay, and Mako. Based on the story "The Last Testament" by Carol Amen, this is an effective, well-made, and well-acted, but extraordinarily depressing, movie about suburban mother Jane Alexander and her family struggling to survive after a nuclear missile hits San Francisco. The audience never learns exactly what has happened or why, only that the power has gone out and that much of the country (and possibly the world) has been wiped out. There's no big buildup or climax here; instead, the town just slowly falls apart. Lucky me, I got to watch this family (including three of the four children) and their neighbors slowly get sick and die from the effects of "invisible radiation." *Testament* is about as far from a laughfest as you can get, and you'll probably need a really stiff drink by the end. It also isn't realistic in its depiction of the aftereffects of the blast. Jane Alexander was nominated for a Best Actress Oscar for her work in this movie. **(GK)**

RARE, OBSCURE, AND LESS IMPORTANT TITLES

Atomic Twister (2002) Made-for-TV

Hiroshima: Out of the Ashes (1990) Made-for-TV

Panic in Year Zero! (1962)

Plague (1978)

Disaster at Silo 7 (1988) Made-for-TV

The Survivalist (1987)

WHAT'S WITH ALL THE LOVE THEMES?

As inappropriate as it may sound, horrible tragedies have been coupled with catchy top-40 singles since the earliest days of disaster films. Time and again, filmmakers have seen fit to include a musical tribute to the end of the world. In the 1930s, these films almost always included a toe-tapping number, usually wailed by the lead actress. *San Francisco* almost qualifies as a musical, the title song is regurgitated so often. Maybe music was intended to raise the spirits of audience members, who might well have been depressed by the death and carnage onscreen. Or perhaps studios believed that, with a number-one hit from their film on the radio, people would be unable to resist seeing the movie that inspired it.

Whatever the reasons, love themes were particularly ubiquitous in disaster films of the '70s. Irwin Allen productions, in particular, almost always included a weepy ballad. There's "The Morning After," from *The Poseidon Adventure*, and "We May Never Love Like This Again," from *The Towering Inferno*, both Oscar winners sung by Maureen McGovern. Actually, "We May Never Love Like This Again" and "Wherever Love Takes Me" (the theme from *Gold*, a thriller/disaster film set in a gold mine), were both sung by McGovern and were both nominated for Oscars in 1974. This led to her being dubbed the "Disaster Queen" at the time.

No matter what the setting—an ocean liner, a skyscraper, or even a plague-infested train—there is always someone crooning the film's "love theme." Helen Reddy belted out the tune "Best Friend" in *Airport 1975*. The filmmakers couldn't quite figure out how to incorporate it into the film, and they instead ran it in the background and over the opening and closing credits. Most of these songs are hysterically inappropriate and just plain strange. Case in point: *The Cassandra Crossing*'s "I'm Still on My Way."

After listening to the melody accompanying this track, you'll feel like the sweaty, boil-covered plague carrier the filmmakers cut to 30 seconds after this song ends.

Think the trend has ended? Think again. Recent releases continue to include love themes and poppy tunes. "No One Needs to Know," Shania Twain's hit from *Twister*, was licensed for the film from one of her earlier records. It doesn't seem to have any connection whatsoever to the events in the film, except that the MTV music video for the song contains some footage from the film. Donna Summer croons with Bruce Robert on "Whenever There Is Love," an original tune written for the film *Daylight*. And, of course, there is *Titanic*'s "My Heart Will Go On," sung by she-who-will-not-be-named. Clearly, "We May Never Love Like This Again" was an influence on the writers of this enormous hit.

And as much as I can't help but like Aerosmith, there's nothing quite as odd as hearing their blaringly loud "love theme" after witnessing the deaths of many major characters and the complete annihilation of major cities around the world in *Armageddon*. But still, this odd juxtaposition seems to work for many audiences. Disaster movies are all about being "big," and what better way to do that than to have a big, over-the-top musical number to go along with them? Well, I suppose I shouldn't think about it too hard, and instead just sit back and enjoy these tunes any way I can. **(GK)**

Mad Bombers, Killer Bees, and Wild Animals

At the height of the disaster movie genre's popularity, producers must have been scouring the newspapers, looking for anything that might form the basis of a disaster film. Surely audiences had grown accustomed to seeing earthquakes, volcanoes, and hurricanes on the big screen, which is what makes the films in this section so much fun. There are the mad bombers who want to blow up roller coasters and buses instead of the typical ships and high-rises. Many of these films are based on true-life incidents; others deal with such strange subject matter as killer wildlife. (When I was little, I remember various news reports telling me that killer bees were making their way north to America, and that this would cause a great disaster, killing crops, animals, and maybe even the odd farmer or two. Killer bees were hard to take all that seriously, but within a year or two, films started popping up based on this "all-too-true" terror.) And then we've thrown in some random, misfit disaster films, like the incomprehensible, psychedelic *The Last Days of Planet Earth*, that simply must be seen to be believed. Expect something a little different from this category of disaster films. **(GK)**

The Bees (1978)

New World Pictures   86 minutes

SO BAD IT'S GOOD

DIRECTOR: Alfredo Zacarias

WRITERS: Alfredo Zacarias, Jack Hill (uncredited)

CAST: John Saxon, Angel Tompkins, John Carradine, Claudio Brook

Obviously trying to capitalize on the "success" of *The Swarm* (which was released that same year), *The Bees* is based on the same premise: killer bees. Like the buzzfest that inspired it, *The Bees* also contains hilarious situations, overacting, bad sets, inappropriate scoring, and poor special effects, not to mention stock footage (that is clearly from a different decade), political incorrectness in the extreme, and one of the most outrageous climaxes I've ever seen in a disaster flick.

Unlike most cheaply produced movies, the filmmakers, perhaps against their better judgment, choose to film many attack sequences and action scenes, which makes this movie fly by reasonably quickly. The film starts with a big attack scene and never lets up—or makes any sense, for that matter. But don't worry, John Saxon's character, Dr. John Norman, a bee scientist/kung fu master, is up to the task of both stopping the insects and impressing his fetching female coworker Sandra, played by Angel Tompkins, with great come-ons like "Why are you so interested in my genes?" Naturally, this works, and before long, Saxon is making time with Tompkins, even in such inappropriate locales as the front seat of a vehicle that is being swarmed by bees. It should be noted the film has a real "one take" feel: there are long takes of Saxon and Tompkins that include overlapping dialogue and unusually delivered lines that don't seem to have been intentionally funny, but that, onscreen, sound hysterical. During one exchange in a lab, Saxon lets out a loud, guttural, jarring "Urngh!" while taking off a lab coat during the middle of a conversation, then continues as if nothing completely unexpected and bizarre had just escaped his lips.

There are many outrageously dopey attack sequences, but the one that sticks out as most offensive occurs at a bench in a park. An old man approaches two young boys who can't act, wanting them to do him "a favor." After some politically incorrect comments, they agree to his terms. He reveals that he has rheumatism, and they collect bees for him in a paper bag, then point and laugh hysterically as he allows the bees to sting his leg. Of course, the swarm arrives seconds later to finish the job, but you'll be stunned by the strange tastelessness of this sequence. You sure can't get away with anything like this today.

The score is also hilarious; it often jumps from genre to genre, the free-form jazz during an attack being my particular favorite. And the movie uses odd wipes (a transition technique in which a line passes across the screen, eliminating the current shot and replacing it with a new one) that wouldn't be out of place in an episode of the old TV show *Batman*. Even more ludicrous is the work of the extras, whose reactions to the sight of a huge cloud of killer bees (staring up blankly, grinding teeth, fainting comically) are inappropriate, to say the least.

Sadly, John Carradine, a once-great actor, is not only almost visibly falling asleep in the middle of a scene, but he also puts on a ridiculous German accent for his role as a scientist nicknamed Ziggy, who "has spent his life in the study of bee communication." Yes, he's a linguist for bees. As if that isn't humorous enough, it's later explained that there has been a misappropriation of funds by the evil U.S. Minister of Agriculture (who has a telephone that is almost as big as his head). He comes to his end when a bee spies on him and presumably reports his evil ways to the queen bee.

That's right folks, the stunning climax features bees capable of rational thought and communication. "They can tink like a man!" Carradine states, his eyes bugging out of his head. All the while, Saxon reveals a plan to turn the bees "into homosexuals," which promptly stalls, leading to a massive attack on New York City. Of course, this leads to the amazing close, in which the bees make their demands for environmental preservation while swarming members of the United Nations.

The Bees is one of those movies that is indefensible, yet appealing in its terribleness. And although it's just as ludicrous as *The Swarm*, it's only half as long. This is a great film to watch and make fun of with friends.

Most Spectacular Moment of Carnage

You get more carnage than you'd expect from a low-budget movie. Highlights include a New York City mugger being stung numerous times, throwing himself through a plate-glass window, picking himself up, throwing himself onto the street, and, finally, being run down by a passing vehicle. The demise of a government official is also good. As he is attacked inside his office, he moves onto the windowsill before throwing himself out backward, and we see him (OK, a dummy of him) crash to the sidewalk below. But my favorite is the scientist who is hit in the head with a large rock, which is thrown by a small Brazilian peasant woman. He's then beaten with a stick by others peasants before being mercifully stung to death. (GK)

Bug (1975)

Paramount Pictures   100 minutes

SO BAD IT'S GOOD

DIRECTOR: Jeannot Szwarc

WRITERS: William Castle, Thomas Page

CAST: Bradford Dillman, Joanna Miles, Richard Gilliland, Jamie Smith Jackson, Alan Fudge, Jesse Vint, Patty McCormack

Those of you who are brave enough to admit having seen William Castle's *Bug* probably don't think that this is really a disaster movie, since, after a rather promising first act that's filled with many familiar signifiers, the film slowly devolves into a heavy-handed allegory. Nonetheless, I was lured by the video box's description of a "massive earth tremor" that "opens a deep crevasse in the California desert." Moreover (again, according to the box), this earthquake releases a "deadly breed of foot-long cockroach, which threatens to destroy the city of Riverside before spreading across the country." This, plus the presence of disaster movie vets Bradford Dillman (*The Swarm*; *Piranha*), Alan Fudge (*Airport 1975*), and Jesse Vint (*Earthquake*), made this movie seem all the more inviting.

All of this is very misleading.

Indeed, the movie opens with an earth tremor, albeit one that's far from massive, with a small church sitting in the epicenter of the quake. Sadly, no one is killed, and though the church is tossed and turned, all the trees outside it are left standing, and all the churchgoers' cars still remain upright. However, the viewer's thirst for blood is satisfied minutes later when a jolly fellow and his pleasantly foulmouthed teenage son (he's got two lines, both of which contain the word *shit*) get charred alive when the truck they're driving stalls and bursts into flame for no apparent reason. It is soon discovered that the tailpipe of the truck was home to a large cockroach, but of course this is no ordinary cockroach: this is a strangely deformed insect that has no eyes, cannot breed, hardly ever moves, and spits fire from its ass. Comical smoldering sounds are to be heard whenever one of these bugs is about to set something ablaze. Why are they doing this? Where do they come from? How is this possible? Who gives a rat's ass?

Someone does, namely the boyfriend of the dead man's daughter, who happens to look out the grimy window of his rural cabin in the middle of the night into pitch-black darkness and notices a dirt-colored cockroach lying perfectly still very far away. He goes to investigate and finds a whole load of these things, which soon set their sights on a hapless little kitty. In what ends up being a very disturbing scene, mainly because it looks like a real cat is being horribly abused, little kitty gets slowly tortured by a bunch of bugs until it finally catches fire. Our young hero stands and watches, obviously too dumbstruck to actually do anything. The viewer, now emboldened by the nasty ways in which victims are dispatched, begins to hunger more vigorously for a continuing body count. Alas, only talking ensues.

The next day, the kid pays a visit to his former teacher, Bradford Dillman, who bears an eerie resemblance to a young Charlton Heston, right down to his hammy voice inflections. Dillman, according to the video box, is supposed to be an entomologist, but he doesn't really do anything to support this claim other than show off his ability to talk to squirrels. After displaying this dubious talent to a room full of perplexed students, our new hero the, um, entomologist, has a short chat with the kid before asking him to join him in the cafeteria for lunch, to which the kid agrees. It is only after Dillman has taken a few bites of food that the kid reveals the rotted cat carcass resting inside of the box he's been carrying for 20 minutes. This prompts Dillman to accompany the boy to the site of the quake, where the earth has violently cracked open, forming a rather tiny crevasse that's suitable for stepping over easily. Due to the abundance of the cockroaches around the crevasse, Dillman decides that the bugs have come from very deep inside the earth, which is in no way a suitable explanation for how it is possible for the bugs to be killing people within mere moments of being churned up from the earth's depths by a mild tremor.

Nonetheless, the discovery of these bugs chills Dillman to the very core of his being, for if it did not, would he utter the disaster movie-esque line "By that time the whole goddamn city could be burned to the ground!"? I think not. However, it should also be noted that by this point in the film, no other deaths have occurred, though apparently some of the bugs end up hitching rides into the city to burn down buildings in spectacular displays of stock footage.

It isn't long before Dillman discovers what he feels is the bugs' key weakness— namely, that due to the differences in atmospheric pressure between the underground world from whence they came and the world aboveground where they currently were, the insects are suffering from "the bends" and that they will, in due time, explode and die. This is where the movie essentially ends (although it does continue for another

45 minutes or so), because once you've discovered that the way to destroy these vicious killer beasts is to do absolutely nothing, what else is there to do but sit around and wait? And that's not very exciting at all.

However, Dillman then decides, for some strange reason, that it might be a good idea to build a pressure tank in which to simulate the atmosphere of the bugs' underground home world so as to keep the bugs alive and prompt them to breed. Although these are clearly the actions of a madman (if he were really interested in saving people from the bugs' destructive ways, he'd want to kill them, not breed them, right?), nobody picks up on the possibility that the guy's insane. Dillman's desire to breed the insects is a bizarre turn of events that isn't even remotely consistent with his behavior up to that point, though it does result in my favorite line, spoken by Dillman to his ex-student after he has requested that the boy build a pressure tank for him (not that we've been given any reason to believe that this small-town hick is able to manufacture such a thing). The boy wisely declines, and decides instead to go check on his girlfriend, who is recuperating after a bug-inflicted injury. Dillman looks him straight in the eye and says, "Isn't she reason enough to build a pressure tank?" Yes, pure gold, not to mention that the last thing anyone trying to kill these bugs would want is a pressure tank.

In the meantime, Dillman drives home, only to discover that he's also brought a few of these bugs with him, as they have attached themselves to the engine and any other part of the car that produces intense heat. Using all of his finely tuned scientific faculties, Dillman sticks a smoldering newspaper into his tailpipe to lure a few of the bugs out, and then proceeds to forget he's only captured two of the three that emerged. Fortunately, this results in his wife falling prey to the missing bug, which crawls onto her head while she is in the kitchen all alone, talking to herself and looking around the room as if others were there. After this bizarre interlude, the bug ignites her head, and she is soon replaced by what is very clearly a male stuntman in a burn suit who proceeds to run from room to room, flailing wildly. Before long he's (I mean, "she's") dead and the house has burned down.

Following this, Dillman flips out and takes residence in a shack in the middle of nowhere with his pressure tank, a tape recorder, and one sweat-stained shirt. He manages to fill the pressure tank with all of the remaining bugs quite easily. One imagines it might be just as easy to pluck the bugs from the ground and stuff them into an incinerator, or drop something extremely heavy on them, or perhaps just pick the bugs off with a rifle. Though these are mutant bugs with the ability to shoot fire from their asses, they are not particularly difficult to kill, and they become less and less menacing as the movie unfolds.

As the film concludes, Dillman has managed to breed the bugs with normal cockroaches, for no apparent reason, resulting in a further mutated breed of bug that exhibits superintelligence, as displayed in the scene where Dillman looks at the wall to see that the bugs have not only escaped from their container (because he failed to attach a lock to the hinged top). but have also grouped themselves together to spell out the letters of his last name. It is at this point where the audience undoubtedly wishes that the bugs would also spell the words *The End*.

We're supposed to think that the increasingly symbiotic relationship between Dillman and the bugs is interesting, but it isn't. It's not remotely consistent with the first half of the film, and it derails all hope that any further disaster movie-type events will occur. The minute director Szwarc (seemingly forgetting that this is a William Castle production) begins to exhibit displays of misguided artistic pretension, all is lost. By attempting to veer into bizarre psychological horror and transform the movie into some kind of parable about the perils of humans trying to play God, the movie succeeds only in becoming more and more incomprehensible, and though this is fun for a while, one's masochism can only go so far. Undaunted, Szwarc would continue to wreak cinematic havoc a few years later with *Jaws 2*.

Most Spectacular Moment of Carnage

The cat torture scene takes the prize, mostly because it is quite clear that the humane society was nowhere near the set when that scene was filmed. **(MR)**

Day of the Animals (1977)

Film Ventures International   97 minutes

AT YOUR OWN RISK

© Film Ventures International, Inc.

DIRECTOR: William Girdler

WRITERS: William Norton, Eleanor Norton

CAST: Christopher George, Leslie Nielsen, Lynda Day George, Richard Jaeckel, Michael Ansara, Ruth Roman

The opening of this ecologically themed disaster film warns that the events depicted in the movie "could happen." And yes, as everyone knows, aerosol cans are indeed very harmful to our ozone layer. But honestly, I think it's extremely unlikely that ultraviolet rays could affect animals that are over 5,000 feet above sea level, causing them to go on a mad rampage and attack campers and park rangers. I'm no scientist, though.

Of course, there's a hiking group being led through the Sierra Mountains just as these animals are affected, leaving the hikers trapped in what seems like the most densely populated national park in the world. Tarantulas, wolves, bears, cougars, hawks, birds, and even ants are primed to attack, and they stare down the travelers throughout much of the first act. All of the bizarre disaster movie caricatures are here as well, including a football player, a news reporter, asshole ad executive Leslie Nielsen, and a Native American trail guide.

Christopher George plays our hero, who is a trail guide. Usually the presence of actors Christopher and Lynda Day George guarantees a bomb (watch *Mortuary* and the extremely sleazy *Pieces* if you don't believe me), but this film is their best in many respects. There's some good widescreen nature photography, and the stars give decent performances. (These two things don't make the movie great, but hell, this is *Citizen Kane* compared to the Georges' other pictures.) Of course, this doesn't stop any of the characters from doing extraordinarily stupid things. After a wolf (or maybe a coyote) viciously attacks a young woman, she is patched up and sent on her way with another friendly hiker in the group. It doesn't take long before she's hawk food. As for the hiker, he discovers a lost little mute girl (don't ask how or why). This bizarre subplot follows the likable hiker and his efforts to protect the girl from the elements. As for the group, no one seems fazed in the least by the attack or takes this as a warning that they should get the hell out of there fast.

Soon, they're all lost in the Sierras and under attack. Made in the late '70s, this flick combines typical disaster movie themes with popular horror movie elements, and there are some disturbing attacks here to keep you interested. Particularly amusing is a scene involving the useless police chief, who is attacked in his own kitchen. He turns away from the kitchen table to the fridge for a second, and when he looks back, numerous rats have magically appeared. A large rats jumps (or is thrown off) of the kitchen table. The chief fights for his life against the rat, which gnaws at his face. Only then does he wisely call for an evacuation of the town.

Other than the surprisingly cruel and brutal attacks, Leslie Nielsen is the main reason to watch this film. In a change of pace from his more recent work, Nielsen plays an insane jerk named Paul Jenson. As the group stumbles around lost and Christopher George tries to come up with some solutions, Nielsen bickers memorably, "You haven't been right so far, hot shot! We can defend ourselves, now can't we, hot shot? I said can't we, hot shot?" using the term "hot shot" more times in a scene—in an entire movie, for that matter—than I have ever heard in my life. George, trying to meet Nielsen's quota, simply responds, "Don't call me hot shot."

Yes, forget the cinematography; there's no scenery left each time Nielsen enters the frame, screaming lines and insults like "You lily-livered punk!" After going absolutely crazy, starting a mutiny, and forming his own group of followers (à la *Lord of the Flies*), Nielsen then goes shirtless, attacks a young female in the group, kills her boyfriend with a spear, and later, wrestles a bear to the death (unfortunately, his own). Yes, Leslie Nielsen wrestles a Kodiak bear; there's something you don't see every day. As for the hiker, he brings the little girl safely into town, but—naturally—finds that the place is overrun with wild animals. He's attacked by a rattlesnake, and before he even gets the chance to react, he's then knocked out of the frame and is presumably torn to bits by a mad dog. The little girl gets to witness all of this. The other characters are attacked by a gang of hungry, roving German shepherds (the Sierras are full of them, I guess—or maybe they could only get the coyote for one day) and attempt to escape to a river during the climax.

Overall, this is cheesy exploitation of the basest of disaster movie elements. You could do much worse, but I wouldn't seek this one out unless you're in a group and want some laughs, or unless you're extremely desperate for a different kind of disaster flick.

Most Spectacular Moment of Carnage
After first being attacked by a worlf (or coyote, or the producer's dog—hell, you make the call), a wounded female hiker is attacked by hawks (you get to see them peck on her fingers). As if that isn't enough, she then falls off of a cliff to a violent death on the rocks below. It's very nasty. **(GK)**

The Jupiter Menace (1981)

Thorn/EMI   80 minutes

SO BAD IT'S GOOD

DIRECTORS: Lee Auerbach, Peter Matulavich

WRITERS: Alan Henry Coats, Peter Matulavich

Although it claims to be a documentary, this howler is clearly a work of fiction, and it presents many dramatic reenactments that are so damn funny that I couldn't help but include the movie in this book. The film even confidently predicts the end of the world. Mark this date on your calendar, friends: May 5, 2000! Still here?

George Kennedy narrates most of the film, although there is an unnecessary second narrator who delivers more useless exposition. Why was he required? Maybe it's because even George Kennedy found some of the lines given to him too preposterous. Instead, he's photographed driving a large 4 x 4 through the desert to the ruins of ancient civilizations like he's in a Mazda commercial, at one point even driving on top of the San Andreas Fault.

After introductions that feature reenactments of Bible prophecies and depict ancient civilizations, Kennedy introduces dubious "scientists" and crackpot "experts" who explain their theories on how the world will come to an end. Personally, I'm convinced that many of these people must be actors. If they aren't, then I suppose it's the ultimate criticism that they can't even play themselves convincingly. It doesn't help when they try to describe the horror of what will come by telling us in earnestness "Dead and dying people are not that much fun to watch." Apparently, the end of the world has something to do with solar alignment. On Christmas Eve, 1982, they conclude, a grand alignment of the planets will (or, in our case, did) occur, triggering worldwide devastation. Kennedy tells us that these events will cause a 20-year cataclysm. Worldwide earthquakes will devastate the earth. Cue Kennedy to drive out to the San Andreas Fault. Now, if George Kennedy really were this concerned about earthquakes, why would he drive directly on top of the fault? After all, it could shift and open up at any moment, right? Anyway, the theory goes that all of these earthquakes have something to do with the gravitational pull of Jupiter, which, when in alignment with Earth, could cause our world's axis to shift.

Even worse, we are told, there will be a grand alignment of all of the planets on May 5, 2000. Kennedy informs us that during this axis shift the Antarctic ice caps may begin to melt and break up, the weight of which will throw the world off kilter. All of this will result in catastrophic earthquakes, tidal waves, and the end of the world when the Earth's axis actually flips over!

Are you still not a believer yet? Kennedy reappears in what is supposed to be some sort of busy scientific lab but what is in reality a television-studio control booth. Early computer digital effects model how all of the tectonic plates under the earth will shift. They even show, via "modern" computer technology, what a 10.0 earthquake will look like. To me, what it looked like was early test footage for that *Star Wars* arcade game where you fly into the trenches of the Death Star and try to blow it up. I was still unconvinced. The documentary shifts to testimonials from various survivalist camps in the United States. Frankly, this part is fascinating; it's like looking through a window into madness. After interviews with the survivalists and militia members, Kennedy admits that they may be extreme, then asks, "But can you blame them?"

As if this weren't convincing enough, more "experts" are interviewed, including a gigantically moustached, eyeliner-and-mascara-wearing male psychic who likes to wander around Central Park at all hours of the day while he explains his premonitions of the coming end of the world. Kennedy suddenly reappears, on a boat off of the coast of Florida, to show hieroglyphics from a pyramid that's supposedly sunk in the Atlantic Ocean. This is intended to prove the theory of catastrophic evolution, meaning that the earth's axis has flipped before, destroying entire races, and that it will again.

Kennedy concludes that if the prophecies of ancient civilizations came true in the past, then there's no reason to doubt them now. Especially when "psychic prediction, Bible prophecy, and Indian beliefs" correlate, Kennedy tells us. These filmmakers must have had some kind of balls to think someone might actually take this amazing crock seriously, especially when they had less than a year from the release of this film for the predictions to come true. As a result, this insane "documentary" is much more fun to watch and mock today than it probably ever was back in 1981.

Most Spectacular Moment of Carnage

May 5, 2000. A day that will live on in infamy—or would have, if anything had actually happened. I suppose the best carnage can be seen in the stock footage of disasters, unless you count the performances of some of the "experts" and interview subjects. (**GK**)

Kingdom of the Spiders (1977)

Dimension Pictures, Inc.   90 minutes

HIGHLY RECOMMENDED

⚠

DIRECTOR: John "Bud" Cardos

WRITER: Alan Caillou

CAST: William Shatner, Tiffany Bolling, Woody Strode, Altovise Davis

Starring the incomparable William Shatner, *Kingdom of the Spiders* has become a highly regarded cult classic in the years since its release. But it's more than that. With a total lack of irony, this feature-length non sequitur weaves a bizarre spell over the viewer as it shifts between B-movie schlock and art film pretension, with nary a moment to spare. Boasting an enormous body count and bleak, fatalistic overtones, this is easily one of the strangest movies you will ever see. And see it you must.

In the blazing summer of 1977, the small Arizona town of Verde Valley (I think that's what it's called; different characters can be heard calling it by different names as the film progresses) is the site of a strange tarantula invasion that begins innocuously enough, but soon explodes into a disaster of epic proportions. Cued to hilariously inappropriate music that's better suited to a '60s British sex romp, the town very slowly falls prey to the deadly spiders. No one is safe!

At first, only a small handful of spiders can be found crawling around in sheds, and no one pays this any mind, but soon, the unthinkable happens: they attack a cow! A rancher, played by Woody Strode, soon calls on the assistance of the local veterinarian, Dr. Robert "Rack" Hansen, aka Captain James T. Kirk, aka William Shatner, Canada's greatest contribution to the world of acting. Strutting around in a just-a-little-too-tight pair of jeans, and with a shit-eating smirk almost constantly pasted on his face, this vet doesn't seem to get much work done, what with all his beer guzzling and leering at women. Shatner looks to be in pretty good shape here, but you still get the feeling that he's working real hard to keep that gut sucked in. One thing's for sure: he doesn't bother trying to mask his character's obvious alcoholism. The way he fixates on beer is reminiscent of a certain Homer Simpson.

Shatner examines Strode's dead animal, but he is unable to identify the cause of death. The possibility of quarantine looms over the men, so he sends blood samples to a lab in Tempe. Soon entomologist Tiffany Bolling (who, according to the back of the video box, is "brilliant" in this movie) drives into town in her Mercedes in search of Shatner. Later she checks into a local motel, which is empty save for a couple in for the local county fair, though they're early by two weeks.

The next day Bolling goes out to meet Shatner and finds him swigging beer with the mayor. The mayor is there only to casually remind Shatner that he has to keep very quiet about the animal death so as not to cause a panic that might jeopardize the success of the fair. When Bolling informs Shatner that Strode's cow was killed by a heavy dose of spider venom, he reacts with disbelief, and then takes the opportunity to make a clumsy pass at her. She rebukes it, but it's obvious she won't be able to resist his pure animal magnetism for long.

The next day Bolling and Shatner take a trip out to Strode's homestead. Strode is looking for his lost dog, and the three men soon find the animal lying dead on the ground. Bolling does a blood test right there that proves that the dog was killed by spider venom. Shatner still doesn't believe her, but he's soon shut up by Strode's amazing revelation that, just a few steps away, there's a gigantic spider hill that has erupted from the ground. Not having considered the possibility of any connection between bizarre animal deaths and the sudden appearance of a swarm of tarantulas in his yard, Strode has left the spider hill untouched. Bolling starts snapping photos of it, contorting her body so as to capture the most dynamic shots possible, as if she was shooting for some spider fashion magazine. After noting that the spiders are 600 miles away from their natural habitat, and that this one hill might contain thousands of spiders, she decides to ask Strode not to destroy the spider hill just yet. He agrees, even though all of his prized livestock is at risk.

In the next thrilling sequence, Shatner goes to visit his dead brother's sister (played by Marcy Lafferty, Shatner's wife at the time) and his young niece. His ex-sister-in-law is very hot for him, and in the dialogue exchange that follows his arrival they liken the act of milking a cow to that of the two of them having sex. (In this particular scenario, she's the cow, by the way.) But he doesn't have time for any of that, because he's hungry! Soon he's speeding down the highway, off to get some chow. Bolling happens to drive past, and he chases her and nearly runs her off the road just so that he can kidnap her in her own car and take her to dinner, which they'll eat right after he enjoys a nice, cold beer. In the restaurant there's some first-rate expository dialogue, including an explanation of how Shatner came to be called by his odd nickname (which I won't bother to explain here other than to say it pretty much doesn't make any sense). Shatner also gets the opportunity to wistfully swallow beer, look out the window, and state that his brother was "killed in 'Nam"—on his second day there!

Later that night, Bolling and Shatner are back in her cabin at the hotel, and she's talking about stuff, but Shatner's not really listening because he just wants to get "busy." They decide, once he's stopped leering at her, that they should probably destroy the spider hill out at Strode's ranch at once. Hey, smart thinking! When they get out there, they see Strode and his wife about to do the same thing. After a brief interlude in which Strode's cherished bull is attacked by spiders and killed, they all go out to the hill, douse it with gasoline, and set it ablaze. What they don't see are all the spiders that have burrowed into the ground, or the others that are escaping out behind the flaming hill. But then, they're not really looking, either.

The next day, Shatner and Bolling take Shatner's niece out for a picnic in the scenic, unforgiving desert. They let her play unattended while they sit out in the sun, all their problems washed away like so much spider venom in the rain. Meanwhile, Strode, who's pissed off about something, decides to go for a drive. As he drives down the lane, listening to bad country music on the radio, a spider crawls up his back. Moments later a bunch of other spiders leap onto his face. He begins to shriek, and then he loses control of the vehicle and drives off the road and down an embankment.

As Shatner and Bolling drive back home, they come across the scene of Strode's accident, though no one has been able to get down to the car, as the wimpy sheriff has declared the trek "too dangerous." Shatner makes it down with ease, however, and he's shocked to discover that Strode's dead body has been cocooned (and, presumably, sucked dry). Back at the lab, Bolling makes the shocking announcement that the venom from these killer tarantulas is five times more toxic than that of a normal spider! But this bad news is topped when they subsequently discover 20 or 30 more spider hills out at Strode's ranch. Faced with this nightmare, the mayor decides the only course of action left is to spray the entire countryside with the deadliest pesticide that exists, in spite of Shatner's and Bolling's protestations. He chooses not to listen to Bolling, who is an actual entomologist, when she says that this will have no effect but to poison the land and the air. He doesn't care what she says. Nothing's gonna stand in the way of his county fair!

So the mayor sends the local crop duster up to spray everything that can be sprayed. Before he takes flight, the pilot grabs a magic marker and scrawls what's supposed to be a drawing of a spider on the side of his plane, but it actually resembles an amoeba, and it possesses far more than the standard eight legs. Unfortunately, just as he begins to spray, he comes to the horrible realization that the plane is full of spiders. He lets out a truly amazing shriek and loses control of the plane (there are some impressive aerobatics displayed here). Finally, he hits the throttle and slams into a gas station, exploding spectacularly (a legitimately good stunt). The spiders win again!

After this, everyone pretty much loses the will to go on. Bolling calls in an investigative team from Tempe, but they won't arrive for a couple of days. No one's been able to reach Strode's wife out at the ranch, so the sheriff decides to take a ride out there. The reason they can't get her on the phone is that she's being attacked by spiders in her bedroom. To fend them off she's using a pistol, blasting them one by one. In a moment I will never forget as long as I live, she sees with horror that a spider has jumped onto her hand. Instead of just shaking her hand and knocking the spider off, she blows her own hand off with the pistol! Now, kids, remember: that is never the right thing to do.

Soon, Shatner and Bolling arrive at Lafferty's house. The place has already been overrun with spiders, and Lafferty lies in the front yard, dead from spider bites. Shatner rescues his niece from inside the house and the three make for the main lodge of the hotel, where they join up with the kindly owner and the creepy couple. The phones, of course, aren't working, since this town still uses an operator to work the switchboard, and if she happens to be killed by tarantulas, then the entire system fails.

But if you think you've seen the best this movie has to offer, you're mistaken. What happens next is absolutely amazing. The sheriff goes downtown to see what's going on and finds out that all hell has broken loose. Screaming people mob the streets, all of them covered with spiders. Cocooned corpses litter the sidewalks. Cars slam violently into other cars and pedestrians, the bloody bodies of the passengers falling out as the doors swing open. Little children collapse to the pavement as spiders bite them to death. Then, in a spectacular conclusion to this orgy of terror, a car loses control and plows into the base of a water tower, which collapses and lands directly on the sheriff's squad car with him inside, crushing him to death! They even throw in a shot of his twisted, bloody body!! I love this movie!!!

Back at the lodge, the power goes off, plunging everyone into darkness, and Shatner volunteers to go down to the basement to check the fuse box. After screwing with it for a while, he finally manages to change the fuses. The lights come back on, but Shatner doesn't have much time to celebrate, as a pile of spiders falls on his head. This prompts him to hilariously contort his body into a dance of pain, which is accompanied by an unsettling moan, and all of this is made even more strange by his refusal to drop the flashlight he's holding, even when he falls to the floor, having been bitten on the face. But hey, he's Shatner, so he doesn't die, but instead manages to climb the stairs and burst into the kitchen, where he promptly falls unconscious.

The next morning when he awakes, still alive, everything is strangely quiet. Shatner peers out the window, and he's shocked at what he sees, as is everyone else. The filmmakers have decided to depict the town cocooned, using a crappy painting! There's no escape for anyone. And as the morbid excellence of this ending sinks in, you realize what an extremely bold choice this was, and that it proves to be the only fitting conclusion for this very unusual film—a film that commits itself so deeply to its own philosophy that, in spite of whatever faults it possesses, it is some kind of masterpiece.

Most Spectacular Moment of Carnage

The one image that stays with me is from the incredible "panic" sequence in the final act. A young boy, covered in spiders, crumples to his death on the pavement. It's just too good. **(MR)**

The Last Days of Planet Earth (1974)

Toho Studios/United Productions of America   88 minutes

SO BAD IT'S GOOD

DIRECTOR: Shiro Moritani

WRITER: Shinobu Hashimoto

CAST: Tetsuro Tamba, Toshio Kurasawa, Kaoro Yumi, Sô Yamamura

Basing a movie on the predictions of Nostradamus is a bad idea. Adapting his theories into a narrative (or an antinarrative, in this case) only makes both him and the filmmakers look all the more ridiculous. Even the predictions of Criswell, the notorious friend of Ed Wood, begin to sound more believable after watching this. While it was released theatrically in some countries in its full length and under its original Japanese title, *The Last Days of Planet Earth* (also known as *Catastrophe 1999: The Prophecies of Nostradamus*) aired only on television in North America, to what must have been stunned audiences. Why were they stunned? Because the film is completely incomprehensible!

The film opens with stock footage and some narration about Nostradamus and his predictions for the end of the world. This narration comes and goes throughout the film, usually popping up whenever things get so confusing that no one could possibly have understood what they were watching anymore. First, giant slugs begin appearing in the Japanese countryside. Soon, food runs short. Nuclear radiation begins causing other problems, like superintelligent children, mutated bats, killer slugs, random explosions, and storm clouds.

Meanwhile, a scientist, his daughter, and her photographer boyfriend (who jumps around the country snapping shots as panicked crowds run by and people are maimed in the chaos) are introduced. The scientist tries in vain to convince world leaders that they're causing the demise of the planet. The world leaders don't go for it. And that's a good thing, because it results in many more disasters, including an amusing flood sequence and a traffic jam that culminates in massive deaths. These events are depicted using miniature models, stock footage, and even still photographs. Of course, I'm talking about Toho Studios, the people who brought you the early Godzilla films. (Some of the footage in this film has *got* to be from the Godzilla films!)

Watch for a nonsensical side trip to New Guinea. A scientific team searches for a lost UN party and ends up fighting off vicious mutated bats. Killer slugs fall from the sky, and one attaches itself to a poor guy's neck. He wails in pain, and his scientist buddies just stand and watch for a moment before removing the slug. Then they give the guy a blood transfusion. I don't know why. Meanwhile, riots ensue as food runs out, leaving world leaders pondering what to do (why don't they just ask the super-intelligent children?).

In the movie's funniest moments, youths form cult groups and decide to commit mass suicide. Out of nowhere, Japanese hippies are introduced, and they're shown dancing around some trees. Then, without explanation, the film returns to typical drawing-room scenes. At that point, I had to scratch my head. Did I just see Japanese hippies dancing through a park? Finally the film returns to the cult groups. The now-cloaked youths sail out into the Pacific Ocean to drown at sea in a Regatta of Death. Better yet, a group of disinterested kids drive their motorcycles off a cliff—in slow motion—and dive (presumably to their deaths) into the water below. Before you have time to register what you just saw and why you saw it, the film moves on to another unconnected event.

Things get really bad for Tokyo when the sky starts reflecting the city below. The heroic scientist makes an impassioned (preachy) plea, even pointing at the camera while begging world leaders to stop nuclear testing or face the consequences. This is where the narration ends. Knowing that audiences might want an ending with their film, the filmmakers present the possibilities of what "might" happen. The movie assaults us with more stock footage of disasters they've already shown, and of the world after this destruction. Mutants roll around the barren earth and fight. The movie ends. As for what happens to the scientist, his daughter, her boyfriend, or the world, your guess is as good as mine. The movie just ends.

It also goes without saying that the film is ineptly dubbed. The characters can barely say a word without sounding ludicrous, and the translated dialogue is also preposterous (it probably was in its original Japanese, too). Scenes are thrown together randomly and the whole thing looks like it was cobbled together out of a bunch of different films. This feature is best viewed with friends while extremely drunk or on narcotics. *The Last Days of Planet Earth* has no redeeming qualities other than the fact that it is staggeringly awful. Without a doubt, it's one of the worst films of the genre.

Most Spectacular Moment of Carnage

All of the frequently shown disasters are, unfortunately, presented in a PG manner. But watch for those punks riding off the cliff. You won't know why it's happening, but you won't be able to look away. (**GK**)

Locusts (2005)

CBS-TV   95 minutes

AT YOUR OWN RISK

DIRECTOR: David Jackson

WRITER: Doug Prochilo

CAST: Lucy Lawless, John Heard, Dylan Neal, Greg Alan Williams, Mike Farrell

"You screw with nature and nature will screw with you."

So says United States Undersecretary of Agriculture Lucy Lawless when she finds out that Virginia-based USDA scientist John Heard has illegally bred a large number of indestructible hybrid locusts in his spare time. These locusts are resistant to all pesticides, and they gestate 10 times faster and have a longer life span than regular locusts. Hey, what a great idea! Heard thinks that this kind of research could prove to be helpful to humans somehow, and that's very nice, but did he have to breed so many of these things? No matter; Lawless has the locusts destroyed. Unfortunately, some shady (and clumsy) military personnel steal several of them before they're killed. The first guy takes a bunch of them from the lab, but in the process he accidentally knocks his locust-containing container into the sink, dropping a few of the bugs down the drain. The rest of of the bugs end up on a Jeep on a military base in California, but a bee smacks into the face of the guy carrying the locusts, causing him to drop the package on the tarmac. It gets run over by another vehicle, and the locusts break free and escape. What will become of Virginia and California? How will this affect the upcoming Visalia Citrus Festival? Who knows?

Fast-forward one month. A California campground is overrun with locusts, which forces any impending sexual activity among the campers to cease and desist immediately. Then a Napa Valley winery is swarmed, causing the migrant Mexican workers to run for the hills. Fortunately, Lawless and her USDA Voracious Insect Mobile Research Lab crew (no shit!) are on the move in California (she's studying mosquitoes, for some reason). Meanwhile, in Virginia, the locusts set their sights on a school bus full of children. During the terrifying ordeal in which the bugs manage to get inside the bus and attack the kids, Heard's daughter is knocked to the floor and ends up in a coma.

Heard witnesses the attack, and he discovers that the bugs are his handiwork. It soon becomes clear that these locusts are traveling in giant, ever-expanding swarms and that their next targets are Pittsburgh and Cleveland, two of America's finest cities.

There's also a huge swarm that continues to move throughout California. Lawless decides to evacuate the aforementioned citrus festival, but she's too late. Men, women, and children alike are overcome with locusts. So are the citizens of downtown Pittsburgh, when a huge locust swarm slams into their city. High-rise windows are smashed, hot dog vendors are sent flying, office birthday parties are ruined. By this time, Heard has driven all the way to the Pittsburgh airport, where he attempts to warn the control tower of the impending disaster. They won't listen to him, and they allow a plane to take off directly into the swarm. In an impressively violent sequence, the engines explode, sending the plane hurtling toward the ground, where it slams into a runway and ignites into a gigantic fireball. Strangely, although a news report (shown later in the movie) informs us that the pilot and copilot were killed instantly, it sheds no light on the fate of the passengers. I think the movie cops out in this regard; there are some extremely vague indications that this was a cargo plane with no passengers, but I prefer to believe that the passengers were, in fact, "raptured" just prior to the crash.

Following this disaster, all branches (or at least some branches) of the U.S. government convene to discuss their options. The locusts are now hundreds of millions strong, and they're converging on the country's heartland where, it is feared, they will consume all available crops. The real fear, you see, is that the locusts will destroy so much of the country's food supply that a worldwide famine could result. If you think that sucks, get this: the locusts have also become carnivorous! Now, neither livestock nor human beings are safe from the bugs' ever-munching little jaws. Faced with this scenario, the government decides it is necessary to take military action. But which weapon of mass destruction to use? Hmm. How about VX gas? It's really deadly, and if they're careful, maybe they won't kill too many people. The officials even go so far as to load up a chopper with the stuff to spray over parts of Ohio. (Hey, aim for Cleveland while you're at it.) But a furious Lawless has already made a call to GNN (you know, that cable news channel that isn't CNN because they can't say CNN and they weren't able to come up with any name better than GNN), and the ensuing bad publicity forces them to call the plan off.

Anyway, in circumstances far too silly to describe, it is discovered that the locusts can be killed by high-voltage electricity. This causes the enactment of a far-fetched plan, in which the country-spanning Continental Power Grid is powered up to full intensity by using *all of the electricity in America at once.* As such, every American is called upon to stop using electricity! As a result of this unlikely scenario, the locust swarm is fried to a golden brown hue as it passes through the intense electrical field, leaving the few surviving locusts sterile and lonely. As far as I know, actual science does not support these events, but the movie had to end sometime. I suppose I can't expect more from a movie directed by the guy who made *Atomic Train.*

Most Spectacular Moment of Carnage

There were not as many deaths as I would have liked. I did enjoy John Heard's death-by-severe-locust-attack, which occurs while he attempts to commit a heroic act (corroborating my first rule of disaster movies: don't be a hero). When they finish with him, he looks like he's just been hit by a car. **(MR)**

Rollercoaster (1977)
Universal   119 minutes

AT YOUR OWN RISK

© Universal Pictures

DIRECTOR: James Goldstone

WRITERS: Sanford Sheldon, Richard Levinson, William Link (based on the film story by Tommy Cook)

CAST: George Segal, Richard Widmark, Timothy Bottoms, Henry Fonda, Harry Guardino, Susan Strasberg, Helen Hunt

I suppose I can understand why a mad bomber might want to focus his attention on destroying roller coasters. In most mad bomber films, the bad guy works underground, planting his device in a garage, an engine room—basically, in some dark, dank, depressing place. The whole amusement park thing would be a refreshing change. You could walk around the park, get some air, enjoy the attractions, buy some cotton candy, win a stuffed monkey (like the villain in this film does), and really have a day of it before sending a roller coaster careening off of the track and dozens of riders to their deaths. Or maybe the mad bomber had, as a child, experienced a bad tummyache on one of the rides or had eaten a stale amusement-park pretzel and is now looking for revenge.

The film gets off to an entertaining start when the bomber, Timothy Bottoms, is shown staking out an amusement park, planting a detonation device, and then casually strolling around. This park even has a live belly dancing exhibit, something that I don't remember ever existing at any park I went to as a kid (and I think that's something I *would* remember). As the coaster rises and dives, the filmmakers do a good job of both manipulating the sound so that every creak is amplified and manipulating the audience into thinking the bomb is about to go off at every single twist and turn. The terrorist sets off the charge, destroying a small piece of the track. The coaster is sent flying off of the rails, and its cars crashing into the midway. It's the best scene in the film, and unfortunately, the rest of the movie never quite lives up to the potential of these first 10 minutes.

Rollercoaster's hero is not a cop or an FBI agent assigned to the case. Instead, we get George Segal as Harry Calder, a Department of Standards and Safety inspector. He's an odd, irritable man whose job is to check amusement park rides to make sure they're safe for use. The first time he's seen, he's in the most bizarre clinic ever filmed, receiving electric shocks to stop smoking (for a while there, I thought I was watching the "Quitters Inc." segment of *Cat's Eye*). This jaw-droppingly strange incident is never even referred to again. As for the bombing, Segal suspects foul play but is told by his boss, Henry Fonda (who makes little more than a cameo in this flick), that he's being paranoid. But after a fire breaks out (offscreen) at another park in Pittsburgh, the major amusement park owners get together for a "secret meeting" in Chicago. I wonder if amusement park owners really do get together for periodic secret meetings to discuss candy formulas and so on. Anyway, it's here that our bomber, Bottoms, makes his motives clear. He wants one million dollars, to be dropped off at a particular amusement park by Segal himself.

What results is a long sequence of Segal being led around the park, briefcase full of money in hand, through ride after ride and attraction after attraction. Whatever park this may be, I feel I have no need to visit it after this sequence, which might have been tense were it not for the fact that it goes on forever. The 20-plus-minute sequence should have been half as long, and the fact that it ends so uneventfully—the money is finally exchanged—makes it all the more frustrating.

Of course, the money is marked. This infuriates Bottoms, who announces that he will blow up another coaster (it's about time!). Segal figures out that the target must be the Revolution, a coaster that is opening, to much media fanfare, at Magic Mountain. Agents race to the event, choosing not to shut down the coaster but instead to search for the bomb and, hopefully, find it before the ride begins. Here's another sequence that is far too long. The agents slowly search the ride, and Bottoms wanders around the park. Nothing happens. But there's enough time for a bad '70s metal band to play two songs for the audience.

Finally, the bomb is located and disarmed. This forces Bottoms to board the coaster for its first ride and plant another one. He then gets off the coaster and faces Segal, who shoots him. Bottoms stumbles onto the tracks and stares blankly at Segal for what must be an eternity before the coaster hits him. Again, you might expect something like this to cause major problems for the ride, not to mention numerous injuries to its passengers, but this does not seem to be the case. In fact, no one in the park seems to mind the fact that a terrorist has just tried to blow up one of the rides and is now a pulpy mess underneath the tracks. Instead, they continue wandering around the amusement park as if nothing has happened. By the way, a young Helen Hunt plays Segal's daughter. There's a subplot that develops their relationship and then places her in the park with Bottoms toward the end of the movie. This subplot seems meticulously set up, but it never pays off. Instead, Segal tells her to go back home, so she does. End of subplot.

The concept of this film is unusual enough to be interesting for a while, the acting is fine (Segal is actually quite likable), and the first explosion is effective, but the movie never really satisfies. For all you techno-buffs out there, one of the big selling features of this film when it was released in theaters was that it was shown in Sensurround.

Most Spectacular Moment of Carnage
The first explosion sends some of the roller coaster's cars flying into other attractions in the park. One car crashes through a neon sign; another simply flips upside down and falls onto the midway, crushing its passengers. **(GK)**

Speed (1994)

Twentieth Century Fox   116 minutes

HIGHLY RECOMMENDED

⚠

DIRECTOR: Jan de Bont

WRITER: Graham Yost

CAST: Keanu Reeves, Dennis Hopper, Sandra Bullock, Joe Morton, Jeff Daniels, Alan Ruck, Glenn Plummer, Richard Lineback, Beth Grant, Hawthorne James, Carlos Carrasco, David Kriegal, Natsuko Ohama, Daniel Villarreal

How does a film that strains your suspension of disbelief beyond its absolute limit manage to be so entertaining? *Speed*, one of the highest-grossing films of 1994, is a nonstop action spectacle that seamlessly incorporates so many disaster film elements that it's really quite remarkable.

The film's first act both introduces us to the leads and places several executives in an elevator. The movie features a full-tilt performance by Dennis Hopper, who is completely gonzo in this movie. His character, Payne, is a mad ex-LAPD Bomb Squad officer. The very first time he's shown onscreen, he manages to drive what is either a screwdriver or a knife into the ear of a security guard. Hopper then jumps into a freight elevator and spends much of the first 25 minutes of the movie staring up at the ceiling toward the camera, with a range of entertaining expressions. He rigs the elevator above his (which happens to be the one carrying the executives) to explode and sets off the first charge, leaving the elevator dangling 30 stories up with only its emergency brakes preventing a free fall. Most of us probably wouldn't have a problem with an elevator full of business executives getting splattered, but the film doesn't allow any time for us to ponder this. And that is the movie's best quality: it moves at such a breakneck speed that there is no time to really think about just how preposterous what's going on really is.

Enter Keanu Reeves as Jack, a gung-ho bomb squad expert, and his obviously doomed partner Harry, played by Jeff Daniels. Reeves makes a much better action star than one would expect; he may have finally been able to shed that whole "Bill and Ted" thing in this film. He's given some good one-liners but otherwise he doesn't actually say a whole lot in this movie; instead, he plays the "man of action." Daniels (who will surely die later in the movie, because hey, this is a disaster film and he's the buddy) is a good foil for Reeves, and the two spend much of the movie bickering at each other about how to handle hostage situations (standard Reeves response: "Shoot the hostage."). You'd think that these scenes would seem a little too light-hearted, considering that director Jan de Bont continually cuts back to the panicking executives who are about to die, but it works.

In the next sequence, Reeves buys a coffee and talks to a large bus driver whom he's friendly with. Next thing you know, the driver and his bus are blown to smithereens by madman Hopper, who informs Reeves that another bus is also armed with a bomb, and that, unless a ransom is paid, the bomb will go off if the bus's speed drops below 50 miles per hour. Reeves quickly follows the endangered bus, no doubt to attempt to save the passengers and avenge the death of his coffee buddy, the bus driver.

In the meantime, passengers on the imperiled bus are introduced, including girl-next-door-type Annie, a star-making role for Sandra Bullock. There's also a sleazy passenger, who's always ready to deliver bad jokes at inappropriate moments, and a petty criminal. Everyone onboard seems to know each other well. Are people in Los Angeles really this friendly? It doesn't really matter, because the chase has already begun. Reeves manages to jump from a car and board the moving bus, where he is forced to contend with an armed passenger who believes he's being arrested for another crime. Jack tries to calm him by telling him (in a most uncool manner) "We're just two cool guys." A hard-hat-wearing construction worker jumps the kid, who, in the struggle, shoots the driver. Of course, the plucky Bullock takes over the driving. A series of near misses follows when the bus runs into traffic as it maneuvers its way through the city. Somehow, despite managing to partially hit almost every vehicle it comes across, its speed remains above 50.

All the while, Dennis Hopper follows the proceedings on several TV screens while eating sandwiches in a loud, exaggerated manner, yelling at the screens, and watching college football at the same time (this is actually a plot point that's developed later). The passengers discover that the highway they are now on isn't finished. What is Reeves's solution? He tells Bullock to floor it and attempt to make the jump across an unfinished highway overpass. This reckless act results in the film's most credibility-straining moment, as the bus takes a *Blues Brothers*–esque jump off of the end of the highway and lands intact on the other side, still running above 50 miles per hour.

Now at LAX, with the bus's gas running low, Reeves comes up with an idea (despite Hopper's continual warning to him: "Do not attempt to grow a brain!") After

Reeves discovers the camera that Hopper has hidden in the bus, Reeves's coworkers take a feed of the inside of the bus, videotape a loop of the passengers, and trick Hopper into thinking he's watching the passengers on the bus in real time, when they are actually being evacuated. Everybody gets out safely, and the bus drives itself into a large plane, causing a spectacular explosion on the runway.

Did I mention that there are some credibility-straining moments in the film? Yet another occurs when Reeves decides to go with the LAPD to the money-drop spot and catch Hopper in person. Against all logic, Reeves decides to take Bullock with him, and she waits in a nearby ambulance. This leads to a rousing, crowd-pleasing finale. Before the close, an out-of-control subway car (with Hopper onboard) crashes through the unfinished subway line and out onto the streets of L.A. But all is well, and the hard-rocking music of Billy Idol leads us out from our seats.

But, you ask, what about Jeff Daniels? How and when did he die? You'll have to see the movie and find out.

Most Spectacular Moment of Carnage

Multitudes of cars are destroyed spectacularly, but our villain's death takes the cake. Decapitated onscreen, Hopper's head flies off. It (presumably) lands behind the subway train, while his limp body remains on top of the train. **(GK)**

The Swarm (1978)

Warner Bros.   156 minutes

SO BAD IT'S GOOD

DIRECTOR: Irwin Allen

WRITER: Stirling Silliphant (based on the novel by Arthur Herzog)

CAST: Michael Caine, Katharine Ross, Richard Widmark, Richard Chamberlain, Olivia de Havilland, Ben Johnson, Lee Grant, José Ferrer, Patty Duke Astin, Slim Pickens, Bradford Dillman, Fred MacMurray, Henry Fonda

Irwin Allen teams with Michael Caine (whom he would work with again the following year in *Beyond the Poseidon Adventure*) in perhaps in their most over-the-top disaster movie yet—this one featuring killer bees! Now bees have never struck me as particularly terrifying cinematic villains. Especially when they can be slapped, squashed, or stomped on so easily. Apparently, Irwin Allen doesn't agree. He should have. Despite being based on a popular and well-received novel by Arthur Herzog, *The Swarm* is nonetheless one of the most hilarious, unbelievable, and ridiculous disaster films ever made. This is great viewing for anyone who is looking for a really bad movie.

The film opens with a government military team (dressed in orange and white space suits that look like they were borrowed from the costuming department of *2001: A Space Odyssey*) that's investigating a seemingly deserted ICBM site. This is one of those great, high-tech '70s sets right out of *Star Trek*, painted bright orange and complete with randomly flashing lights and knobs and buttons that seem to serve no real purpose. It even has a giant screen that lowers for important messages from Washington (who needs that meddlesome phone?).

The heavily armed military team soon discovers that all of the officers at the site are dead. Out of nowhere, Michael Caine waltzes in as the sunflower-eating ("High in potassium, low in sodium!") entomologist Bradford Crane, telling everybody that a moving swarm of killer bees with lethal stinging capabilities are the responsible party. Despite the facts that all of the dead officers must be covered from head to toe with bee stings and that radar shows a large mass moving at 7 miles per hour, the commanding general Slater (played by Richard Widmark) is skeptical.

Widmark sends (model) choppers out to assess the situation. Here is where we finally get our first glimpse of the swarm, and it's a rather poor effect to boot. In fact, it looks like someone smeared coffee grounds over the top half of the frame. At least Irwin chose to use real bees for the close-ups. In fact, the best shots in the movie are of the actors (or more likely, beekeepers standing in for the actors) having bees blown on them via offscreen fans. After the choppers crash, Katharine Ross emerges as a local doctor who has been successfully hiding at the site along with some other survivors, completely unnoticed by the military. She gets to deliver wonderful lines like "I need antitoxins!" while Caine and Widmark bicker over who's in charge. On the order of the president, entomologist Caine is given complete command of the situation, much to the Widmark's dismay.

Meanwhile, in what seems like a completely different film, a family is out picnicking in a park. Irwin employs a hilarious shot from the point of view of a stalking bee. When the mother finally attempts to use bug spray, it's all over for the family. With the exception of the panicked young son, they are stung to death despite their spastic gyrations of defense. The boy manages to escape, and he drives a vehicle to nearby Marysville, which is actually holding a flower festival. Many more annoying subplots are then introduced, most notable of which is a sickly sweet, geriatric love triangle between school superintendent Olivia de Havilland, town mayor Fred MacMurray, and retired good ol' boy Ben Johnson. At least this subplot comes to a gleefully tragic end later.

Having been stung, the boy is hospitalized. He's suffering from hallucinations—and what hallucinations they are! In fact, everyone in the movie who is stung experiences the same visions of a superimposed giant bee looming above them. Despite the fact that a team of doctors are working to cure the boy, entomologist/military strategist/pseudo-psychiatrist Caine walks in, stands next to the superimposed stinger, and quickly convinces the young boy that the image is, indeed, only a hallucination. He also manages to engage the fetching Ross in a budding romantic relationship. But how is Caine dealing with the major problem at hand? You know, the millions of killer bees that are poised to attack? Very poorly, it seems, as an entertaining attack sequence follows in which the swarm bears down on the town. How does our leader Caine handle the situation? By driving into town minutes before the strike and screaming in a panicked tone, "Get inside! The killer bees are coming!" This is all right, though, because it does lead to numerous shots of townspeople being swarmed and stung to death. Particularly nasty are the deaths of many schoolchildren playing outside. In fact, *The Swarm* holds the record for having the greatest number of dead children in a disaster film.

Despite all the bee carnage, Caine does his best to chew all scenery in some memorable exchanges with Widmark. There's nothing funnier than seeing two actors furiously debate killer-bee tactics, all the while dropping information for those dumb viewers who might not know anything about the subject. In fact, Caine's and Widmark's arguments take up much of this film's screen time. After scientists locate and capture a few stray bees, Widmark warns, "When that swarm finds out that some of their friends have been taken captive, they might come back to Marysville!" Yikes! Guess you don't need to take an IQ test to be a general. Not in an Irwin Allen movie, anyway.

The movie's poster advertises such celebrities as Slim Pickens, Patty Duke Astin, Lee Grant, and José Ferrer. Where are they, you might be wondering? Well, in one scene Pickens appears at the ICBM site and insists on knowing what has happened to his son. He is led to his son's carcass, where he emotes while hugging the body bag. He then lifts the body bag, carries it out of the morgue as Caine and the other scientists watch, baffled, and is never to be seen again. Patty Duke Astin has a heavily cut (one can only assume, despite the film's 156-minute running time) role as a grief-stricken, pregnant café owner who later disappears. Lee Grant plays a news reporter who appears in a couple of scenes and then vanishes without a trace. And José Ferrer, who gets perhaps the funniest bit in this movie, has a scene as a nuclear plant manager. In less than two minutes of screen time, he is both introduced and swarmed, just as the plant explodes and an entire town of over 36,000 people is wiped out.

After Marysville is attacked and hundreds die, a train carrying survivors and evacuees is swarmed and crashes spectacularly. I don't know about you, but I'm beginning to have some doubts about our so-called hero, Caine. By now, he is responsible for the unnecessary deaths of over 37,000 people, and the swarm is closing in on an evacuated Houston! Finally, Caine is demoted and Widmark takes over. Unfortunately, his equally inept plan fails; trapping all the remaining characters in a skyscraper as the city is attacked. Oops! What to do now? Widmark orders Houston burned to the ground, and the bees with it. Naturally, the swarm gets into the skyscraper and kills numerous stuntmen, one of whom falls roughly 40 stories to his "death" below in the fiery climax.

The film takes an oddly religious turn at this point. Characters converse philosophically about what is happening, spouting lines that explain the swarm as "part of the Creator's plan." Caine saves the audience from further torture and gets an idea. It's an obvious idea that anyone would have thought of in the first 30 minutes of the film, but by this point I was relieved it had finally dawned on him. The killer bees are attracted to the sound of sonic alarms, which they mistake for a mating call (so all these bees really wanted to do was mate?). Before you can say "How the hell did they get out of that skyscraper alive?" (or the flaming city of Houston, for that matter), Caine and Ross are somehow beamed to an airfield.

This leads to the loopy wrap-up, which involves an oil slick, missiles, and a giant explosion (but not the ensuing environmental disaster that would have occurred in the process). The survivors even manage to stand (in a studio, in front of superimposed flames hundreds of feet high) and converse, no doubt just so they have a reason to watch the toxic cloud they've created grow larger and larger over them. *The Swarm* is recommended, but for all the wrong reasons.

Most Spectacular Moment of Carnage

In a worthy segment of nastiness, our geriatric love triangle (which has been so monotonously set up) ends in tragedy when the train they're traveling on is swarmed, flips, rolls down a mountain, and explodes. What a horrible end! Don't worry about MacMurray and Johnson, though; their bodies are thrown out the train window as it rolls down the mountain, so we can safely assume that they were crushed beyond recognition well before the train exploded. (*GK*)

The Trigger Effect (1996)

Gramercy/Universal   95 minutes

AT YOUR OWN RISK

DIRECTOR: David Koepp

WRITER: David Koepp

CAST: Kyle MacLachlan, Elisabeth Shue, Dermot Mulroney, Richard T. Jones, Bill Smitrovich, Michael Rooker, Philip Bruns

The Trigger Effect certainly begins with the promise of a real disaster, but along the way it gets sidetracked by its lofty (and extremely obvious) aspirations. In this film, social purpose and meaning take center stage, overshadowing its disaster elements. The concept, an original one at the time, concerns the effects of an unexplained power outage in the city of L.A. (and, it is implied, the surrounding area as well) and one couple's growing panic and unfounded suspicion. With no electricity, phone lines, bank machines, or computers running, it's almost like the Great 2003 Northeast Blackout, except with fewer barbecues, beer drinking, and people having a good time. Regardless, it still sounds interesting, doesn't it? Well, it isn't. You're expecting mad crowds looting and panic in the streets, right? You won't find any of that in this movie.

Our leads, played by Elisabeth Shue and Kyle MacLachlan, are a couple in need of medication for their sick newborn. MacLachlan avoids confrontation at all cost. Shue is from the wrong side of the tracks, and she seems to be bored with the marriage (or maybe the role) and missing the excitement of her previous life. The couple finds they have little cash on hand, and of course they won't be able to access a bank machine. (It is strange, though, that they would actually go to a bank, present their bank books and financial records, and not be able to get at least *some* money.)

Then Dermot Mulroney arrives, playing a "friend" of the couple. He spends much of the movie flirting with Shue, irking MacLachlan, and making ridiculous suggestions like going downtown to see the riots and driving into the desert and heading for a remote cabin, even though they don't have enough gas to get there (thereby implying that they'll have to steal some from either an unoccupied car or another traveler). The couple seems to think that these are great ideas. Even this might be interesting for the viewer if any of these central characters had any qualities that were remotely likable. However, from the moment they were introduced, I hated them. Actually, all of the characters seem angry and irritated. The film opens with a tense argument involving MacLachlan and noisy theatergoer Richard T. Jones. From this point on, he continually runs into this guy, to the point of parody—at a gun shop, on a street corner, in a restaurant, and even while attempting to find help. Los Angeles is a city of over 20 million, and the suggestion that every single time he leaves his house MacLachlan runs into the same guy quickly becomes preposterous. And each time he sees him, MacLachlan reacts by cowering and trying to hide from the guy. I mean, come on, their argument may have been heated, but that's all it was. Of course, it's MacLachlan's racial prejudices that actually cause him to fear the man, who is black. They also cause the viewer to despise MacLachlan, who eventually points a gun at the guy.

The couple's neighbors are no less unstable. Everyone's behavior becomes increasingly paranoid. After the leads head out to a cabin and fire a gun at an odd but harmless driver (Michael Rooker) during their trip, there is no longer a reason to care about them or their predicament. MacLachlan does eventually come to question his own behavior, but that just isn't enough to make us empathize with him. I suppose the director was attempting to show, via all these angry, devious characters, just how horrible things have become within the modern city—that society can break down almost instantly. It's as though L.A. is a volcano of tension and violence that is ready to erupt. All of the characters bicker and argue to the end, at which point MacLachlan and the black man meet again, finally learn to trust one another, and work together to help save the life of a wounded Mulroney. Then the power returns, and everything is hunky-dory again. Some filmmakers have a talent for keeping their audiences entertained with insignificant and sometimes horrible characters. David Koepp, who is a talented writer/director, doesn't succeed on this occasion. As well meaning as it might be, the message is so heavy-handed and obvious that it becomes tedious.

There are some effective and tense scenes. MacLachlan attempts to steal medication for his child from his rude and intimidating pharmacist by sneaking behind the counter and searching the goods while the pharmacist stands only feet away. The opening shot involves a well-orchestrated steadi-cam that introduces and follows many of the main characters, who are in a movie-theater setting. However, the good scenes are few and far between, and the film ends up being rather dull. In addition, because its leads are so dislikable to begin with, one wishes that they had been killed very early in the film. In light of the events that occurred during an actual blackout in 2003 (or nonevents, to be more accurate; nothing particularly bad happened), this flick looks all the more overbaked.

Most Spectacular Moment of Carnage

Because its characters are cut off from any means of mechanized communication with others, the film never depicts what is going on within the city. There's only a hint of a panicked crowd in a few scenes, and there's only one on-screen death—that of a burglar, who is shot unnecessarily. **(GK)**

BRIEF REVIEWS

Dead Ahead: The Exxon Valdez Disaster (1992)
Best Film and Video   90 minutes

AT YOUR OWN RISK

This unusual, low-budget (but effective) made-for-TV movie depicts the complicated politics surrounding the famous Alaskan oil spill. Why did it take so long for the spill to be contained (actually, it never was) and clean-up to begin? Who's to blame? The answer is complicated, and it gives rise to many new questions. The information is interesting and well relayed, and the cast is great (except for some of the boat crew, who must have been local players who had never acted before). Unfortunately, those wanting sadistic thrills had best avoid this movie, because all you'll see are disturbing stock-footage shots of various animals struggling or lying dead in the sludgy oil that's washing upon the shores. Directed by Paul Seed, the film stars Christopher Lloyd, John Heard, Rip Torn, Michael Murphy, Bob Gunton, David Morse, and Mark Metcalf. **(GK)**

RARE, OBSCURE, AND LESS IMPORTANT TITLES

...And Millions Die! (1973)

The Deadly Bees (1966)

The Death of Ocean View Park (1979) Made-for-TV

Disaster on the Coastliner (1979)

Flying Virus (2001) Straight-to-video

Killer Bees (1974) Made-for-TV

The Night the Bridge Fell Down (1983) Made-for-TV

Path to Paradise: The Untold Story of the World Trade Center Bombing (1997) Made-for-TV

The Savage Bees (1976) Made-for-TV

Terror out of the Sky (1978)

Tokyo Blackout (1987)

Train of Events (1949)

THE HIGHEST-GROSSING DISASTER MOVIES OF ALL TIME
(or at least as of 2005, as I write this)

Domestic

1	*Titanic* (1997)	$601 million
2	*Independence Day*	$306 million
3	*Twister*	$242 million
4	*War of the Worlds* (2005)	$232 million
5	*Armageddon*	$202 million
6	*The Day After Tomorrow*	$186 million
7	*The Perfect Storm*	$183 million
8	*Deep Impact*	$140 million
9	*Speed*	$121 million
10	*Die Hard 2*	$117 million

International

1	*Titanic* (1997)	$1.2 billion
2	*Independence Day*	$505 million
3	*Armageddon*	$353 million
4	*War of the Worlds* (2005)	$349 million
5	*The Day After Tomorrow*	$341 million
6	*Twister*	$253 million

7	Deep Impact	$208 million
8	Speed	$162 million
9	The Perfect Storm	$141 million
10	Die Hard 2	$120 million

Worldwide

1	Titanic (1997)	$1.8 billion
2	Independence Day	$811 million
3	War of the Worlds (2005)	$581 million
4	Armageddon	$554 million
5	The Day After Tomorrow	$527 million
6	Twister	$495 million
7	Deep Impact	$348 million
8	The Perfect Storm	$324 million
9	Speed	$283 million
10	Die Hard 2	$237 million

Those Darn Aliens!

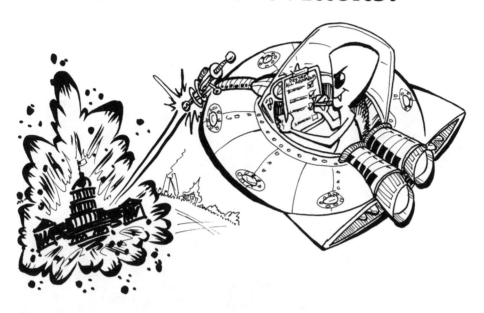

So many alien invasion movies were made in the late '50s and early '60s, and so many movies in this subgenre straddle the line between monster movie and disaster movie, that it was tough to decide which films to include here. We determined that a film like *The War of the Worlds* (as well as its remake), for example, should be included because, among other signifiers, there is so much emphasis on the destruction of the world, and this destruction is depicted with elaborate and groundbreaking special effects. Buildings collapse, things catch fire, and of course, people run through the streets in terror, being vaporized. In addition, consider the films that *The War of the Worlds* inspired years later—films like *Independence Day*, which follows the disaster formula to a T and is unquestionably a disaster film.

Of course, I can't share any personal stories of being abducted by aliens or experiencing an alien attack. These films are pure demented fantasy. **(GK)**

Independence Day (1996)

Twentieth Century Fox   145 minutes

AT YOUR OWN RISK

© Twentieth Century Fox

DIRECTOR: Roland Emmerich

WRITERS: Dean Devlin, Roland Emmerich

CAST: Bill Pullman, Mary McDonnell, Jeff Goldblum, Judd Hirsch, Margaret Colin, Will Smith, Vivica A. Fox, Randy Quaid, Robert Loggia, James Rebhorn, Harvey Fierstein, Adam Baldwin, Brent Spiner, James Duval, Harry Connick, Jr.

If ever there was the cinematic equivalent of eating a big bag of potato chips, *Independence Day* is that movie. You certainly enjoy it while you're eating it, but afterward you feel bloated and greasy. It's a ruthlessly engineered piece of pure entertainment, and judged on that basis, it succeeds spectacularly. But try to look for something deeper and you'll discover instead the film's entirely hollow core: there is not one moment of genuine emotion; not one bit of suspense that isn't painfully contrived; not one bit of narrative logic that holds together. In spite of this, the film moves forward with great momentum, and it is to the filmmaker's credit that you don't even realize how empty and meaningless the experience is until it's all over.

A gigantic alien mothership parks itself just outside Earth's orbit and sends a fleet of warships into our atmosphere. The ships take up strategic positions in cities all over the world, including Washington, D.C., New York City, Houston, and Los Angeles. Eventually they also put one in Nevada (but not in Las Vegas! Maybe the aliens are big Wayne Newton fans). Proving that these creatures have a sense of humor, their ships are first seen hovering over the cities on July 2. Within the context of the events that unfold, this is nearly a dare on their part to force all humankind to fight for its life on the 4th of July.

The ships take their positions, poising themselves (for the most part) over significant landmarks like the Empire State Building and the Statue of Liberty. And then, nothing happens. This allows time to introduce the cast of characters, which includes President Bill Pullman. The country's leader is beleaguered by the press for having had a boring, uneventful term in office. Wonder what could turn things around for him? Hmm, how about a war to end all wars?

One of Pullman's aides, Margaret Colin, used to be married to cable-company worker and MIT graduate Jeff Goldblum, but she left him to pursue her political ambitions. Goldblum, twitchy as ever, essays the nebbishy braniac-who-saves-the-day role so common in Emmerich-Devlin movies (see James Spader in *Stargate* and Matthew Broderick in 1998's *Godzilla* if you're not convinced. Actually, don't.) Judd Hirsch is well cast as Goldblum's father, but I'm not sure how Harvey Fierstein made it into the movie as one of Goldblum's coworkers. But hey, stunt casting works every time.

About a half hour in, cocky fighter pilot Will Smith appears. Smith lives in a really nice house with his stripper girlfriend, Vivica A. Fox, and her young son. Smith's best friend is played (in a performance that can only be described as "cringeworthy") by singer Harry Connick, Jr. The two of them talk in a manly shorthand punctuated by high fives, munch on cigars, and point at each other while uttering "You the man!" Randy Quaid rounds out the central cast as an alcoholic Vietnam vet who now makes his living as a crop duster. He and his three kids live in a Winnebago and, oh yes, he claims to have been abducted by aliens 10 years earlier, and he thirsts for revenge.

Anyway, though the top minds in Washington and within the intelligence community are all at work trying to figure out what these spacecraft are going to do and why satellite communications have been disrupted, only Jeff Goldblum has the answer. Though it is never shown how he discovers this, he comes to the startling realization that all the ships are being controlled by a central computer on a mother ship, and that they are using our satellites to maintain a communication link between each one. This, of course, is ridiculous. Having found a way to build spaceships of enormous size, and also having devised a propulsion system that is far beyond the understanding of humankind, the best these aliens can do to maintain communication with each other is to rely on our satellites? Even if that was the only way these ships could keep in contact, you'd think some actual scientist would have figured it out. How about the still-living Arthur C. Clarke, who helped invent the communications satellite? Maybe he'd have suggested that the best course of action would be to remotely shut the satellites down, or to blow them up! That would surely have had a disastrous impact on the aliens' attack plans.

But, no, only Goldblum has been able to detect a signal emitting from the satellites—a signal that, he believes, is a countdown leading to an attack. At no time is it understood what devices he has used to discover these signals or what technology he's using to decode them, nor does anyone ask, not even the president, who instead takes one look at Goldblum's PowerMac as it counts down and immediately decides to leave Washington. I'd imagine this would make Goldblum eligible for a Nobel Prize of some sort, or at least a raise back at the cable company.

Just as the president steps onto Air Force One, the countdown ends and all the warships simultaneously deploy their primary weapons, which for some reason are designed only to point straight down. For maximum effect, large buildings are targeted as ground zero for each attack, and this detonation creates a gigantic fireball that radiates outward, consuming everything in its path. The same thing happens in different cities, and the devastation is incredible. Cars and trucks fly through the air like toys, buildings exploding spectacularly, and people run away, become engulfed in flames, are thrown through the air or crushed by cars or other things. And in a now-famous shot, the White House is completely destroyed.

Meanwhile, back in L.A., Fox, her son, and their dog run from the fireball and end up in a commuter tunnel, where she kicks open a locked steel door that leads to a maintenance room. For some reason, the fireball just sweeps past instead of filling the room with flames. As well, much is made of the fact that the dog just narrowly escapes death.

The attack ends and the ships fall dormant. For some reason, the aliens send no ground troops to mop up the mess and sweep for survivors. In fact, there is no further activity from any of the ships until they're provoked later in the film. This makes it very difficult to figure out what their plan actually is, or even if they have one, for that matter.

Meanwhile, Smith and his squadron prepare to attack the nearest warship, while Goldblum et al ride safely in Air Force One. Oh yes, I should point out that Smith has aspirations of becoming an astronaut and piloting the space shuttle. Anyway, he and his squadron head off in their fighter planes and launch rockets at the ship, only to watch them disintegrate harmlessly in the ship's protective energy shield. A fleet of small fighter crafts then emerge from the ship and engage Smith and crew in combat (just for fun, it would seem, as our guys certainly pose no threat to them). Among the unfortunate pilots to be killed is our friend Harry Connick, Jr., which prompts Will Smith to go completely insane and engage one of the alien crafts in a dogfight that bears absolutely no resemblance to anything that occurs in *Star Wars: Episode V—The Empire Strikes Back.*

© Twentieth Century Fox

Finally, Smith ejects himself from his plane in order to force the alien craft to crash. On the ground, he opens up the damaged ship's cockpit and punches the alien pilot out cold. Obviously having forgotten about the recent death of his best friend, he lights up a cigar and makes various inappropriate quips to himself.

On Air Force One, Judd Hirsch starts laying into the president, the secretary of defense, and anyone else who will listen for not having prepared for such an alien invasion. He cites the 1946 crash of an alien spacecraft in Roswell, New Mexico, and the presence of "secret" installation Area 51. The president scoffs at this and proceeds to tell Hirsch that not only did no such crash occur, but Area 51 does not even exist. Now, it's true that no one knows what exactly happened in Area 51, but it's no secret that the installation is there, out in the Nevada desert. It would seem that President Bill Pullman is the only man on earth who believes that Area 51 is a myth. Perhaps he's never watched the Fox network, or been apprised by his defense advisors of the photos being taken of the base by Russian satellites. Anyway, he finds out that the base is real and that, indeed, an alien spacecraft has been kept there for 50 years, along with three alien corpses. What's more, it's the same type of craft as those that engaged the air force in combat earlier. And here's where the movie totally falls apart.

See, if these aliens visited us in 1946, a full 50 years before their attack, in the same kind of spacecraft that they're still using in 1996, it means that they would have had every opportunity to attack us then. Since the ship that crashed was a short-range fighter vehicle, the only way to transport it to Earth would have been inside one of their mother ships. Obviously these aliens had the means to build these ships and travel across the universe at least 50 Earth years before they decided to come back and destroy us. So why would they send a mother ship to Earth in 1946, but not attack? Apparently, according to the movie, these creatures move from planet to planet, destroying each one as they go. When they move, their entire civilization moves, and it's an enormous undertaking with a clear military objective. Under these conditions, they would not have come to Earth in '46 just to screw around and buzz New Mexico dirt farmers. But I guess we're supposed to believe that's what they did—that they just went away, allowing our population to explode and our war machine to advance sufficiently to improve our chances of fighting back. While I'm sure the filmmakers thought they were being clever by referencing Roswell, this was actually a bad idea because it's implausible. But that's just one of the sloppy examples of a particular plot point being used to solve some immediate story problem, even as it undermines the structure of the story.

I wish I could say that the rest of the movie isn't as stupid as what's come before, but that would be a lie. To condense a few of the subsequent events: Smith meets up with Quaid and a large group of other families in motor homes, and they all head off to Area 51. Once there, they're brought deep inside the underground bunker to keep them safe from alien attack, for there's a warship preparing to move directly over the site and blow it up (again, due to the impractical nature of their primary weapon, blowing anything up is a very slow, time-consuming process for these aliens). At the same time, the small alien craft that's been stored here secretly and that has been dormant for 50 years suddenly comes to life, as it's been reactivated by the presence of its mother ship. (Another reason to assume that it could not have traveled to Earth in '46 without the mother ship near: its power comes from a central computer in the mother ship.)

A very drunk Goldblum comes to some amazing realization about how to deactivate the energy shield around the spaceships. Yet, instead of explaining his realization, he distracts everyone with sleight of hand and a Coke can and odd line readings so that no one questions the fundamental impossibility of what he suggests. And what he suggests is to fly the old alien ship that's in their possession out into space, where they will dock with the mother ship. Following this, Goldblum will connect his PowerMac to the mother ship's computer and set off a nuclear explosion in the mother ship while, down on Earth, our military readies itself to strike. Now, theoretically, if all he has to do is disable the mother ship in order to shut the shields down, then instead of screwing around with computers, they could just load up their alien craft with nuclear warheads and launch 'em all once they dock. But no, he's gonna go up there, link his computer—which is from Earth—with their alien computer, upload a virus, and then launch the nuclear weapon he's bringing with him. I would like to state here that the movie never explains how it is possible to link a Macintosh computer to that of the aliens, nor does it explain how the virus works or how it is possible for Goldblum to know what kind of virus to write that would work in an alien computer platform that he does not understand and has never seen.

And, of course, to fly the ship we have none other than Will Smith, who seems to have no problem piloting it because, as he explains, he's "well aware of its maneuvering capabilities." I did think it was odd that neither Goldblum nor Smith brings a spacesuit, a helmet, or oxygen with them when they embark; they just assume that they'll be able to breathe when they leave Earth's atmosphere. Once they dock inside the mother ship, Goldblum immediately uploads the virus, while Quaid and the president himself prepare a climactic attack on the warship as it moves over Area 51.

This is a film in which every central character, in the end, gets exactly what he or she wants, including redemption. Smith wants to be an astronaut, and he gets his wish. Pullman wants to distinguish himself as president, and he gets to help save the planet by spearheading the attack against the aliens. Goldblum, who's wasted his superhuman intelligence until now, gets to put it to good use while reconciling with his ex-wife. Quaid has been a failure as a husband, a father, and a crop duster, but he gets to have his moment as the man who makes it possible—against all odds—to destroy the alien warship. Hell, even the stripper gets to save lives and explain to the first lady why stripping is a good job. Everyone gets what they want—except the audience. But is it fun to watch? Yes, because it takes hold of the on/off switch in your brain and sets it to "off" before you even have a chance to think. There's a director's cut of the movie that's a few minutes longer—I'm sure it's a revelation.

Most Spectacular Moment of Carnage

None of the central characters die bloodily. The film can't even muster the energy to kill its few human "villains," like the scheming secretary of defense, in inventive ways. So, if you're thirsting for blood, this is not the movie for you, other than to cheer the timely end of Harry Connick, Jr., for his crimes against acting. **(MR)**

Mars Attacks! (1996)

Warner Bros.   126 minutes

HIGHLY RECOMMENDED

⚠

DIRECTOR: Tim Burton

WRITER: Jonathan Gems

CAST: Jack Nicholson, Glenn Close, Annette Bening, Pierce Brosnan, Danny DeVito, Martin Short, Sarah Jessica Parker, Michael J. Fox, Rod Steiger, Tom Jones, Jim Brown, Lukas Haas, Natalie Portman, Pam Grier, Lisa Marie, Sylvia Sidney, Jack Black, Paul Winfield, Joe Don Baker

Released in December 1996, Tim Burton's *Mars Attacks!* was the antithesis of that summer's self-important, ridiculous alien invasion movie *Independence Day*. *Mars Attacks!* did it right, by both parodying and paying homage to the '50s sci-fi B-picture as well as to the '70s disaster movie genre. In the tradition of '50s flicks, the film is composed in eye-popping CinemaScope and features a bug-eyed alien threat that neither science nor the U.S. military can stop, all scored to a theremin-heavy Danny Elfman soundtrack. And in the tradition of '70s movies, virtually every person in the large cast of stars is killed spectacularly as the movie progresses. Luckily, the filmmakers also make good use of '90s film technology to convincingly—and hilariously—bring the alien creatures to life. Plus, how can you go wrong with a movie that features an exclamation mark as part of the title?

The movie opens with flaming cows, and that's always a good sign. Shooting deadly laser bolts from their silver flying saucers, their brains exposed and their mouths fixed in gleeful grins, the martians of *Mars Attacks!* have no grand plan to dominate Earth, and no desire to colonize our planet; instead, they're sadistic pranksters, laying waste to everything and everyone in their path just for fun.

After amassing what appears to be their entire fleet of saucers in pyramid-shaped formations on a course to Earth, the martians break into a television broadcast to announce their apparently peaceful intentions to meet with president Jack Nicholson. Military advisor Rod Steiger suspects otherwise, but scientist Pierce Brosnan is ceaselessly optimistic, and the president agrees to meet with them. Large crowds of onlookers and media are brought to the desert outside of Las Vegas where the aliens will land, and the president sends ambassador Paul Winfield to greet with them. Winfield is backed by a giant military contingent, and he's armed with a silly machine that can translate English into Martian and vice versa, albeit badly. However, the arranged meeting is just a set-up for the martians to kill everyone in the crowd and to kidnap vapid television personality Sarah Jessica Parker. This scene is also notable for depicting the deaths of not only Winfield but also Michael J. Fox, who is hit by a disintegrating death ray, leaving behind only a green skeleton and his disembodied, smoldering hand in Parker's clutching fingers.

After this massacre, the president is advised by Brosnan that the entire event could have been only a "cultural misunderstanding," and the president broadcasts an announcement into space that he would still like to extend the olive branch of peace. Of course, by this time the martians, who are now hovering in a ship above Earth, have begun to perform a series of bizarre experiments on their captive TV star, which culminate with her head being grafted onto the body of a dog. Also glimpsed in the alien ships are large glass spheres containing various creatures in suspended animation, including cows and a circus clown. When not performing these experiments, the martians enjoy reading old issues of *Playboy* and watching really bad television, specifically *The Dukes of Hazzard*.

The martians agree to meet with the Americans again, but this time they send their alien ambassador to address Congress. Again, the president does not attend this meeting, and again, the crowd is massacred. Scientist Brosnan is kidnapped this time, and he ends up being taken aboard the orbiting spacecraft and decapitated. The aliens keep his head and what's left of his bleeding, raggedly severed neck alive by a machine of some kind.

While all of this is happening, we're introduced to other characters who will prove to be important over the course of the film. Lukas Haas is a trailer-park kid whose brother, Jack Black, is one of the soldiers killed during the first attack. His father, Joe Don Baker, is a militant redneck, and his grandmother, Sylvia Sidney, is a dottering old woman who lives in a nursing home and listens to nothing but Slim Whitman records. Meanwhile, in Vegas there's a somewhat slimy entrepreneur, also played by Jack Nicholson, and his girlfriend Annette Bening, who are both friends with ex-boxer-turned-hotel-performer Jim Brown. Later, when Vegas is attacked, Bening and Brown team up with obnoxious gambler Danny DeVito and singer Tom Jones (who plays himself) and try to escape. Movie director Barbet Schroeder portrays the doomed French president; back in Washington, Glenn Close is the first lady, Natalie Portman is the presidential daughter, and Martin Short is the oversexed White House press secretary who is eventually seduced by Lisa Marie, who plays a martian disguised as a beautiful woman. Also in Washington is Jim Brown's semi-estranged wife Pam Grier and their two kids. All Brown wants is to get back there to see them, come hell or high water.

After this second attack, the martians begin a full-scale assault on Washington and later, the world, and the movie really hits its stride. The trailer park is destroyed by a gigantic robotic monster; Las Vegas is decimated; Washington is hammered. Even some kids on a class trip aren't safe, and a flying saucer uses its death ray to topple the Washington Monument onto them. Easter Island's ancient sculptures are knocked over like bowling pins; Paris is set ablaze; the Taj Mahal is incinerated, and in England, Big Ben is blown to smithereens. One key to possibly stopping the aliens comes when a dead martian is examined by scientists and it is discovered that, when not wearing protective helmets, they chew a gum consisting of various ingredients that appear to keep them alive in our atmosphere. However, this is merely a red herring; it's later discovered that the easiest way to kill these aliens is to force them to listen to Slim Whitman music, which causes their exposed brains to burst. Armed with this weapon, humankind eventually eliminates the martian threat, but not before Rod Steiger is shrunk to a tiny size and stepped on, and not before the president, after delivering an impassioned speech for peace, is impaled through the back by a martian flag.

The visual inventiveness of *Mars Attacks!* is fantastic, and the absurd energy that fuels the film is boosted by excellent performances, music, visual effects, and direction. It is wacky without being superficial and satirical without being merely a spoof—meaning that there is substance within the hilarity and chaos. Tim Burton is that rare director who can make large-scale, effects-heavy movies, imbue them with his personal stamp, and not alienate the audience with technical coldness. Though it was unfairly rejected by audiences when it was originally released, *Mars Attacks!* has since attracted a following of fans who see it in the spirit in which was intended.

Most Spectacular Moment of Carnage

I really like the painful-looking disintegration that occurs when people are hit by the martians' death rays; the flesh appears to melt off of the skeleton. I also like the exploding martian brains. However, I believe that the carnage level of *Mars Attacks!* can only be measured by how many of the movie's stars are left standing at the end. By that standard, this film boasts an enormous body count. Sylvia Sidney, Lukas Haas, Natalie Portman, Jim Brown, Pam Grier, Tom Jones, and Annette Bening survive. Everyone else bites it. Jack Nicholson even manages to die twice, which is no small feat. Danny DeVito, Michael J. Fox, Jack Black, Barbet Schroeder, and Paul Winfield are all disintegrated; Pierce Brosnan and Sarah Jessica Parker are beheaded and experimented upon, but die only when their spacecraft crashes into the ocean; Joe Don Baker is crushed when his trailer home is smashed to bits by a giant robot; Glenn Close is flattened by a large chandelier; Martin Short has a finger bitten off and is then bludgeoned; and Rod Steiger is shrunk and then stepped on. In his role of the Vegas businessman, Nicholson is run over by a giant metal sphere, which then careens, with him on it, out of a collapsing hotel's topmost window; as the president, he is impaled through the back by a metal rod. And of course, many hundreds of other people die horribly as well. It doesn't get any better than this! **(MR)**

The War of the Worlds (1953)

Paramount   85 minutes

HIGHLY RECOMMENDED

⚠

DIRECTOR: Byron Haskin

WRITERS: Barré Lyndon (based on the novel by H. G. Wells)

CAST: Gene Barry, Ann Robinson, Les Tremayne, Robert Cornthwaite, Sandro Giglio, Lewis Martin, Houseley Stevenson, Jr., Paul Frees, William Phipps, Vernon Rich, Jack Kruschen, Paul Birch

Forget about the no-name cast of this sci-fi classic; this can definitely be classified as a disaster flick, especially after watching its scenes of panicked crowds, mass chaos, and the spectacular destruction of many cities on Earth. The film starts with a voiceover and newsreel footage of the first two world wars before our narrator introduces this invasion as one that's being "fought with terrible weapons of super science." Like all the best '50s movies of this kind, the filmmakers feel the need to educate viewers about the galaxy. It's as though people wouldn't accept the concept unless the filmmakers absolutely convinced them that Earth really was ripe for attacking. The narrator explains, moving planet by planet, why the martians would rather take Earth than any of the nearby planets. Saturn, he describes like a travel agent, is an attractive world (am I to suppose he's been there recently?), but at 220 degrees below zero, it's much too cold. Shots of each planet appear as its terrain and climate are described. As in the similar film *When Worlds Collide*, the other planets in outer space are animated, and they look like something out of a cartoon.

The movie really begins when a comet crashes in a small town. The whole town goes out to inspect the glowing meteorite, and they put out the small fires that surround it. Luckily for them, that brilliant scientist Gene Barry happens to be fishing nearby. He's one of those great old movie heroes who acts stiffly, speaks with deep authority, and accurately predicts all of the troubles that the characters will soon face, despite having no real reason to know anything about them. Barry's Geiger counter goes off the scales as he looks around the site, and he soon realizes that the radiation is coming from the downed comet. This disappoints many of the now-irradiated townspeople, who were planning to turn the site into a tourist attraction. Ann Robinson plays the love interest, a teacher of library science at USC. She introduces herself, along with her uncle, a local pastor played by Lewis Martin, to Barry. Martin immediately agrees to put Barry up for the night as he waits for the meteorite to cool, and the three head off just in time to join in a local square dance and drink some "soda water."

But their wild night out is cut short when it's revealed that the meteorite actually hides an alien machine with a laser beam, which fires and vaporizes three townspeople who are watching the site. The "machine" looks something like a red taillight on a cobra-shaped metallic arm. When it fires, it makes a noise similar to that which my car makes when I start it up on a cold winter morning (can any mechanics out there tell me what to do about it?). This picture has a beautiful look and style to it. The large alien machines look amazing. They emit vibrant, colored light that looks like something from a neon sign. The film practically glows, and its visual style was very advanced for its time. The vaporization of characters in this movie also looks phenomenal. When they're hit, the people glow before dissolving, leaving only a black cinder mark on the ground.

As more "comets" fall from the sky, the army is called in. Barry begins advising them and explains that the alien machines must be "navigated by a gyroscopic mechanism." If I were an army general, I'd be wondering at this point how this scientist guy knows so much about martians, and I would begin to wonder if maybe Mr. Smartypants was a martian himself. This never becomes an issue, because Barry's advice is always sound, and these dense army guys must figure they'd be totally lost without him. As more machines hover in the countryside and the army waits to attack, pastor Martin decides that he must inform these guests that Earth means them no harm. This does nothing but get him quickly vaporized and start a spectacular, full-scale assault between the army and the martians. The army is no match for the might of the aliens, and we're treated to some great shots of screaming soldiers covered in flames during the battle.

Barry knows enough to get the hell out of there, and he quickly takes Robinson to a nearby plane and heads up into the air. Rather unwisely, he flies right into the martians' line of sight and crashes the plane nearby. What to do now? The two decide to go home, clean up, and grab themselves a hearty breakfast. Robinson proves to be quite a cook, and she fries up some delicious-looking eggs. Seeing those eggs got me thinking how great it must have been 50 years ago to get up each morning and eat a plate full of pancakes, sausages, and eggs. Mmmm, sure beats plain old cereal, doesn't it? Even Barry nods in approval at the eggs and states, "We're doing all right." Who wouldn't be, with eggs like those?

But breakfast is short lived when another comet crashes nearby, almost taking down the house. Trapped inside, Barry and Robinson scramble to get out, using an ax. There's even a brief glimpse of a martian, who actually looks kind of sweet, what with its big head, long thin arms, and suction cups on the ends of its three fingers. It quickly runs out of the house when Barry throws the ax at it. The two escape the house just before it is blown up behind them.

The narrator returns, along with stock footage of various cities around the world. The footage is dissolved with martian war machines and explosions. This simple effect actually works very well, and it gives the film a bigger sense of scope. By this point it is determined that the aliens will take over the world in a matter of six days. Barry, Robinson, and the army general watch as they attempt to use an atomic bomb (don't worry about them; they're wearing goggles), but they find it has no effect. L.A. is evacuated as the machines approach. As vehicles drive up and down the streets, a voice booms through loudspeakers, "The martians are coming this way." Indeed they do, and the audience is treated to more spectacular footage of L.A. ablaze and lasers blowing up various buildings. On the streets, Barry is separated from Robinson and the rest of his scientific staff. Before he drives out of the city, he is attacked by an angry mob who are clearly unhappy that their homes are being blown to bits by aliens. "Fools!" Barry screams dramatically, "They cut their own throats!" The mob destroys all of Barry's research and punches Barry in the face, knocking him out. His bad day becomes even worse when he finds a license plate torn from the bus holding Robinson and his coworkers.

Barry races through the city streets, avoiding falling debris as he runs past the looming machines to search all of the churches in the city and find Robinson. The martians die out immediately after Robinson is found, and the film wraps up with narration stating that "bacteria" killed them. Like many films of this era, it takes on a puritanical religious slant, and the narrator thanks "the little things that God, in his wisdom, had put upon this earth" as the music swells and the film ends. Apparently I should be relieved that God had it in for the martians, too.

This is a fun, fast-paced, highly entertaining disaster/sci-fi classic that should be seen. Clearly, it deserved the Oscar it won for special effects, and it definitely stands out as one of the slickest, most visually impressive films of its era.

Most Spectacular Moment of Carnage

The flaming soldiers are a high point, but the best death goes to the army lieutenant who, after ordering everyone out of the bunker, is suddenly vaporized. He glows a
bright green, and his skeleton is visible for an instant before he fades into dust. **(GK)**

War of the Worlds (2005)
Paramount/Dreamworks   117 minutes

HIGHLY RECOMMENDED

⚠

DIRECTOR: Steven Spielberg

WRITERS: Josh Friedman, David Koepp (based on book by H. G. Wells)

CAST: Tom Cruise, Dakota Fanning, Justin Chatwin, Miranda Otto, Tim Robbins, Morgan Freeman (narrator)

I can't believe it didn't happen sooner. Mass chaos and destruction, spectacular action and special effects—why hadn't anyone thought of wheeling several trucks full of money to Steven Spielberg and indoctrinating him into the disaster movie genre years ago? This film isn't just a remake of the 1953 classic *The War of the Worlds*; it's a veritable smorgasbord of disaster film staples. In one scene, the ground shakes and opens up à la *Earthquake*; in another, a plane crashes; in yet another, a ship is overturned and sinks. We get it all in this entertaining flick.

The film opens with narration, just like the original did, but it shifts gears quickly by focusing on one particular family: Tom Cruise and his two children, played by Dakota Fanning and Justin Chatwin. During the course of the alien invasion, this family must travel to Boston to find Cruise's ex-wife and her new husband, whom they are unable to contact due to the attack. Of course, there has to be tension: the relationship between Cruise and his kids is particularly strained, and the three are placed in claustrophobic sets to amplify the tension between them. The point of view never shifts as the threesome moves from one incredibly dangerous situation to the next (to the point where it almost becomes comical—at certain points in the film, death would seem like a sweet relief, although I don't think this was the point Spielberg was trying to make). Over the course of the film, they come into contact with various people, each of whom reacts differently to the events unfolding—the idea here being to contrast the different emotions and responses to the alien invasion, thereby transforming what could have just been a series of impressively mounted, but emotionally empty, special effects into a more identifiable human story. The invasion itself has been altered somewhat from the original. Instead of a meteor that hides an alien ship landing on Earth, in this film the alien "tripods" are already here, buried in the ground. An alien-induced electrical storm shoots the machines' pilots down to begin the invasion. It seems a bit unnecessarily complicated compared to having comets simply hurtle to the ground, but OK.

For a movie with this much action, it's surprising how many long takes, which Spielberg employs to great effect, are also in the film. These help to build the tension and allow the actors' performances to carry the momentum of each scene to a climax. During the first invasion scene, there are incredible shots of the panicked crowd racing through the streets and vaporized buildings exploding in flames behind them. This footage is shot in a vein similar to that found in Spielberg's *Saving Private Ryan* (1998), and it delivers a visceral kick. It feels almost as if you're running along with them. The acting is great all around, although I've always had a bit of a problem with the "smart-aleck kid" syndrome that many Hollywood movies employ. I think the filmmakers intend for the children to appear cute and sometimes precocious, but it often just comes off as bratty. Thankfully, there is justification for the behavior in this film.

With only a single viewing under my belt, I did find it difficult to figure out what, exactly, the alien angle was with this invasion. Writers Josh Friedman and David Koepp (who directed *The Trigger Effect*) keep things vague as to what exactly is going on. After the initial blackout, there are suggestions that it is an EMP effect (a nuclear disaster film staple, by the way) that is causing the darkness, but that's all the explanation that is given, and even that is merely suggested. One character offers the possibility that the aliens have been waiting millions of years to attack. (The problem with this theory, which so often pops up in this type of movie, is that nobody's come up with a good reason why the aliens would wait until society had progressed this far to carry out its plans.) As it turns out, it seems that humans are needed for some sort of harvesting purpose (are they food, or a fuel source?), although if that's the case, the aliens sure are pretty wasteful, seeing as how they blowup a lot of people just, it seems, for kicks. Regardless, the harvesting makes for some deliciously creepy visuals of areas covered in a vibrantly red, pulpy, bloody, plantlike substance. Whatever the aliens' objective is, it really doesn't matter—what this film is really about is Cruise and his family learning to work together as a group and with others. Fortunately, everything is so well-paced and riveting that the minute details of the invasion become unimportant.

After numerous terrifying sequences, the remnants of the family end up locked in a basement with Tim Robbins, an extremely creepy survivalist who is losing his mind. By far the most claustrophobic in the film, this sequence depicts the darkest and most disturbing moments in the family's struggle for survival, and it ends in a surprisingly dark manner for a summer blockbuster, with the suggestion of a brutal murder. Perhaps the creepiest thing about *War of the Worlds* is how vividly it portrays the rapid crumbling of society amid disaster.

Unfortunately, unlike the best disaster films of the Irwin Allen era, there are no elaborate deaths for any of the major characters. It's a minor complaint, because there is plenty of violence happening around them, but all the same, it would have been a real shock to see Tom Cruise or one of the kids get abruptly vaporized by an alien ray. Oh well, at least the son is beaten up by an angry mob. The climax, which should surprise no one who has read the book or seen the original movie, leads to my only other complaint: it's a tacked-on happy ending in which, amid a completely destroyed city, all of the people who are important to the story find one another on a perfectly preserved city block. Perhaps this was all done simply to allow the leads from the original movie to make guest appearances (that's Gene Barry and Ann Robinson as Otto's parents), but it was, for me, the only false note in the film. The rest of this flick knocked my socks off.

Most Spectacular Moment of Carnage

Citizens are blasted with alien beams. This causes them to explode into dust spectacularly, leaving only bits of clothing floating eerily behind. People in a panicked crowd turn on each other, leading to a nasty shooting. A ferry capsizes and passengers are crushed by vehicles and fall into the ship's rotor blades (unfortunately, this is depicted very tastefully and is not particularly graphic). A human victim is "harvested" by the aliens and, although the action is obscured, we are left with the distinct impression that the body's contents are being sucked out, and that some of those contents are then sprayed over the ground. But the winner is the sequence in which Fanning wanders out to a nearby stream. She sees a body float by, and moments later, in a wonderfully morbid and disturbing scene, an uncountable number of bodies float past the little girl. Way to go, Steve! **(GK)**

The Day of the Triffids (1962)
Security Pictures Ltd.   93 minutes

RECOMMENDED

Based on the classic novel by John Wyndham, this unusual film features giant alien plants that attack and take over the world. As goofy as that sounds (and is), the movie's quite entertaining. Technically the film is more sci-fi than disaster, but it's worth checking out all the same. This flick is due for a feature-film remake, in my opinion. (**GK**)

The Lost Missile (1958)
United Artists   70 minutes

AVOID AT ALL COSTS

A hydrogen missile from space enters our atmosphere and begins spinning around the globe. On a collision course with New York City, it's expected to hit in less than one hour. All the while, narration is used to try and make sense of all the stock footage, cheap effects, and generally disjointed nature of the movie. At least this disaster film holds the record for killing Canadians: the missile flies across the Canadian wilderness, destroying forests, taking out the Canadian air force (not that that's much of an accomplishment), and wiping out entire families. What to do? Send in a young bomb specialist, a pre-raspy-voiced Robert Loggia. Manhattan is saved, but not before Ottawa is completely obliterated. Can't save 'em all, I suppose. With the exception of Loggia's talents, this is pretty much a total waste of time. Directed by Lester Wm. Burke. Not available on video or DVD. (**GK**)

RARE, OBSCURE, AND LESS IMPORTANT TITLES

Assignment Outer Space (1960)

Battle of the Worlds (1961)

The Day of the Triffids (1981) Made-for-TV

Grand Tour: Disaster in Time (1992) Made-for-TV

H. G. Wells' War of the Worlds (2005) Straight-to-video

The Time Shifters (1999) Made-for-TV

MOVIES THAT SOUND LIKE THEY'RE DISASTER FILMS, BUT AREN'T

Don't be fooled. These titles may sound like disaster movies, but pop the tape into your VCR and you'll see no sign of screaming, panicked crowds being crushed by falling buildings. And what good is that?

Cyclone (1987)
This flick is about a superpowered motorcycle, which is driven by Heather Thomas. Sadly, despite its heavy artillery, the bike does not possess the power to actually create cyclones.

Day the World Ended (1956)
The world doesn't end in this Roger Corman monster movie cheapie. In fact, the film takes place after an atom bomb has detonated, leaving a group of survivors alone in a mountain cabin, fending off the attacks of a radiated mutant, or something like that.

The Hurricane (1999)
Denzel Washington plays a boxer known as Hurricane Carter. He spends most of the movie in prison, making it extraordinarily difficult to get himself caught in any sort of storm.

Hurricane Smith (1992)

The only hurricane in this film is the fighting frenzy of action star Carl Weathers.

The Ice Storm (1997)

You'd think this movie might depict some sort of horrific hailstorm of epic proportions. Instead, you'll get a weird drama, set in the late '60s, about wife swapping.

Night of the Flood (1996)

It's some kind of interpretive dance movie. From what I gather, nobody in this flick dances during a flood or anything. So why bother?

Quicksand: No Escape (1992)

Expecting to see an expedition group in the jungles of South America become trapped in sinking quicksand? Well, neither was I, but we can hope, can't we? Instead, this is just some thriller with Donald Sutherland.

Storm of the Century (1999)

This Stephen King miniseries is set against the backdrop of a winter storm, but the weather is of little consequence in the supernatural tale of a male witch bumping off the townspeople.

Under the Volcano (1984)

This drama features Albert Finney, as an alcoholic, and Jacqueline Bisset. Although it's set in Mexico, there are no erupting volcanoes to speak of. I suppose Bisset got her fill of that in *When Time Ran Out.…* **(GK)**

Disaster Movie Parodies

Given the over-the-top nature of disaster movies, you would think the genre would be ripe for spoofing. However, there haven't been as many parodies made as you would expect. Maybe it's because these films almost seem like self-parodies already. Every once in a while you'll see a disaster movie reference pop up in a film. *Titanic* gags, for example, have occurred in movies and television shows, from the series *Futurama* to the 1998 Leslie Nielsen vehicle *Wrongfully Accused* to the hilarious "That's Armageddon" segment in 1977's *The Kentucky Fried Movie*. But few satirical films that specifically parody disaster movies have been made. Fortunately, many of the ones that have been made are classics (the others, well . . .). **(GK)**

Airplane! (1980)

Paramount   88 minutes

HIGHLY RECOMMENDED

⚠

DIRECTORS: Jim Abrahams, David Zucker, Jerry Zucker

WRITERS: Jim Abrahams, David Zucker, Jerry Zucker

CAST: Robert Hays, Julie Hagerty, Lloyd Bridges, Leslie Nielsen, Robert Stack, Peter Graves, Lorna Patterson, Stephen Stucker, Kareem Abdul-Jabbar, Barbara Billingsley, David Leisure, Ethel Merman, Jimmie Walker

Easily one of the funniest movies I've ever seen, this warped disaster movie parody may arguably be the best film reviewed in this book. Taking the well-used airplane-in-peril scenario, the filmmakers exploit all of the disaster movie clichés to maximum effect. Apparently, the 1957 disaster movie *Zero Hour!* was this movie's direct inspiration, but even if you haven't seen that hard-to-find title, you'll recognize elements from later films like *Airport 1975* and others. The film has a very classic '50s feel, and many of its "insider" jokes pay homage to pictures from both the '50s and the '70s, with one scene offering up its own take on 1953's *From Here to Eternity*, and the next spoofing 1977's *Saturday Night Fever*.

The film opens with a great *Jaws* parody in which the fin-like tail of the airplane in question is visible above the clouds. There's also a great gag in which the taxi-driver hero, Robert Hays, screeches to a halt in front of the airport and races inside, ignoring his new customer. The film repeatedly cuts back to the customer throughout the movie, sitting in the running taxi and waiting patiently for Hays to return. Hays finds Julie Hagerty, his stewardess girlfriend, who has decided to leave him. After a series of rapid-fire gags, they both end up on the flight, and it is revealed that Hays was a pilot in "the War" who has refused to get back into the cockpit since losing seven of his squadron members in battle, including the often-referred-to George Zip. Also onboard is a sickly girl who is scheduled for a heart transplant; a singing, guitar-toting nun (shades of Helen Reddy in *Airport 1975*); a hilariously straight-faced doctor, played by

Leslie Nielsen; and a pair of jive-talking "brothers," whose dialogue is translated via subtitles.

Using hilarious flashbacks (the best involving their first meeting, at a dive bar/disco as the Bee Gees' "Stayin' Alive" blares from the speakers), Hays explains his long history with Hagerty to several passengers, who do everything from hanging themselves to dousing themselves with gasoline to avoid his soppy story. After a fish dinner is served to the crew and many of the passengers, food poisoning takes hold, leaving no one to fly the plane. Our reluctant hero must overcome his fear of flying and his drinking problem to rise to the occasion, save the day, and win just one—"for the Zipper." Back on the ground, Lloyd Bridges and Hays's ex-captain, Robert Stack, attempt to talk him down. The shot of a glazed Bridges hanging upside down in the control tower, high from sniffing glue, is one of the funniest images ever committed to film.

The model airplanes used in the film are cheesy enough to get a laugh, but they actually aren't that phony-looking (in fact, they look better than the models used in many other disaster films). The music perfectly emulates the themes of these types of movies. The Zuckers always manage to put multiple jokes into the same frame, which often results in consistently steady laughs, as well as new laughs when multiple viewings reveal previously missed gags. If one joke fails, there's always some other funny thing going on, and that's what makes this one of the best films ever.

Besides appearing on the AFI's Best Comedy Films list, *Airplane!* was nominated for a Golden Globe for Best Motion Picture, Musical/Comedy, which it should have won. As you should with all Zucker Brothers' films, stay through the credits. There are always funny ones thrown in, such as one for Gripology, and Charles Dickens as the author of *A Tale of Two Cities*. Watch for yet another gag after the credits roll. If you haven't seen this classic comedy, do yourself a favor and rent it.

Most Spectacular Moment of Carnage

There isn't anything particularly violent in this film. What looks like the most painful event involves a large wooden guitar, which is carried to the back of the plane by a flight attendant and which loudly hits the head of every person sitting on the aisle. But the winner goes to Robert Stack, who, using a series of punches, elbows, and kicks, single-handedly beats the hell out of every panhandler who approaches him in the airport. **(GK)**

Airplane II: The Sequel (1982)

Paramount   84 minutes

RECOMMENDED

© Paramount Pictures

DIRECTOR: Ken Finkleman

WRITER: Ken Finkleman

CAST: Robert Hays, Julie Hagerty, Lloyd Bridges, Chad Everett, Peter Graves, Chuck Connors, William Shatner, Raymond Burr, John Vernon, Stephen Stucker, Kent McCord, James A. Watson, Jr., John Dehner, Rip Torn, Sonny Bono, Al White, David Leisure, David Paymer, Pat Sajak, Hervé Villechaize, George Wendt (uncredited)

While it isn't the full-blown masterpiece that *Airplane!* is, *Airplane II: The Sequel* is very, very funny in its own right. Yes, it does reprise some of the original's best gags, but it also adds many more. In fact, it's easily the best Zucker Brothers knockoff you'll ever see. And it has one thing that even the original doesn't: William Shatner, in perhaps his best role ever.

As the flick opens to the musical strains of *Battlestar Galactica*, it becomes clear that the filmmakers will also see fit to parody science fiction titles like 1982's *E.T. the Extra-Terrestrial*, 1956's *Invasion of the Body Snatchers*, and 1977's *Star Wars*. The movie begins with an increasingly sexually suggestive crawl about a princess in another universe (this is no doubt from a completely different film), and then makes its way back to the airport. A title card appears, stating that this is Houston—The Future, despite the use of present-day stock-footage shots (which may have come from the first movie) of the city. A barrage of jokes follows, and while some of the more dated references don't play as well today (I couldn't remember what they were parodying), many are extremely funny.

Picking up where the first story left off, the luckless Robert Hays has been moved to the Ronald Reagan Hospital for the Mentally Ill. While there, he learns that the XR-2300 ("No, not the muffler bracket for a '79 Pinto; the lunar shuttle") is about to fly. Apparently, having test-piloted and crashed the same model of a commercial passenger lunar shuttle to be used for travel to the moon, Hays believes that the ship's faulty wiring will put the inaugural voyage in danger. Unfortunately, Hagerty, the computer officer onboard the ship, will not speak with him. She is now engaged to marry Chad Everett, who is also on the flight (although I'm not entirely sure just what his job entails). After escaping from the institute and buying a ticket for the flight from a nearby scalper, Hays boards the craft. Also expressing concern about the shuttle are a cigar-chomping Chuck Connors (as "the Sarge") and Rip Torn, who plays a worried executive on the ground. Beginning every sentence with "The boys on the board," Torn explains that these "boys on the board" will be very upset if the flight doesn't go as planned. The payoff comes when the boys on the board turn out to literally be boys. I know, it's an obvious gag, but I laughed.

In my favorite scene, Hays grasps Hagerty and pleads with her to turn the shuttle around, yelling, "This shuttle could blow up at any second." There are Japanese

© Paramount Pictures

tourists standing directing behind them during this exchange, one of whom does a large spit-take upon hearing the news. He explains what he heard to his friend, who does a spit-take some 10 seconds later. Director Ken Finkleman must have a thing for spit-takes, as four appear in the movie. All of them are well timed, are photographed differently (one comes from offscreen; another is in the background; and so on), and are hilariously effective.

The computer, a HAL-like talking computer named ROCK, soon overheats and shorts out, but it refuses to be shut down, rerouting the shuttle into the sun. It kills the crew members one by one, leaving Hays to fly the plane, reverse its course, and land it on the moon. Sonny Bono is also onboard, as an impotent passenger who's carrying a bomb. "A bah . . . ?" the frightened flight attendant asks Hays, who responds, "No, not a bah. A bomb." All of these events are bad, but even worse—the ship is running low on coffee! And worst of all is landing a plane that's "cracking up." Hays stoically explains in one of the film's best bits of dialogue: "Elaine, we're going to have to come in pretty low to land this thing. Sure, it's difficult. Coming in low is part of every textbook approach. It's just something you have to do . . . when you land."

Running things on the moon is William Shatner, an ex-pilot who flew with Hays in "the War." This sequel introduces an even more detailed backstory about Hays's history as a fighter pilot. His fear of flying all started when he lost most of his squad over Macho Grande during "the War." As this story is related, the filmmakers fade to hilarious black-and-white stock footage of fighter planes crashing. Just which war was this?

Shatner quickly gets down to business, ordering, "I want a six-foot trench dug around the entire base, fill it with gasoline . . . get the women and children to the lower shelters, contact the Japanese ambassador . . . get me a complete file on everyone who's seen *The Sound of Music* more than four times." Shatner goes absolutely crazy during the 15 minutes he's in the picture, and he screams many of his lines, each one of which is pure gold for the audience.

In the end, there's no way that the disaster movie genre could be parodied better than it was in both *Airplane!* and this underrated sequel. Watch for a couple of funny fake credits at the close of the film, particularly the credit that follows the one for Best Boy, when Worst Boy credit is given to Adolf Hitler. Shatner reemerges after the credits for another quick joke, leaving you with a smile.

Most Spectacular Moment of Carnage
Reprising a similar joke in the first film, in which a woman attempts to put on some lipstick during a stormy flight, this time a passenger decides that he needs a shave while the shuttle attempts to land. He passes out after patting aftershave on his grotesque, heavily nicked face. **(GK)**

The Big Bus (1976)

Paramount   88 minutes

AT YOUR OWN RISK

© Paramount Pictures

DIRECTOR: James Frawley

WRITERS: Lawrence J. Cohen, Fred Freeman

CAST: Joseph Bologna, Stockard Channing, John Beck, Rene Auberjonois, Ned Beatty, Bob Dishy, José Ferrer, Ruth Gordon, Harold Gould, Larry Hagman, Sally Kellerman, Richard Mulligan, Lynn Redgrave, Richard B. Shull, Stuart Margolin, Howard Hesseman, Vic Tayback

"There have been movies about big earthquakes. There have been movies about big boats sinking. Movies about big buildings burning. Movies about big German balloons bursting. And now, a movie about . . . the Big Bus."

So starts the first disaster movie parody ever made, *The Big Bus*. Most people I've talked to who remember this film saw at a drive-in theater, and they describe it as being hilarious. Unfortunately, in my opinion that card at the beginning of the movie is the funniest gag in the entire picture, and most of the cast spends the entire time bugging out their eyes and trying too hard to be hysterically funny. It might be fun to watch if only to see what "rapid-fire comedy" looked like before the Zucker Brothers took it to its height in *Airplane!*, but just don't expect to laugh a whole lot at the dated humor.

After an explosion injures the driving crew of a new, double-decker nuclear-powered bus during the first press conference about the vehicle, a new driver must be found. Joseph Bologna stars as Dan Torrance, a down-on-his-luck bus driver who has been accused of cannibalizing all 110 of his passengers during an ill-fated trip years earlier. At a local bus-driver bar, he denies the charges, admitting only to accidentally eating one foot, which results in a large and mostly unfunny bar fight. At least there's one absurd gag that seems to work here: Bologna's slow buddy Shoulders O'Brien, played by John Beck, brandishes a broken milk carton like a beer bottle, swinging it around recklessly.

Meanwhile, bus designer Kitty Baxter, played by Stockard Channing, and her scientist father (who has been injured by the explosion, can't move, and is forced to lie out in the parking lot and bark orders for the remainder of the movie) ready the vehicle's inaugural launch. Onboard are a wacky old lady, a bickering couple, and a faithless priest. There's also a piano-playing lounge singer, who I did think was funny. While most viewers will probably find this character annoying, I personally hold bad lounge singers as a guilty pleasure, and clearly, this guy's purpose in the film is to parody the overuse of musical numbers in the genre. Most importantly, there's a villainous gas baron, played by José Ferrer, who wants to stop nuclear power from spreading and stealing his profits. He's therefore planted a bomb on the nuclear-powered vehicle.

There are numerous sequences inside the bus: the characters are shown splashing in a pool, drinking at a bar, and so on. This is all supposed to be hilarious, and maybe it would be, were it not for the fact that many of these conveniences actually exist in buses today. In fact, there are many scenes in the movie that, more than 25 years later, don't seem to have any identifiable jokes left in them. Anyway, Bologna must diffuse the bomb and control the runaway bus when it won't slow down. As it speeds around Harbinger Curve, a 1953 Chevy pickup suddenly crashes into the side of it, and the bus crashes to a halt on the edge of a cliff.

Most of the dialogue from this point on is screaming and yelling; Bologna is particularly guilty of screaming and barking his lines. The film applies the "overacting for the sake of overacting is funny" principle, when of course it almost always isn't. Stockard Channing, who all of a sudden appears baking a pie in the bus's kitchen (that's supposed to get a big laugh, I'm guessing), accidentally knocks herself unconscious. Bologna attempts to weigh the back end of the bus down by firing a gun at soda dispensers and filling the kitchen with cola. Learning that Channing is still in there, Bologna crawls across the top of the bus and jumps in, swimming around in the pop and rescuing Channing. Bologna and Beck then work together to wheel the bus back to safety, and they resume the drive toward their destination. There's a quick gag that shows the bus splitting in two, and then, jarringly, the credits roll. This movie is choppy and it doesn't make a lot of sense to begin with, but to actually end the film before they reach their destination is stunning. It's as if the filmmakers sat with a stopwatch, deciding to end the film when it hit 82 minutes, wherever that might be within the story.

The final sequence (with Bologna on top of the bus) is well shot, and the cast must have been expensive. But part of the problem is that, once the movie gets moving, it really isn't any more exaggerated or ridiculous than the films it parodies. None of the gags are particularly well-timed, either, and the ones you haven't seen coming don't make any sense anyway. What's worse for viewers today is that, while the idea of a runaway bus probably sounded ludicrous at the time, 20 years later *Speed* would be made. And that picture would take the same concept a little more seriously and actually end up being an entertaining film. Go figure.

Most Spectacular Moment of Carnage
Nothing dies in this film (except maybe a few careers). Stockard Channing almost drowns in soda pop, which I suppose would be the closest thing to carnage in the flick. (GK)

Hero (1992)

Columbia Pictures   112 minutes

AT YOUR OWN RISK

Not well received upon its release, this misfire does have a few funny moments. Dustin Hoffman plays the "hero" of the title, a rather abrasive, obnoxious guy who manages to rescue the trapped passengers of a crashed airliner. Directed by Stephen Frears, the movie also features Geena Davis, Andy Garcia, Joan Cusack, Kevin J. O'Connor, Maury Chaykin, Stephen Tobolowsky, and Tom Arnold, with cameos by Chevy Chase and Edward Herrmann. **(GK)**

Thumbtanic (2002)

O Entertainment   26 minutes

RECOMMENDED

Perhaps it's just me, but after enduring so many earnest, overbaked *Titanic* flicks, this short, which was written and produced by comedy writer/director Steve Oedekerk, struck me as very entertaining. Playing out like a condensed parody of James Cameron's *Titanic* but with, well, thumbs, the movie flies by with its rapid-fire gags that include everything from direct riffs on the film to Elvis and monkey gags, and an even ear-bleedingly accurate Celine Dion impersonation. The whole "thumb" thing is a bizarre concept, to be sure, but I got used to the oddity of thumbs having conversations in goofy accents, wandering around, and even making love, and I found the likenesses to be striking and the novelty of it all more than amusing. Some of the digital effects are actually as good as those found in some of the genre's recent titles (particularly those for the direct-to-video market). The miniature work is excellent as well and fun to look at (the sets and props are built from doll houses and toy accessories). This is definitely a good little short, with plenty of yuks to clean your palate after viewing a sinking-ship movie that's overloaded with its own seriousness. Who says the sinking of the *Titanic* can't be a load of laughs? (**GK**)

Whoops Apocalypse (1986)
MGM   94 minutes

AVOID AT ALL COSTS

Whoops is right. This supposed Cold War nuclear comedy has one good gag involving an insane British prime minister who believes that evil pixies are responsible for the rising unemployment in the United Kingdom. Otherwise, there are zero laughs here (despite, or maybe because of, a cast that includes Alexei Sayle and Rik Mayall), and there are no apocalypses as promised (onscreen, anyway). With Loretta Swit, Peter Cook, Michael Richards, Ian Richardson, and Herbert Lom. Don't even think about checking out this flick; this is no *Dr. Strangelove*. (**GK**)

OUR ULTIMATE DISASTER MOVIE LISTS

Yes, here they are. There are many, many disaster movies out there that are worth seeing, but these lists present our favorites. The first list is of films we believe are some of the best that the genre has to offer, and the second lists those we love because they encompass all the qualities that make a film so bad it's good.

Our All-Time Favorite Disaster Movies

Airplane! (1980)

Alive (1993)

Die Hard 2 (1991)

Earthquake (1974)

The Flight of the Phoenix (1965)

Kingdom of the Spiders (1977)

The Last Voyage (1960)

Mars Attacks! (1996)

Speed (1994)

A Night to Remember (1958)

Titanic (1997)

The Towering Inferno (1974)

The War of the Worlds (1953)

War of the Worlds (2005)

Our Favorite "So Bad They're Good" Disaster Flicks

Beyond the Poseidon Adventure (1979)

Bug (1975)

The Concorde: Airport '79 (1979)

Firestorm (1998)

The Jupiter Menace (1981)

The Last Days of Planet Earth (1974)

Meteor (1979)

The Swarm (1978)

The Bees (1978)

When Time Ran Out... (1980)

So, there you have it. We hope this book has given you some ideas for films to check out, and that it leaves you with a greater knowledge of the disaster movie genre—arguably the biggest, baddest, greatest, most successful genre in the history of film. See you at the next disaster flick!

INDEX

Bold page numbers denote the main review of the movie.

A

A&E Network Studios, 99
ABC, 48, 241, 304
ABC Circle Films, 302
ABC Pictures, 122
Abdul-Jabbar, Kareem, 372
Abrahams, Jim, 372
Abrams, J. J., 173
Acceptable Risks (1986), **302**
Accident, The (1983), 13, **88–90**, 98
Adams, Lynne, 18, 36
Aerosmith, 307
Affleck, Ben, 173–176
After the Shock (1990), **76**
Aftershock: Earthquake in New York (1999), **54–55**
Agar, John, 272
Aguilar, Luz Maria, 40, 63
Agutter, Jenny, 42–43
Aherne, Brian, 159
Ahray, Sonsee, 162
Air Rage (2001), 49
Airplane! (1980), 4, 48, 84, **372–373**, 376, 382
Airplane II: The Sequel (1982), 4, 84, **374–376**
Airport '77 (1977), **13–14**, 37, 47, 83, 133
Airport (1970), 3–4, **9–10**, 22, 83
Airport 1975 (1974), **11–12**, 82, 83, 133, 306, 312, 372
Airspeed (1998), **18–19**
Albert, Eddie, 15–17, 224
Albert, Edward, 119
Albertson, Jack, 147–148
Aldrich, Robert, 28, 31
Aldrich, William, 28, 30
Alexander, Jane, 304–305
Aliens, 173

Alive: 20 Years Later (1993), 21
Alive (1993), 5, **20–21**, 40, 229, 382
Allen, Corey, 91
Allen, Irwin, 3, 79–80, 85, 122, 129–130, 147, 168, 218, 221, 225, 232, 234, 305, 338–340
Allen, Karen, 247
Allen, Ronald, 144
Alliance Entertainment, 267
Alliance/Rhombus, 211
Ambler, Eric, 144
Ambrose, David, 42
Ameche, Don, 207–209
Amen, Carol, 304–305
American International Pictures, 184
Amici, Rosa, 7
Amiel, Jon, 106
Amis, Suzy, 165, 204–206
Amos, John, 22
And I Alone Survived (1978), 49
. . . And Millions Die! (1973), 84, 346
Anderson, Donna, 303
Anderson, William C., 241
Andersson, Bibi, 15
Andrews, Dana, 11, 48, 56–57
Andrews, Harry, 154
Andromeda Strain, The (1971), 260
Angela, Piero, 267
Anglim, Philip, 304
Anglin, Anne, 88
Ansara, Michael, 169, 316
Anwar, Gabrielle, 168
Anything to Survive (1990), 103
Apocalypse, The (1997), **192**
Archer, Anne, 152
Arenberg, Lee, 192
Arkin, Adam, 227

Arkoff, Samuel Z., 184
Armageddon (1998), 5, 53, 82, 171, **173–177**, 181, 307, 347, 348
Armstrong, Jerome, 113
Arnold, Tom, 380
Artisan Entertainment, 54
Asner, Edward, 47, 235–236
Assignment Outer Space (1960), 368
Astaire, Fred, 218, 303
Asteroid (1997), **178–179**
Astin, Patty Duke, 201–202, 225, 338, 340
Astor, Mary, 238
Atherton, William, 22, 35, 289, 291
Atlantic (1929), 2, 169. *See also Titanic: Disaster in the Atlantic*
Atlantis Films, 245
Atomic Train (1999), **261**, 331
Atomic Twister (2002), 305
Attenborough, Richard, 28–29
Auberjonois, Rene, 35, 377
Auerbach, Lee, 319
Avalanche (1969), 103, 200
Avalanche (1978), 15, **91–93**, 185–186
Avalanche (1994), 136
Avalanche (1999), 103
Avalanche Express (1979), **94–95**
Avalon, Frankie, 169
AVCO Embassy Pictures, 264
Avengers, The, 173
Ayres, Robert, 144

B
Bachman, Randy, 212
Back from Eternity (1956), 49
Bad Boys, 173
Bailey, G. W., 298–300
Baird, Stuart, 24
Baker, Bart, 187
Baker, Carroll, 229
Baker, Diane, 122
Baker, Joe Don, 356–357, 359
Baker, Roy, 144
Baldwin, Adam, 350
Baldwin, Alec, 276
Baldwin, Stephen, 168
Ballhaus, Michael, 344
Balmer, Edwin, 189
Bancroft, Anne, 35
Bannen, Ian, 28–29
Barbeau, Adrienne, 286
Barr, Jean-Marc, 284

Barry, Gene, 360–362, 366
Barry, Ian, 222
Bartlett, Hall, 48
Bartold, Norman, 152
Barwood, Hal, 369
Basehart, Richard, 232
BASEketball, 175
Bates, Kathy, 165, 167, 304
Battle of the Worlds (1961), 368
Battlefield Earth, 205
Battlestar Galactica, 37, 375
Bay, Michael, 173, 175
BBC, 292
Beatty, Ned, 85, 132–133, 377
Beck, John, 47, 377–379
Bedelia, Bonnie, 22
Bees, The (1978), **309–311**, 383
Begley, Ed, Jr., 15, 33
Behrens, Sam, 20
Bellamy, Earl, 201, 232
Bellamy, Ralph, 48, 225
Ben-Hur, 82
Benguigui, Jean, 267
Bening, Annette, 356–358
Berger, William, 267
Bernhard, Sandra, 192
Berry, Halle, 24–25
Bertram, Laura, 245
Besch, Bibi, 269
Best, Eve, 99
Best Film and Video, 345
Beyond the Poseidon Adventure (1979), 4, 80, **129–131**, 338, 383
Biehn, Michael, 178
Big Bus, The (1976), **377–379**
Big One, The: The Great Los Angeles Earthquake (1990), 78
Bigelow, Kathryn, 139
Billingsley, Barbara, 372
Birch, Paul, 360
Bisset, Jacqueline, 9–10, 119–120, 370
Black, Jack, 314, 356–357, 359
Black, Karen, 11–12
Blackman, Honor, 144
Blackmer, Sidney, 76
Blair, Charles, Jr., 40
Blair, Linda, 11–12
Blakely, Susan, 15–17, 218
Blazing Tower, The. *See Terror on the 40th Floor*
Bloom, Claire, 59–61

Blue Lagoon, The, 244
Blues Brothers, The, 336
Boehm, Sydney, 189
Boen, Earl, 272
Bohem, Leslie, 59, 108
Bolling, Tiffany, 321–324
Bologna, Joseph, 377–379
Bond, Timothy, 245
Bonnaire, Sandrine, 284–285
Bonnard, Mario, 111
Bono, Sonny, 48, 374, 376
Booker, Jessica, 211
Booth, Bronwen, 18
Booth, James, 13–14
Boothby, Loren, 54
Borgnine, Ernest, 4, 28–30, 85, 119, 121, 147–148, 150, 201–203
Bosley, Tom, 47
Boston Strangler, The (1968), 83
Bottoms, Timothy, 243, 332, 334
Bower, Tom, 22
Boyde, Charmaine, 88
Boyle, Peter, 129–130, 223
Brackett, Charles, 159
Branagh, Kenneth, 99
Brand, Neville, 201
Brandon, Michael, 286–288
Brannigan, Steve, 287
Brantley, Betsy, 180
Bravos, Peter, 28
Breen, Richard, 159
Brenneman, Amy, 59–61
Brent, George, 70–71
Brett, Jonathan, 44
Breznahan, Kevin, 20
Bridges, Beau, 52
Bridges, Jeff, 26–27
Bridges, Lloyd, 372–373, 374
Brierly, David, 292
British International Pictures, 2
British Lion-Pax, 198
Brittain, Donald, 88
Brittanic (2000), 169
Broderick, Matthew, 436
Bromfield, Louis, 70
Brook, Claudio, 309
Brosnan, Pierce, 108–110, 356–357, 359
Broughton, June, 292
Brown, Clarence, 70
Brown, Jim, 356–358
Brown, Tom, 208

Bruckheimer, Jerry, 173
Bruneau, Laura, 88
Bruns, Philip, 342
Buchholz, Horst, 94
Bug (1975), **312–315**, 383
Bujold, Geneviève, 63–65, 211
Bullock, Sandra, 156–158, 335–337
Bulwer-Lytton, Edward George, 1–2, 16, 111, 122
Bunker, Eddie, 273336
Burger, Robbyn, 178
Burke, Lester Wm., 367
Burning Rage (1984), 224
Burns, Edward, 31
Burr, Raymond, 374
Burton, Tim, 22, 356, 358
Buscemi, Steve, 173, 175–176
Busch, Niven, 207
Busey, Jake, 256
Bushell, Anthony, 144
Butler, Robert, 44
Buttons, Red, 4, 119, 121, 147–149

C

Caesar, Sid, 11
Caffrey, Stephen, 289
Caillou, Alan, 321
Caine, Michael, 129–131, 338–341
Cairney, John, 144
Calder, Harry, 413
Cameron, James, 127, 145, 159, 165, 167, 380
Camp, Colleen, 156
Campanella, Joseph, 184, 214–217
Campbell, Bruce, 250–252
Campbell, Graeme, 117
Campbell, Martin, 101
Camus, Albert, 284
Canaan, Christopher, 52
Canal+, 284
Cannon, J. D., 152
Cardona, René, 40
Cardona, René, Jr., 40, 229
Cardos, John "Bud", 321
Cariou, Len, 24
Carlin, Lynn, 214
Carlos, Valdemar, 283
Carlson, Richard, 47
Carney, Art, 123
Carpathia, The, 31
Carpenter, Jake, 20

Carradine, David, 132–133
Carradine, John, 238–239, 309–311
Carrasco, Carlos, 335
Carrera, Barbara, 119
Carroll, Barbara, 111
Carson, Lisa Nicole, 54
Cassandra Crossing, The (1976), 64, 81, **264–266**, 306
Castel, Lou, 264
Castle, William, 312, 315
Catastrophe (1978), 224
Catastrophe 1999: The Prophecies of Nostradamus. See The Last Days of Planet Earth
Cat's Eye, 333
Cave-In! (1983), 80, 84, 225
CBC, 77, 88
CBS-TV, 329
Chain Reaction, The (1980), 78
Challenger (1990), 49
Chamberlain, Richard, 179, 218–220, 338
Channing, Stockard, 377–379
Chapman, Lonny, 241–242
Charles in Charge, 258
Charles, Zachary, 178
Charo, 15–17
Chase, Barrie, 28
Chase, Chevy, 380
Chatwin, Justin, 364
Chaykin, Maury, 380
Cheadle, Don, 113–114
Chernobyl: The Final Warning (1991), **302–303**
Chiba, Sonny, 295
Chiles, Lois, 156
China Syndrome, The (1979), 260
Chinatown, 173
Christensen, Ronnie, 52
Ciclone. See Cyclone (1978)
Cinecetta, 267
Cinemania, 284
City on Fire (1979), 64, 80, 81, 84, 85, 88, **195–197**
Claire, Cyrielle, 267
Clark, Susan, 11–12, 195–196
Clarke, Arthur C., 437
Clary, Robert, 35
Clean and Sober (1988), 81
Cleopatra Jones (1973), 85
Clooney, George, 247–248
Close, Glenn, 356–357, 359

Coats, Alan Henry, 319
Coby, Fred, 67
Coffin, Tristam, 67
Cohen, Lawrence J., 377
Cohen, Rob, 59–60
Coleman, Dabney, 220
Colin, Margaret, 350–351
Collins, Gary, 9
Columbia Pictures, 67, 192
Columbia/Tri-Star, 101, 132
Comer, Anjanette, 214
Compagnie Francaise Cinematographique, 284
Compton, O'Neal, 180
Computer Wore Tennis Shoes, The, 46
Concorde, 257
Concorde Affair '79 (1979), 49
Concorde, The: Airport '79 (1979), **15–17**, 83, 121, 383
Condominium (1980), 225
Connery, Sean, 184–186
Connick, Harry, Jr., 350, 353, 355
Connors, Chuck, 295–297, 374–375
Connors, Mike, 94
Conqueror, The (1956), 53
Conrad, Robert, 226
Conrad, William, 224
Conti, Tom, 168
Control (1987), 5, **267–268**, 271
Convy, Bert, 225
Conway, Tim, 156, 158
Cook, Peter, 381
Cook, Robin, 289356
Cook, Tommy, 332
Corbett, John, 226
Corbin, Barry, 289
Corbucci, Sergio, 111
Cord, Alex, 201–202
Core, The (2003), 6, **106–107**
Corman, Roger, 91, 184–185, 257, 369
Cornthwaite, Robert, 360
Cortese, Dan, 117–118
Cortese, Valentina, 119
Cosmatos, George Pan, 264, 266
Costigan, James, 154
Costner, Kevin, 304
Cotten, Joseph, 13, 42
Cotter, Chris, 307
Cox, Ronny, 132, 134
Crack in the World (1965), 3, **56–58**, 106
Crash: The Mystery of Flight 1501 (1990), 49

Crash (1978), 49, 84
Crash Landing: The Rescue of Flight 232 (1992), 49
Crawford, Katherine, 47
Crawley, Amos, 245
Creepshow (1982), 115
Crichton, Michael, 253
Cristal, Linda, 280, 283
Cristaldifilm, 267
Cromwell, James, 180
Cronenberg, David, 211–212
Crosby, Denise, 180, 272–273
Cross, Ben, 44–45
Crowded Sky, The (1961), 49
Cruise, Tom, 364–366
Cubitt, David, 52
Cuibul Salamandrelor (1976). *See Oil*
Cullum, John, 269
Culp, Robert, 232–234
Cuoco, Kaley, 52
Curran, Tony, 31
Curry, Tim, 162–163
Cusack, Joan, 380
Cussler, Clive, 152
Cuthbert, Elisha, 18–19
Cyclone (1978), 20, **229–231**, 265
Cyclone (1987), 369

D
Daemian, Amiel, 187
Dafoe, Willem, 156–158
Dalton, Audrey, 159
Daniels, Jeff, 335–337
Danning, Sybil, 15
Dante, Joe, 257
Dante's Peak (1997), 5, **108–110**, 117, 192
Darnell, Linda, 48
David, Keith, 113, 173
Davidson, John, 15–16
Davidtz, Embeth, 99
Davies, Jeremy, 253–254
Davis, Altovise, 321
Davis, Eddie, 280
Davis Entertainment, 117
Davis, Geena, 380, 473
Davis, Kristin, 261
Davis, Ossie, 304
Day After, The (1983), 4, 262, **269–271**, 292
Day After Tomorrow, The (2004), 6, **96–98**, 347, 348

Day of the Animals (1977), 84, **316–318**
Day of the Triffids, The (1962), **367**, 368
Day the Earth Caught Fire, The (1961), **198–200**
Day the Earth Moved, The (1974), 78
Day the Earth Stood Still, The (1951), 35
Day the Sky Exploded, The (1958), 3, 193
Day the World Ended (1956), 369
Daylight (1997), **59–62**, 109, 171, 307
de Bont, Jan, 156, 253, 255, 335–336
De Concini, Ennio, 111
de Havilland, Olivia, 13, 338, 340
De Jarnatt, Steve, 272
De Lancie, John, 26
De Laurentiis, Dino, 243
De Mornay, Rebecca, 377
de Souza, Steven E., 22
Dead Ahead: The Exxon Valdez Disaster (1992), **345**
Deadly Bees, The (1966), 346
Death of Ocean View Park, The (1979), 346
Death Race 2000 (1975), 92
Dee, Ruby, 304
Deep Impact (1998), 5, 81, 122, **180–183**, 189, 347, 348
Dehner, John, 374
DeKoker, Richard, 135
Del Toro, Benecio, 26
Delaney, Kim, 52–53
Delon, Alain, 15
Delta Force, The (1986), 83
Deluge (1933), 2, **76**
DeMornay, Rebecca, 304
Dempsey, Patrick, 276–277
DeMunn, Jeffrey, 44, 298–300
Dennehy, Brian, 302
Derr, Richard, 189–190
Devane, William, 286–287, 289, 304
DeVito, Danny, 356–357
Devlin, Dean, 350–351
DiCaprio, Leonardo, 165–167, 171
DiCenzo, George, 37
Dickens, Charles, 464
Dickinson, Angie, 47
Die Hard 2 (1991), 5, **22–23**, 347, 348, 382
Dillman, Bradford, 257, 312–315, 338
Dimension Pictures, Inc., 321
Dinsdale, Reece, 292–293
Dion, Celine, 380
Disaster at Silo 7 (1988), 305
Disaster on the Coastliner (1979), 84, 346

Discovery Channel, The, 129
Dishy, Bob, 377
Dixon, Jill, 144
Doel, Francis, 91
Donaldson, Roger, 108
Donlevy, Brian, 208, 210
Doomsday Flight, The (1966), **47**
Douglas, Illeana, 20
Downs, Jane, 144
Doyle, Mike, 162
Dr. Strangelove, 381
Dreamworks, 364
Driver, Minnie, 235–236
Driving Miss Daisy (1989), 81
Duff, Howard, 280–283
Duffy, Patrick, 241–242
Dukes of Hazzard, The, 119
Dunaway, Faye, 218
Duncan, Michael Clarke, 173
Dunne, Philip, 70
Durning, Charles, 35
Duryea, Dan, 28
Dutton, Charles S., 54
Duval, James, 350
Duvall, Robert, 180, 182, 284
Duvall, Wayne, 235
Dworet, Laurence, 276
Dye, Cameron, 192
Dykstra, John, 59
Dyrenforth, James, 144
Dysart, Richard, 298–300
Dysart, Richard A., 35, 184, 235–236

E

Earthquake (1974), 6, 10, 51, **63–66**, 81, 82,
    83, 94, 179, 200, 218, 221,
    312, 364, 382
Earthquake in New York (1998), 78
Eason, Bo, 250
Eastwood, Clint, 372
Ebsen, Buddy, 226
Eckhart, Aaron, 106
Eden, Barbara, 168, 225
Edwards, Anthony, 171, 272–274
Ekipazh (1980), 78
Eldard, Ron, 180
Electric Company, The, 380
Eleniak-Goglia, Erika, 54
Elevator, The (1974), 82, 225
Elfman, Danny, 444
Eliason, Joyce, 162

Elizondo, Hector, 44–45
Elwes, Cary, 253–255
Emannuele, Luigi, 111
EMI, 154, 319
Emmerich, Roland, 5, 96, 98, 350–351
Epicenter (2000), 78
Erwin, Jhene, 245
Estrada, Erik, 11, 201–202
E.T. the Extra-Terrestrial (1982), 375
Evans, Art, 22
Evans, Charles, 67
Evans, Gene, 201
Evans, Linda, 94
Everett, Chad, 374–375
Executive Decision (1996), **24–25**
Exorcist, The, 12

F

Falling from the Sky: Flight 174 (1995), 49
Family Channel, 245
Fanning, Dakota, 364, 366
Farentino, James, 225
Farrell, Mike, 329
Farrow, Mia, 91–92, 243–244
Fate Is the Hunter (1964), 49
Favreau, Jon, 180
Fawcett, Farrah, 48
Faye, Alice, 207–209
Fearless (1993), **26–27**
Feist, Felix E., 76
Fell, Norman, 11
Fernando, Larranaga, 63
Ferrel, Pablo, 40
Ferréol, Andréa, 267
Ferrer, José, 338, 340, 377–378
Ferrer, Miguel, 304
Ferry, David, 245
Fichtner, William, 173, 176, 247
Field, Sally, 129–130
Field, Todd, 253–254
Fierstein, Harvey, 350–351
58 Minutes (book), 22
Film Ventures International, 316
Final Descent (1997), 49
Final Voyage (1999), 169
Finch, Peter, 28–29
Findlater, John, 9
Fingaz, Sticky, 31
Finkleman, Ken, 374–375
Finn, John, 44, 261
Finney, Albert, 370

Fire! (1977), 79, **201–203**, 234
Fire and Rain (1989), **47**, 83
Firestorm (1998), **204–206**, 383
Fisher, Brian, 7
Fisher, Frances, 165
Fisher, Joely, 227
Flight into Danger (1956), 49
Flight of the Phoenix (2004), **31–34**
Flight of the Phoenix, The (1965), 3, **28–30**, 83, 382
Flood! (1976), 79, 200, **232–234**
Florek, Dan, 235
Flying Virus (2001), 346
Foley, Jeremy, 108
Fonda, Henry, 80, 184, 195–196, 332–333, 338
Fonda, Peter, 90
Fontaine, Joan, 168
Forbes, Colin, 94
Forbidden Planet (1956), 84
Ford, Glenn, 295–299
Ford, Harrison, 139–140
Ford, John, 2, 238–239, 241
Foreman, Carl, 119
Forrest, Steve, 225
Forster, Robert, 91–92
Forsyth, Rosemary, 132
Forsythe, John, 214–216
Forsythe, William, 204–206
Foster, Preston, 122
Fox, Colin, 59–60
Fox, George, 63
Fox, Michael J., 356–357, 359
Fox, Vivica A., 350–352
Foxworth, Robert, 13
Francis, Connie, 30
Franciscus, James, 119–121, 195–196
Franken, Steve, 91
Franklin, Don, 178
Franz, Dennis, 22–23
Fraser, Ronald, 28–29
Frawley, James, 377
Frears, Stephen, 380
Freeman, Fred, 377
Freeman, Morgan, 80–81, 180–182, 235–236, 276, 278
Frees, Paul, 360
French Connection, The, 148
Fresco, Rob, 261
Frewer, Matt, 304
Friedman, Josh, 364–365

From Here to Eternity (1953), 372
Frost, Terry, 67
Fudge, Alan, 312
Fukasaku, Kinji, 295
Fuller, Kurt, 272, 289
Fuller, Penny, 47
Furness, George, 141
Futurama, 371

G

Gable, Clark, 73–74
Gale, Dorothy, 315
Gale Force (1992), 258
Gallagher, Peter, 162–163
Gallico, Paul, 129, 147
Gammell, Robin, 211
Garard, Gil, 13–14
Garber, Victor, 165
Garcia, Andrés, 229
Garcia, Andy, 380
Gardner, Ava, 4, 63–65, 81, 195–196, 264–265, 303
Garland, Judy, 315
Garner, Jennifer, 54
Garrett, Oliver H. P., 238
Garrett, Peter, 132
Garris, Mick, 304
Gazzara, Ben, 267–268
Geer, Will, 241–242
Gems, Jonathan, 356
George, Christopher, 316–317
George, Lynda Day, 316–317
Gerard, Gil, 13–14
Gertz, Jamie, 253
Ghost of Flight 401, The (1978), 49
Gibb, Cynthia, 117
Gibson, Tyrese, 31
Gidding, Nelson, 35, 129
Gielgud, John, 257
Giglio, Sandro, 360
Gilligan's Island, 59, 242
Gilliland, Richard, 312
Girdler, William, 316
Glass Inferno, The, 379
Glave, Karen, 211
Gleeson, Brendan, 44–45
Glenn, Scott, 101–102, 204–205
Gless, Sharon, 11
Glory (1989), 81
Gold (1974), 32, **257**, 306
Goldblum, Jeff, 350–355

Goldstein, Jenette "Vasquez", 274
Goldstone, James, 119, 332
Gone with the Wind, 271
Gooding, Cuba, Jr., 276, 278–279
Goodliffe, Michael, 144
Goorjian, Michael A., 235
Gordon, Ruth, 377
Gortner, Marjoe, 7, 63–64
Goudreau, Richard, 18
Gough, Bill, 88
Gould, Harold, 377
Graham, Sam, 245
Graham, William A., 47
Gramercy Pictures, 342
Grand Tour: Disaster in Time (1992), 368
Grant, Kathryn, 67–69
Grant, Lee, 13–14, 338, 340
Grapes of Wrath, The (1940), 80
Graves, Peter, 372, 374
Gray Lady Down (1978), 82, **132–134**, 168
Greene, David, 132
Greene, Graham, 77
Greene, Lorne, 63–65, 170, 257
Greenlaw, Linda, 307
Greenleaf, Raymond, 67
Greenwood, Bruce, 106
Grier, Pam, 356
Griffith, Kenneth, 144
Guardino, Henry, 332
Guest, Val, 198
Guillaume, Robert, 47
Guillerman, John, 218
Guinness, Alec, 152
Gunton, Bob, 247, 345
GUO, 42
Guttenberg, Steve, 269–270
Gyllenhaal, Jake, 96–98

H

H. G. Wells' War of the Worlds (2005), 368
Haas, Lukas, 304, 356–358
Hackman, Gene, 147–151, 170
Hagerty, Julie, 372–373, 374–375
Hagerty, Michael C., 156
Haggerty, Dan, 225
Hagman, Larry, 241–242, 377
Haid, Charles, 47
Hailey, Arthur, 48
Hale, Alan, 122
Hale, Barbara, 9
Hale, William, 154, 286

Hall, Jack, 126
Hall, James Norman, 238, 243
Hall, John, 238–239
Hallahan, Charles, 108
Hallier, Lori, 245
Hallmark Entertainment, 54, 162, 250
Halloran, Teri, 67
Hamel, Veronica, 119, 129, 131
Hamilton, Josh, 20
Hamilton, Linda, 108, 110
Hanging by a Thread (1979), 80, 225
Hansen, Peter, 189
Hard Rain (1998), 81, **235–237**
Hardin, Ty, 201
Harlin, Renny, 22–23
Harmon, Mark, 129
Harper, Tess, 37
Harris, Ed, 304
Harris, Richard, 135–138, 264–266
Harris, Ricky, 235
Harris, Ross, 304
Hart, Roxanne, 187
Harvey, Don, 22
Hashimoto, Shinobu, 326
Haskin, Byron, 360
Hasselhoff, David, 47
Hawke, Ethan, 20
Hawkes, John, 247
Hawthorne, James, 335
Hayden, Sterling, 48
Hayes, Helen, 9–10
Hayes, Terry, 101
Hays, Robert, 372–373, 374–376
Hayward, David, 286
Hayward, Susan, 53
Hazlegrove, Jane, 292
Healy, Ted, 73
Heard, John, 329–331, 345
Heat Wave! (1974), 82, 225
Heche, Anne, 113–115
Hecht, Ben, 238
Hedaya, Dan, 59–60
Heflin, Van, 9
Heineman, Laurie, 214–215
Heller, Lukas, 28, 31
Helmond, Katherine, 35
Hemdale, 257, 272
Hemmings, David, 42, 135
Henner, Marilu, 162
Hensleigh, Jonathan, 173
Herbert, James, 42

Hero (1992), **380**
Herrmann, Edward, 261, 380
Hershey, Barbara, 232–233
Herzog, Arthur, 338
Heslov, Grant, 108
Hesseman, Howard, 377
Heston, Charlton, 4, 11–12, 19, 63–65, 82, 132–134, 170, 173, 176, 222
Hicks, Catherine, 44–45
High and the Mighty, The (1954), 49
Hill, Bernard, 165
Hill, Dulé, 52
Hill, Jack, 195, 309
Hindenburg, The (1975), **35–36**
Hines, Barry, 292
Hiroshima: Out of the Ashes (1990), 305
Hirsch, Elroy "Crazylegs", 48
Hirsch, Judd, 350–351
Hockin, Esther, 88
Hoffman, Dustin, 276–279, 380
Hoffman, Elizabeth, 108
Hoffman, Philip Seymour, 253–254
Hoffmann, Gaby, 113
Hoffmann, Pato, 187
Hogan, Michael, 88
Holden, William, 119–121, 218–219
Hole, Jeremy, 267
Holly, Lauren, 44–45
Holm, Ian, 96–97, 135–136, 154
Holt, Jack, 73
Hooks, Robert, 13
Hopkins, Anthony, 135–137
Hopkins, Josh, 247
Hopkins, Robert E., 73
Hopper, Dennis, 192, 280–281
Horror at 37,000 Feet (1973), 84
How the West Was Won (1962), 80
Howard, Trevor, 184, 243
Hoyt, John, 189–190
Hubbell, Chris, 245
Hubley, Whip, 24
Hudson, Ernie, 250–252
Hudson, Rock, 91–92
Hughes, Eric, 152
Hughes, Helen, 245
Hulce, Tom, 26–27
Hume, Edward, 269
Hunt for Red October, The, 276
Hunt, Helen, 253–255, 332
Hunt, Peter, 257
Hunter, Thomas, 264

Hurd, Gale Anne, 173
Hurricane (1974), 37, 82, 154, 225, **241–242**
Hurricane (1979), 238, **243–244**
Hurricane Smith (1992), 370
Hurricane, The (1937), 2, **238–240**, 241
Hurricane, The (1999), 369
Hurt, William, 284–285
Hussey, Olivia, 295–297
Hutton, Lauren, 37–38
Hyde, Jonathan, 165

I
Ice Storm, The (1997), 370
In Old Chicago (1937), 2, **207–210**
Independence Day (1996), 5, 98, 171, 347, 348, 349, **350–355**, 356
Inferno (1998), **222**
Ingalls, Don, 11, 232
Innes, Laura, 180
International Airport (1985), 83
Into Thin Air: Death on Everest (1997), 103
Invasion of the Body Snatchers (1956), 375
Ironside, Michael, 247–248
It's a Wonderful Life, 190

J
Jackson, David, 261, 329
Jackson, Jamie Smith, 312
Jackson, Mick, 113, 292
Jaeckel, Richard, 316
James, Clifton, 135
Jameson, Jerry, 11, 37, 47, 82–83, 152, 214, 225, 241
Janssen, David, 154
Jaws (1975), 463
Jeffreys, Anne, 280
Jenkins, Rebecca, 52
Jenkins, Richard, 106
Johns, Harriette, 144
Johnson, Ben, 338, 340–341
Johnson, Michelle Anne, 192
Johnson, Van, 47
Jones, Dean, 47
Jones, Freddie, 135, 169
Jones, Jennifer, 218, 220–221
Jones, L. Q., 171, 250
Jones, O-Lan, 272
Jones, Richard T., 342
Jones, Shirley, 129
Jones, Tom, 356–358

Jones, Tommy Lee, 108, 113–116, 226
Jordan, Richard, 152–153
Josephson, Erland, 267
Josephson, Julien, 70
Joyce, Brenda, 70–71
Judd, Edward, 198–200
Juggernaut (1974), **135–138**, 171
Julia, Raul, 284–285
Jung, Calvin, 269
Junger, Sebastian, 247
Jupiter Menace, The (1981), 83,
   319–320, 383

K
K-19: The Widowmaker (2002), 6, **139–140**
Kane, Carol, 224
Ka'ne, Dayton, 243
Karras, Alex, 119
Karyo, Tchéky, 106
Katkov, Norman, 201
Katsulas, Andreas, 24
Katz, Robert, 264
Kaufman, Christine, 111
Keach, Stacy, 132–133
Keach, James, 243
Keating, Larry, 189
Keith, Brian, 122, 184
Kellerman, Sally, 377
Kelley, DeForest, 226
Kelly, Terence, 88
Kennedy, Adam, 152
Kennedy, Arthur, 229
Kennedy, George, 4, 9, 11–12, 13–14, 15–16,
   28–29, 63–64, 83, 295–296, 319–320
Kennedy, Merle, 192
Kentucky Fried Movie, The, 371
Kerwin, Brian, 117
Khanjian, Arsinée, 211
Kier, Udo, 173, 176
Kihlstedt, Rya, 180
Killer Bees (1974), 346
Killer on Board (1977), 169
King, Charmion, 211
King, Harold, 286
King, Henry, 207
King Kong, 122–123
King, Perry, 96–97
King, Robert, 101
King, Stephen, 304, 370
Kingdom of the Spiders (1977), 84,
   321–325, 382

Kinnear, Roy, 135, 169
Klimek, Darrin, 187
Knapp, Gregory, 295
Knight, Shirley, 129, 135
Knox, Alexander, 56
Koepp, David, 342–343, 364–365
Komatsu, Sakyo, 295
Konchu Daisenso (1968), 225
Kotto, Yaphet, 76, 298–299
Kozak, Harley Jane, 162
Krakatoa, East of Java (1969), **122**
Kramer, Stanley, 303
Kriegel, David, 20, 335
Kristel, Sylvia, 15
Krüger, Hardy, 28–30, 31
Kruschen, Jack, 141, 360
Kubrick, Stanley, 255
Kurasawa, Toshio, 326
Kusakari, Masao, 295–297
Kyle, Christopher, 139

L
La Frenière, Céline, 195
LaBelle, Patti, 47
Lafferty, Marcy, 322, 324
Lafia, John, 52
LaFortune, Roc, 18
LaManna, Ross, 162
Lamour, Dorothy, 238–239
Lancaster, Burt, 9, 264–266, 267
Landau, Martin, 184
Landis, Jesse Royce, 9
Lane, Diane, 247–248
Lane, Nicholas, 292
LaPaglia, Jonathan, 222
Larrañaga, Fernando, 40
Last Days of Planet Earth, The (1974), 308,
   326–328, 383
Last Days of Pompeii, The (1913), 2, 123
Last Days of Pompeii, The (1935), 2,
   122–123
Last Days of Pompeii, The (1959), **111–112**
Last Days of Pompeii, The (1984), 123
Last Night (1998), **211–213**
Last Voyage, The (1960), 3, **141–143**, 382
Lavallee, David, 132
Law, John Phillip, 264
Lawless, Lucy, 329
Lawrence, Sharon, 54
Layne, Cooper, 106
Lazareno, Norma, 40

Lea, Nicholas, 101
Leachman, Cloris, 154
Learned, Michael, 241–242
Leder, Mimi, 180
Lee, Christopher, 13–14
Leguizamo, John, 22
Leigh, Janet, 226
Leisure, David, 372, 374
Lemmon, Jack, 13–14
Leone, Sergio, 111–112
Leoni, Téa, 180–183
Les Films Ariane, 267
Leslie, William, 67–69
Lester, Richard, 135, 138
Lester Wm., Burke, 459
Lethal Weapon 3, 115
Levien, Sonya, 207
Levinson, Richard, 332
Lewis, David P., 195
Lewis, Monica, 13–14
Lieberman, Robert, 162
Linden, Hal, 37–39
Lindo, Delroy, 106
Lineback, Richard, 335
Link, William, 332
Lions Gate Films, 18
Liotta, Ray, 44–46
Lithgow, John, 269–270
Littman, Lynne, 304
Lloyd, Christopher, 345
Locusts (2005), **329–331**
Logan, John, 250
Loggia, Robert, 350, 367
Lolita (1962), 85
Long, Howie, 204–206
Loos, Anita, 73
Lord, Jack, 47
Lord of the Flies, 240
Lord, Walter, 3, 144–145
Loren, Sophia, 264–265
Lorre, Peter, 168
Lost! (1986), 226
Lost in Space, 80, 173
Lost Missile, The (1958), **367**
Lovelock, Ray, 264
Lowe, Rob, 261–262, 304
Lowry, Dick, 261
Loy, Myrna, 11, 70–71
Lyndon, Barré, 360
Lynley, Carol, 147, 232–233

M
MacDonald, Jeanette, 73–74
MacLachlan, Kyle, 342–343
MacMurray, Fred, 338, 340–341
Madigan, Amy, 269
Majors, Lee, 37–39
Mako, 304
Malden, Karl, 129–130, 184–186
Malkovich, John, 20
Malone, Dorothy, 141
Mankiewicz, Tom, 264
Mankowitz, Wolf, 198
Mann, Stanley, 184
Mantegna, Joe, 18–19
Marcovicci, Andrea, 15
Margolin, Stuart, 377
Marie, Lisa, 356, 358
Marihugh, Tammy, 141
Markham, Monte, 13
Marquand, Christian, 28–29
Mars Attacks! (1996), 5, **356–358**, 382
Marshall, Frank, 20
Marston, Joel, 141
Martin, Anne-Marie, 253
Martin, Dean, 9
Martin, Lewis, 360–361
Martin, Pamela Sue, 147–148
Marton, Andrew, 56
Marvin, Lee, 94
Massey, Raymond, 238
Mastrantonio, Mary Elizabeth, 247–248
Mastroianni, Armand, 289
Maté, Rudolph, 189
Matheson, Tim, 222
Matthau, Walter, 63–64
Matthews, Dakin, 289
Matulavich, Peter, 319
Maxwell, Roberta, 211
May, Bradford, 178
May, Rita, 292
Mayall, Rik, 381
Mayes, Wendell, 147
McCambridge, Mercedes, 15
McCardie, Brian, 156
McCarthy, Sheila, 22
McClanahan, Rue, 76
McClane, John, 41
McCord, Kent, 374
McCormack, Mary, 180
McCormack, Patty, 312

McCormick, Randall, 156
McCoy, Leonard "Bones", 280
McCoy, Matt, 192
McDonald, Christopher, 247–248
McDonnell, Mary, 350
McDowall, Roddy, 147–148, 225, 232–233
McDowell, Malcolm, 227
McGavin, Darren, 13
McGovern, Maureen, 306
McKellar, Don, 211–212
McKern, Leo, 198–199
McLanahan, Rue, 105
McMullen, Trent, 211
McNally, Stephen, 280
McQueen, Steve, 218–221
Meagher, Karen, 292–293
Meaney, Colm, 22
Meoli, Christian J., 20
Meredith, Burgess, 35, 119, 121
Meredith, Don, 214–216
Merman, Ethel, 372
Metcalf, Mark, 345
Meteor (1979), 80, 122, **184–186**, 383
Meteorites! (1998), **187–188**
MetroMedia Productions, 214
Meyer, Nicholas, 269
MGM, 73, 141, 303, 381
Midway (1976), 82
Mihok, Dash, 96, 247
Miles, Joanna, 312
Miles, Vera, 201–203, 226
Milland, Ray, 37, 225, 257
Million Dollar Baby (2004), 81
Mills, Donna, 201, 225, 226
Milner, Martin, 232–234, 241
Mineo, Sal, 122
Miracle Landing (1990), 49
Miracle Mile (1988), 5, 171, **272–275**
Miracle on Interstate 880 (1993), 78
Mirren, Helen, 154
Mitchell, Cameron, 225, 232–233
Mitchell, Thomas, 238
Mizzy, Vic, 269
Montagne, Edward, 214
Montaldo, Guiliano, 267
Montoya, Alex, 28–29
Mooney, Michael M., 35
Moore, Brian, 267
Moore, John, 31
Moore, Kieron, 56–58
Moore, Roger, 257

Moorehead, Agnes, 53
Morales, Esai, 261
More, Kenneth, 144
Moricone, Ennio, 330
Morita, Pat, 119–121
Moritani, Shiro, 326
Morning Departure (1950), 169
Morris, Greg, 47
Morris, Kathryn, 222
Morrison, Temuera, 101, 156
Morse, David, 345
Mortensen, Viggo, 59–60
Morton, Joe, 24, 335
Moses, Rick, 91
Mote, D. Brent, 261
Moxon, Henry, 292
MTM, 245
Mulligan, Richard, 377
Mulroney, Dermot, 342–343
Munroe, Janet, 198–200
Murder on Flight 502 (1975), **48**
Murnik, Peter, 235
Murphy, Michael, 345
Myers, Paul Eric, 54

N
Nachmanoff, Jeffrey, 96
Naked Gun, The: From the Files of Police Squad!
  (1988), 83, 84
Namath, Joe, 94–95
Napier, Marshall, 187
Nathanson, Jeff, 156
Natteford, Jack, 67
NBC, 52, 178, 261
Neal, Dylan, 329
Neame, Ronald, 147, 184
Neeson, Liam, 139
Negulesco, Jean, 159
Nelligan, Kate, 267
Nelson, Barry, 9
Nelson, Ed, 11
Nemec, Corin, 222, 304
Nero, Franco, 22
NeverEnding Story, The, 276
New World Pictures, 91, 309
Newman, Barry, 59–60, 195–196
Newman, Paul, 119–121, 218–221
Newman, Randy, 151
Newton, John, 20
Nichols, Dudley, 238
Nicholson, Jack, 356–357, 359

Nielsen, Leslie, 84, 147–148, 195–196, 225, 316–318, 371, 372–373
Night of the Flood (1996), 370
Night of the Iguana, The (1964), 81
Night of the Lepus (1972), 226
Night of the Twisters (1996), **245–246**
Night the Bridge Fell Down, The (1983), 84, 346
Night the World Exploded, The (1957), 3, **67–69**, 106
Night to Remember, A (1958), 3, 128, **144–146**, 382
Nippon Chinbotsu (1973), 33, 257
Niznik, Stephanie, 222
Nolan, Jeanette, 91
Nolan, Lloyd, 9, 63, 201
Nordhoff, Charles, 238, 243
Norman, Maidie, 13
Norstar, 292
North, Edmund H., 184
Norton, Eleanor, 316
Norton, William, 316
Noseworthy, Jack, 20
Nosseck, Noel, 250
Nykvist, Sven, 243

O

O Entertainment, 380
O'Brien, Edmond, 47, 141
Occhipinti, Andrea, 267
O'Connell, Arthur, 147
O'Connell, Dierdre, 26
O'Connor, Kevin J., 380
O'Donnell, Chris, 101–102
Oedekerk, Steve, 380
Oh, Sandra, 211–212
Ohama, Natsuko, 335
Oil (1976), 226
O'Keefe, Michael, 132
Olmos, Edward James, 295–299
Olson, Eric, 232
Olson, Nancy, 11
Omega Man, The (1971), 82
On Golden Pond (1981), 80
On Hostile Ground (2000), 226
On the Beach (1959), 4, 81, **303**
Once Upon a Time in the West (1968), 80
Orion Pictures, 37
Otto, Miranda, 31–32, 364
Outbreak (1995), 81, **276–279**
Owen, Chris, 10

P

Page, Anthony, 303
Page, Thomas, 312
Pal, George, 2, 189
Palance, Jack, 222–223
Panic in the City (1968), **280–283**
Panic in Year Zero! (1962), 305
Paramount Pictures, 40, 56, 76, 106, 139, 165, 180, 187, 189, 192, 235, 243, 286, 304, 312, 360, 364, 372, 374, 377
Parker, Sarah Jessica, 356–357, 359
Parnell Films, 123, 159
Path to Paradise: The Untold Story of the World Trade Center Bombing (1997), 346
Patrick, Jason, 156–158
Patrick, Robert, 22
Patterson, Lorna, 372
Patton, Will, 173, 175–176
Paul, Adrian, 227
Paxton, Bill, 165, 253–255
Paymer, David, 374
Payne, Allen, 247
Peck, Gregory, 303
Pelé, 79
Penitentiary II, 252
Penningroth, Phil, 261
Pennsylvania Miner's Story, The (2002), 78
Pepper, Barry, 204–205
Pepper Prince Company Ltd., The, 284
Perez, Rosie, 26–27
Perfect Storm, The (2000), 6, 171, **247–249**, 347, 348
Perilous Voyage (1976), 84, 169
Perkins, Anthony, 303
Perry, Frank, 88
Perry, Luke, 227
Persoff, Nehamiah, 82, 280
Peters, Kelly Jean, 214
Petersen, Wolfgang, 6, 247, 276
Phipps, William, 360
Pickens, Slim, 129–130, 338, 340
Pidgeon, Walter, 168
Piranha, 312
Plague (1978), 305
Plague, The (1992), **284–285**
Planet of the Apes (1968), 82, 293
Planet on the Prowl (1966), 3, 193
Platt, Oliver, 24–25
Plummer, Glenn, 156, 335

Pola, Claude, 91
Polley, Sarah, 211
Polonsky, Abraham, 94
Ponton, Yvan, 18
Pool, Robert Roy, 276
PorchLight Entertainment, 245
Portman, Natalie, 356–357
Portrait of a Lady, The (1996), 85
Poseidon Adventure, The (1972), 3–4, 6, 13, 79, 84, 85, 129, **147–151**, 170, 305
Postlethwaite, Pete, 77
Powell, Charles, 18
Powell, Dick, 53
Powell, Robert, 42–43
Power, Tyrone, 70–71, 207–209
Pressman, Lawrence, 47
Primus, Barry, 91
Principal, Victoria, 7, 63–64
Prochilo, Doug, 329
Puenzo, Luis, 284
Pullman, Bill, 350–351, 353
Punch-McGregor, Angela, 42
Puzo, Mario, 63

Q
Quaid, Dennis, 31–32, 96–97
Quaid, Randy, 171, 235–236, 350–355
Quake (1993), 78
Qualls, D. J., 106
Quicksand: No Escape (1992), 370
Quinlan, Kathleen, 13–14, 298–301

R
Radiotelevisione Italiana, 267
Rains Came, The (1939), 2, **70–72**, 112, 238
Raise the Titanic (1980), 37, 83, 127, 130, **152–153**
Rakoff, Alvin, 195
Ralph, Jessie, 73
Ramsay, Bruce, 20
Rank Film, 144
Rathbone, Basil, 122
Ray, Billy, 113
Raye, Martha, 15–16
Read, Piers Paul, 20
Rebhorn, James, 350
Red Alert (1977), **286–288**
Reddy, Helen, 11–12, 306, 372
Redgrave, Lynn, 377
Redgrave, Vanessa, 180–181

Reed, Marshall, 67
Rees, Roger, 162
Reeve, Christopher, 132
Reeves, Keanu, 335–337
Reeves, Steve, 111–112
Reid, Fiona, 88
Reid, Kate, 267
Reilly, John C., 247–249
Reisch, Walter, 159
Remains of the Day, 154
Remar, James, 222
Rennie, Callum Keith, 211–212
Rey, Fernando, 111
Ribisi, Giovanni, 31–33
Rich, David Lowell, 15
Rich, Vernon, 360
Richards, Michael, 381
Richardson, Doug, 22
Richardson, Ian, 381
Ring of Fire (1961), 223
Ringwald, Molly, 304
Ritter, Thelma, 159
RKO Radio Pictures, 76, 105, 122
Robards, Jason, 152, 243–244, 269–270, 302
Robbins, Matthew, 298
Robbins, Tim, 364–365
Robert, Bruce, 307
Robin Cook's Virus (1995), **289–291**
Robinson, Ann, 360–362, 366
Robinson, Frank M., 218
Robson, Mark, 63, 94
Rock, The, 173
Rogers, John, 106
Rollercoaster (1977), 80, **332–334**
Rolston, Mark, 235
Roman, Ruth, 316
Rooker, Michael, 342–343
Rose, Alan, 10
Rose, Barbara, 10
Rose, Kathryn, 10
Rosellini, Isabella, 26–27, 46
Rosenberg, Alan, 272334
Rosenberg, Frank P., 132
Roshan, Seth, 169
Ross, Beverly, 154
Ross, Katharine, 338–339
Rossovich, Rick, 298
Rossum, Emmy, 96
Roth, Eric, 15
Roundtree, Richard, 7, 63–64

Rubin, Bruce Joel, 180
Ruck, Alan, 253–254, 335
Ruckman, Ivy, 245
Rush, Barbara, 189–190
Russell, Kurt, 24–25
Russo, Rene, 276–279
Ruttan, Susan, 47
Ryan, Mitch, 54
Rysher Entertainment, 44, 68

S
Sackler, Howard, 132
Sadler, William, 22–23
Saint, Eva Marie, 162
Saint James, Susan, 154
Sajak, Pat, 374
Salomon, Mikael, 54–55, 235
Samuel Goldwyn Company, 238
San Francisco (1936), 2, **73–75**, 238, 306
San Giacomo, Laura, 192, 304
Sanders, George, 141–143
Sanders, Jay O., 59–60, 96
Sands, Andrew, 18
Santa Claus Conquers the Martians, 200
Sarrazin, Michael, 47
Saturday Night Fever (1977), 372
Savage Bees, The (1976), 346
Savage, Charles E., 280
Savage, Paul, 67
Savalas, Telly, 129–131
Saving Private Ryan (1998), 455
Sawa, Devon, 245
Saxon, John, 47, 309–311
Sayle, Alexei, 381
Scalia, Jack, 76
Scannell, Frank J., 67
Scarborough, Chuck, 54
Scheff, Michael, 13
Scheider, Roy, 373
Schell, Maximilian, 94–95, 122, 180–183
Schiff, Richard, 180
Schneider, John, 52, 245–246
Schoedsack, Ernest B., 122
Schofield, Annabel, 223
Schroeder, Barbet, 357, 359
Schwarzenegger, Arnold, 5
Sciorra, Annabella, 178–179
Scortia, Thomas N., 218
Scorupco, Izabella, 101
Scott, Dougray, 180
Scott, George C., 35–36, 162

Scott, Janette, 56–58
Scott, Martha, 11
Scott, Pippa, 214
Se7en (1995), 81
Seagal, Steven, 24–25
Sears, Fred F., 67
Seaton, George, 9
Seberg, Jean, 9
Security Pictures Ltd., 367
Seed, Paul, 345
Segal, George, 332–334
Seger, John, 320
Segurini, Lavinia, 267
Selby, David, 152–153
Selena Audiovisuel, 267
Semler, Dean, 204
Semple, Lorenzo, Jr., 243
Sergei, Ivan, 52
Serling, Rod, 47
Seth, Roshan, 135, 137–138
Seven in Darkness (1969), 49
Shackleton (2002), **99–100**
Shampoo, 173
Shanley, John Patrick, 20
Sharif, Omar, 135–137
Shatford, Bobby, 305
Shatner, William, 84, 321–325, 374–376
Shattered City: The Halifax Explosion
   (2003), **77**
Shaw, Robert, 94
Shawshank Redemption, The (1994), 81
Shea, Eric, 147–150
Sheen, Martin, 227, 264–266
Sheldon, Sanford, 332
Sheridan, Jamey, 304
Sheridan, Nicollette, 289–291
Sherman, Gary, 76
Shining, The, 255
Ship That Couldn't Stop, The (1961), 169
Short, Martin, 356, 358–359
Show Boat (1951), 81
Shrapnel, Lex, 139
Shue, Elisabeth, 342
Shull, Richard B., 377
Siddig, Alexander, 101
Sidney, Sylvia, 356–358
Siedow, Jim, 286–287
Sierra, Gregory, 220
Silliphant, Stirling, 85, 119, 147, 218, 338
Silva, Henry, 295–296
Silver, Joel, 24

Simpson, O. J., 218–219, 264–266
Sinise, Gary, 303
Skerritt, Tom, 54
Ski Lift to Death (1978), 103
Skyjacked (1972), 82
Slater, Christian, 235–236
Sling Blade, 176
Slotnick, Joey, 253
Slue, Errol, 88
Smash-Up on Interstate 5 (1976), 226
Smight, Jack, 11
Smith, C. Aubrey, 238
Smith, Charles Martin, 180
Smith, Jamie Renée, 108
Smith, Kurtwood, 180
Smith, Lois, 253
Smith, Will, 350–353
Smithee, Alan, 168, 222
Smitrovich, Bill, 342
Snowbound: The Jim and Jennifer Stolpa Story (1994), 103
Sobieski, Leelee, 180, 182
Solar Crisis (1990), 82, **222–223**
Sonic Impact (1999), 49
Sorenson, Stephen, 81
S.O.S. Titanic (1979), **154–155**
Soth, Chris, 204
Sound of Music, The, 35, 376
Soylent Green (1973), 82
Spacey, Kevin, 276, 278–279
Spano, Vincent, 20
Spector, Craig, 117
Spector, David, 13
Speed (1994), 115, **335–337**, 347, 348, 382
Speed 2: Cruise Control (1997), **156–158**
Spielberg, Steven, 6, 364–365
Spiner, Brent, 350
SST: Death Flight (1977), 49
St. Helens (1981), **123**
Stack, Robert, 48, 141–142, 372–373
Stallone, Sage, 59–60
Stallone, Sylvester, 5, 59–62, 109, 171
Stamper, Harry, 217
Stand, The (1994), **304**
Stander, Lionel, 229–230, 264–265
Stanwyck, Barbara, 159–160
Stapleton, Maureen, 9–10
Star Trek, 168, 339
Star Trek: The Next Generation, 35, 148
Star Wars: Episode V-- The Empire Strikes Back, 353

Star Wars (1977), 12, 37, 375
Starflight: The Plane That Couldn't Land (1983), **37–39**, 83
Stark, Anthony, 222
Starship Troopers, 177
Steele, Vanessa, 187
Steiger, Rod, 356, 358–359
Sterling, Robert, 169
Stern, Richard Martin, 218
Stern, Sandor, 286
Stevens, David, 54
Stevens, Stella, 148, 150
Stevenson, Houseley, Jr., 360
Stewart, Don, 47
Stewart, James, 13–14, 28–30, 31
Stiglitz, Hugo, 40, 229
Stiller, Jerry, 11
Stone, Andrew L., 141
Storch, Larry, 11
Storey, June, 208
Storke, Adam, 304
Storm (1999), 227
Storm of the Century (1999), 370
Stormare, Peter, 173, 175
Strasberg, Lee, 264
Strasberg, Susan, 332
Strickland, Gail, 37
Strode, Woody, 141, 321–324
Stuart, Gloria, 165
Stucker, Stephen, 372, 374
Sturgeon, Scott, 178
Sturgess, Shannon, 250–251
Sturridge, Charles, 99
Sub Down (1997), **168**
Submerged (2000), 49
Submersion of Japan, The. See *Nippon Chinbotsu*
Suchet, David, 24
Sudak, Joe, 10
Sullivan, Barry, 241
Summer, Donna, 307
Sumner, Peter, 42
Sumpter, Donald, 139
Superdome (1978), 82–83
Survivalist, The (1987), 305
Survive! (1976), 20, **40–41**
Survive the Savage Sea (1992), 169
Survivor, The (1981), **42–43**
Sutherland, Donald, 276, 278
Sutton, Frank, 241–242
Suvari, Mena, 261

Svenson, Bo, 156, 295–297
Swank, Hilary, 106
Swanson, Gloria, 11
Swarm, The (1978), 4, 79, 80, 309–310, 312, **338–341**, 383
Swit, Loretta, 381
Szwarc, Jeannot, 312, 315

T

Tailspin: Behind the Korean Airliner Tragedy (1989), 49
Takada, Kôji, 295
Tamba, Tetsuro, 326
Tanner, Antwon, 222
Tate, John, 303
Tayback, Vic, 377
Taylor, Leo, 187
Taylor, Robert, 101
10.5 (2004), **52–53**
Tenant, The (1976), 85
Tennant, Victoria, 284
Tentacles (1977), 85
Terminator, The, 173
Terror in the Sky (1971), 74
Terror on the 40th Floor (1974), 37, 82, **214–217**, 225
Terror Out of the Sky (1978), 346
Terror Storm. See Cyclone (1978)
Tessari, Duccio, 111
Testament (1983), 271, **304–305**
Texas Chainsaw Massacre, 287
Thinnes, Roy, 11, 35
Thirst (1998), 227
Thomas, Heather, 369
Thomas, Jim, 24
Thomas, John, 24
Thompson, Chris, 187
Thompson, Fred Dalton, 22
Thomson, Scott, 253
Thorn/EMI, 319
Thornton, Billy Bob, 173, 176
Threads (1984), 4, 98, 262, 271, **292–294**
Thulen, Ingrid, 264, 267
Thumbtanic (2002), **380–381**
Ticotin, Rachel, 44, 54
Tidal Wave: No Escape (1998), 258
Tidal Wave (1975), **257**
Time Shifters, The (1999), 368
Time Tunnel, The, 80
Tinnel, Robert, 18
Tinti, Gabriele, 28–29

Titanic: Disaster in the Atlantic, 2.
    See also Atlantic (1929)
Titanic: The Animated Movie (401), 169
Titanic (1943), 2, 169
Titanic (1953), 3, 142, **159–161**
Titanic (1996), 46, **162–164**
Titanic (1997), 5, 159, **165–167**, 171, 307, 347, 348, 380, 382
Tobolowsky, Stephen, 380
Toho Studios, 33, 295, 326
Tokyo Blackout (1987), 346
Tolkin, Michael, 180
Tompkins, Angel, 309
Torn, Rip, 345, 374–375
Tornado! (1996), 54, 171, **250–252**
Tornado. See Cyclone (1978)
Torrence, Dan, 470
Touch of Evil, 82
Touchstone Pictures, 20, 173
Towering Inferno, The (1974), 10, 79, 170, 214, **218–221**, 306, 382
Towne, Robert, 173
Tracy, Spencer, 73–74
Tragedy of Flight 103, The: The Inside Story (1990), 50
Train of Events (1949), 346
Trainor, Mary Ellen, 24
Trans-World Entertainment, 88
Tremayne, Les, 360
Trevor, Elleston, 28, 31
Trigger Effect, The (1996), **342–344**, 365
Trimark, 222, 261, 276
Triumph Over Disaster: The Hurricane Andrew Story (1993), 258
Troell, Jan, 243
Trotti, Lamar, 207
True Lies (1994), 82
Trump, Marla Maples, 24
Tucci, Stanley, 106
Tunney, Robin, 101–102
Turbulence (1997), 5, 18, **44–46**
Turbulence 2: Fear of Flying (2000), 50
Turbulence 3: Heavy Metal (2001), 50
Turkel, Ann, 264
Turley, Jack, 214, 241
Turner Home Entertainment, 302, 374
Turturro, John, 26
Twain, Shania, 307
12 Angry Men (1957), 80
Twentieth Century Fox, 22, 28, 31, 70, 94, 96, 113, 147, 152, 156, 159, 168, 195, 204,

207, 218, 298, 335, 350
Twister (1996), 250, **253–256**, 347, 348
2001: A Space Odyssey, 339
Tycus (1998), **192**
Tyler, Liv, 173–175
Tyler, Steven, 218
Tyne, Billy, 305
Tyson, Cicely, 15, 54

U
Under the Volcano (1984), 370
Underwood, Blair, 180
Unforgiven (1992), 81
United Artists, 111, 135, 303, 367
United Pictures Corporation, 280
United Productions of America, 326
Universal Pictures, 9, 11, 13, 15, 59, 63, 108, 132, 253
Universal Studios, 35, 332, 342
Universal TV, 47

V
Vaccaro, Brenda, 13
Valdemar, Carlos, 229
Valdez, Juan, 64
Valentine, Scott, 76
Valli, Alida, 264
Van Dyke, W. S., 73
Vargas, Jacob, 31
Vaughn, Robert, 170, 218, 295–296
VelJohnson, Reginald, 22
Vernon, John, 374
Vertical Limit (2000), **101–103**
Viacom Productions, 222
Villarreal, Daniel, 335
Villechaize, Hervé, 374
Vint, Jesse, 312
Virus (1980), 83, **295–297**
Viva Knievel! (1977), 84
Void, The (2001), 227
Voight, John, 302
Volcano: Fire on the Mountain (1997), **117–118**
Volcano (1997), 5, 108, **113–116**, 117, 171
von Bargen, Daniel, 222
von Sydow, Max, 243
Von Trier, Lars, 53
Von Zernick Sertner Films, 250, 289
Voyage of Terror (1998), 169
Voyage to the Bottom of the Sea (1961), 80, **168–169**

W
Wager, Walter, 22
Wagner, Robert, 115–117, 159–161, 218, 221
Wahlberg, Mark, 247–248
Waite, Ralph, 286–288
Walker, Jimmie, 15–16, 372
Walsh, J. T., 24, 278
Walsh, M. Emmet, 13, 152, 286–287
Walston, Ray, 304
Walter, Jessica, 241–242
War of the Worlds (2005), 6, 81, 347, 348, 349, **364–366**, 382
War of the Worlds, The (1953), 2, 5, 189, 270, 349, **360–363**, 382
Ward, Fred, 52–53
Ward, Luci, 67
Ward, Sela, 96
Warden, Jack, 129
Warner Bros., 24, 26, 48, 119, 129, 201, 218, 232, 247, 253, 276, 338, 356
Warner, David, 15, 154, 165–166
Warning Sign (1985), 259, **298–301**
Washington, Denzel, 369
Waterston, Sam, 298–300
Watson, James A., Jr., 374
Wayne, John, 53
Weathers, Carl, 370
Webb, Clifton, 159
Webber, Timothy, 88
Weekend at Bernie's, 39
Weir, Peter, 26
Weiss, Arthur, 201
Weitz, Bruce, 180
Weller, Fred, 54
Wells, H. G., 360, 364
Welsh, Jonathan, 245
Wendt, George, 374
Werntz, Gary, 180
Whalen, Sean, 253
When Time Ran Out... (1980), 4, 80, **119–121**, 370, 383
When Worlds Collide (1951), 2–3, 6, **189–191**, 360
White, Al, 374
White, Betty, 235–236
White, John Manchip, 56
Whitman, Stuart, 226
Whittaker, James, 132
Who Is Killing the Great Chefs of Europe?, 30
Whoops Apocalypse (1986), **381**
Widmark, Richard, 332, 338–341

Woodward, Tim, 139
Wopat, Tom, 187, 224
Wrecking Crew, The (1969), 80
Wright, Teresa, 232
Wright, Tracy, 211
Wrongfully Accused (1998), 371
Wyndham, John, 367
Wynter, Dana, 9

Y

Yamamura, Sô, 326
Yglesias, Rafael, 26
York, Francine, 232
York, Susannah, 257
Yost, Graham, 235, 335
Young, Gig, 35
Young, John Sacret, 305
Young, Karen, 59–60
Young, Robert M., 37
Young, Roger, 289
Young, William Allen, 269
Yumi, Kaoro, 326

Z

Zacarias, Alfredo, 309
Zagarino, Frank, 192
Zal, Roxana, 304
Zane, Billy, 165–167
Zero Hour! (1957), **48**, 372
Zeta-Jones, Catherine, 162–163
Zimbalist, Efrem, Jr., 11
Zimet, Julian, 56
Zimmer, Hans, 218
Zucker, David, 372–373
Zucker, Jerry, 372–373